WONDER WOMAN

EYES OF THE GORGON

WONDER WOMAN
EYES OF THE GORGON

GREG RUCKA WRITER

DREW JOHNSON   JAMES RAIZ   SEAN PHILLIPS PENCILLERS

RAY SNYDER   SEAN PHILLIPS INKERS

RICHARD & TANYA HORIE COLORISTS

TODD KLEIN LETTERER

WONDER WOMAN CREATED BY WILLIAM MOULTON MARSTON

DAN DIDIO VP-EXECUTIVE EDITOR
IVAN COHEN EDITOR-ORIGINAL SERIES
ANTON KAWASAKI EDITOR-COLLECTED EDITION
ROBBIN BROSTERMAN SENIOR ART DIRECTOR
PAUL LEVITZ PRESIDENT & PUBLISHER
GEORG BREWER VP-DESIGN & DC DIRECT CREATIVE
RICHARD BRUNING SENIOR VP-CREATIVE DIRECTOR
PATRICK CALDON SENIOR VP-FINANCE & OPERATIONS
CHRIS CARAMALIS VP-FINANCE
TERRI CUNNINGHAM VP-MANAGING EDITOR
STEPHANIE FIERMAN SENIOR VP-SALES & MARKETING
ALISON GILL VP-MANUFACTURING
RICH JOHNSON VP-BOOK TRADE SALES
HANK KANALZ VP-GENERAL MANAGER, WILDSTORM
LILLIAN LASERSON SENIOR VP & GENERAL COUNSEL
JIM LEE EDITORIAL DIRECTOR-WILDSTORM
PAULA LOWITT SENIOR VP-BUSINESS & LEGAL AFFAIRS
DAVID MCKILLIPS VP-ADVERTISING & CUSTOM PUBLISHING
JOHN NEE VP-BUSINESS DEVELOPMENT
GREGORY NOVECK SENIOR VP-CREATIVE AFFAIRS
CHERYL RUBIN SENIOR VP-BRAND MANAGEMENT
JEFF TROJAN VP-BUSINESS DEVELOPMENT, DC DIRECT
BOB WAYNE VP-SALES

WONDER WOMAN: EYES OF THE GORGON

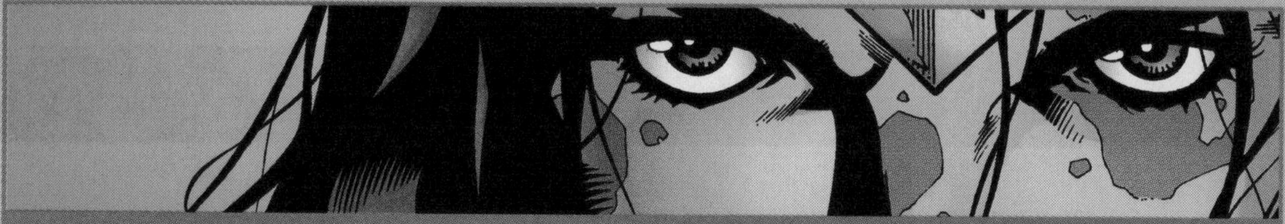

OUR STORY SO FAR...

Diana of the floating island of Themyscira, home of the Amazons, came to "Man's World" years ago. Acting as an ambassador of peace, also known as Wonder Woman, she hoped to teach the ways of her just and harmonious civilization to a violent world. A Themysciran embassy was eventually set up in New York, and a large staff now runs it so that Diana can concentrate on the important work of bringing unity. In order for her teachings to reach as many people as possible, Diana penned a book — *Reflections: A Collection of Essays and Speeches* — which ended up sparking a firestorm of controversy almost immediately upon publication.

Doctor Veronica Cale — a pharmaceutical CEO with an axe to grind — initiated a plan to discredit the Amazon, hiring a public relations firm to scour the book for quotes that could be used against Wonder Woman. Cale also helped in securing the release of Doctor Psycho — a diminutive adversary of Wonder Woman's with extremely dangerous mental abilities.

Diana began a tour to promote and sign copies of her book and came across the organization known as "Protect Our Children" — a group, led by one Darrel Keyes, that had been heatedly at odds with the philosophies Diana had espoused in Reflections.

Later, Diana went to visit her recovering friend Vanessa Kapatelis, who was recovering from the trauma of the physical and mental transformation into the new superbeing, the Silver Swan — only to find that Vanessa had mysteriously vanished.

Reeling from that discovery, Diana next confronted War God Ares about the growing rumors that he was planning a move against the Amazons. But with the lasso of truth around him, the Olympian swore to Diana that no harm would come to the Amazons from his hand.

Soon Diana found demonstrators outside the embassy that were both for and against her. But there were other forces at work that used the protests as a staging ground, and Keyes ended up becoming the victim of an assassination on the steps of the embassy. Violence broke out between Wonder Woman's supporters and detractors, spurred on by a Cale-controlled Doctor Psycho, who watched from the sidelines. Before Diana could get a handle on the situation, she was attacked by the vengeful Silver Swan — another obstacle thrown Diana's way due to Cale.

Meanwhile, on Mount Olympus, Ares was stirring up mischief in Zeus's love life. The War God employed his son Eros to manipulate Zeus's emotions. Hera caught her husband gazing at the Amazon Artemis through a viewing pond. In an unexpected jealous rage, Hera kicked at the pond, causing the entire floating island of Themsycira to go crashing into the ocean.

Back on Earth, Wonder Woman managed to subdue Silver Swan, promising to never abandon her friend and to get her help. She brought the Swan — now near death because her body was rejecting her cybernetic implants — back to Themyscira, only to discover the fate that had befallen the Amazons. But it soon became apparent that the disaster had yielded an unexpected, fearful consequence: the fall to the ocean caused a tsunami that was headed towards the Carolinas. Wonder Woman, with the help of the shape-shifting alien Lansanarian "Wonder Dome," managed to beat back the deadly tidal wave — but at a price. The Lansanarian sacrificed its life force to stop the wave, transforming at the last minute into an invisible jet — which became its permanent state.

ON ANOTHER SIDE OF THE ISLAND, THE DESTRUCTION LED TO THE GORGON STHENO BEING FREED FROM CAPTIVITY, WHILE WONDER WOMAN'S IMPRISONED NEMESIS, CIRCE, WAS HURLED INTO THE SEA. STHENO REALIZED THAT BY RESCUING CIRCE, SHE COULD PLACE THE WITCH IN HER DEBT. STHENO WAS REUNITED WITH HER SISTER EURYALE, AND THE TWO GORGONS EXPLAINED TO CIRCE WHAT THEY WISHED IN REPAYMENT: THE RESURRECTION OF THEIR DEAD SISTER, THE MURDEROUS MEDOUSA.

MEANWHILE, WITH SO MUCH TO DEAL WITH AT ONCE, DIANA DIDN'T HAVE TIME TO FOCUS ON THE MURDER OF DARREL KEYES, AND SO ENLISTED THE HELP OF HER JLA TEAMMATE BATMAN. WITH THE DARK KNIGHT ON THE CASE, DIANA WAS FREE TO SEEK HELP FOR VANESSA. DIANA TURNED TO SPECIALIST DR. LESLIE ANDERSON — A WOMAN WHO HAPPENED TO BE THE BUSINESS PARTNER OF VERONICA CALE.

THE WORLD'S GREATEST DETECTIVE QUICKLY DISCOVERED A CONNECTION BETWEEN KEYES' DEATH AND ANOTHER MURDER VICTIM: A DIRECTOR OF SECURITY FOR CALE'S PHARMACEUTICAL COMPANY. IN THE MEANTIME, CALE WAS ABDUCTED BY DR. PSYCHO. THE PSYCHIC PROCEEDED TO USE HIS MENTAL POWERS TO IMPERSONATE NUMEROUS PEOPLE, INCLUDING CALE HERSELF — WHOM HE HELD HOSTAGE IN REVENGE FOR HER EARLIER ABUSE OF HIM AS A PRISONER. WONDER WOMAN FINALLY CONFRONTED PSYCHO AND A BATTLE ENSUED. WHILE CALE WAS RESCUED, PSYCHO MANAGED TO SLIP AWAY. BOTH DIANA AND DR. ANDERSON REMAIN UNAWARE OF CALE'S INVOLVEMENT IN SO MANY OF WONDER WOMAN'S RECENT TROUBLES.

AMONG THE RUINS, IN AN ANCIENT PLACE OF MAGIC, AN UNSPEAKABLE HORROR WAS BEING REBORN. MEDOUSA WAS ALIVE ONCE AGAIN! AND SHE HAD ONE BLOODTHIRSTY MISSION ON HER MIND: TO KILL WONDER WOMAN...

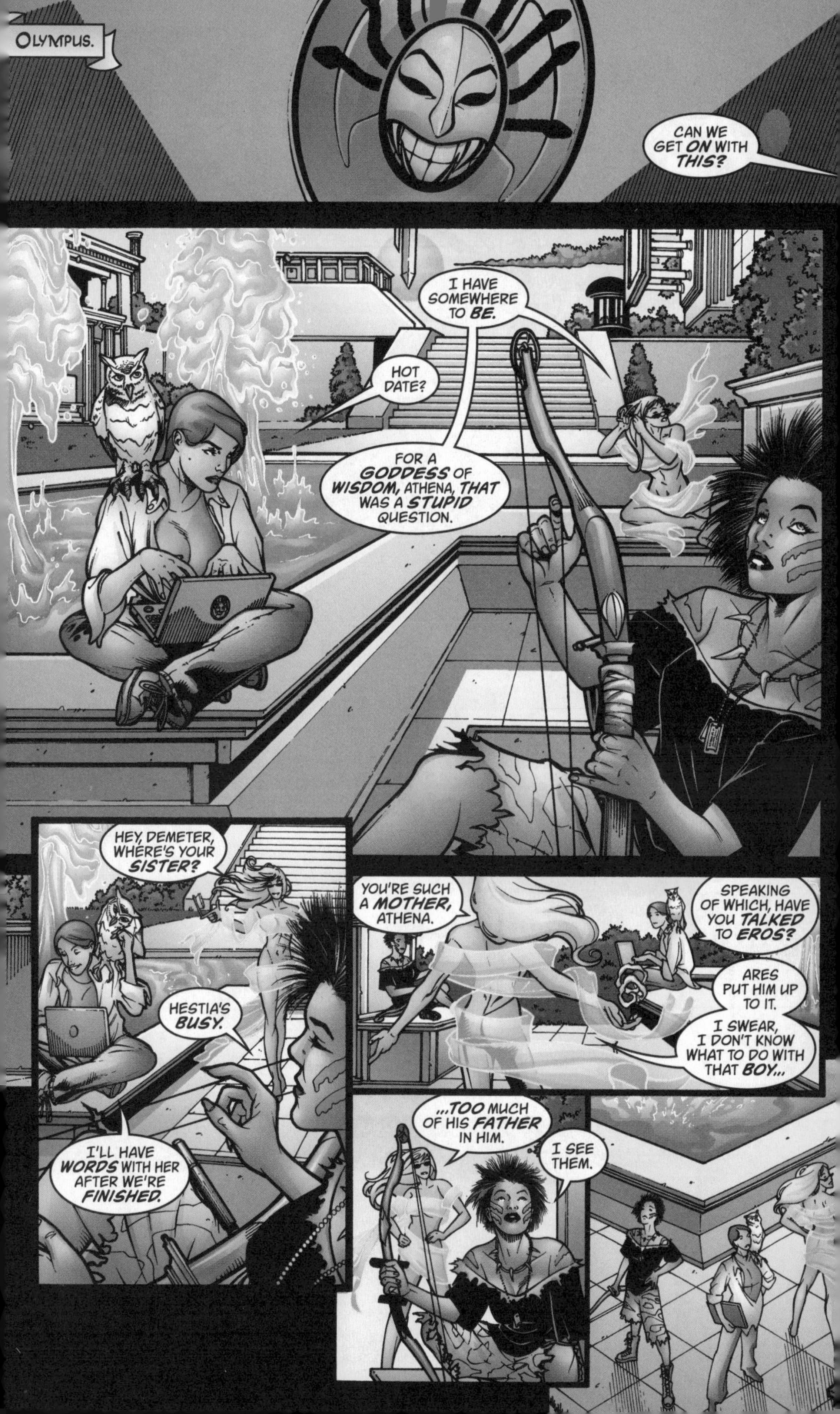
OLYMPUS.
CAN WE GET ON WITH THIS?
I HAVE SOMEWHERE TO BE.
HOT DATE?
FOR A GODDESS OF WISDOM, ATHENA, THAT WAS A STUPID QUESTION.
HEY, DEMETER, WHERE'S YOUR SISTER?
HESTIA'S BUSY.
I'LL HAVE WORDS WITH HER AFTER WE'RE FINISHED.
YOU'RE SUCH A MOTHER, ATHENA.
SPEAKING OF WHICH, HAVE YOU TALKED TO EROS?
ARES PUT HIM UP TO IT.
I SWEAR, I DON'T KNOW WHAT TO DO WITH THAT BOY...
...TOO MUCH OF HIS FATHER IN HIM.
I SEE THEM.

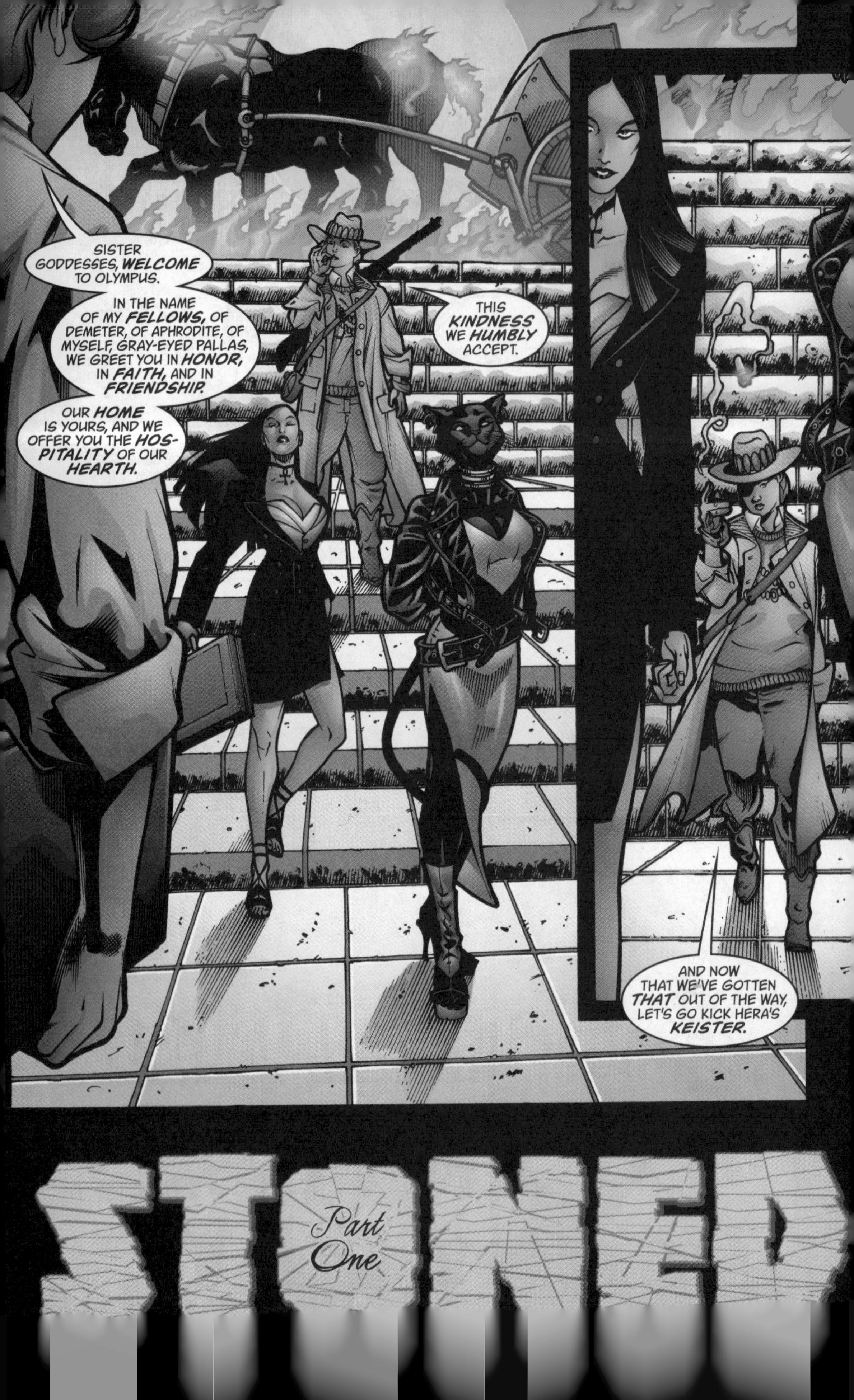
SISTER GODDESSES, WELCOME TO OLYMPUS.
IN THE NAME OF MY FELLOWS, OF DEMETER, OF APHRODITE, OF MYSELF, GRAY-EYED PALLAS, WE GREET YOU IN HONOR, IN FAITH, AND IN FRIENDSHIP.
OUR HOME IS YOURS, AND WE OFFER YOU THE HOS-PITALITY OF OUR HEARTH.
THIS KINDNESS WE HUMBLY ACCEPT.
AND NOW THAT WE'VE GOTTEN THAT OUT OF THE WAY, LET'S GO KICK HERA'S KEISTER.
STONED
Part One

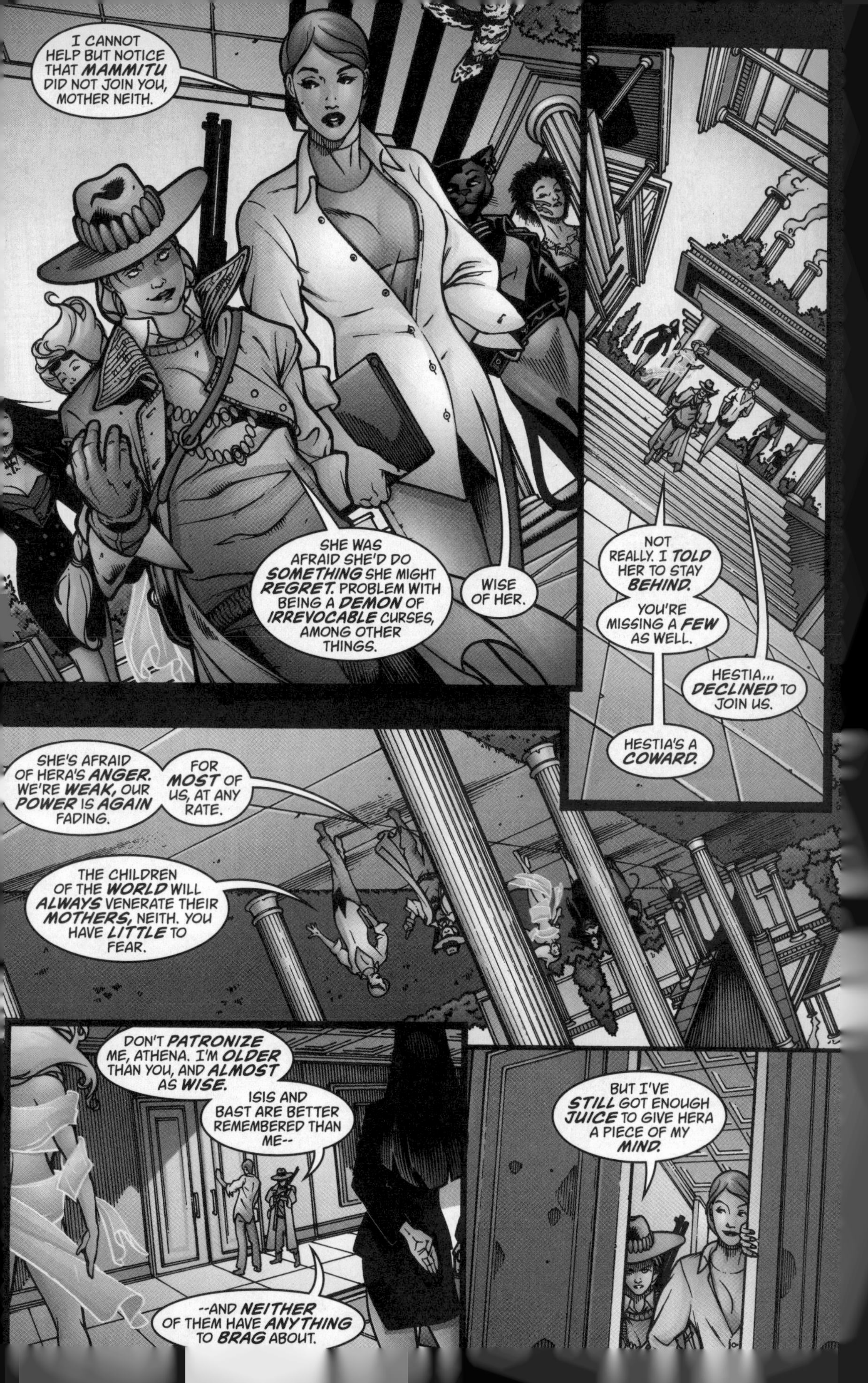
I CANNOT HELP BUT NOTICE THAT MAMMITU DID NOT JOIN YOU, MOTHER NEITH.
SHE WAS AFRAID SHE'D DO SOMETHING SHE MIGHT REGRET. PROBLEM WITH BEING A DEMON OF IRREVOCABLE CURSES, AMONG OTHER THINGS.
WISE OF HER.
NOT REALLY. I TOLD HER TO STAY BEHIND.
YOU'RE MISSING A FEW AS WELL.
HESTIA... DECLINED TO JOIN US.
HESTIA'S A COWARD.
SHE'S AFRAID OF HERA'S ANGER. WE'RE WEAK, OUR POWER IS AGAIN FADING.
FOR MOST OF US, AT ANY RATE.
THE CHILDREN OF THE WORLD WILL ALWAYS VENERATE THEIR MOTHERS, NEITH. YOU HAVE LITTLE TO FEAR.
DON'T PATRONIZE ME, ATHENA. I'M OLDER THAN YOU, AND ALMOST AS WISE.
ISIS AND BAST ARE BETTER REMEMBERED THAN ME--
--AND NEITHER OF THEM HAVE ANYTHING TO BRAG ABOUT.
BUT I'VE STILL GOT ENOUGH JUICE TO GIVE HERA A PIECE OF MY MIND.

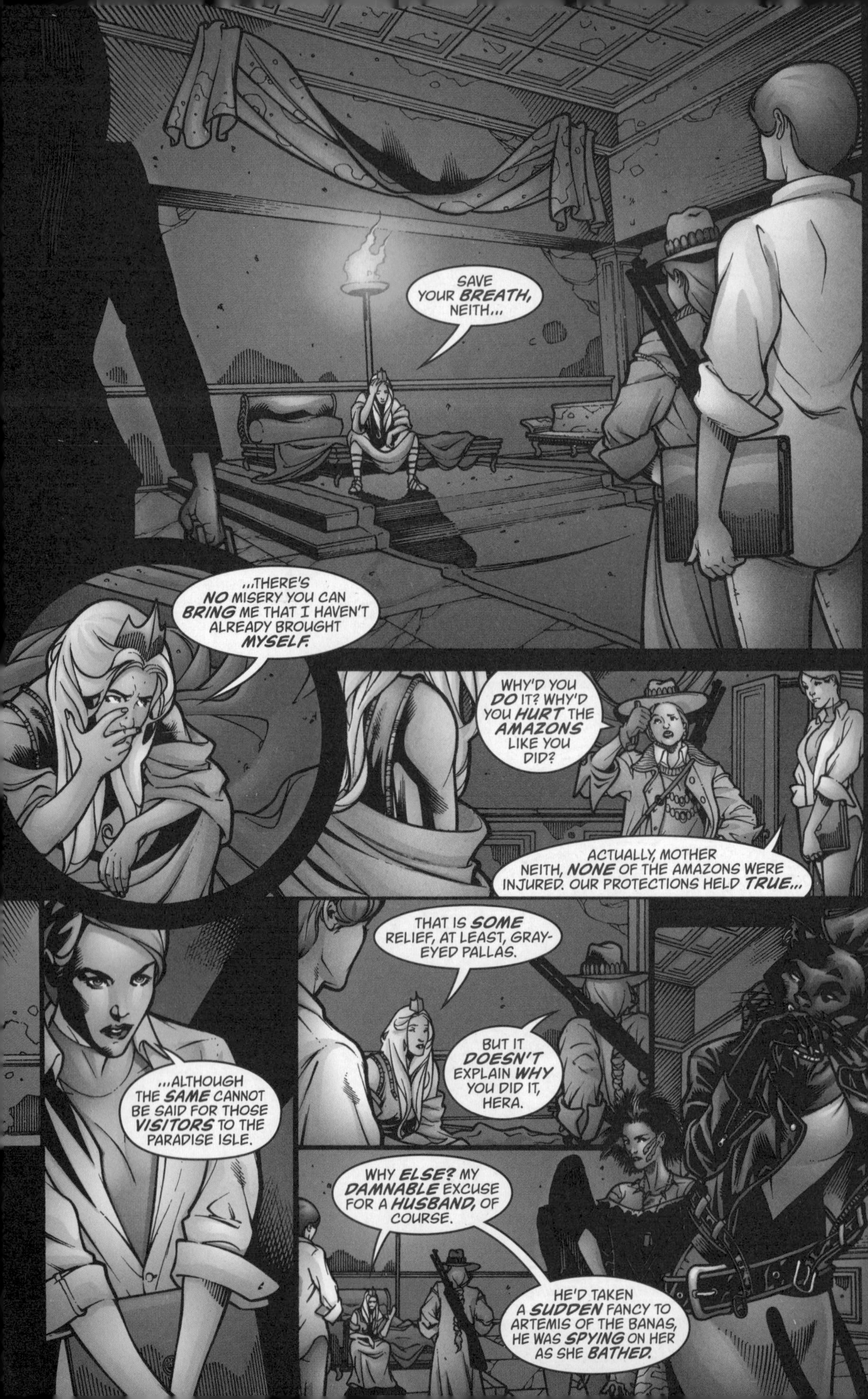
SAVE YOUR BREATH, NEITH...
...THERE'S NO MISERY YOU CAN BRING ME THAT I HAVEN'T ALREADY BROUGHT MYSELF.
WHY'D YOU DO IT? WHY'D YOU HURT THE AMAZONS LIKE YOU DID?
ACTUALLY, MOTHER NEITH, NONE OF THE AMAZONS WERE INJURED. OUR PROTECTIONS HELD TRUE...
...ALTHOUGH THE SAME CANNOT BE SAID FOR THOSE VISITORS TO THE PARADISE ISLE.
THAT IS SOME RELIEF, AT LEAST, GRAY-EYED PALLAS.
BUT IT DOESN'T EXPLAIN WHY YOU DID IT, HERA.
WHY ELSE? MY DAMNABLE EXCUSE FOR A HUSBAND, OF COURSE.
HE'D TAKEN A SUDDEN FANCY TO ARTEMIS OF THE BANAS, HE WAS SPYING ON HER AS SHE BATHED.

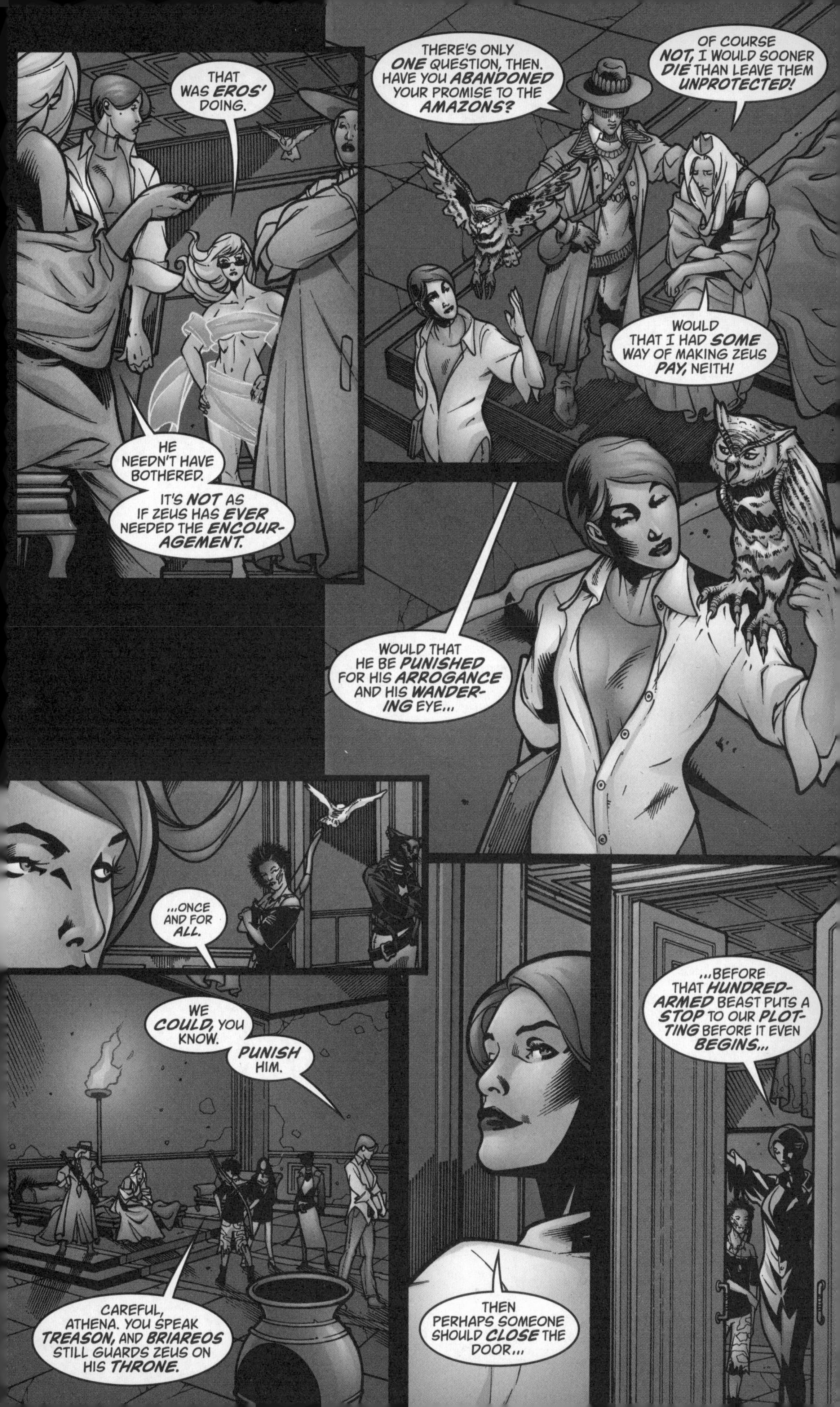
THAT WAS EROS' DOING.
HE NEEDN'T HAVE BOTHERED.
IT'S NOT AS IF ZEUS HAS EVER NEEDED THE ENCOURAGEMENT.
THERE'S ONLY ONE QUESTION, THEN. HAVE YOU ABANDONED YOUR PROMISE TO THE AMAZONS?
OF COURSE NOT, I WOULD SOONER DIE THAN LEAVE THEM UNPROTECTED!
WOULD THAT I HAD SOME WAY OF MAKING ZEUS PAY, NEITH!
WOULD THAT HE BE PUNISHED FOR HIS ARROGANCE AND HIS WANDERING EYE...
...ONCE AND FOR ALL.
WE COULD, YOU KNOW.
PUNISH HIM.
CAREFUL, ATHENA. YOU SPEAK TREASON, AND BRIAREOS STILL GUARDS ZEUS ON HIS THRONE.
THEN PERHAPS SOMEONE SHOULD CLOSE THE DOOR...
...BEFORE THAT HUNDRED-ARMED BEAST PUTS A STOP TO OUR PLOTTING BEFORE IT EVEN BEGINS...

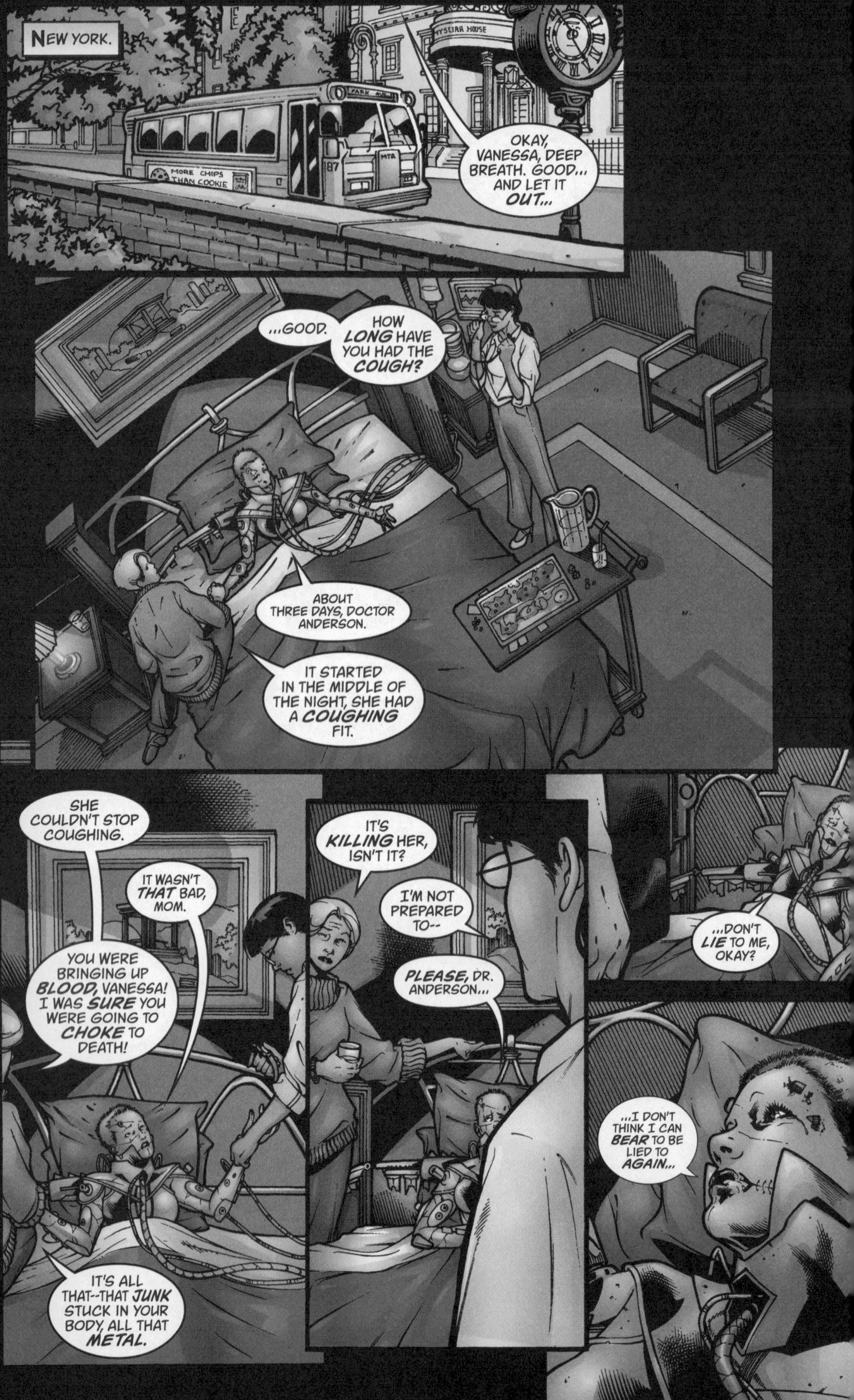
NEW YORK.
MYSTIAH HOUSE
PARK AVE
MORE CHIPS THAN COOKIE
OKAY, VANESSA, DEEP BREATH. GOOD... AND LET IT OUT...
...GOOD.
HOW LONG HAVE YOU HAD THE COUGH?
ABOUT THREE DAYS, DOCTOR ANDERSON.
IT STARTED IN THE MIDDLE OF THE NIGHT, SHE HAD A COUGHING FIT.
SHE COULDN'T STOP COUGHING.
IT WASN'T THAT BAD, MOM.
YOU WERE BRINGING UP BLOOD, VANESSA! I WAS SURE YOU WERE GOING TO CHOKE TO DEATH!
IT'S ALL THAT--THAT JUNK STUCK IN YOUR BODY, ALL THAT METAL.
IT'S KILLING HER, ISN'T IT?
I'M NOT PREPARED TO--
PLEASE, DR. ANDERSON...
...DON'T LIE TO ME, OKAY?
...I DON'T THINK I CAN BEAR TO BE LIED TO AGAIN...

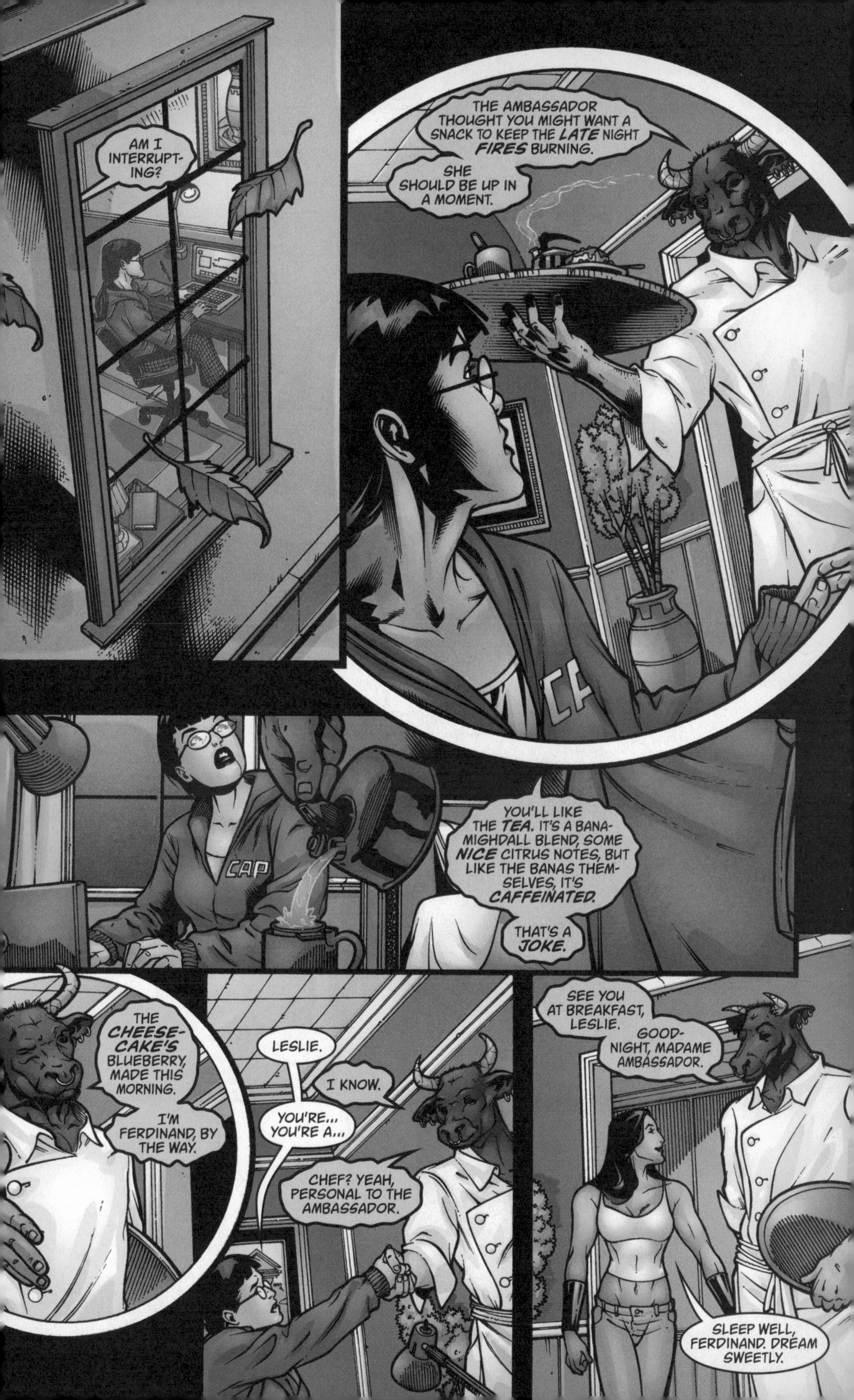
AM I INTERRUPTING?
THE AMBASSADOR THOUGHT YOU MIGHT WANT A SNACK TO KEEP THE LATE NIGHT FIRES BURNING.
SHE SHOULD BE UP IN A MOMENT.
YOU'LL LIKE THE TEA. IT'S A BANAMIGHDALL BLEND, SOME NICE CITRUS NOTES, BUT LIKE THE BANAS THEMSELVES, IT'S CAFFEINATED.
THAT'S A JOKE.
THE CHEESECAKE'S BLUEBERRY, MADE THIS MORNING.
I'M FERDINAND, BY THE WAY.
LESLIE.
I KNOW.
YOU'RE... YOU'RE A...
CHEF? YEAH, PERSONAL TO THE AMBASSADOR.
SEE YOU AT BREAKFAST, LESLIE.
GOOD-NIGHT, MADAME AMBASSADOR.
SLEEP WELL, FERDINAND. DREAM SWEETLY.

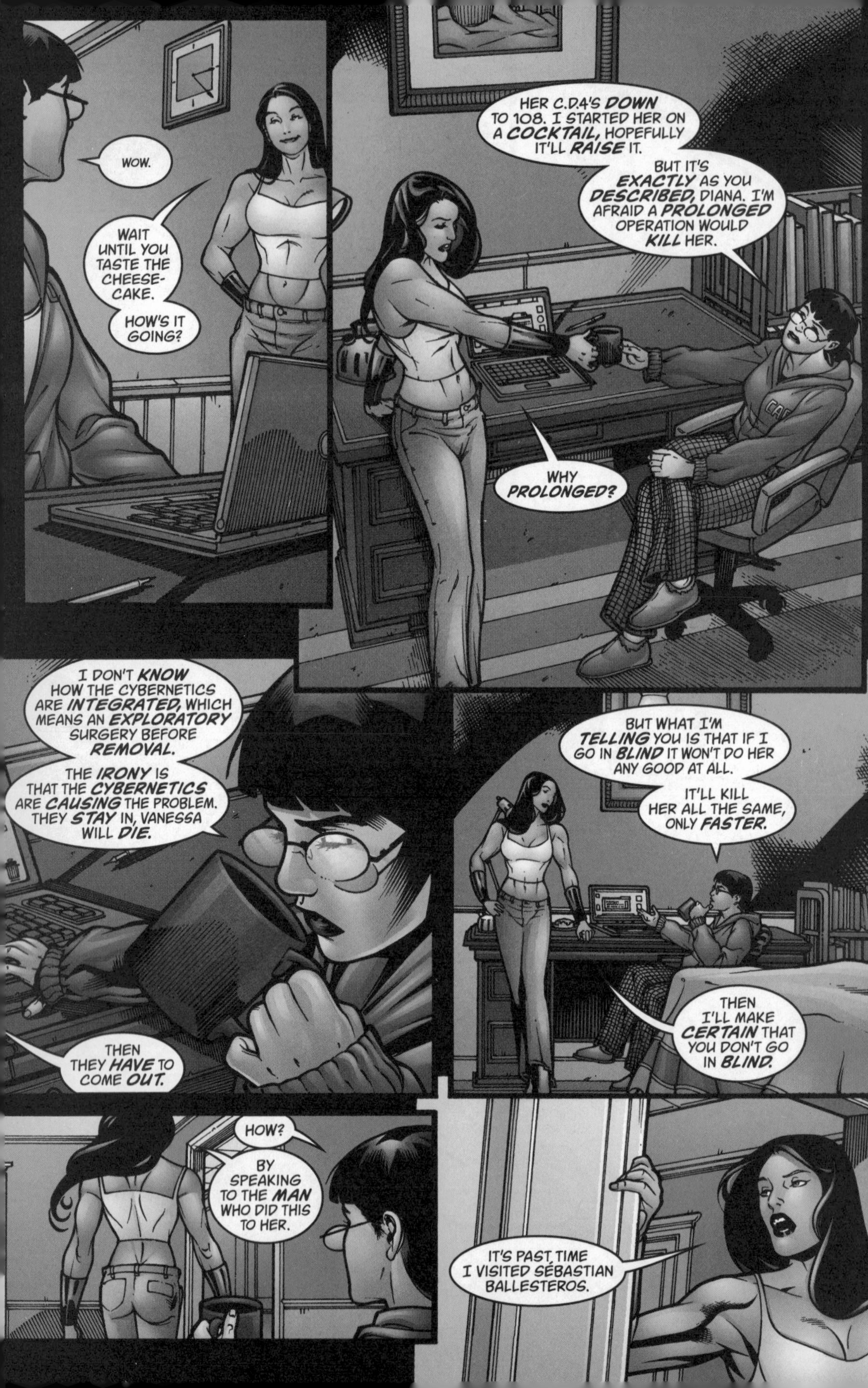

WOW.
WAIT UNTIL YOU TASTE THE CHEESE-CAKE.
HOW'S IT GOING?
HER C.D.4'S DOWN TO 108. I STARTED HER ON A COCKTAIL, HOPEFULLY IT'LL RAISE IT.
BUT IT'S EXACTLY AS YOU DESCRIBED, DIANA. I'M AFRAID A PROLONGED OPERATION WOULD KILL HER.
WHY PROLONGED?
I DON'T KNOW HOW THE CYBERNETICS ARE INTEGRATED, WHICH MEANS AN EXPLORATORY SURGERY BEFORE REMOVAL.
THE IRONY IS THAT THE CYBERNETICS ARE CAUSING THE PROBLEM. THEY STAY IN, VANESSA WILL DIE.
THEN THEY HAVE TO COME OUT.
BUT WHAT I'M TELLING YOU IS THAT IF I GO IN BLIND IT WON'T DO HER ANY GOOD AT ALL.
IT'LL KILL HER ALL THE SAME, ONLY FASTER.
THEN I'LL MAKE CERTAIN THAT YOU DON'T GO IN BLIND.
HOW?
BY SPEAKING TO THE MAN WHO DID THIS TO HER.
IT'S PAST TIME I VISITED SÉBASTIAN BALLESTEROS.

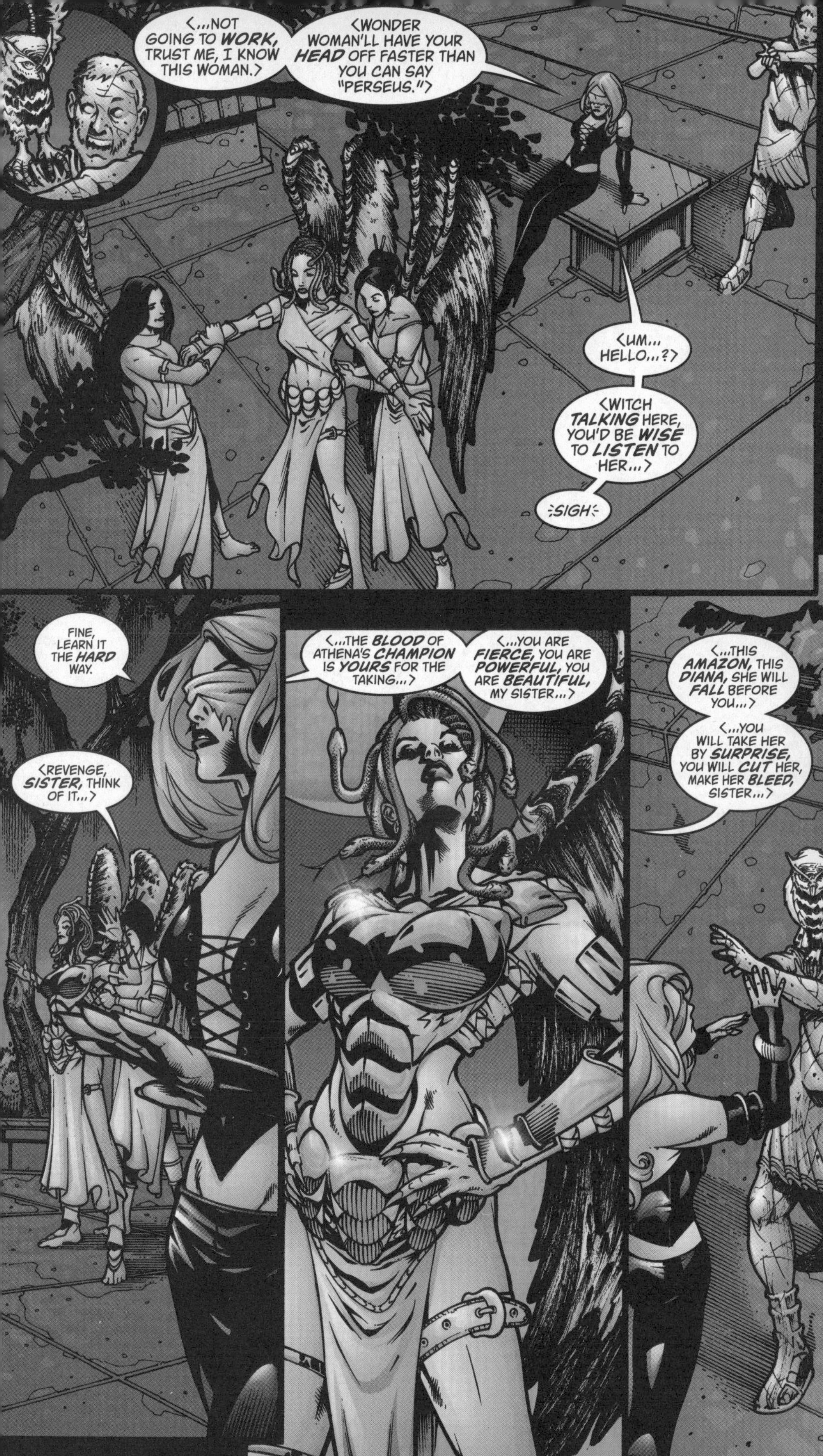
<...NOT GOING TO WORK, TRUST ME, I KNOW THIS WOMAN.>
<WONDER WOMAN'LL HAVE YOUR HEAD OFF FASTER THAN YOU CAN SAY "PERSEUS.">
<UM... HELLO...?>
<WITCH TALKING HERE, YOU'D BE WISE TO LISTEN TO HER...>
SIGH
FINE, LEARN IT THE HARD WAY.
<REVENGE, SISTER, THINK OF IT...>
<...THE BLOOD OF ATHENA'S CHAMPION IS YOURS FOR THE TAKING...>
<...YOU ARE FIERCE, YOU ARE POWERFUL, YOU ARE BEAUTIFUL, MY SISTER...>
<...THIS AMAZON, THIS DIANA, SHE WILL FALL BEFORE YOU...>
<...YOU WILL TAKE HER BY SURPRISE, YOU WILL CUT HER, MAKE HER BLEED, SISTER...>

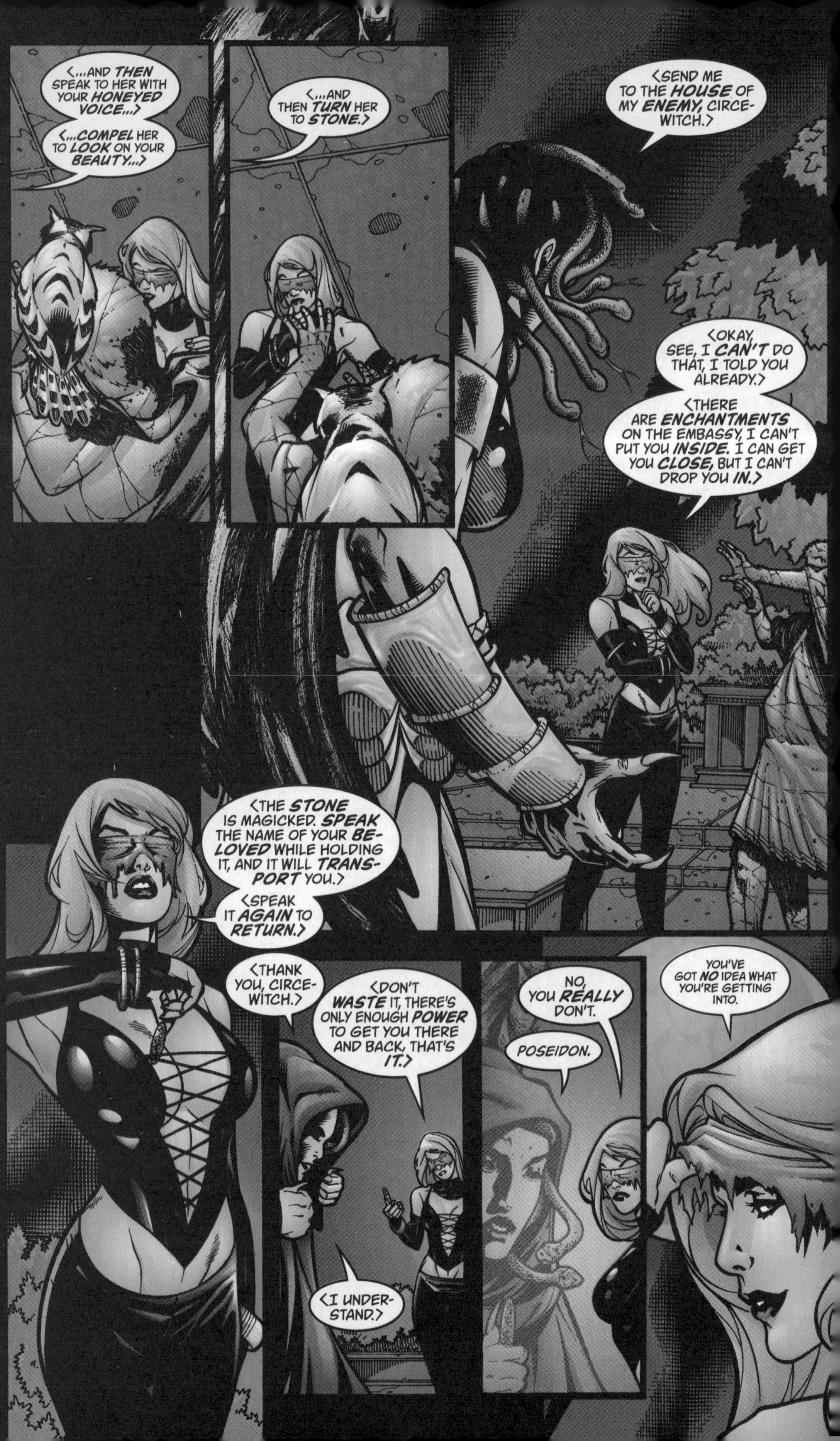

<...AND THEN SPEAK TO HER WITH YOUR HONEYED VOICE...>
<...COMPEL HER TO LOOK ON YOUR BEAUTY...>
<...AND THEN TURN HER TO STONE.>
<SEND ME TO THE HOUSE OF MY ENEMY, CIRCE-WITCH.>
<OKAY, SEE, I CAN'T DO THAT, I TOLD YOU ALREADY.>
<THERE ARE ENCHANTMENTS ON THE EMBASSY, I CAN'T PUT YOU INSIDE. I CAN GET YOU CLOSE, BUT I CAN'T DROP YOU IN.>
<THE STONE IS MAGICKED. SPEAK THE NAME OF YOUR BELOVED WHILE HOLDING IT, AND IT WILL TRANSPORT YOU.>
<SPEAK IT AGAIN TO RETURN.>
<THANK YOU, CIRCE-WITCH.>
<DON'T WASTE IT, THERE'S ONLY ENOUGH POWER TO GET YOU THERE AND BACK, THAT'S IT.>
<I UNDERSTAND.>
POSEIDON.
NO, YOU REALLY DON'T.
YOU'VE GOT NO IDEA WHAT YOU'RE GETTING INTO.

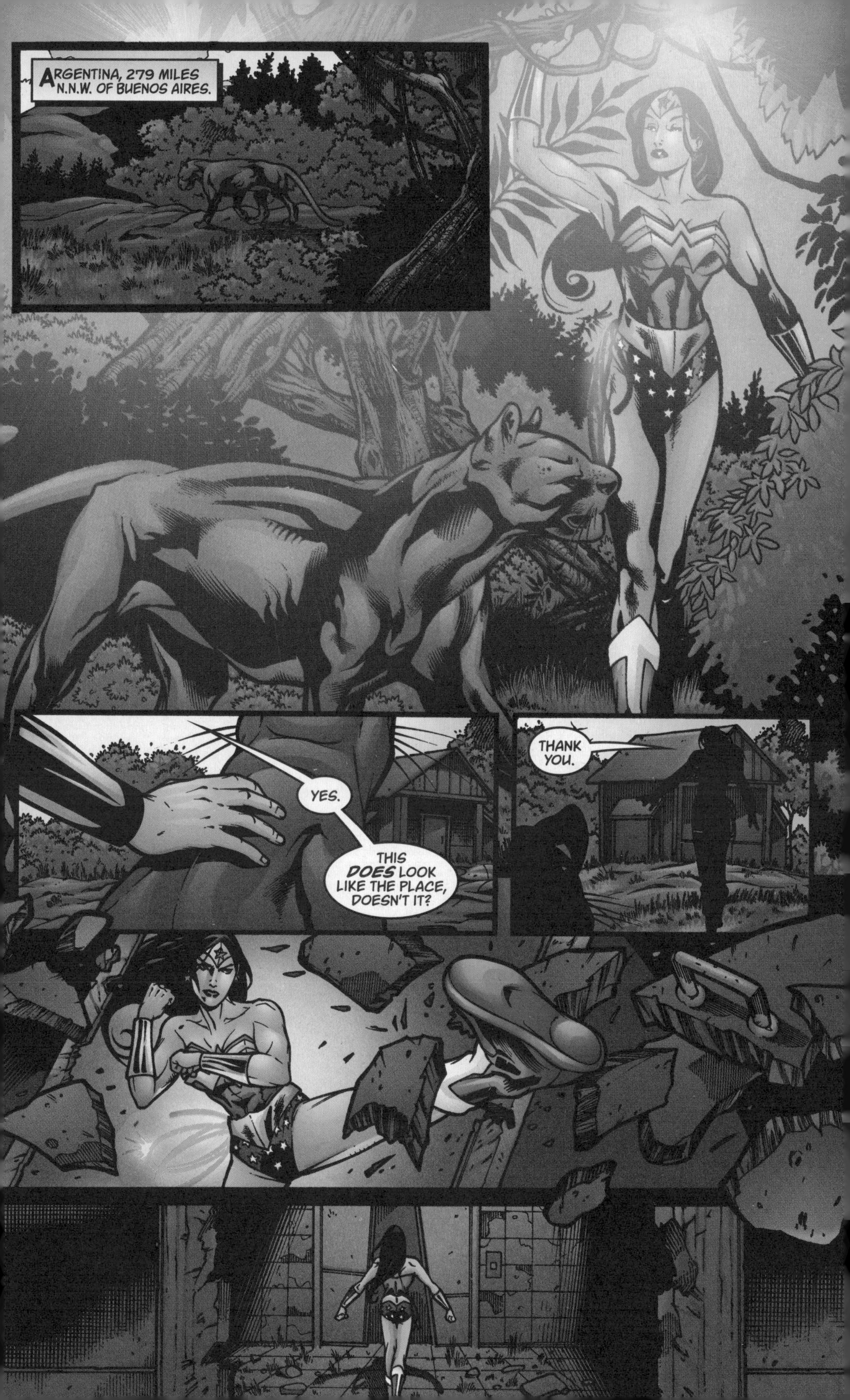
ARGENTINA, 279 MILES N.N.W. OF BUENOS AIRES.
YES.
THIS DOES LOOK LIKE THE PLACE, DOESN'T IT?
THANK YOU.

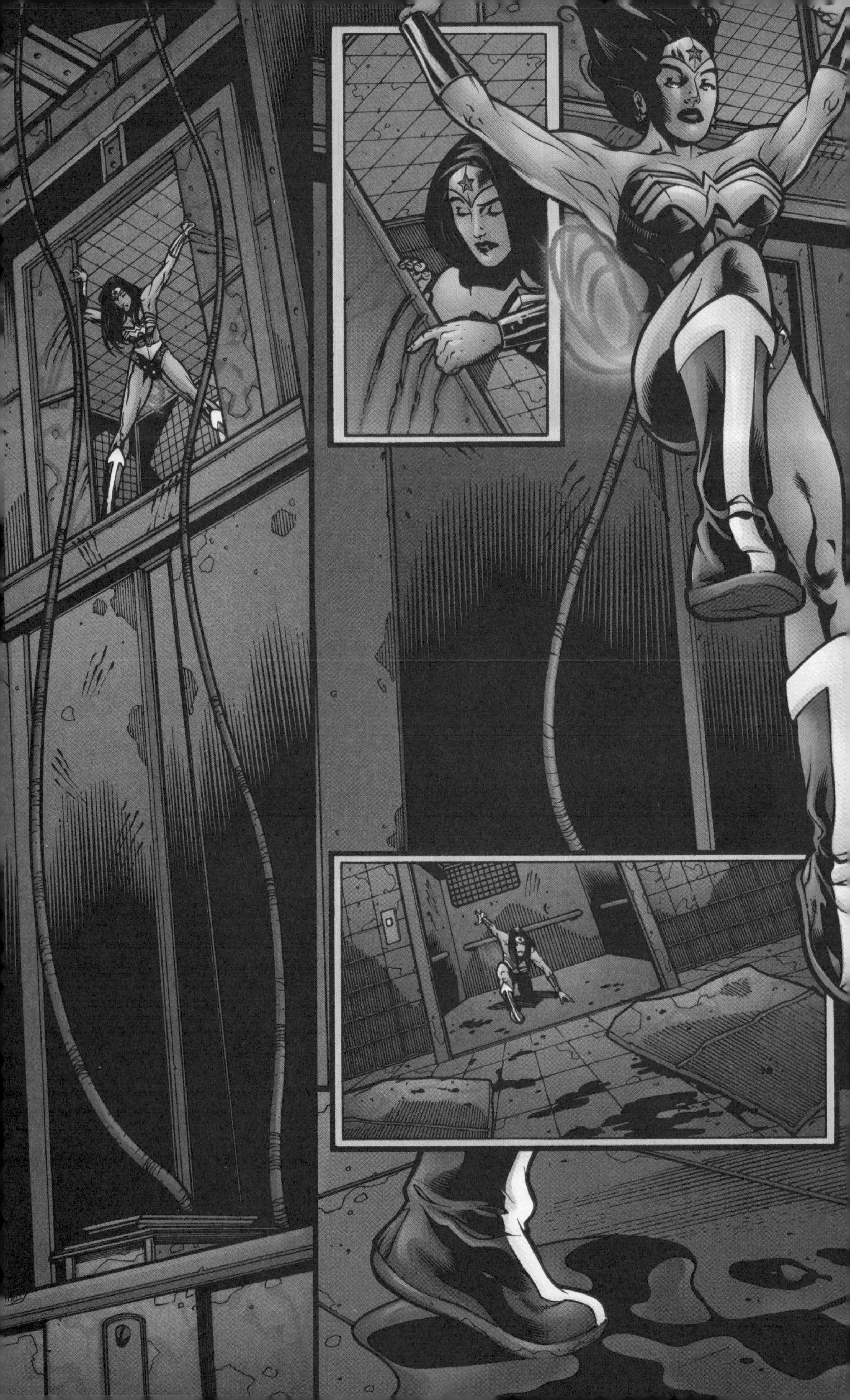

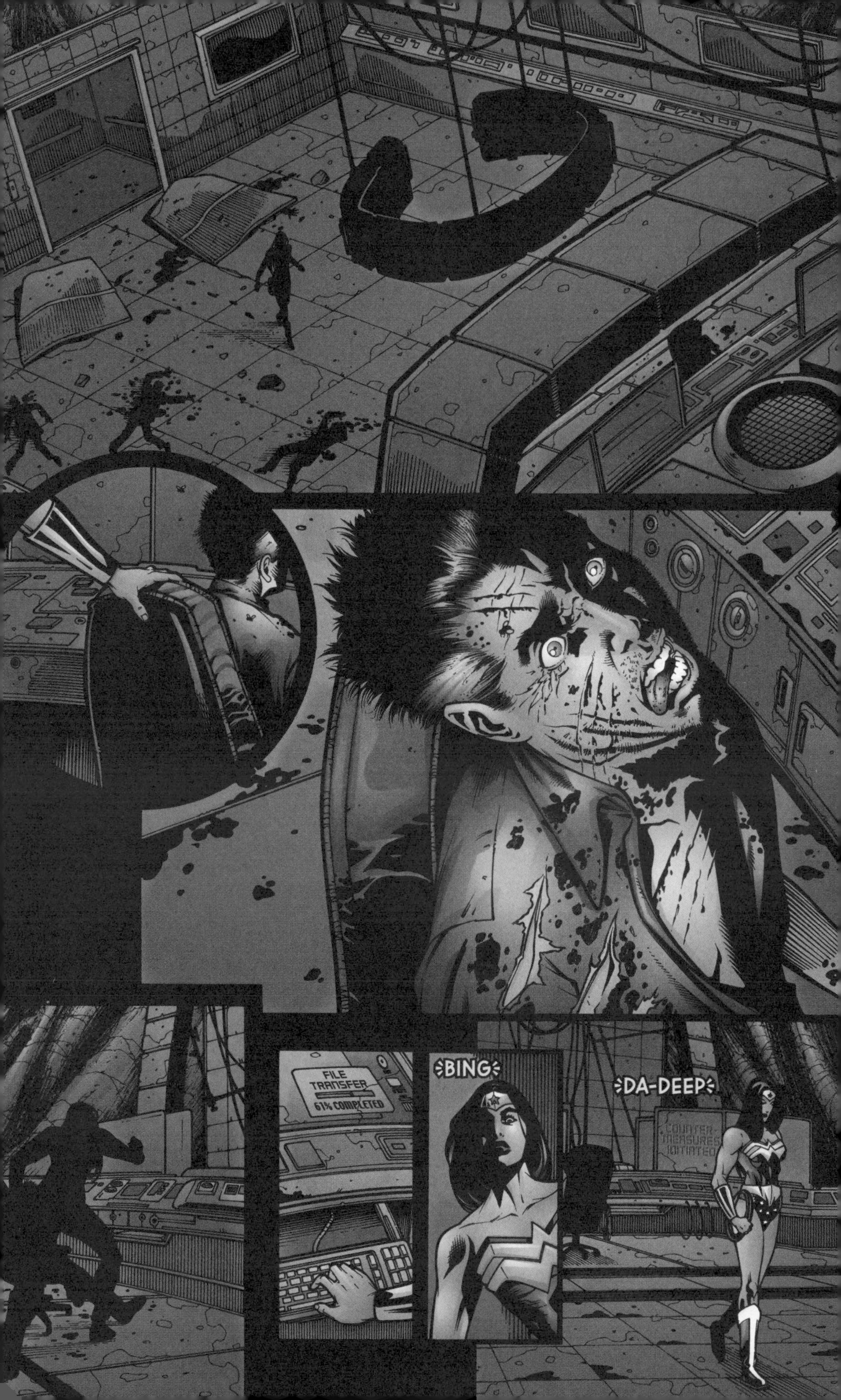

FILE TRANSFER
61% COMPLETED
BING
DA-DEEP
COUNTER-MEASURES INITIATED

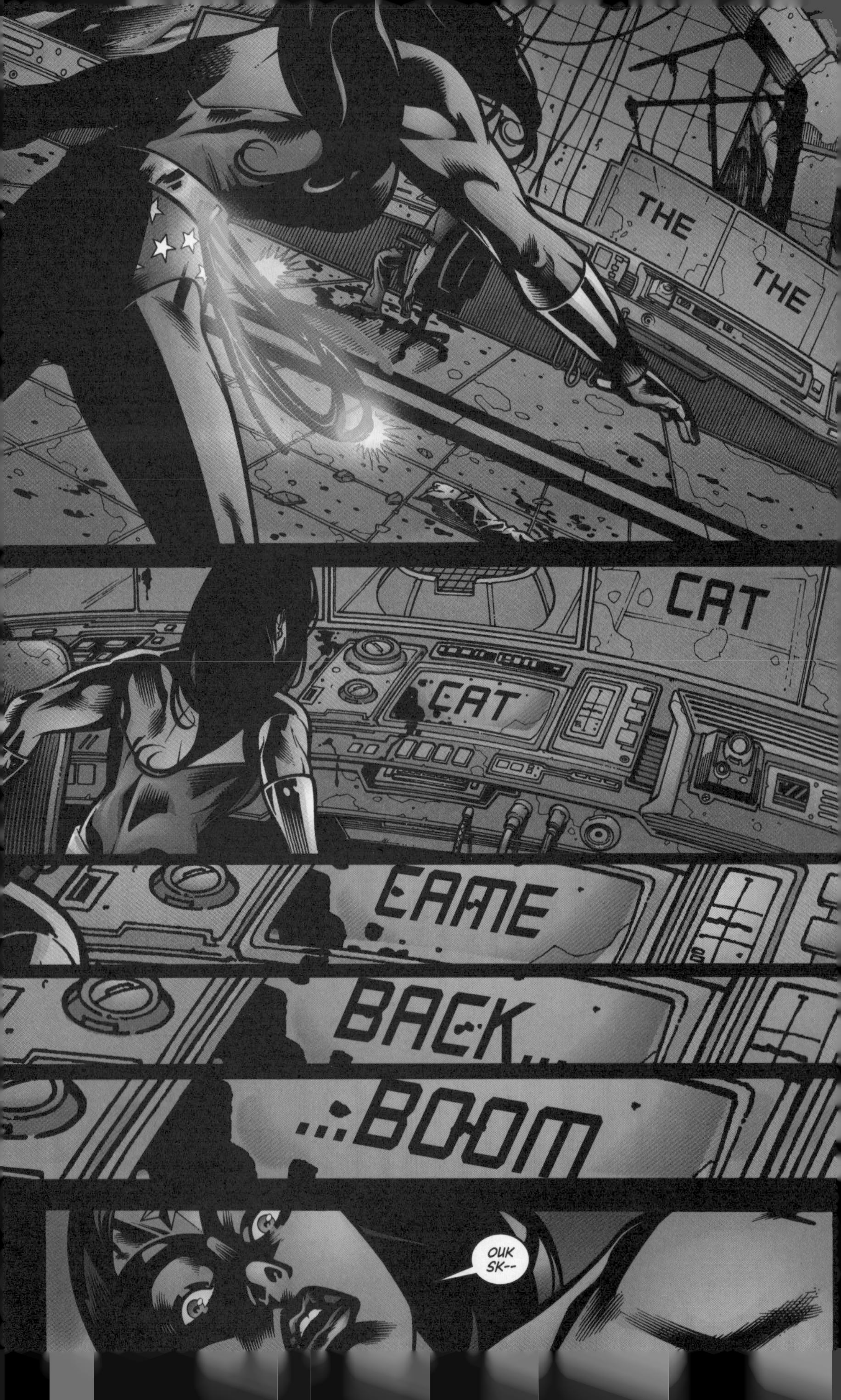
THE
THE
CAT
CAT
CAME
BACK...
...BOOM
OUK SK--

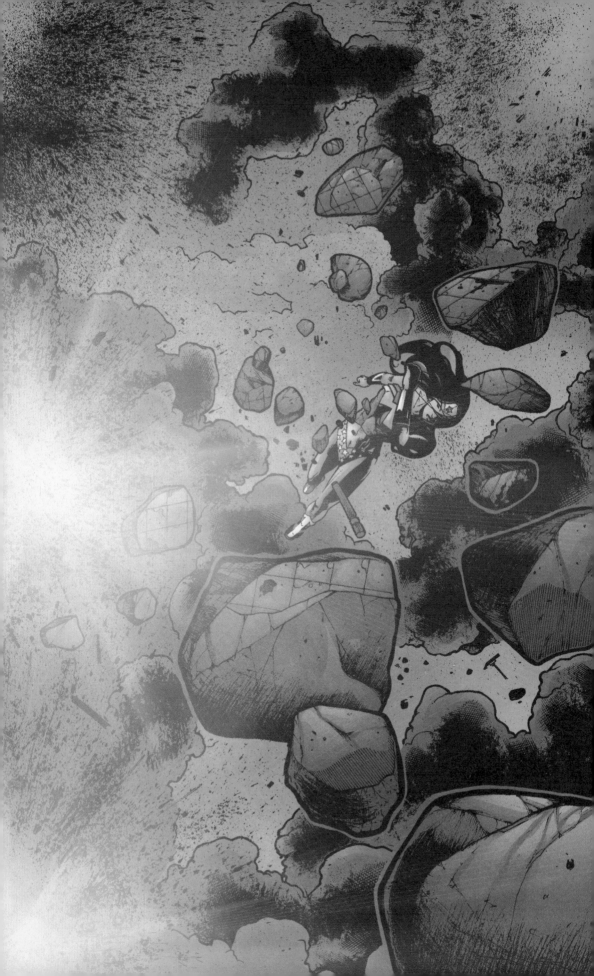

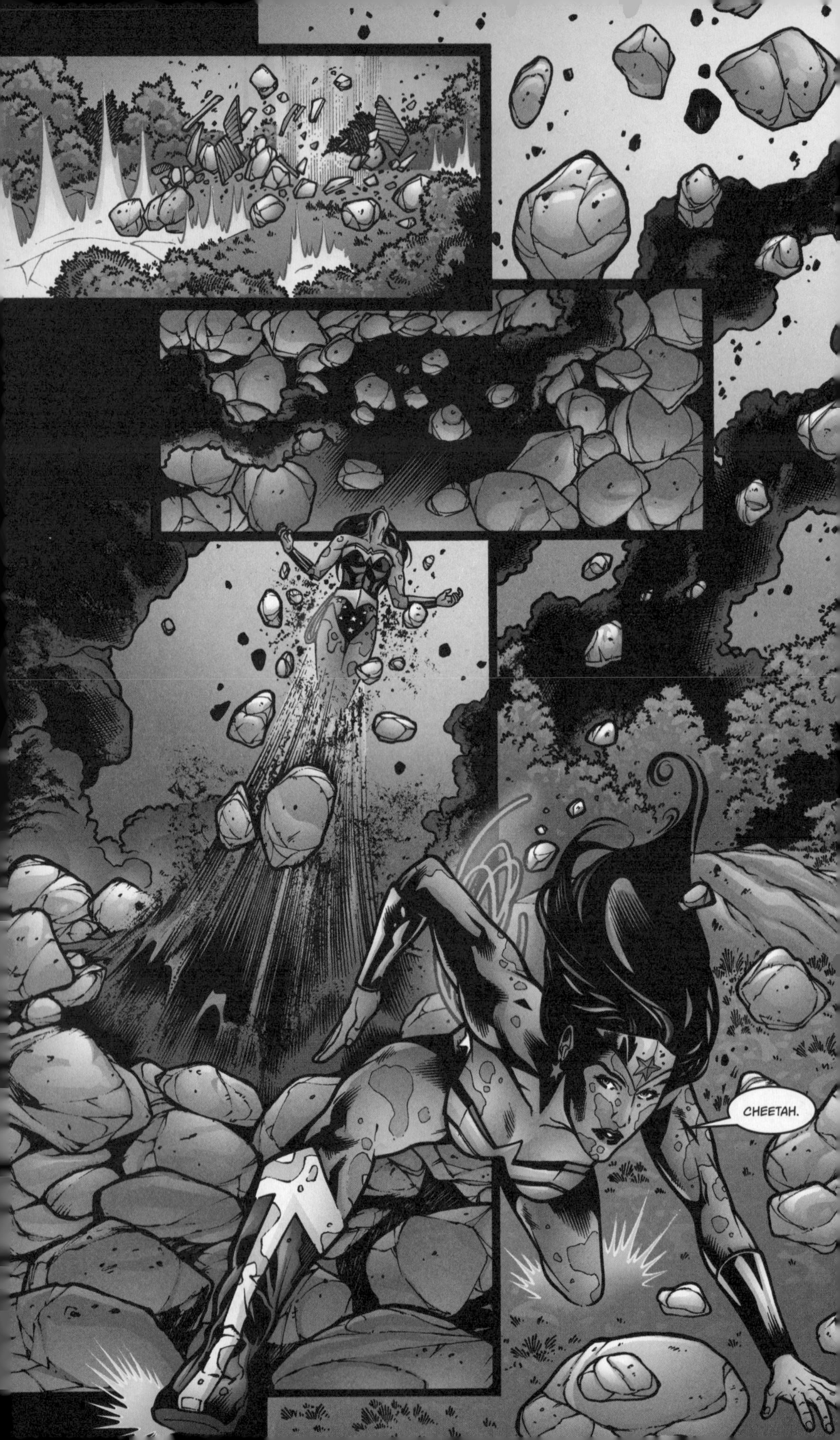
CHEETAH.

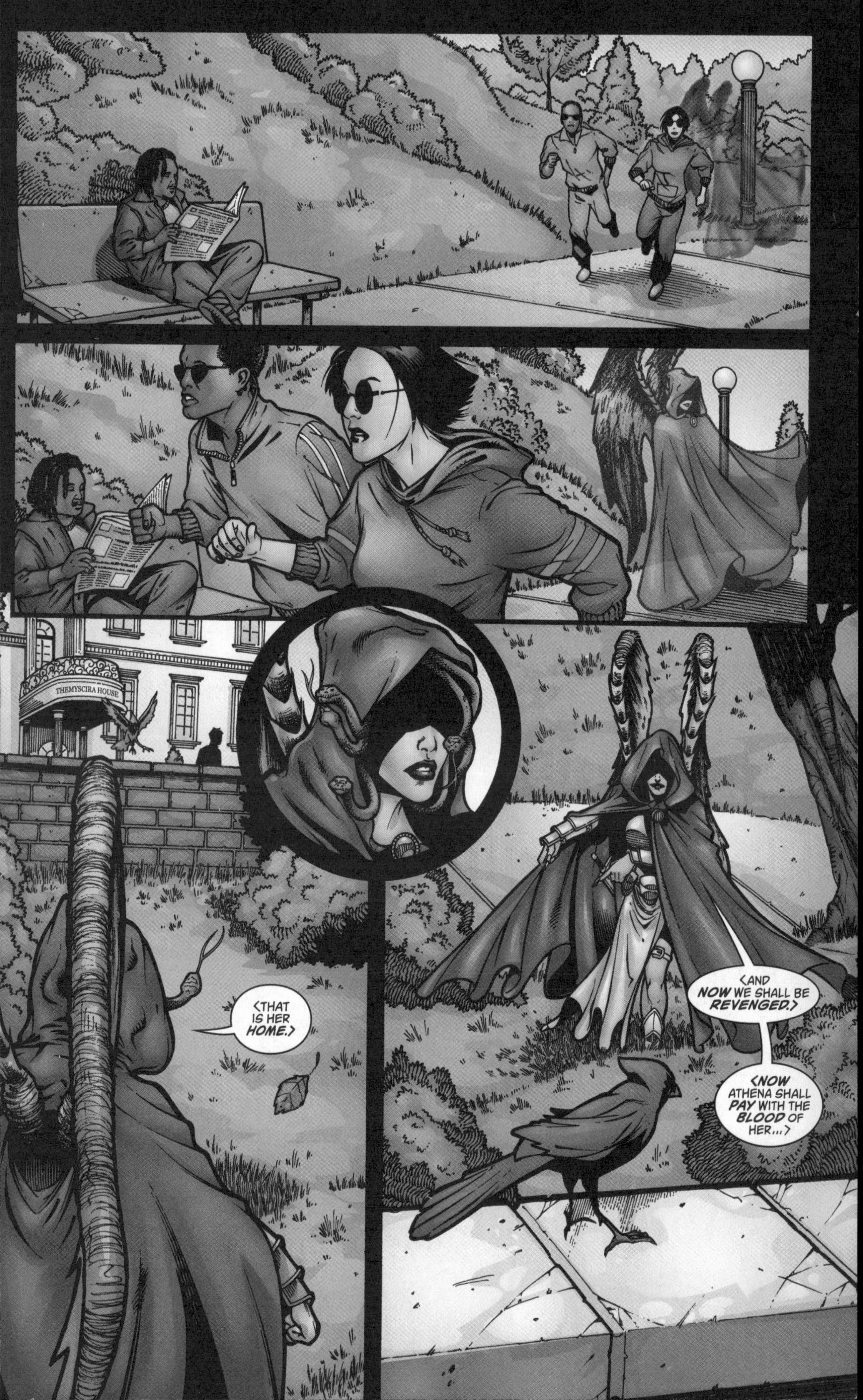
THEMYSCIRA HOUSE
<THAT IS HER HOME.>
<AND NOW WE SHALL BE REVENGED.>
<NOW ATHENA SHALL PAY WITH THE BLOOD OF HER...>

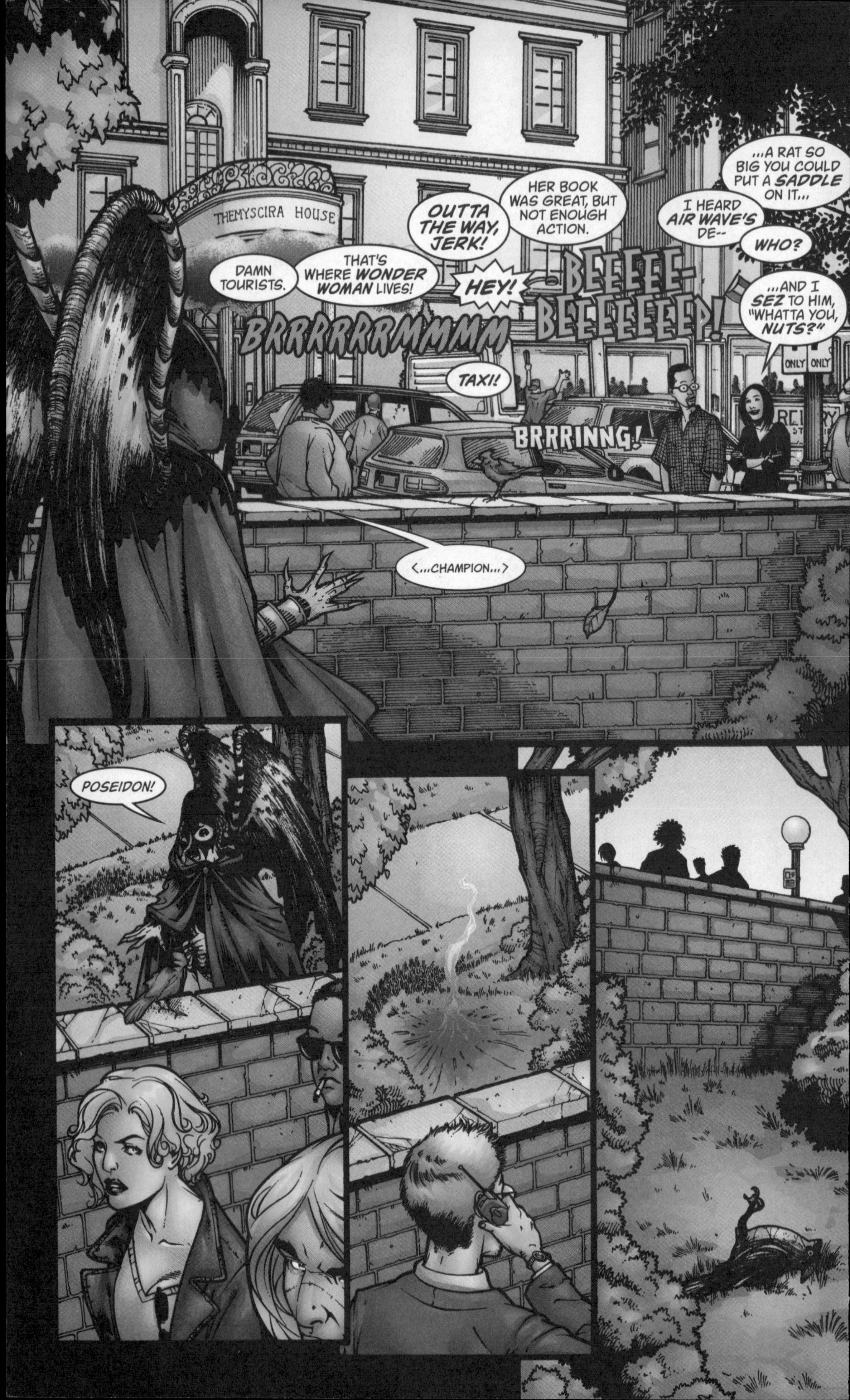
THEMYSCIRA HOUSE
DAMN TOURISTS.
THAT'S WHERE WONDER WOMAN LIVES!
BRRRRRRMMMMM
OUTTA THE WAY, JERK!
HEY!
HER BOOK WAS GREAT, BUT NOT ENOUGH ACTION.
BEEEEE-BEEEEEEEP!
TAXI!
I HEARD AIR WAVE'S DE--
...A RAT SO BIG YOU COULD PUT A SADDLE ON IT...
WHO?
...AND I SEZ TO HIM, "WHATTA YOU, NUTS?"
ONLY ONLY
BRRRINNG!
<...CHAMPION...>
POSEIDON!

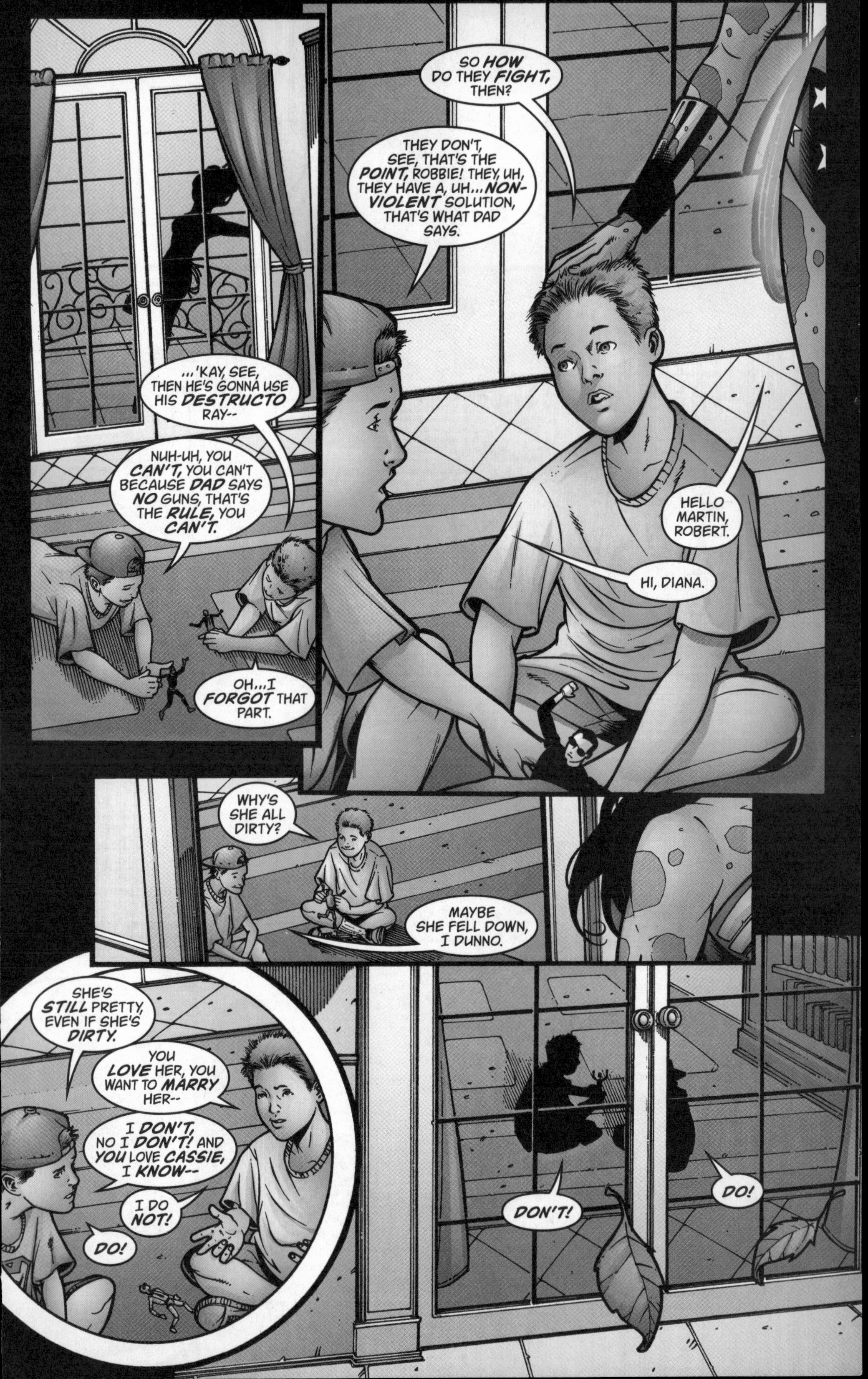
SO HOW DO THEY FIGHT, THEN?
THEY DON'T, SEE, THAT'S THE POINT, ROBBIE! THEY, UH, THEY HAVE A, UH... NON-VIOLENT SOLUTION, THAT'S WHAT DAD SAYS.
...'KAY, SEE, THEN HE'S GONNA USE HIS DESTRUCTO RAY--
NUH-UH, YOU CAN'T, YOU CAN'T BECAUSE DAD SAYS NO GUNS, THAT'S THE RULE, YOU CAN'T.
OH...I FORGOT THAT PART.
HELLO MARTIN, ROBERT.
HI, DIANA.
WHY'S SHE ALL DIRTY?
MAYBE SHE FELL DOWN, I DUNNO.
SHE'S STILL PRETTY, EVEN IF SHE'S DIRTY.
YOU LOVE HER, YOU WANT TO MARRY HER--
I DON'T, NO I DON'T! AND YOU LOVE CASSIE, I KNOW--
I DO NOT!
DO!
DON'T!
DO!

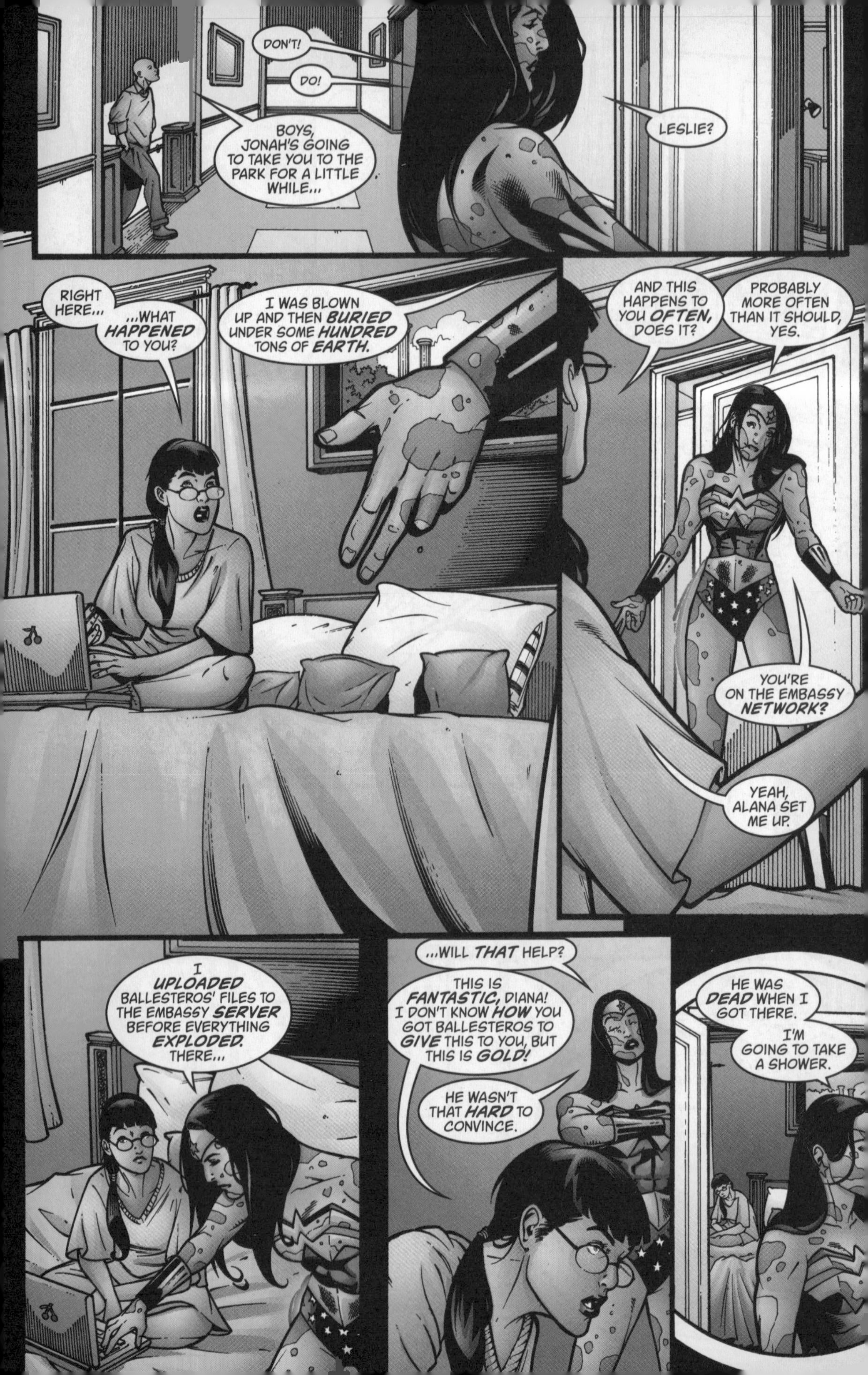

DON'T!
DO!
BOYS, JONAH'S GOING TO TAKE YOU TO THE PARK FOR A LITTLE WHILE...
LESLIE?
RIGHT HERE...
...WHAT HAPPENED TO YOU?
I WAS BLOWN UP AND THEN BURIED UNDER SOME HUNDRED TONS OF EARTH.
AND THIS HAPPENS TO YOU OFTEN, DOES IT?
PROBABLY MORE OFTEN THAN IT SHOULD, YES.
YOU'RE ON THE EMBASSY NETWORK?
YEAH, ALANA SET ME UP.
I UPLOADED BALLESTEROS' FILES TO THE EMBASSY SERVER BEFORE EVERYTHING EXPLODED. THERE...
...WILL THAT HELP?
THIS IS FANTASTIC, DIANA! I DON'T KNOW HOW YOU GOT BALLESTEROS TO GIVE THIS TO YOU, BUT THIS IS GOLD!
HE WASN'T THAT HARD TO CONVINCE.
HE WAS DEAD WHEN I GOT THERE.
I'M GOING TO TAKE A SHOWER.

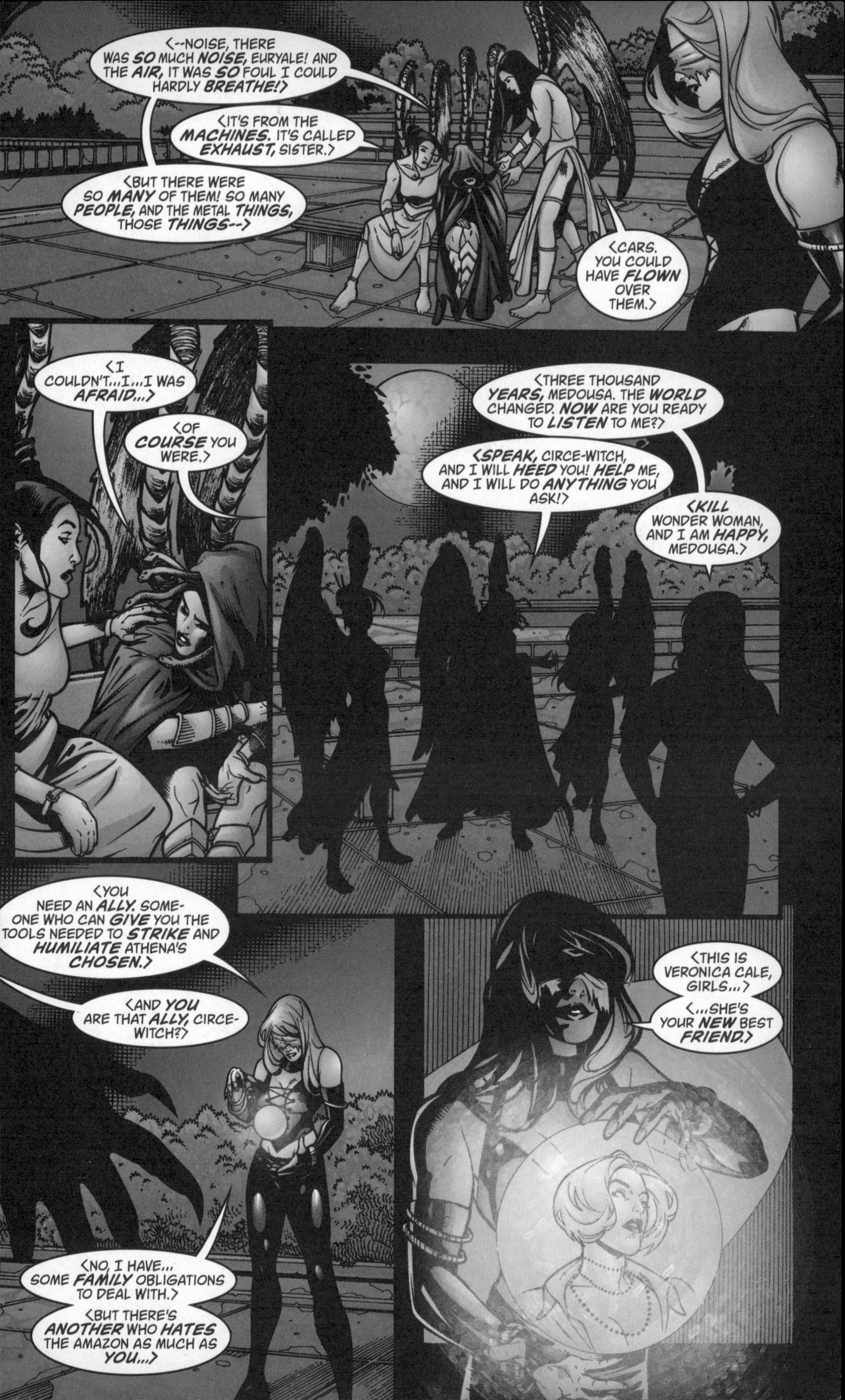
<--NOISE, THERE WAS SO MUCH NOISE, EURYALE! AND THE AIR, IT WAS SO FOUL I COULD HARDLY BREATHE!>
<IT'S FROM THE MACHINES. IT'S CALLED EXHAUST, SISTER.>
<BUT THERE WERE SO MANY OF THEM! SO MANY PEOPLE, AND THE METAL THINGS, THOSE THINGS-->
<CARS. YOU COULD HAVE FLOWN OVER THEM.>
<I COULDN'T...I...I WAS AFRAID...>
<OF COURSE YOU WERE.>
<THREE THOUSAND YEARS, MEDOUSA. THE WORLD CHANGED. NOW ARE YOU READY TO LISTEN TO ME?>
<SPEAK, CIRCE-WITCH, AND I WILL HEED YOU! HELP ME, AND I WILL DO ANYTHING YOU ASK!>
<KILL WONDER WOMAN, AND I AM HAPPY, MEDOUSA.>
<YOU NEED AN ALLY. SOME-ONE WHO CAN GIVE YOU THE TOOLS NEEDED TO STRIKE AND HUMILIATE ATHENA'S CHOSEN.>
<AND YOU ARE THAT ALLY, CIRCE-WITCH?>
<NO, I HAVE... SOME FAMILY OBLIGATIONS TO DEAL WITH.>
<BUT THERE'S ANOTHER WHO HATES THE AMAZON AS MUCH AS YOU...>
<THIS IS VERONICA CALE, GIRLS...>
<...SHE'S YOUR NEW BEST FRIEND.>

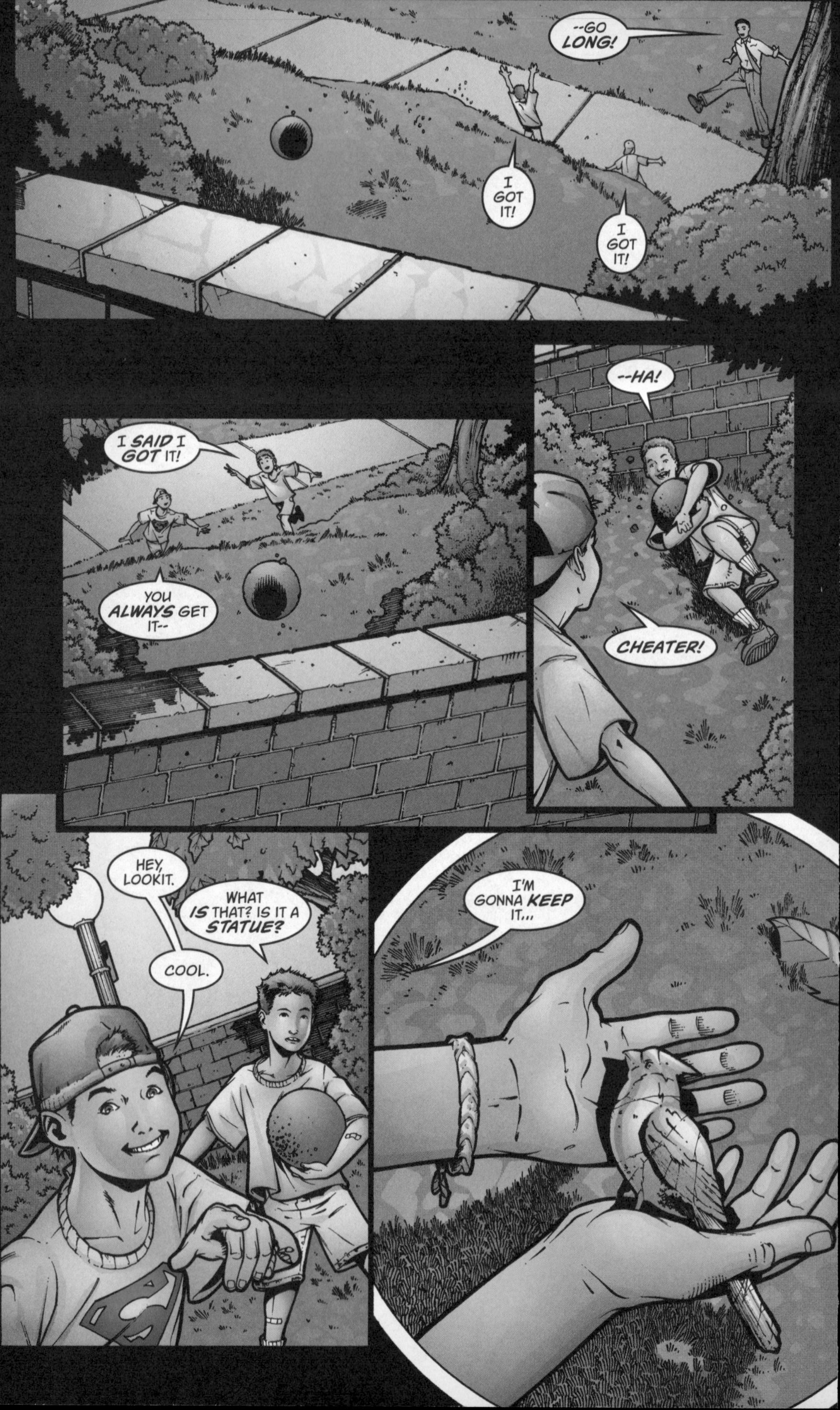
--GO LONG!
I GOT IT!
I GOT IT!
I SAID I GOT IT!
YOU ALWAYS GET IT--
--HA!
CHEATER!
HEY, LOOKIT.
WHAT IS THAT? IS IT A STATUE?
COOL.
I'M GONNA KEEP IT...

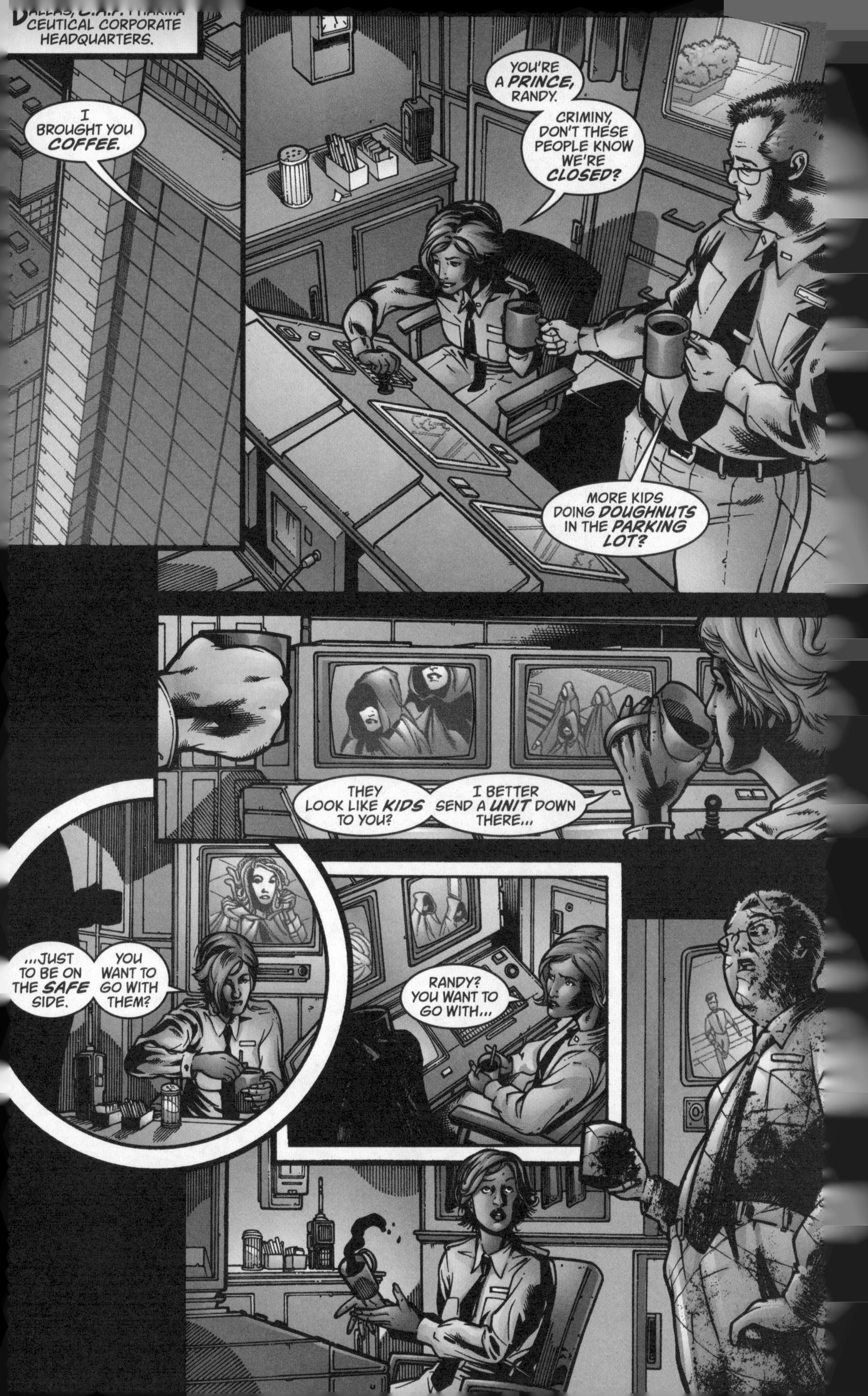
CEUTICAL CORPORATE HEADQUARTERS.
I BROUGHT YOU COFFEE.
YOU'RE A PRINCE, RANDY.
CRIMINY, DON'T THESE PEOPLE KNOW WE'RE CLOSED?
MORE KIDS DOING DOUGHNUTS IN THE PARKING LOT?
THEY LOOK LIKE KIDS TO YOU?
I BETTER SEND A UNIT DOWN THERE...
...JUST TO BE ON THE SAFE SIDE.
YOU WANT TO GO WITH THEM?
RANDY? YOU WANT TO GO WITH...

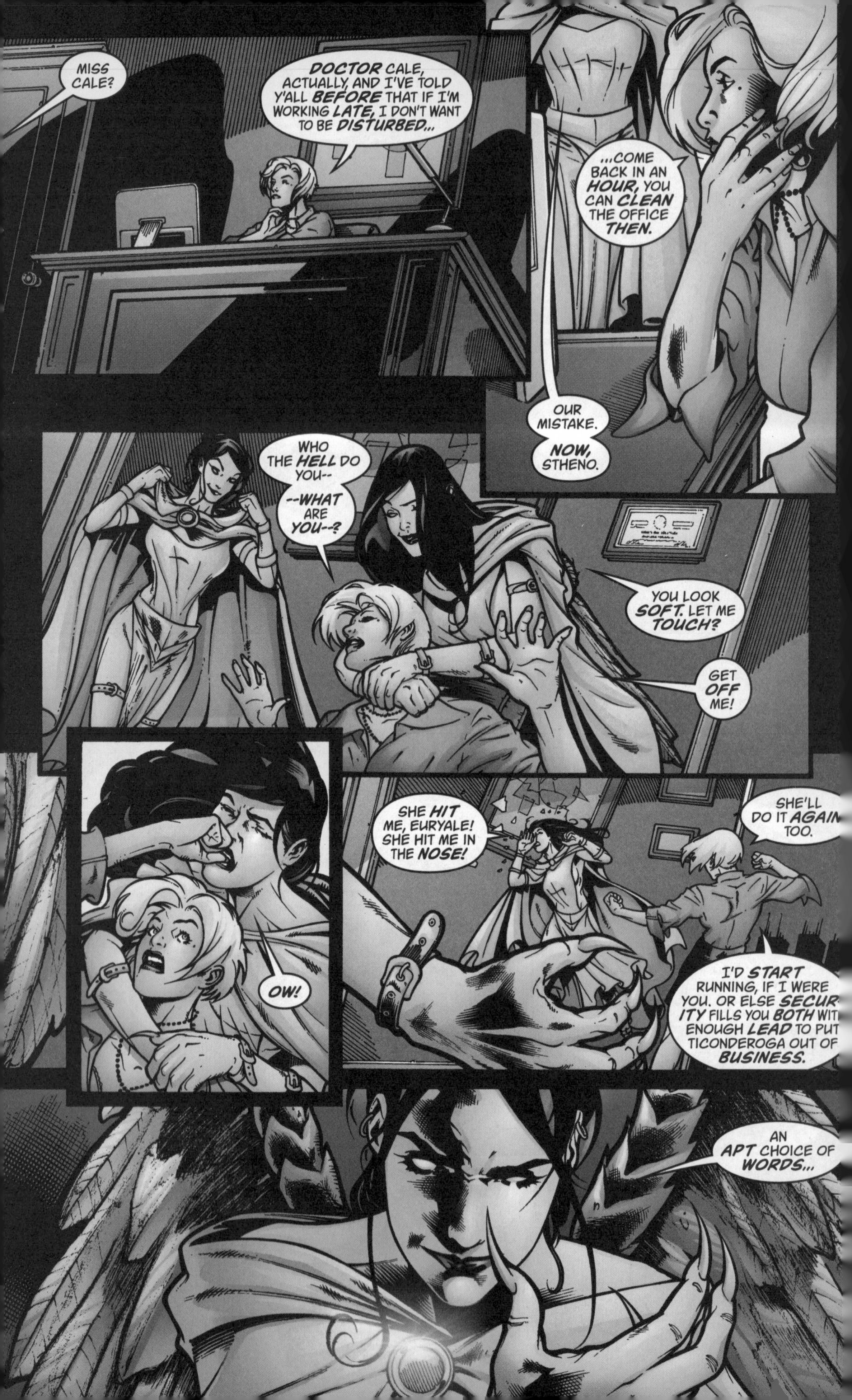
MISS CALE?
DOCTOR CALE, ACTUALLY, AND I'VE TOLD Y'ALL BEFORE THAT IF I'M WORKING LATE, I DON'T WANT TO BE DISTURBED...
...COME BACK IN AN HOUR, YOU CAN CLEAN THE OFFICE THEN.
OUR MISTAKE.
NOW, STHENO.
WHO THE HELL DO YOU--
--WHAT ARE YOU--?
YOU LOOK SOFT. LET ME TOUCH?
GET OFF ME!
OW!
SHE HIT ME, EURYALE! SHE HIT ME IN THE NOSE!
SHE'LL DO IT AGAIN TOO.
I'D START RUNNING, IF I WERE YOU. OR ELSE SECURITY FILLS YOU BOTH WITH ENOUGH LEAD TO PUT TICONDEROGA OUT OF BUSINESS.
AN APT CHOICE OF WORDS...

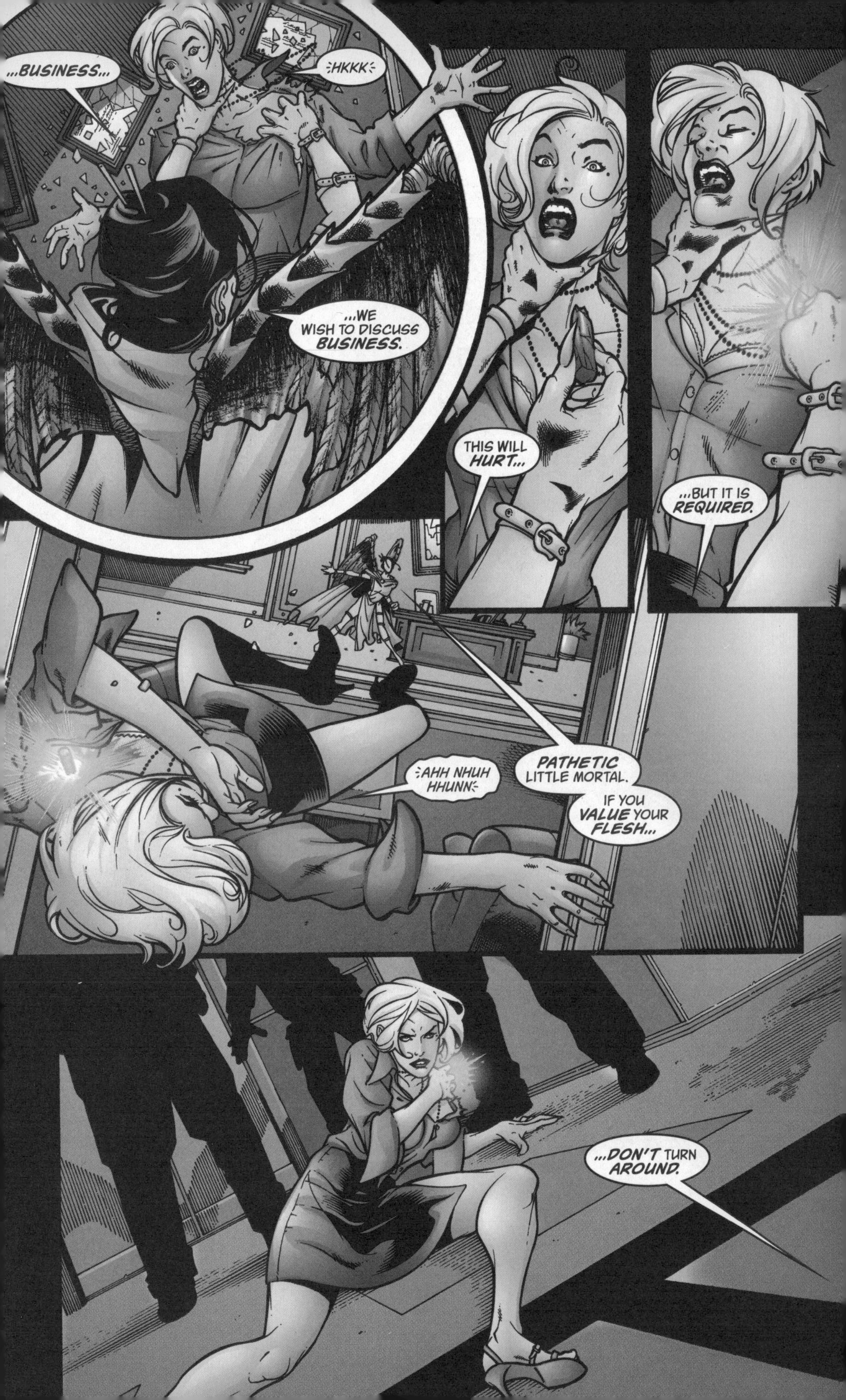

...BUSINESS...
HKKK
...WE WISH TO DISCUSS BUSINESS.
THIS WILL HURT...
...BUT IT IS REQUIRED.
AHH NHUH HHUNN
PATHETIC LITTLE MORTAL.
IF YOU VALUE YOUR FLESH...
...DON'T TURN AROUND.

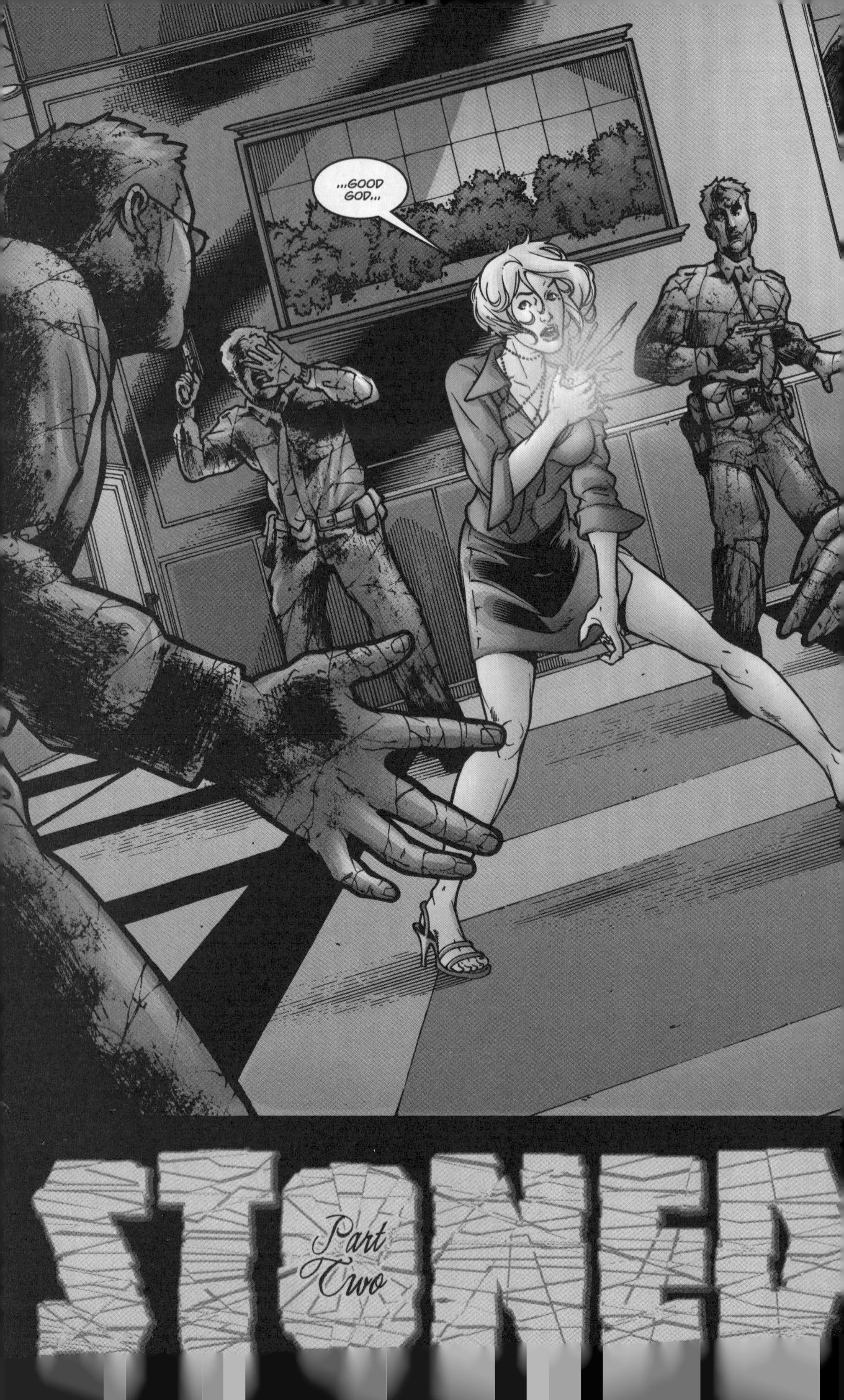
...GOOD GOD...
STONED
Part Two

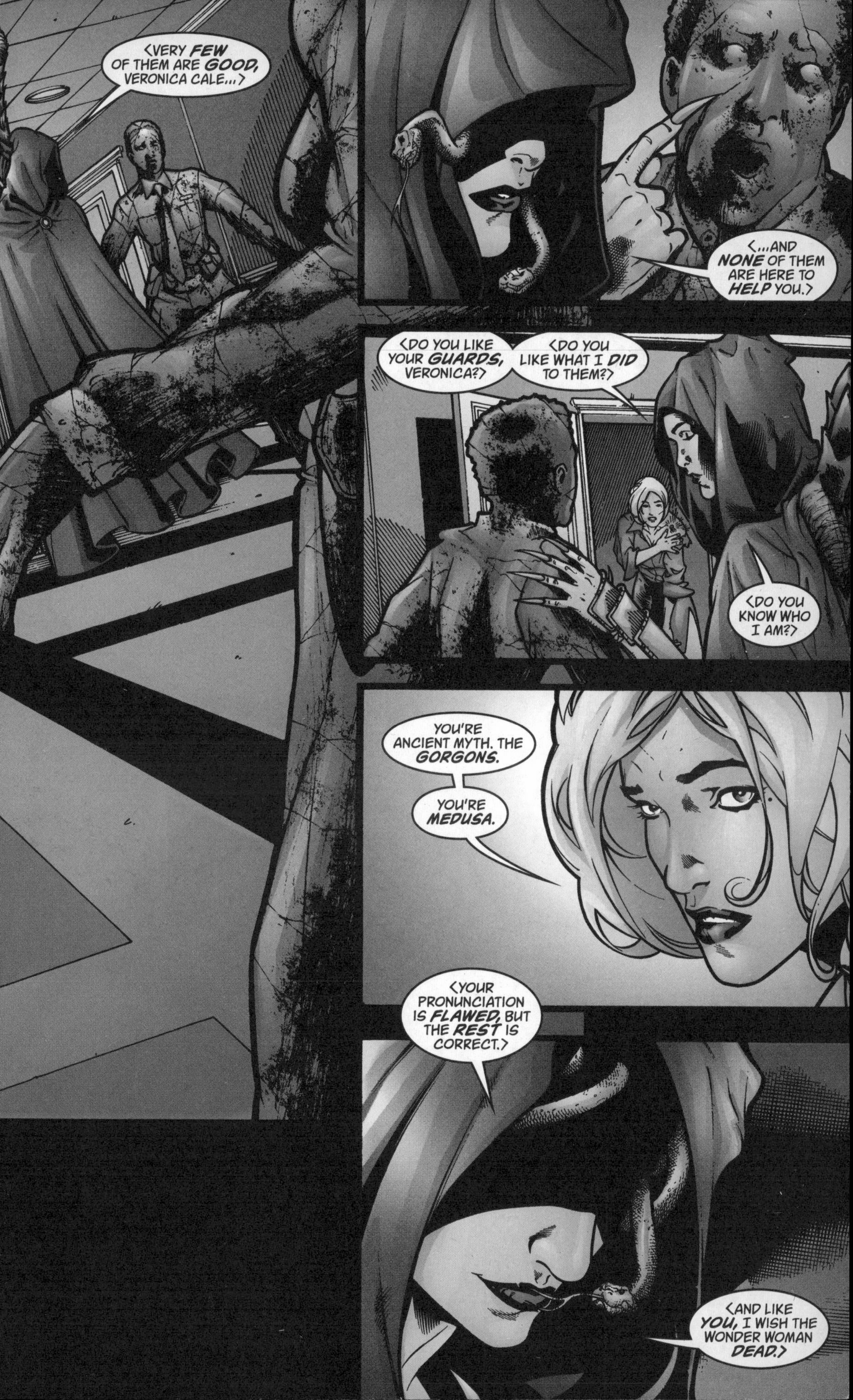
<VERY FEW OF THEM ARE GOOD, VERONICA CALE...>
<...AND NONE OF THEM ARE HERE TO HELP YOU.>
<DO YOU LIKE YOUR GUARDS, VERONICA?>
<DO YOU LIKE WHAT I DID TO THEM?>
<DO YOU KNOW WHO I AM?>
YOU'RE ANCIENT MYTH. THE GORGONS.
YOU'RE MEDUSA.
<YOUR PRONUNCIATION IS FLAWED, BUT THE REST IS CORRECT.>
<AND LIKE YOU, I WISH THE WONDER WOMAN DEAD.>

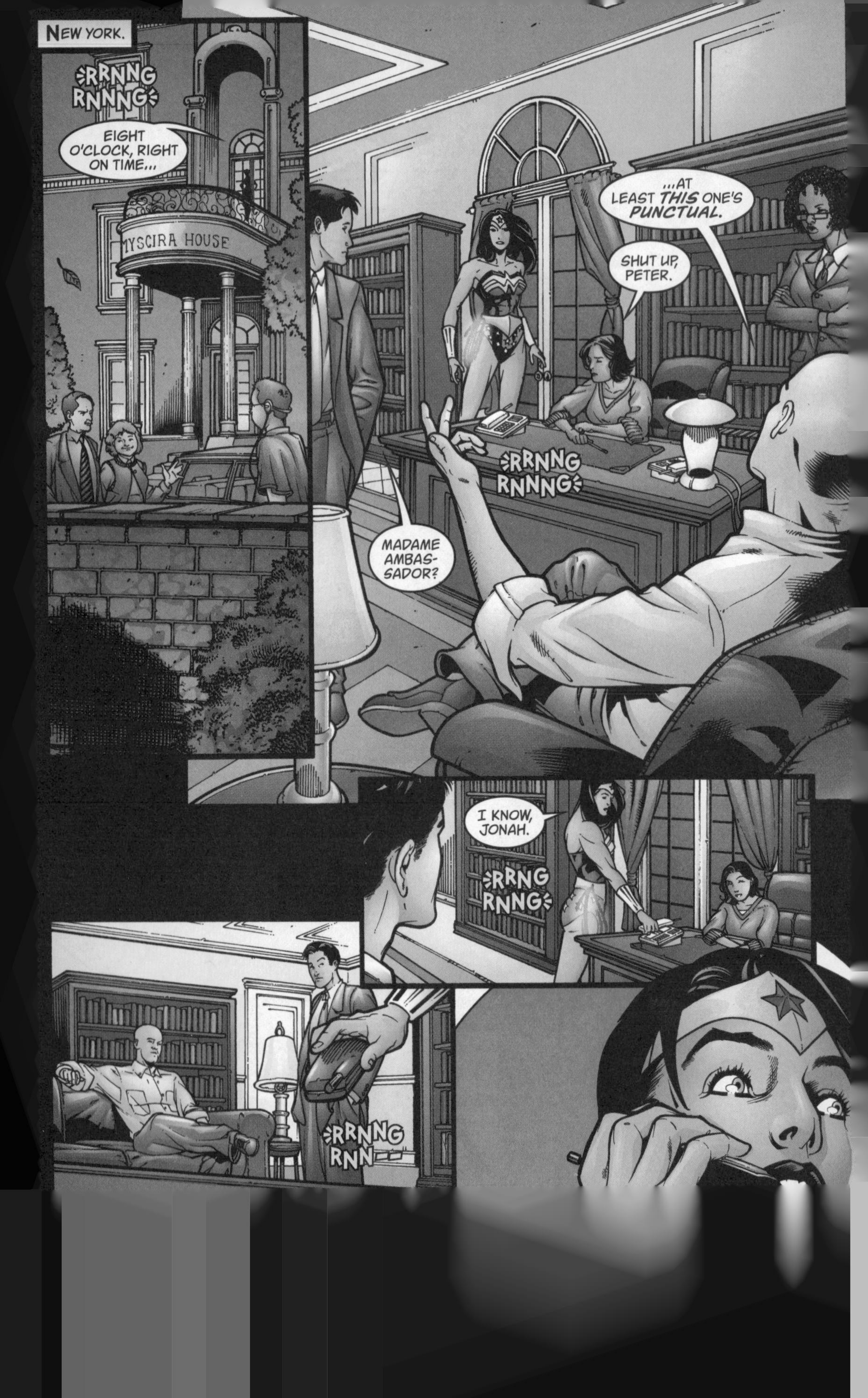
NEW YORK.
RRNNG RNNNG
EIGHT O'CLOCK, RIGHT ON TIME...
MYSCIRA HOUSE
...AT LEAST THIS ONE'S PUNCTUAL.
SHUT UP, PETER.
RRNNG RNNNG
MADAME AMBAS-SADOR?
I KNOW, JONAH.
RRNG RNG
RRNNG RNN

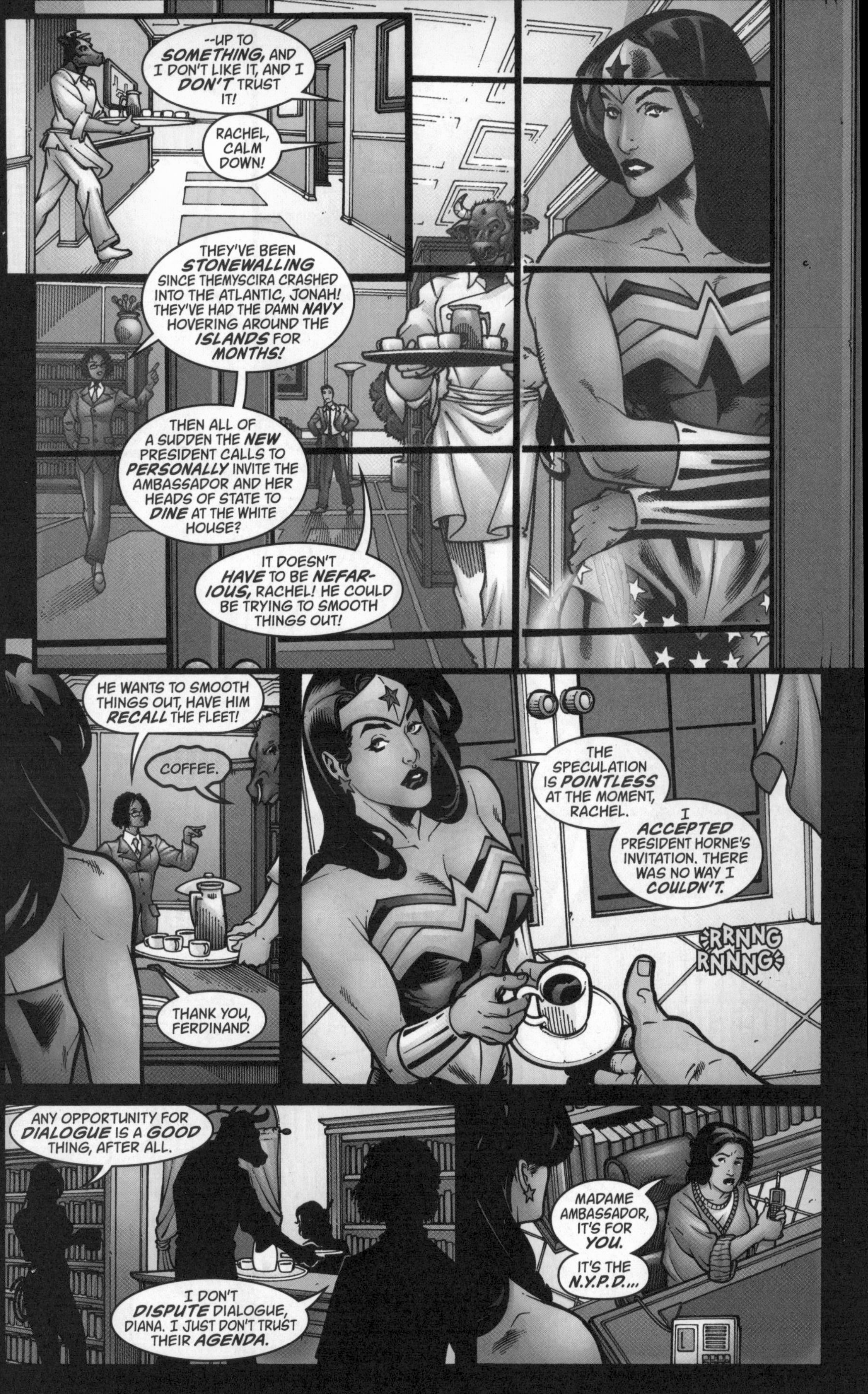
--UP TO SOMETHING, AND I DON'T LIKE IT, AND I DON'T TRUST IT!
RACHEL, CALM DOWN!
THEY'VE BEEN STONEWALLING SINCE THEMYSCIRA CRASHED INTO THE ATLANTIC, JONAH! THEY'VE HAD THE DAMN NAVY HOVERING AROUND THE ISLANDS FOR MONTHS!
THEN ALL OF A SUDDEN THE NEW PRESIDENT CALLS TO PERSONALLY INVITE THE AMBASSADOR AND HER HEADS OF STATE TO DINE AT THE WHITE HOUSE?
IT DOESN'T HAVE TO BE NEFARIOUS, RACHEL! HE COULD BE TRYING TO SMOOTH THINGS OUT!
HE WANTS TO SMOOTH THINGS OUT, HAVE HIM RECALL THE FLEET!
COFFEE.
THANK YOU, FERDINAND.
THE SPECULATION IS POINTLESS AT THE MOMENT, RACHEL.
I ACCEPTED PRESIDENT HORNE'S INVITATION. THERE WAS NO WAY I COULDN'T.
RRNNG RNNNG
ANY OPPORTUNITY FOR DIALOGUE IS A GOOD THING, AFTER ALL.
I DON'T DISPUTE DIALOGUE, DIANA. I JUST DON'T TRUST THEIR AGENDA.
MADAME AMBASSADOR, IT'S FOR YOU.
IT'S THE N.Y.P.D....

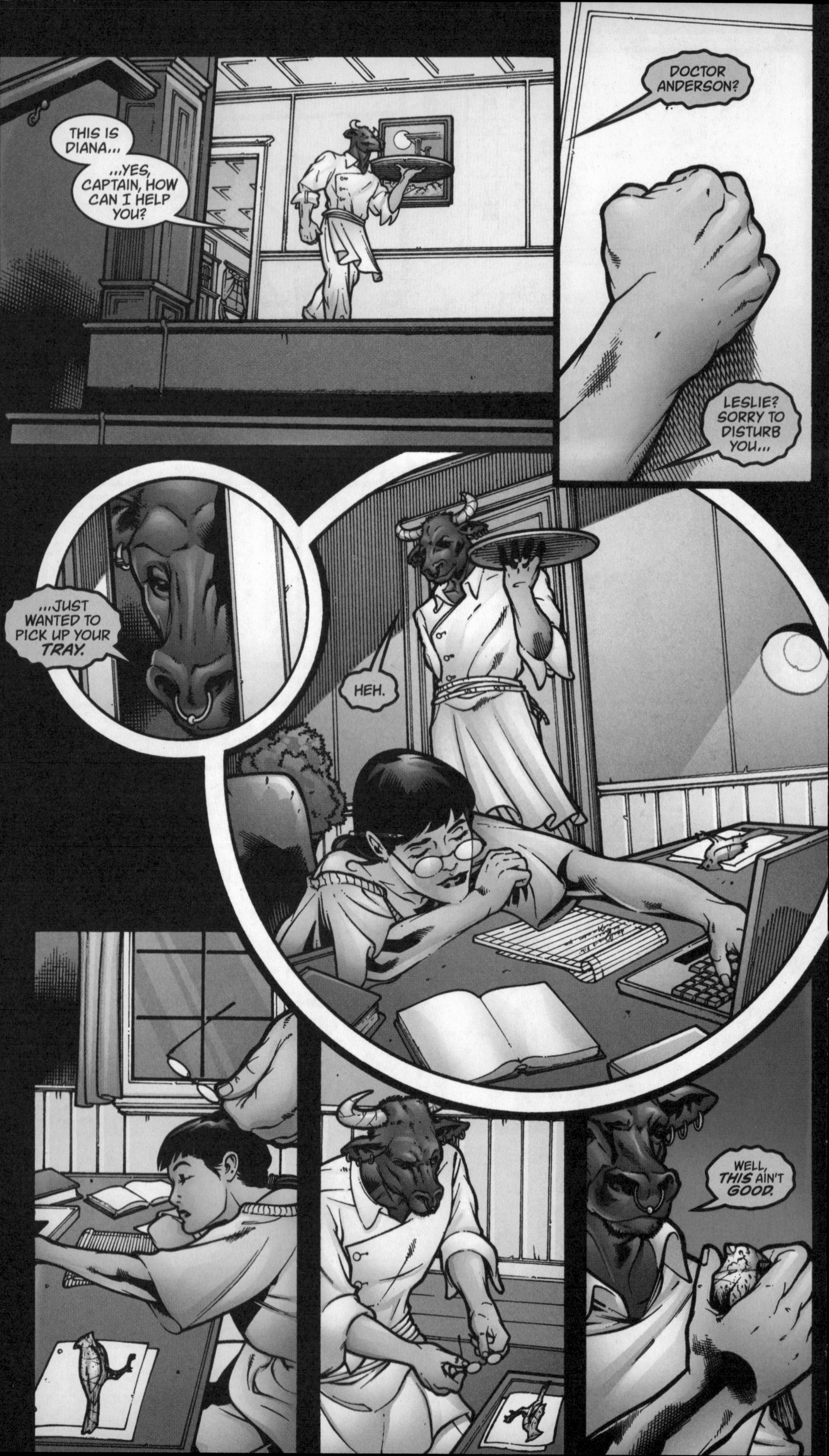
THIS IS DIANA...
...YES, CAPTAIN, HOW CAN I HELP YOU?
DOCTOR ANDERSON?
LESLIE? SORRY TO DISTURB YOU...
...JUST WANTED TO PICK UP YOUR TRAY.
HEH.
WELL, THIS AIN'T GOOD.

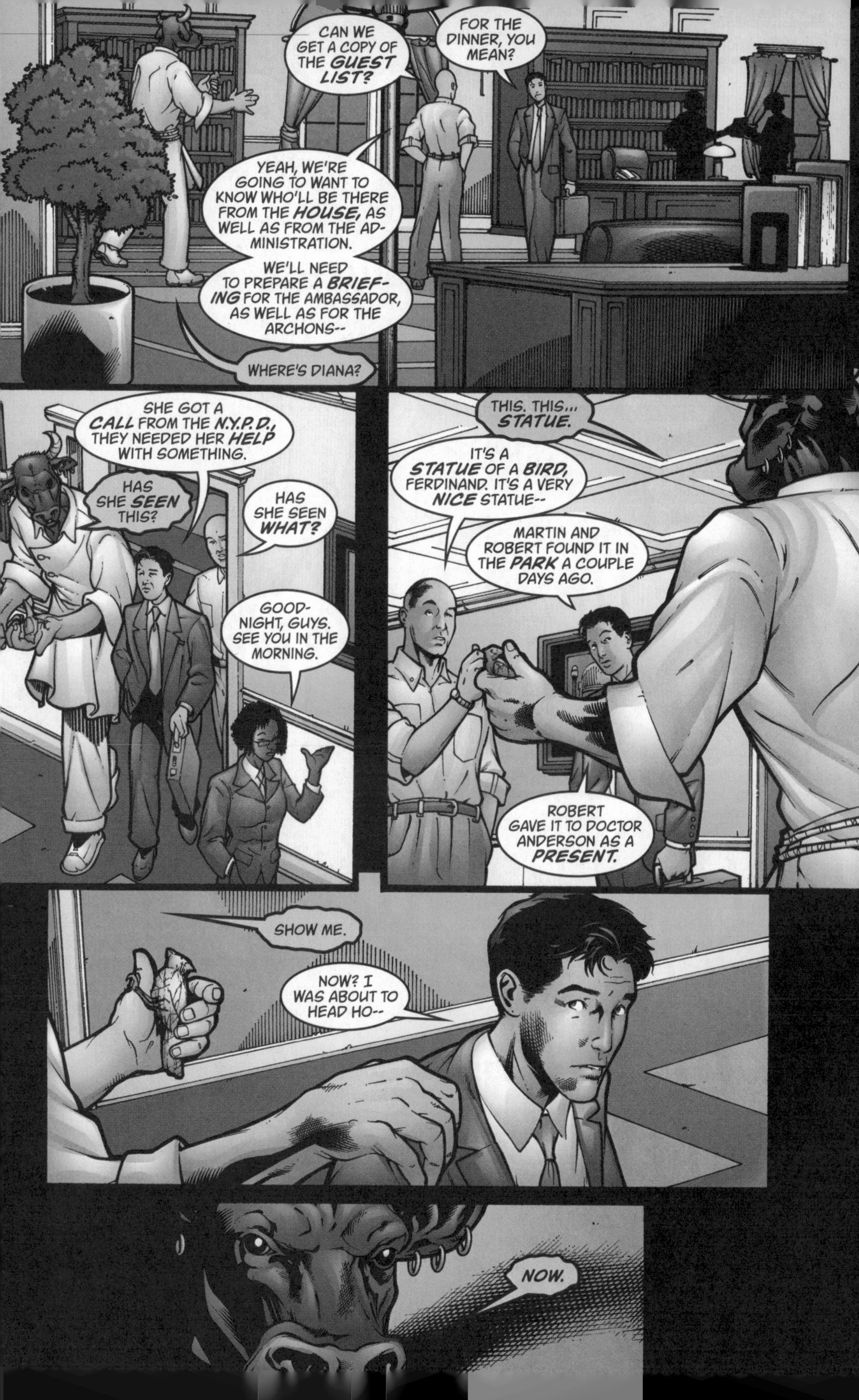
CAN WE GET A COPY OF THE GUEST LIST?
FOR THE DINNER, YOU MEAN?
YEAH, WE'RE GOING TO WANT TO KNOW WHO'LL BE THERE FROM THE HOUSE, AS WELL AS FROM THE ADMINISTRATION.
WE'LL NEED TO PREPARE A BRIEFING FOR THE AMBASSADOR, AS WELL AS FOR THE ARCHONS--
WHERE'S DIANA?
SHE GOT A CALL FROM THE N.Y.P.D., THEY NEEDED HER HELP WITH SOMETHING.
HAS SHE SEEN THIS?
HAS SHE SEEN WHAT?
GOOD-NIGHT, GUYS. SEE YOU IN THE MORNING.
THIS. THIS... STATUE.
IT'S A STATUE OF A BIRD, FERDINAND. IT'S A VERY NICE STATUE--
MARTIN AND ROBERT FOUND IT IN THE PARK A COUPLE DAYS AGO.
ROBERT GAVE IT TO DOCTOR ANDERSON AS A PRESENT.
SHOW ME.
NOW? I WAS ABOUT TO HEAD HO--
NOW.

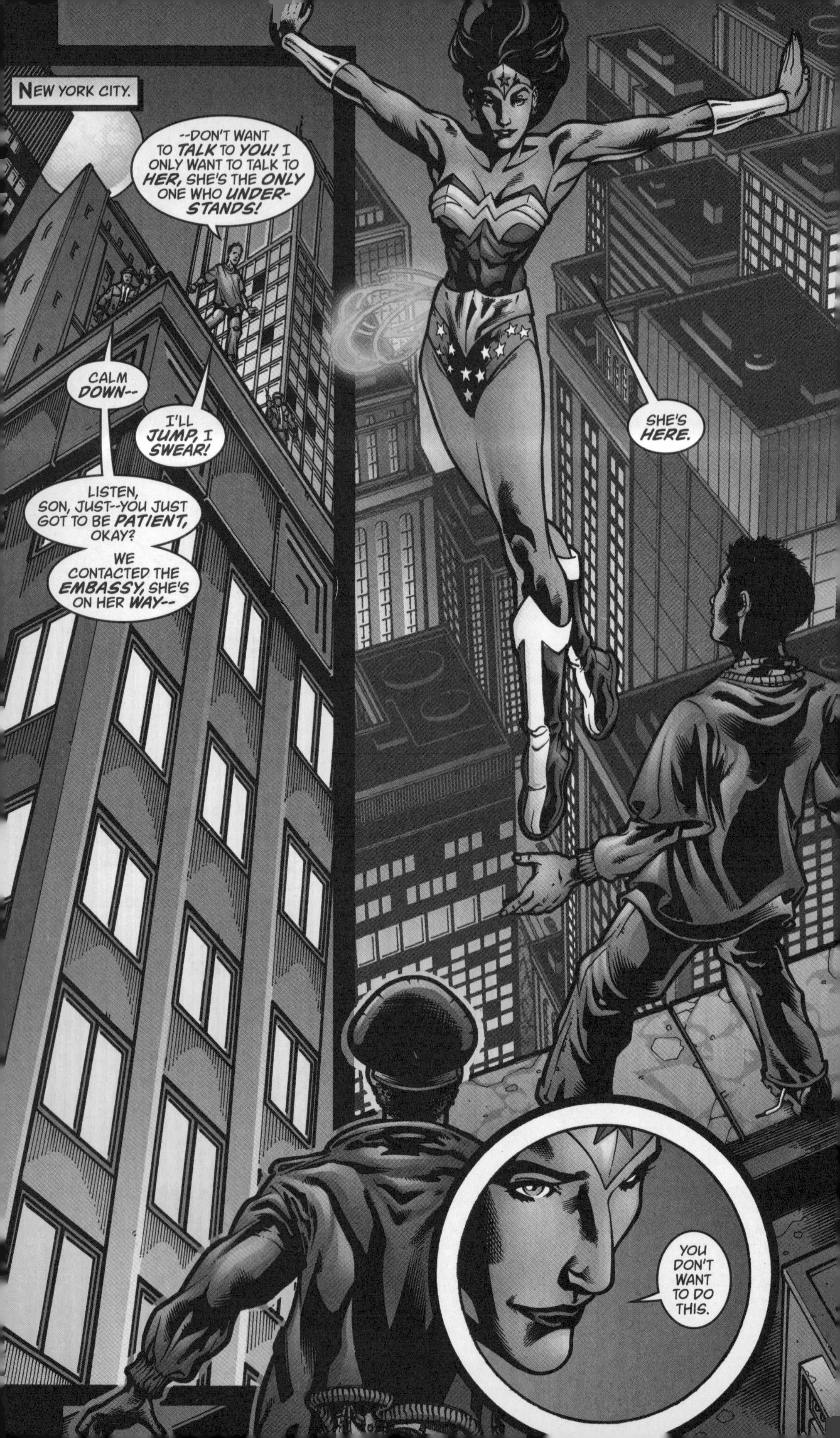

NEW YORK CITY.
--DON'T WANT TO TALK TO YOU! I ONLY WANT TO TALK TO HER, SHE'S THE ONLY ONE WHO UNDER-STANDS!
CALM DOWN--
I'LL JUMP, I SWEAR!
LISTEN, SON, JUST--YOU JUST GOT TO BE PATIENT, OKAY?
WE CONTACTED THE EMBASSY, SHE'S ON HER WAY--
SHE'S HERE.
YOU DON'T WANT TO DO THIS.

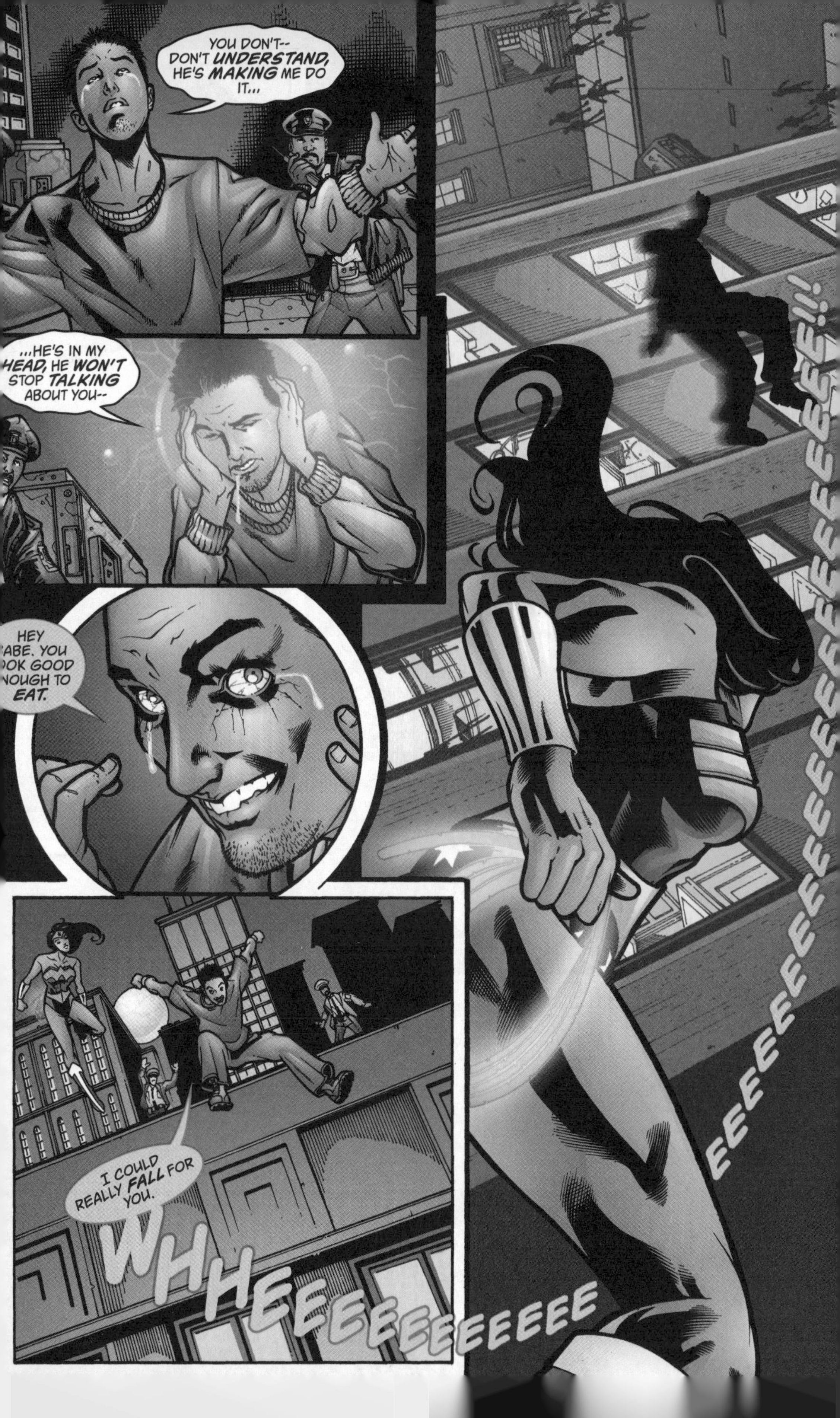
YOU DON'T-- DON'T UNDERSTAND, HE'S MAKING ME DO IT...
...HE'S IN MY HEAD, HE WON'T STOP TALKING ABOUT YOU--
HEY ABE. YOU OOK GOOD NOUGH TO EAT.
I COULD REALLY FALL FOR YOU.
WHHEEEEEEEEEEE
EEEEEEEEEEEEEEEEEEE!!!

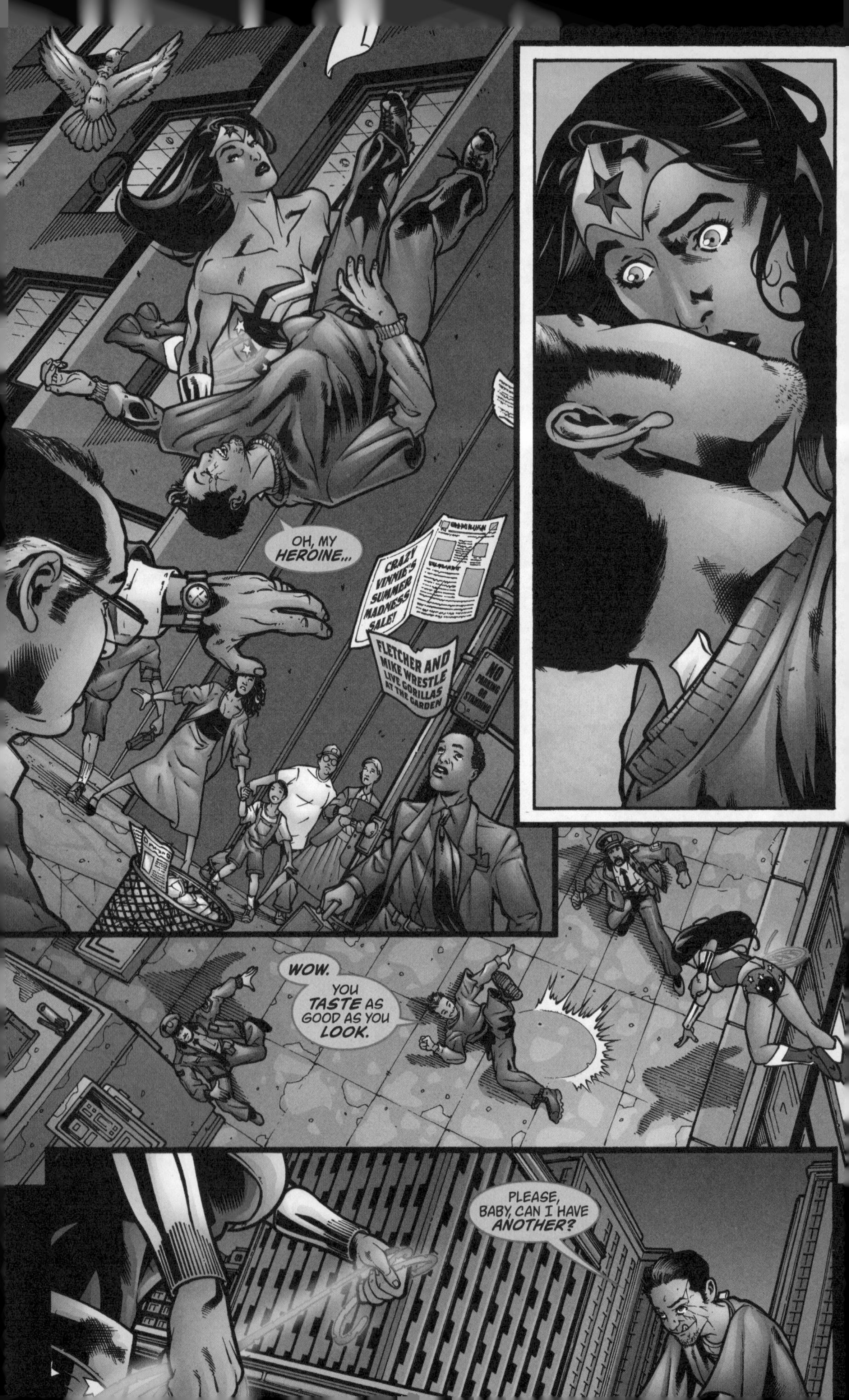
OH, MY HEROINE...
CRAZY VINNIE'S SUMMER MADNESS SALE!
FLETCHER AND MIKE WRESTLE LIVE GORILLAS AT THE GARDEN
NO PARKING OR STANDING
WOW.
YOU TASTE AS GOOD AS YOU LOOK.
PLEASE, BABY, CAN I HAVE ANOTHER?

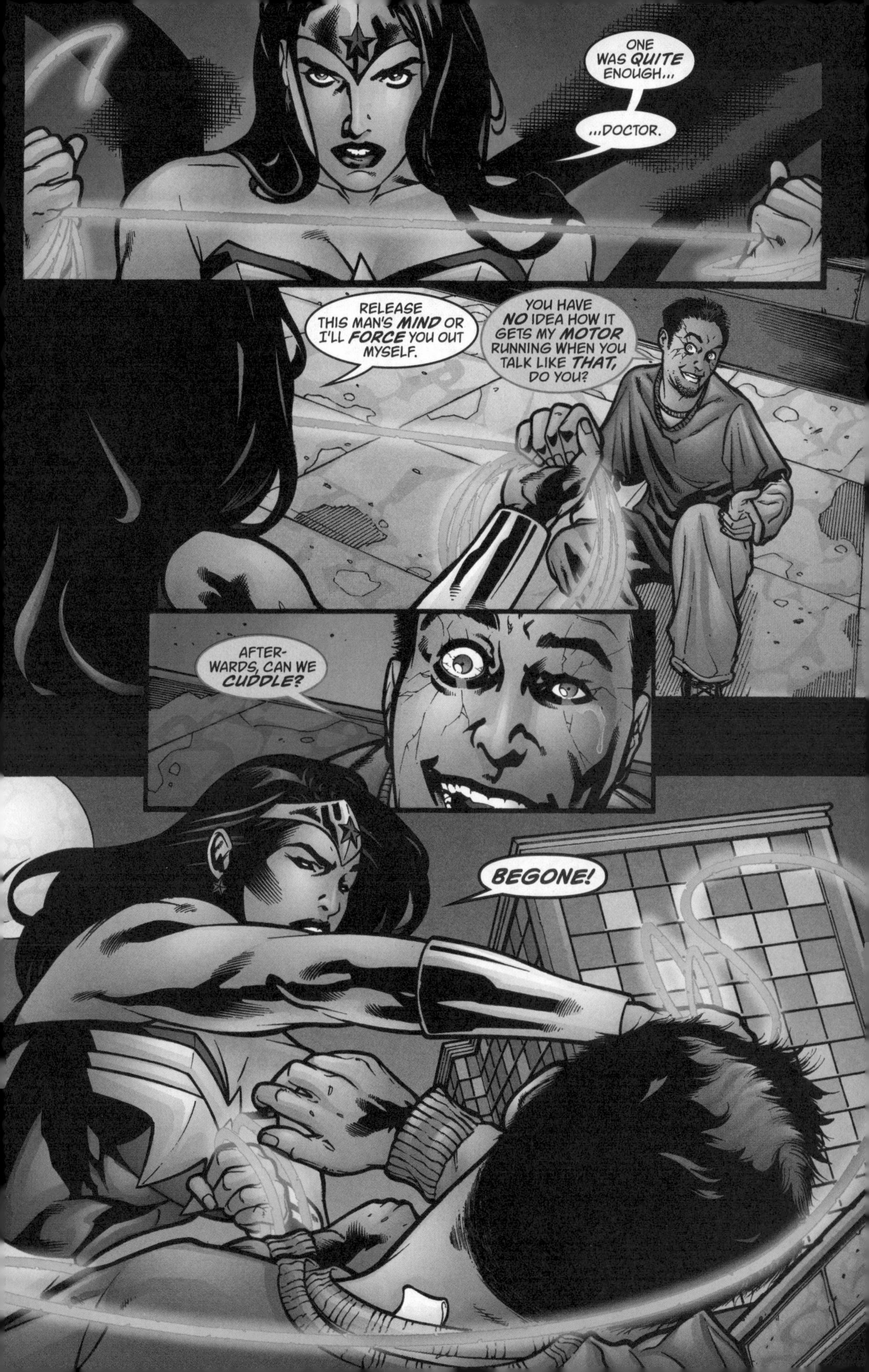
ONE WAS QUITE ENOUGH...
...DOCTOR.
RELEASE THIS MAN'S MIND OR I'LL FORCE YOU OUT MYSELF.
YOU HAVE NO IDEA HOW IT GETS MY MOTOR RUNNING WHEN YOU TALK LIKE THAT, DO YOU?
AFTER-WARDS, CAN WE CUDDLE?
BEGONE!

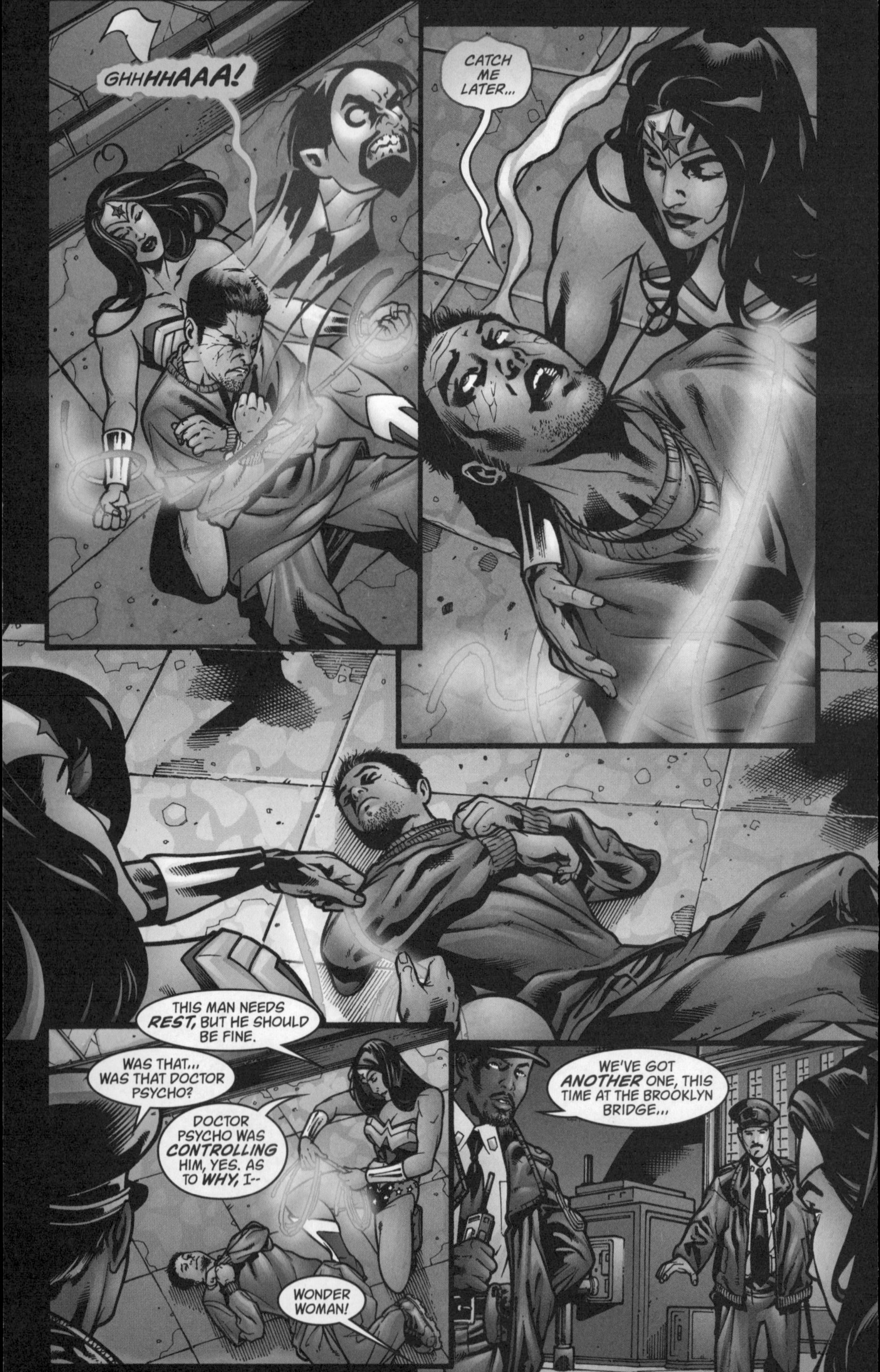
GHHHHAAA!
CATCH ME LATER...
THIS MAN NEEDS REST, BUT HE SHOULD BE FINE.
WAS THAT... WAS THAT DOCTOR PSYCHO?
DOCTOR PSYCHO WAS CONTROLLING HIM, YES. AS TO WHY, I--
WONDER WOMAN!
WE'VE GOT ANOTHER ONE, THIS TIME AT THE BROOKLYN BRIDGE...

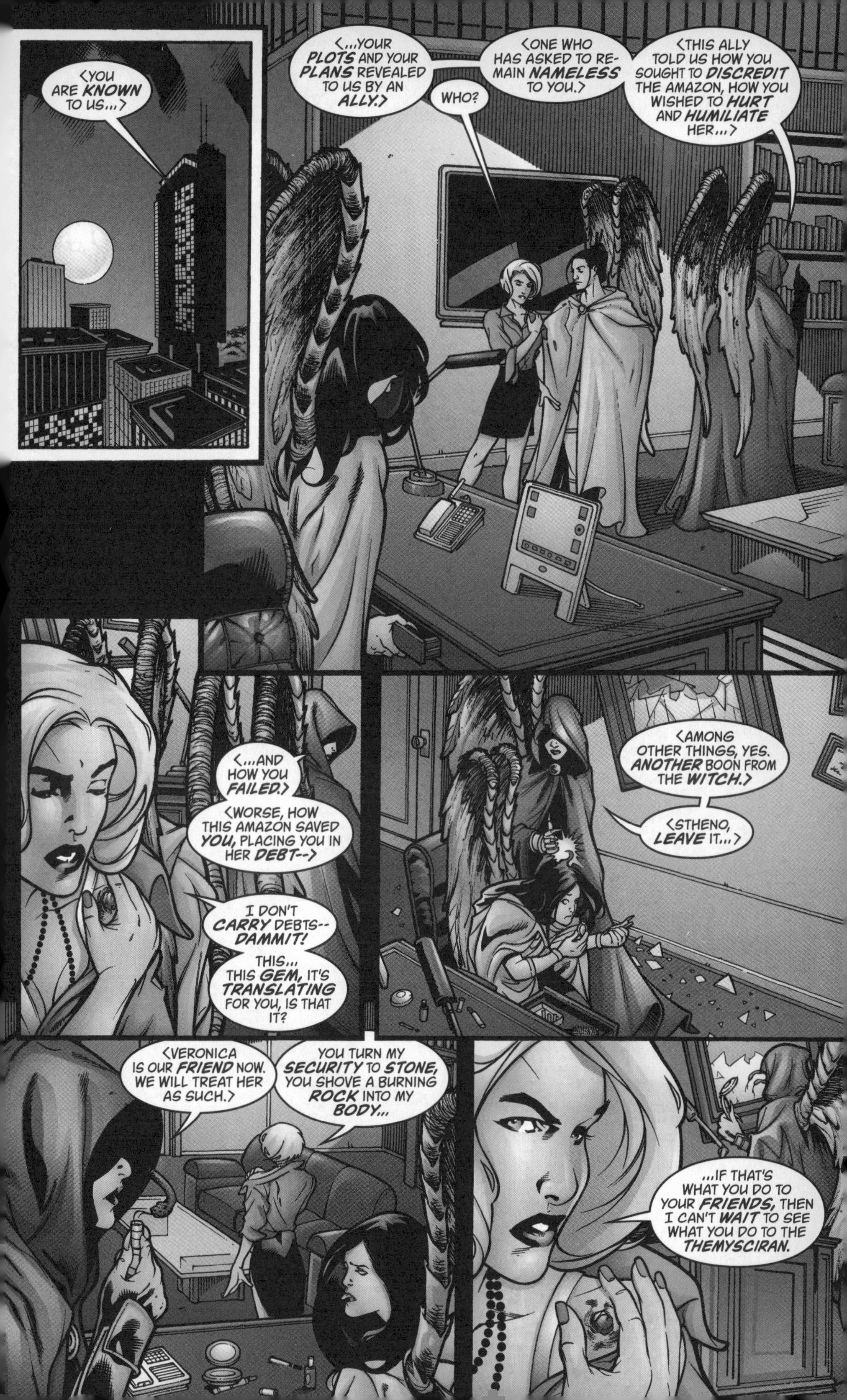
<YOU ARE KNOWN TO US...>
<...YOUR PLOTS AND YOUR PLANS REVEALED TO US BY AN ALLY.>
WHO?
<ONE WHO HAS ASKED TO RE-MAIN NAMELESS TO YOU.>
<THIS ALLY TOLD US HOW YOU SOUGHT TO DISCREDIT THE AMAZON, HOW YOU WISHED TO HURT AND HUMILIATE HER...>
<...AND HOW YOU FAILED.>
<WORSE, HOW THIS AMAZON SAVED YOU, PLACING YOU IN HER DEBT-->
I DON'T CARRY DEBTS-- DAMMIT!
THIS... THIS GEM, IT'S TRANSLATING FOR YOU, IS THAT IT?
<AMONG OTHER THINGS, YES. ANOTHER BOON FROM THE WITCH.>
<STHENO, LEAVE IT...>
<VERONICA IS OUR FRIEND NOW. WE WILL TREAT HER AS SUCH.>
YOU TURN MY SECURITY TO STONE, YOU SHOVE A BURNING ROCK INTO MY BODY...
...IF THAT'S WHAT YOU DO TO YOUR FRIENDS, THEN I CAN'T WAIT TO SEE WHAT YOU DO TO THE THEMYSCIRAN.

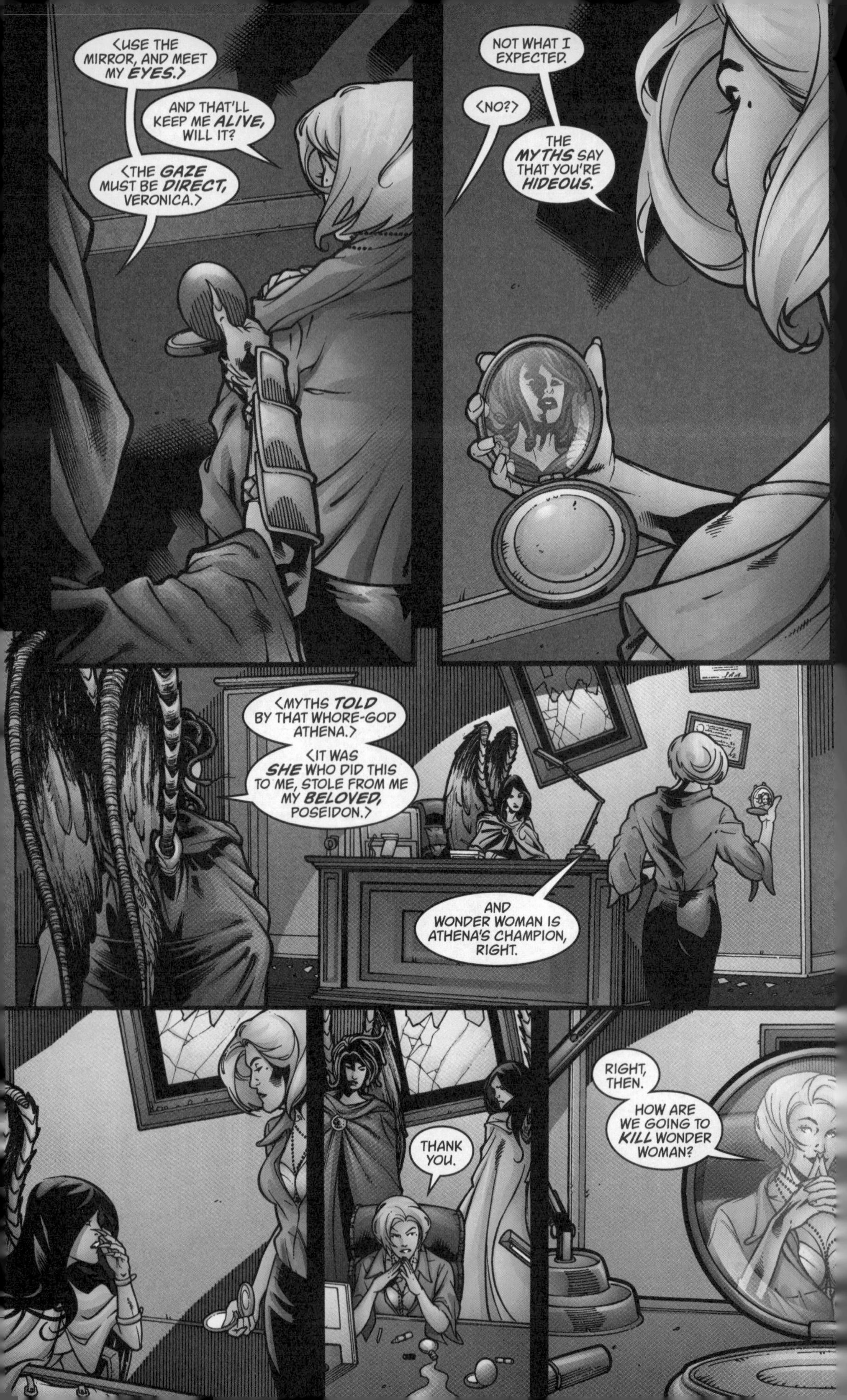
<USE THE MIRROR, AND MEET MY **EYES**.>
AND THAT'LL KEEP ME **ALIVE**, WILL IT?
<THE **GAZE** MUST BE **DIRECT**, VERONICA.>
NOT WHAT I EXPECTED.
<NO?>
THE **MYTHS** SAY THAT YOU'RE **HIDEOUS**.
<MYTHS **TOLD** BY THAT WHORE-GOD ATHENA.>
<IT WAS **SHE** WHO DID THIS TO ME, STOLE FROM ME MY **BELOVED**, POSEIDON.>
AND WONDER WOMAN IS ATHENA'S CHAMPION, RIGHT.
THANK YOU.
RIGHT, THEN.
HOW ARE WE GOING TO **KILL** WONDER WOMAN?

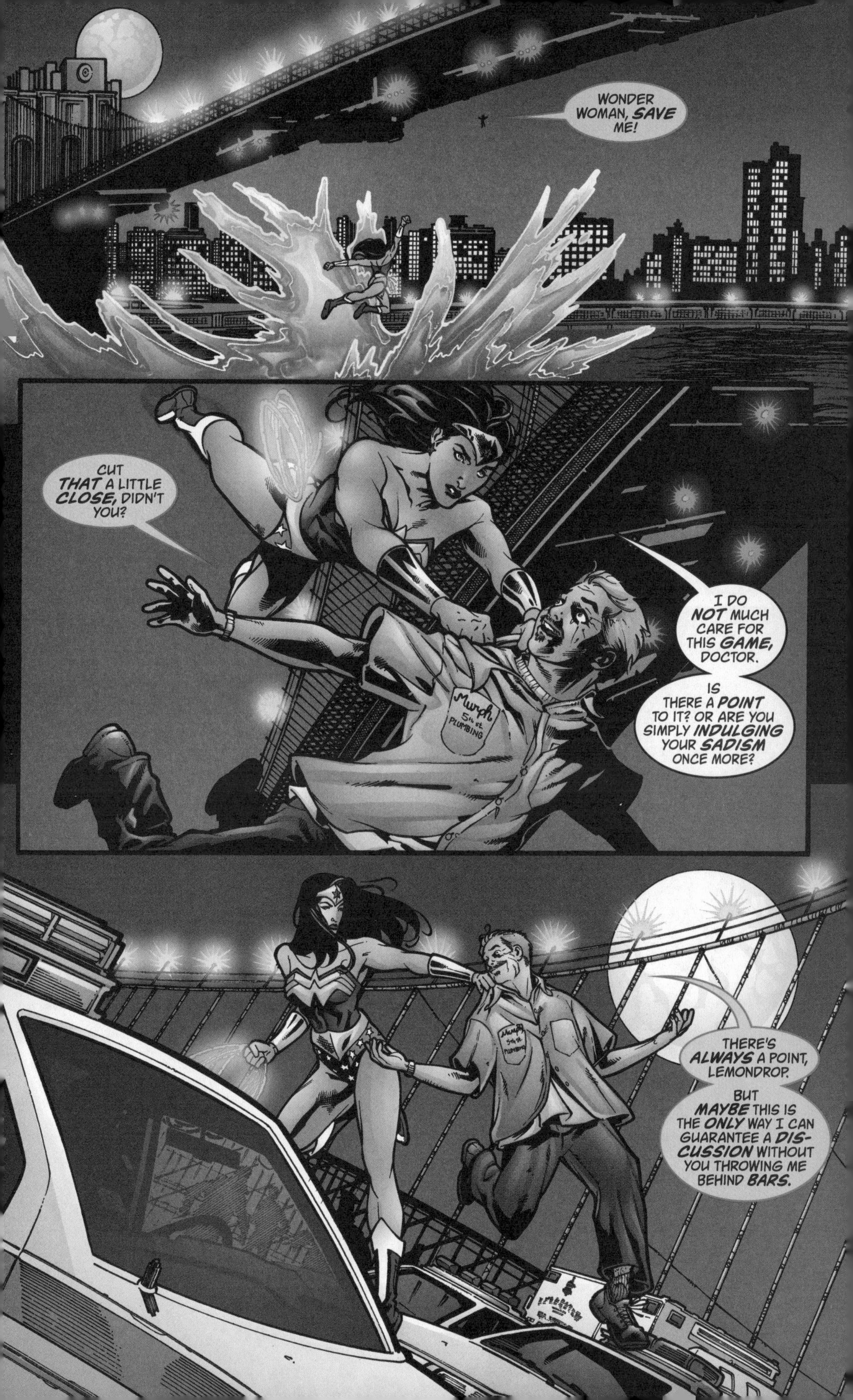
WONDER WOMAN, SAVE ME!
CUT THAT A LITTLE CLOSE, DIDN'T YOU?
I DO NOT MUCH CARE FOR THIS GAME, DOCTOR.
IS THERE A POINT TO IT? OR ARE YOU SIMPLY INDULGING YOUR SADISM ONCE MORE?
THERE'S ALWAYS A POINT, LEMONDROP.
BUT MAYBE THIS IS THE ONLY WAY I CAN GUARANTEE A DIS-CUSSION WITHOUT YOU THROWING ME BEHIND BARS.

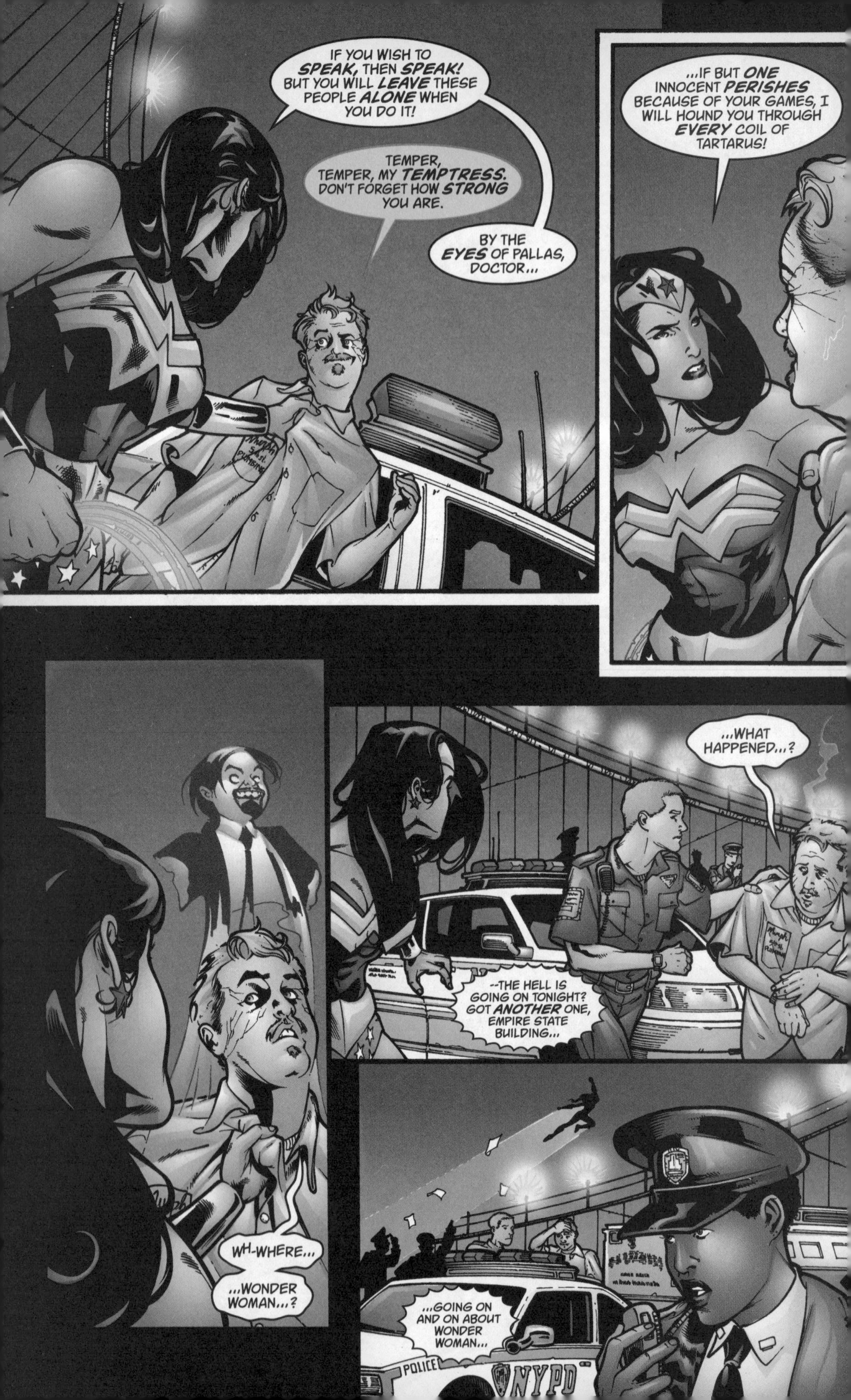
IF YOU WISH TO SPEAK, THEN SPEAK! BUT YOU WILL LEAVE THESE PEOPLE ALONE WHEN YOU DO IT!
TEMPER, TEMPER, MY TEMPTRESS. DON'T FORGET HOW STRONG YOU ARE.
BY THE EYES OF PALLAS, DOCTOR...
...IF BUT ONE INNOCENT PERISHES BECAUSE OF YOUR GAMES, I WILL HOUND YOU THROUGH EVERY COIL OF TARTARUS!
WH-WHERE...
...WONDER WOMAN...?
...WHAT HAPPENED...?
--THE HELL IS GOING ON TONIGHT? GOT ANOTHER ONE, EMPIRE STATE BUILDING...
...GOING ON AND ON ABOUT WONDER WOMAN...
POLICE
NYPD

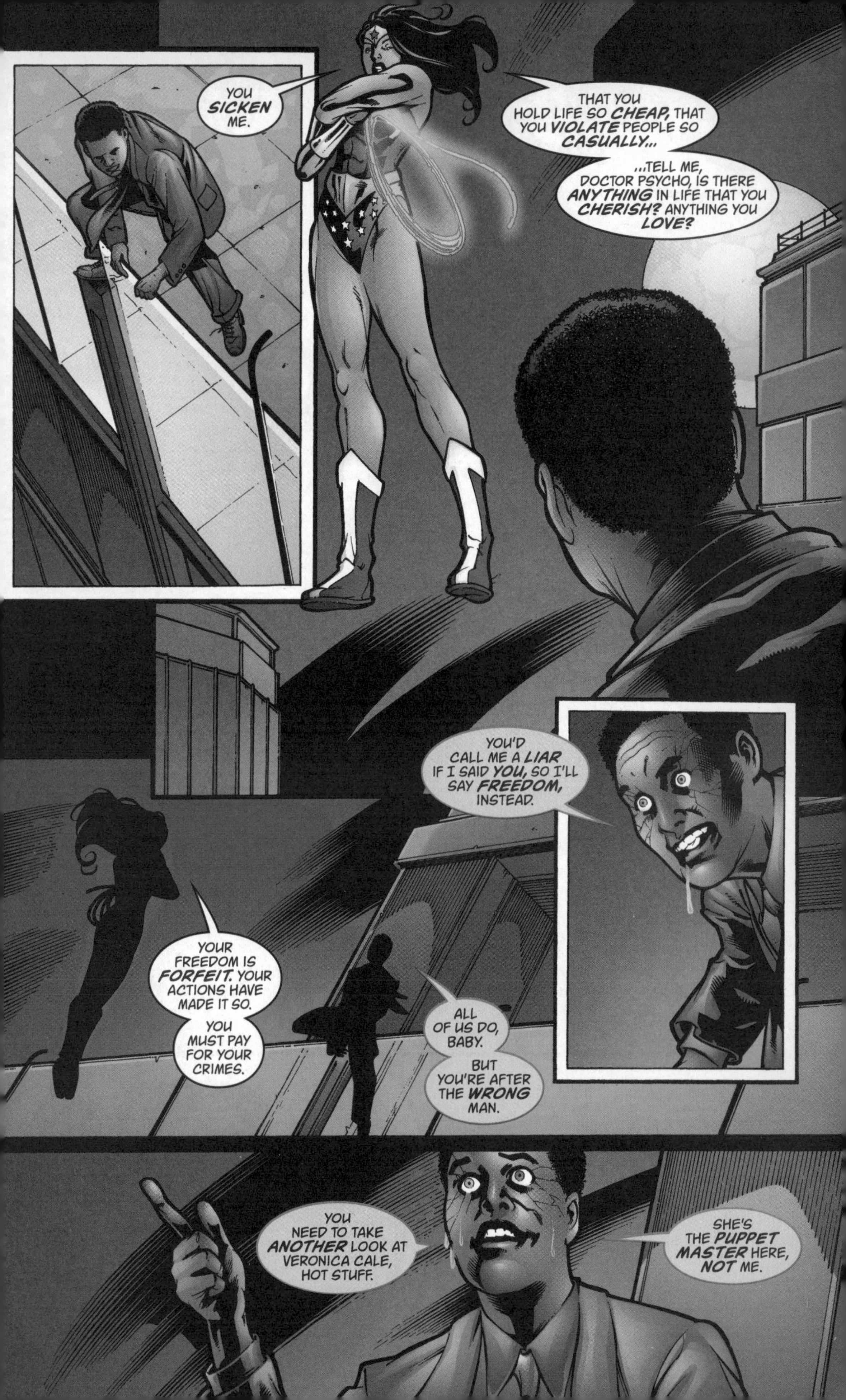
YOU SICKEN ME.
THAT YOU HOLD LIFE SO CHEAP, THAT YOU VIOLATE PEOPLE SO CASUALLY...
...TELL ME, DOCTOR PSYCHO, IS THERE ANYTHING IN LIFE THAT YOU CHERISH? ANYTHING YOU LOVE?
YOU'D CALL ME A LIAR IF I SAID YOU, SO I'LL SAY FREEDOM, INSTEAD.
YOUR FREEDOM IS FORFEIT. YOUR ACTIONS HAVE MADE IT SO.
YOU MUST PAY FOR YOUR CRIMES.
ALL OF US DO, BABY.
BUT YOU'RE AFTER THE WRONG MAN.
YOU NEED TO TAKE ANOTHER LOOK AT VERONICA CALE, HOT STUFF.
SHE'S THE PUPPET MASTER HERE, NOT ME.

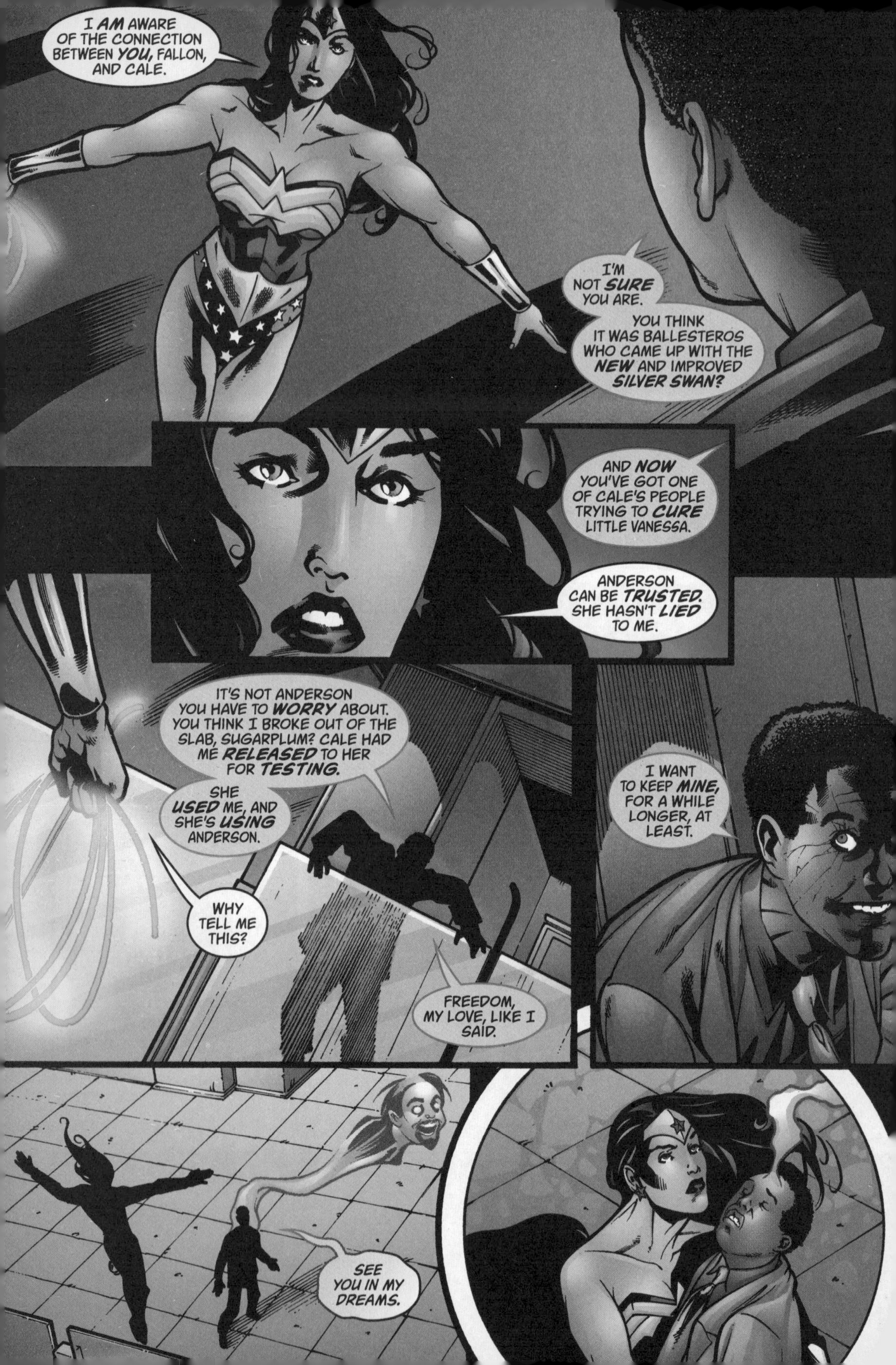
I AM AWARE OF THE CONNECTION BETWEEN YOU, FALLON, AND CALE.
I'M NOT SURE YOU ARE.
YOU THINK IT WAS BALLESTEROS WHO CAME UP WITH THE NEW AND IMPROVED SILVER SWAN?
AND NOW YOU'VE GOT ONE OF CALE'S PEOPLE TRYING TO CURE LITTLE VANESSA.
ANDERSON CAN BE TRUSTED. SHE HASN'T LIED TO ME.
IT'S NOT ANDERSON YOU HAVE TO WORRY ABOUT. YOU THINK I BROKE OUT OF THE SLAB, SUGARPLUM? CALE HAD ME RELEASED TO HER FOR TESTING.
SHE USED ME, AND SHE'S USING ANDERSON.
WHY TELL ME THIS?
I WANT TO KEEP MINE, FOR A WHILE LONGER, AT LEAST.
FREEDOM, MY LOVE, LIKE I SAID.
SEE YOU IN MY DREAMS.

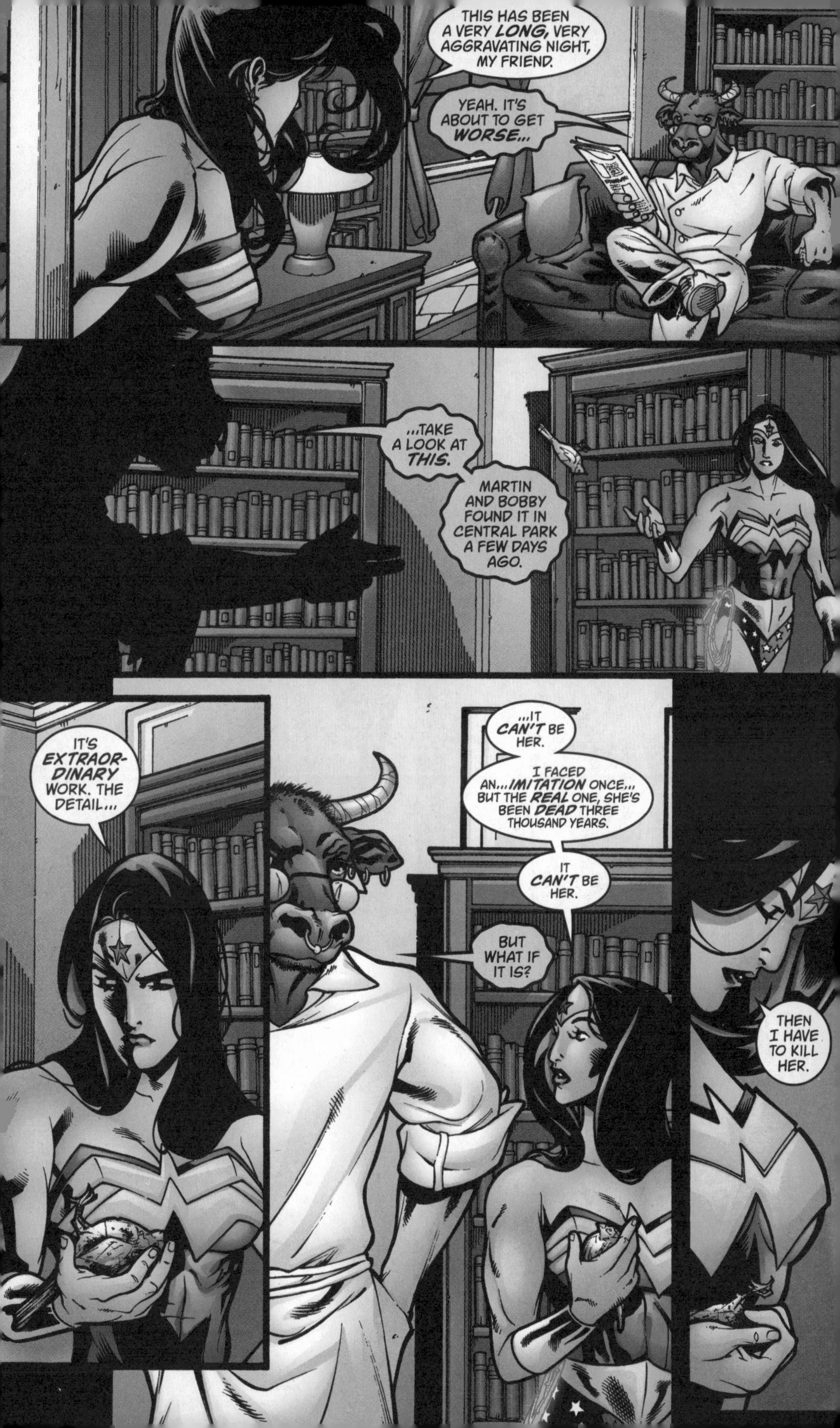

THIS HAS BEEN A VERY LONG, VERY AGGRAVATING NIGHT, MY FRIEND.
YEAH. IT'S ABOUT TO GET WORSE...
...TAKE A LOOK AT THIS.
MARTIN AND BOBBY FOUND IT IN CENTRAL PARK A FEW DAYS AGO.
IT'S EXTRAORDINARY WORK. THE DETAIL...
...IT CAN'T BE HER.
I FACED AN...IMITATION ONCE... BUT THE REAL ONE, SHE'S BEEN DEAD THREE THOUSAND YEARS.
IT CAN'T BE HER.
BUT WHAT IF IT IS?
THEN I HAVE TO KILL HER.

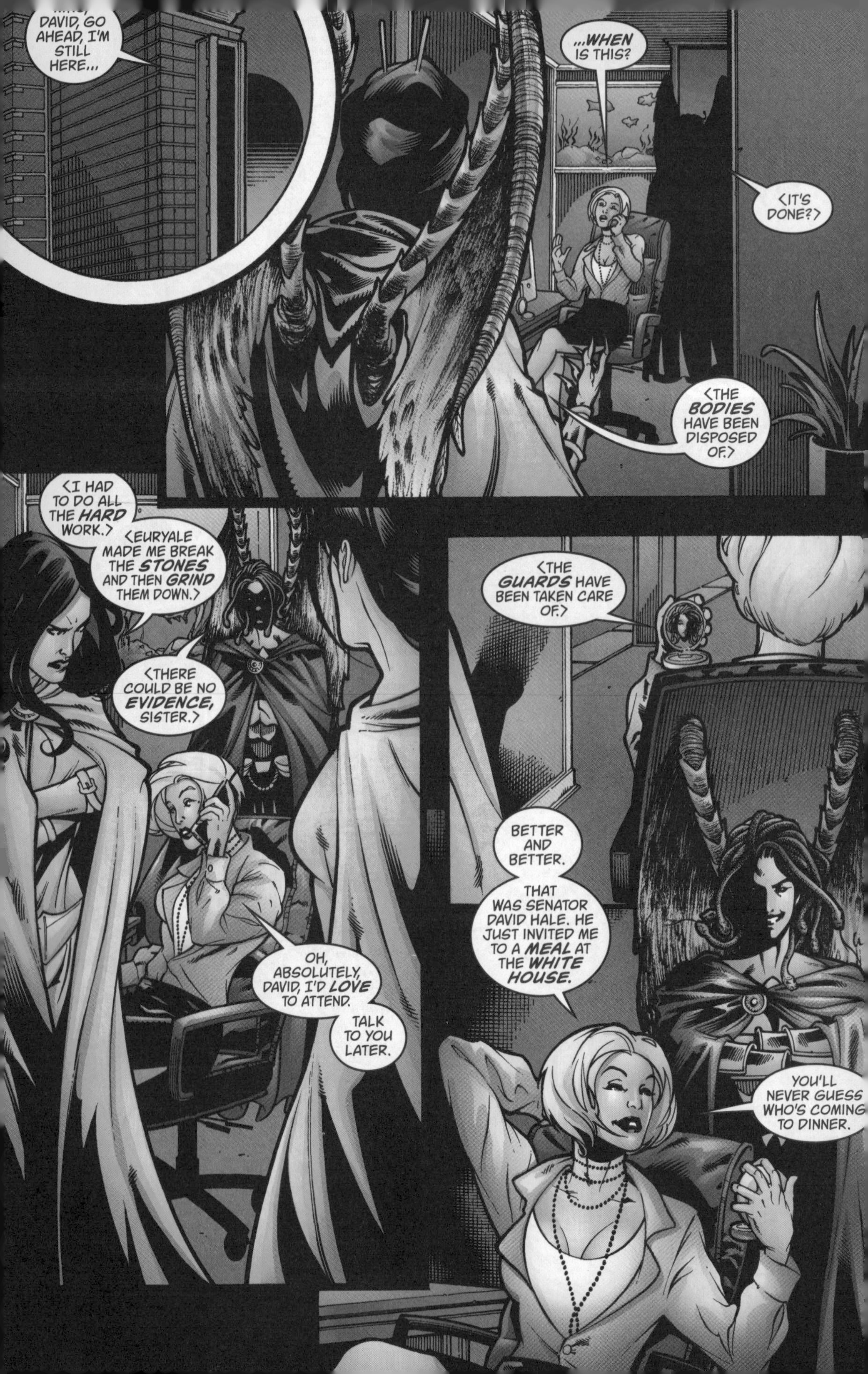
DAVID, GO AHEAD, I'M STILL HERE...
...WHEN IS THIS?
<IT'S DONE?>
<THE BODIES HAVE BEEN DISPOSED OF.>
<I HAD TO DO ALL THE HARD WORK.>
<EURYALE MADE ME BREAK THE STONES AND THEN GRIND THEM DOWN.>
<THERE COULD BE NO EVIDENCE, SISTER.>
OH, ABSOLUTELY, DAVID, I'D LOVE TO ATTEND.
TALK TO YOU LATER.
<THE GUARDS HAVE BEEN TAKEN CARE OF.>
BETTER AND BETTER.
THAT WAS SENATOR DAVID HALE. HE JUST INVITED ME TO A MEAL AT THE WHITE HOUSE.
YOU'LL NEVER GUESS WHO'S COMING TO DINNER.

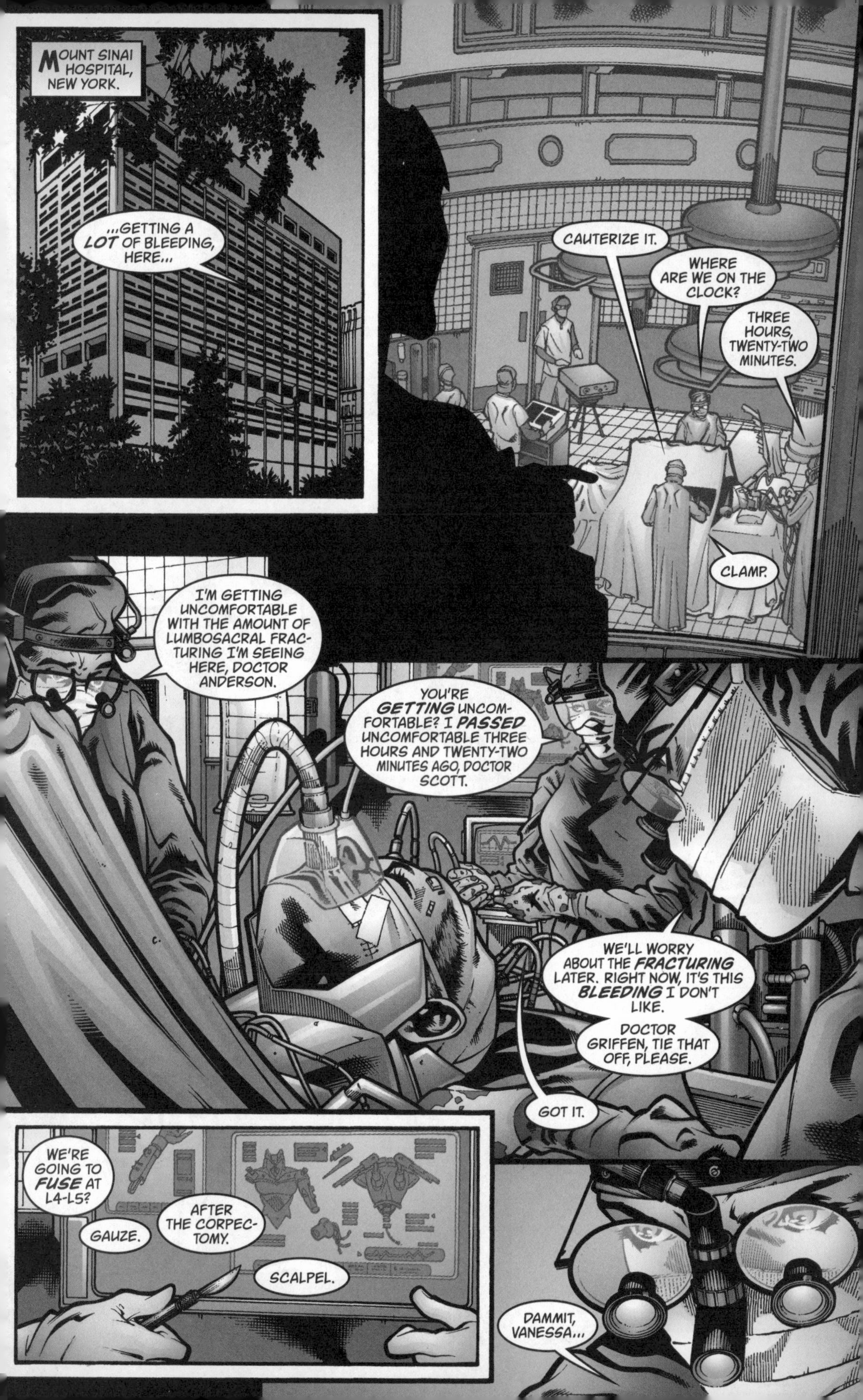
MOUNT SINAI HOSPITAL, NEW YORK.
...GETTING A LOT OF BLEEDING, HERE...
CAUTERIZE IT.
WHERE ARE WE ON THE CLOCK?
THREE HOURS, TWENTY-TWO MINUTES.
CLAMP.
I'M GETTING UNCOMFORTABLE WITH THE AMOUNT OF LUMBOSACRAL FRACTURING I'M SEEING HERE, DOCTOR ANDERSON.
YOU'RE GETTING UNCOMFORTABLE? I PASSED UNCOMFORTABLE THREE HOURS AND TWENTY-TWO MINUTES AGO, DOCTOR SCOTT.
WE'LL WORRY ABOUT THE FRACTURING LATER. RIGHT NOW, IT'S THIS BLEEDING I DON'T LIKE.
DOCTOR GRIFFEN, TIE THAT OFF, PLEASE.
GOT IT.
WE'RE GOING TO FUSE AT L4-L5?
GAUZE.
AFTER THE CORPECTOMY.
SCALPEL.
DAMMIT, VANESSA...

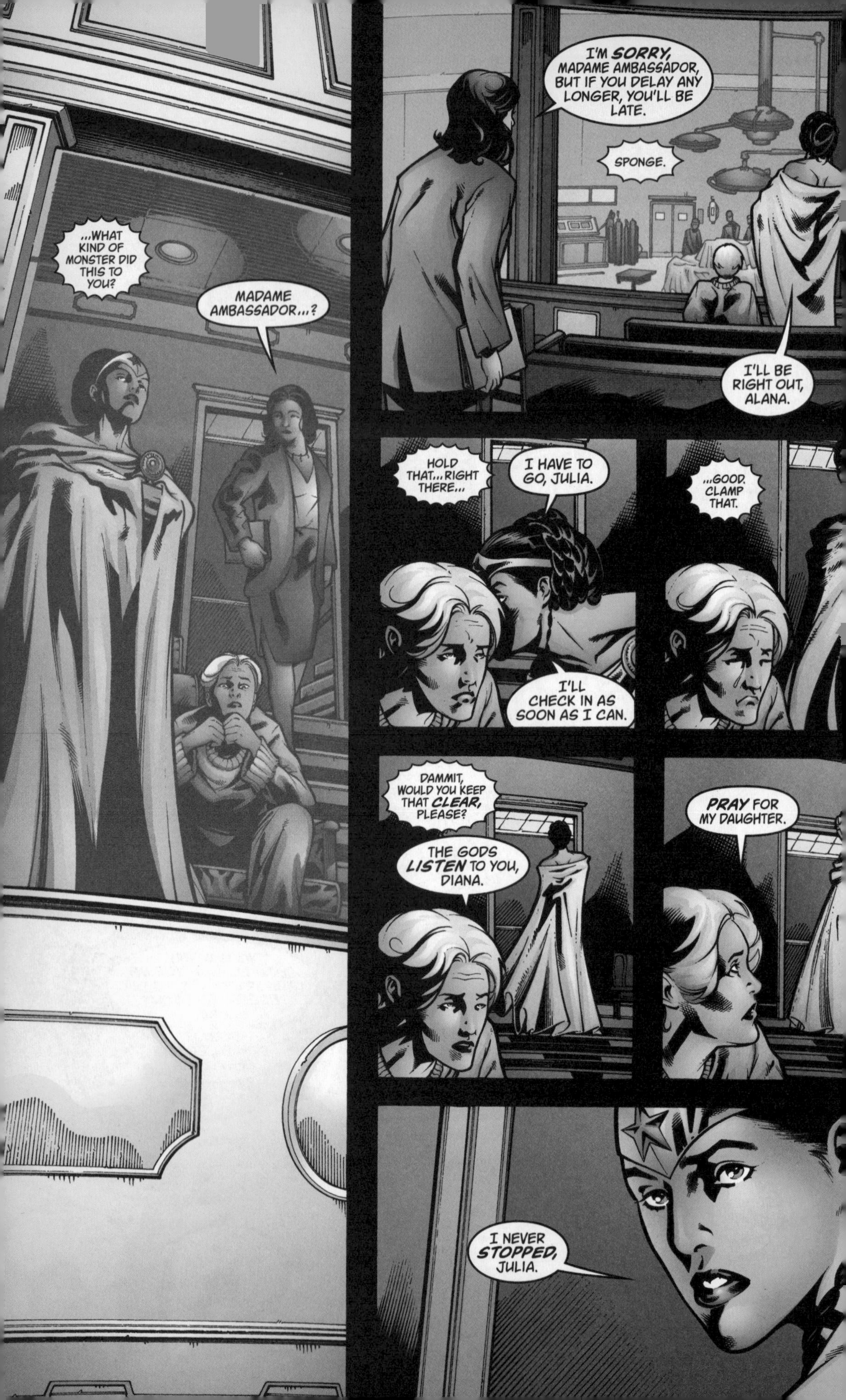
...WHAT KIND OF MONSTER DID THIS TO YOU?
MADAME AMBASSADOR...?
I'M SORRY, MADAME AMBASSADOR, BUT IF YOU DELAY ANY LONGER, YOU'LL BE LATE.
SPONGE.
I'LL BE RIGHT OUT, ALANA.
HOLD THAT... RIGHT THERE...
I HAVE TO GO, JULIA.
I'LL CHECK IN AS SOON AS I CAN.
...GOOD. CLAMP THAT.
DAMMIT, WOULD YOU KEEP THAT CLEAR, PLEASE?
THE GODS LISTEN TO YOU, DIANA.
PRAY FOR MY DAUGHTER.
I NEVER STOPPED, JULIA.

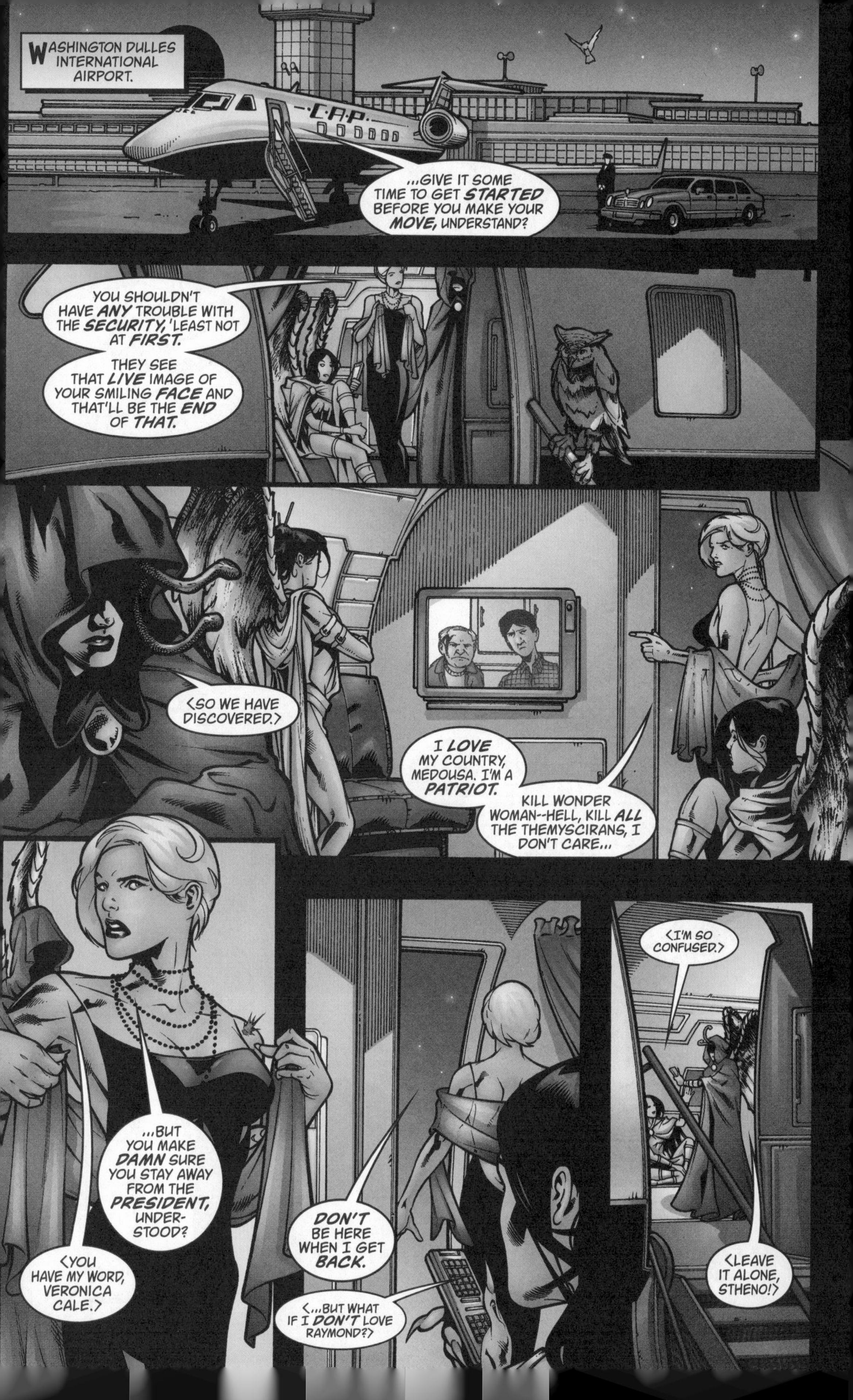
WASHINGTON DULLES INTERNATIONAL AIRPORT.
...GIVE IT SOME TIME TO GET STARTED BEFORE YOU MAKE YOUR MOVE, UNDERSTAND?
YOU SHOULDN'T HAVE ANY TROUBLE WITH THE SECURITY, 'LEAST NOT AT FIRST.
THEY SEE THAT LIVE IMAGE OF YOUR SMILING FACE AND THAT'LL BE THE END OF THAT.
<SO WE HAVE DISCOVERED.>
I LOVE MY COUNTRY, MEDOUSA. I'M A PATRIOT.
KILL WONDER WOMAN--HELL, KILL ALL THE THEMYSCIRANS, I DON'T CARE...
...BUT YOU MAKE DAMN SURE YOU STAY AWAY FROM THE PRESIDENT, UNDER-STOOD?
<YOU HAVE MY WORD, VERONICA CALE.>
DON'T BE HERE WHEN I GET BACK.
<...BUT WHAT IF I DON'T LOVE RAYMOND?>
<I'M SO CONFUSED.>
<LEAVE IT ALONE, STHENO!>

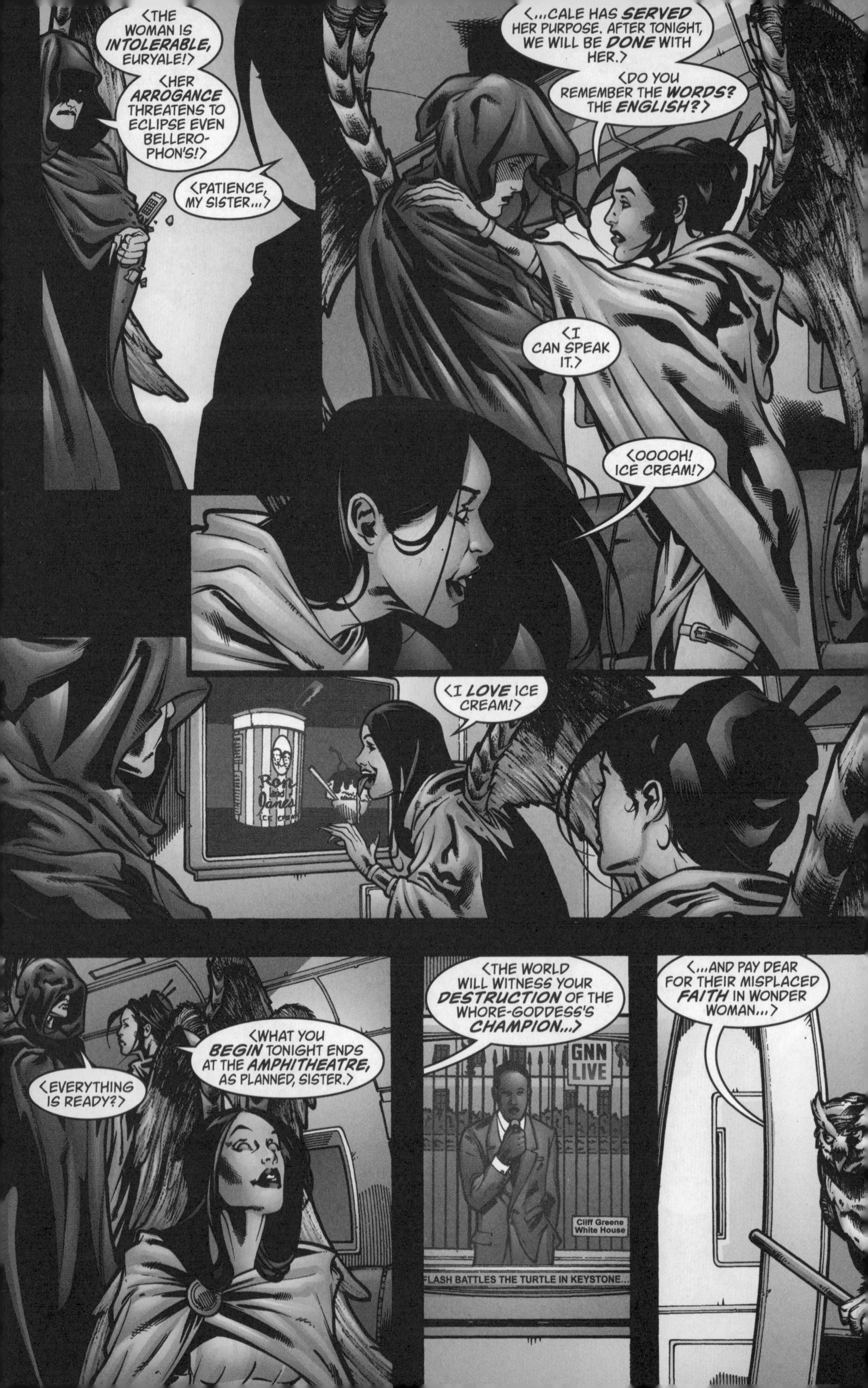

<THE WOMAN IS INTOLERABLE, EURYALE!>
<HER ARROGANCE THREATENS TO ECLIPSE EVEN BELLEROPHON'S!>
<PATIENCE, MY SISTER...>
<...CALE HAS SERVED HER PURPOSE. AFTER TONIGHT, WE WILL BE DONE WITH HER.>
<DO YOU REMEMBER THE WORDS? THE ENGLISH?>
<I CAN SPEAK IT.>
<OOOOH! ICE CREAM!>
<I LOVE ICE CREAM!>
<EVERYTHING IS READY?>
<WHAT YOU BEGIN TONIGHT ENDS AT THE AMPHITHEATRE, AS PLANNED, SISTER.>
<THE WORLD WILL WITNESS YOUR DESTRUCTION OF THE WHORE-GODDESS'S CHAMPION...>
GNN LIVE
Cliff Greene White House
FLASH BATTLES THE TURTLE IN KEYSTONE...
<...AND PAY DEAR FOR THEIR MISPLACED FAITH IN WONDER WOMAN...>

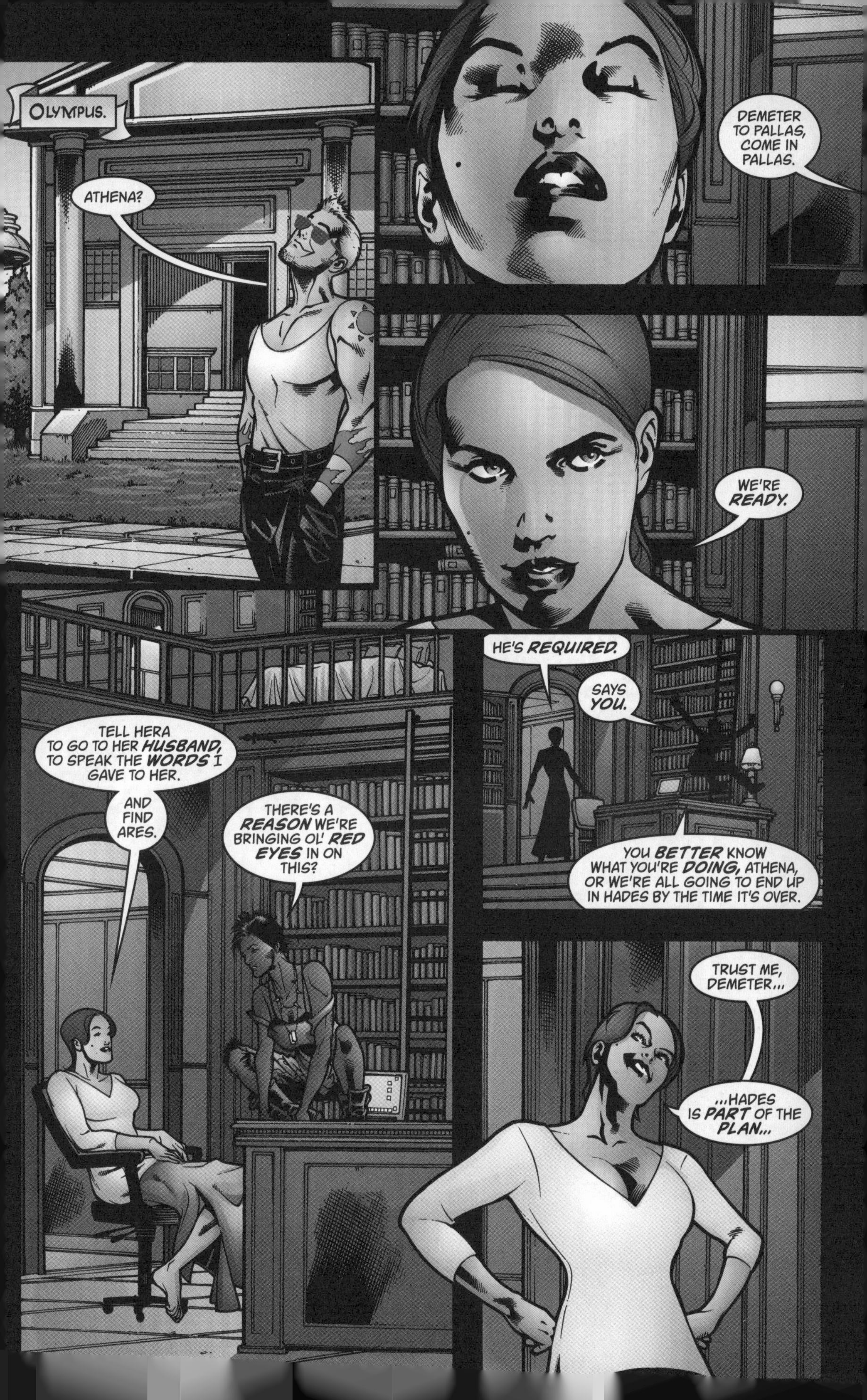
OLYMPUS.
ATHENA?
DEMETER TO PALLAS, COME IN PALLAS.
WE'RE READY.
TELL HERA TO GO TO HER HUSBAND, TO SPEAK THE WORDS I GAVE TO HER.
AND FIND ARES.
THERE'S A REASON WE'RE BRINGING OL' RED EYES IN ON THIS?
HE'S REQUIRED.
SAYS YOU.
YOU BETTER KNOW WHAT YOU'RE DOING, ATHENA, OR WE'RE ALL GOING TO END UP IN HADES BY THE TIME IT'S OVER.
TRUST ME, DEMETER...
...HADES IS PART OF THE PLAN...

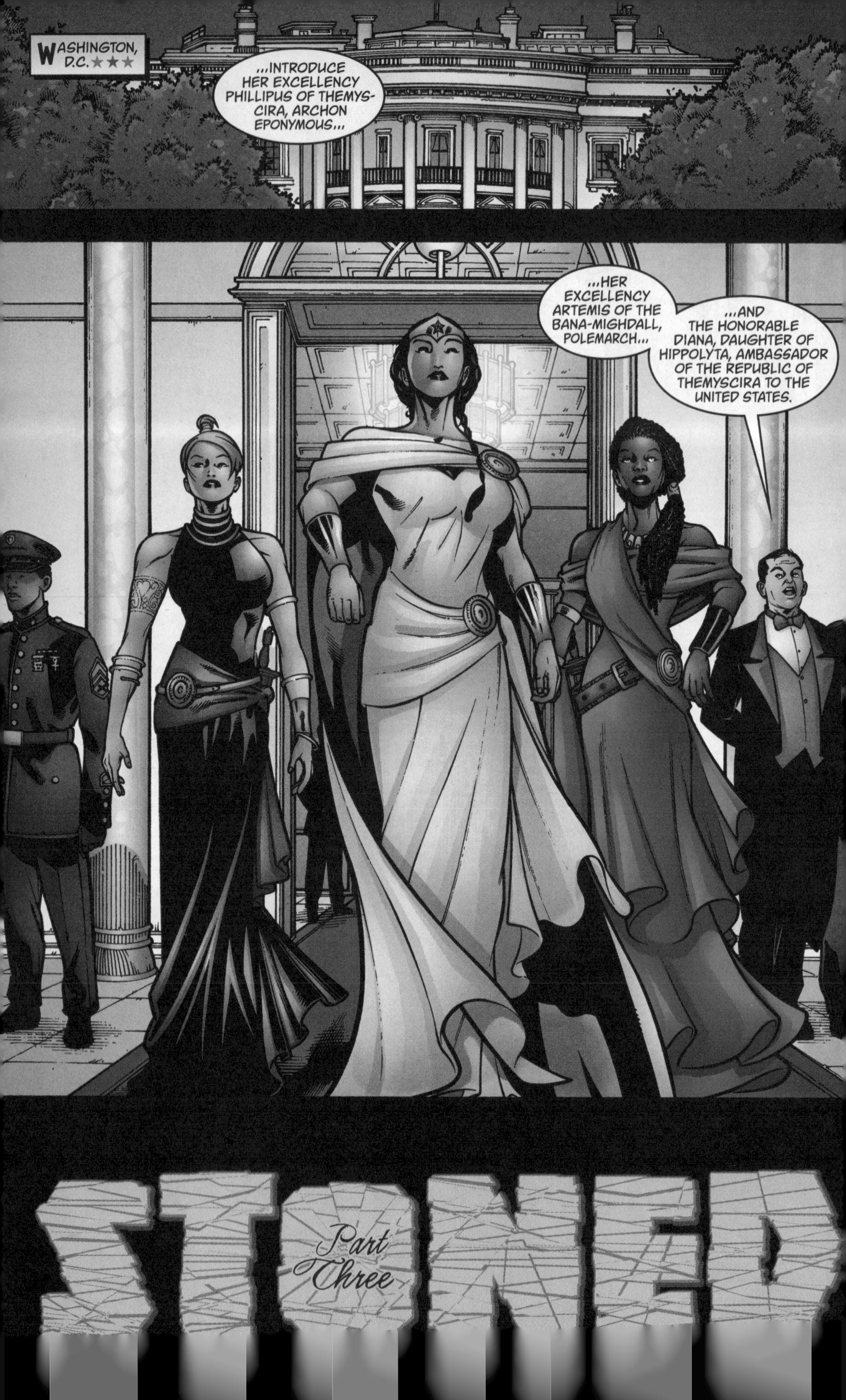
WASHINGTON, D.C.★★★
...INTRODUCE HER EXCELLENCY PHILLIPUS OF THEMYSCIRA, ARCHON EPONYMOUS...
...HER EXCELLENCY ARTEMIS OF THE BANA-MIGHDALL, POLEMARCH...
...AND THE HONORABLE DIANA, DAUGHTER OF HIPPOLYTA, AMBASSADOR OF THE REPUBLIC OF THEMYSCIRA TO THE UNITED STATES.
STONED
Part Three

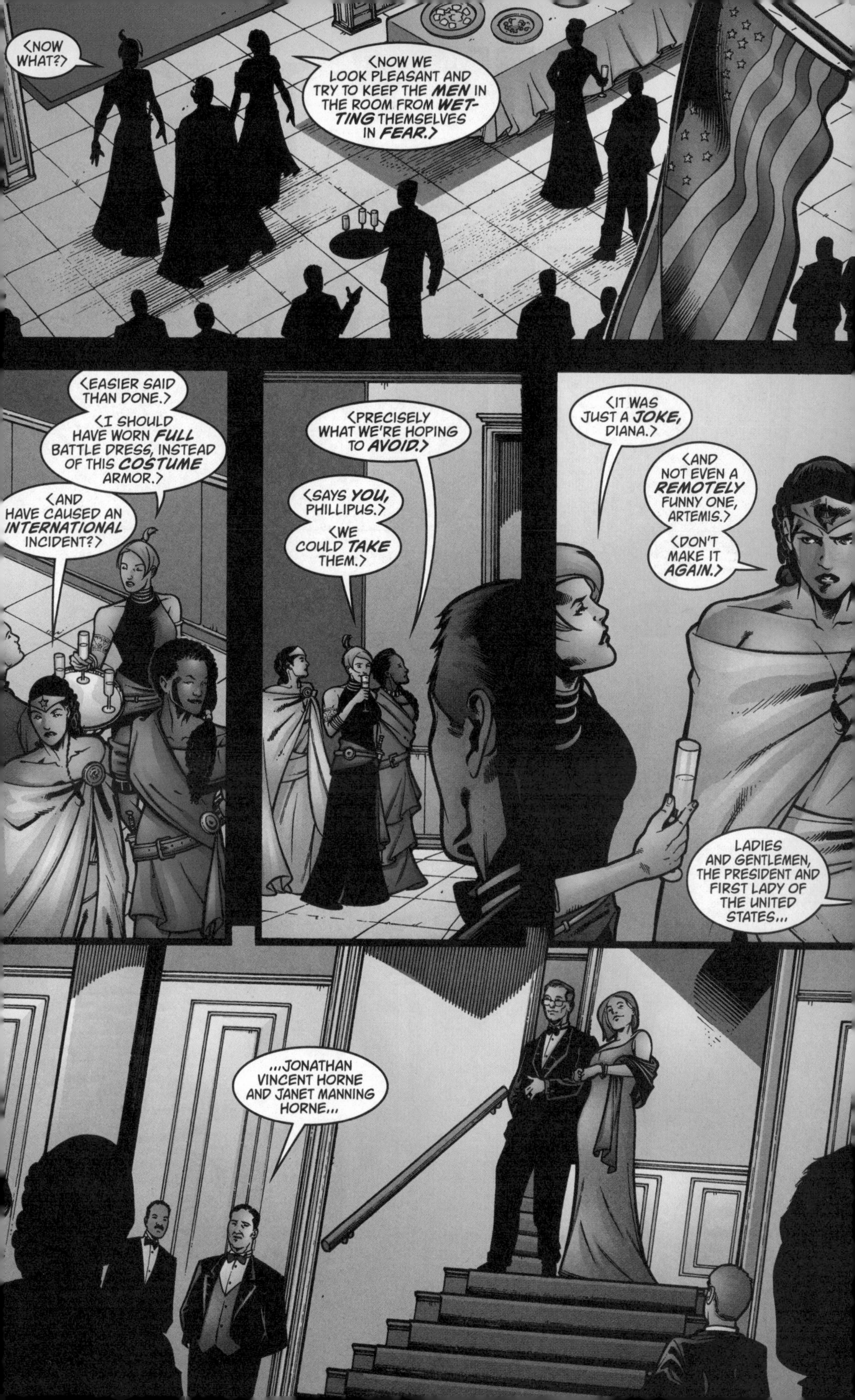
<NOW WHAT?>
<NOW WE LOOK PLEASANT AND TRY TO KEEP THE MEN IN THE ROOM FROM WETTING THEMSELVES IN FEAR.>
<EASIER SAID THAN DONE.>
<I SHOULD HAVE WORN FULL BATTLE DRESS, INSTEAD OF THIS COSTUME ARMOR.>
<AND HAVE CAUSED AN INTERNATIONAL INCIDENT?>
<PRECISELY WHAT WE'RE HOPING TO AVOID.>
<SAYS YOU, PHILLIPUS.>
<WE COULD TAKE THEM.>
<IT WAS JUST A JOKE, DIANA.>
<AND NOT EVEN A REMOTELY FUNNY ONE, ARTEMIS.>
<DON'T MAKE IT AGAIN.>
LADIES AND GENTLEMEN, THE PRESIDENT AND FIRST LADY OF THE UNITED STATES...
...JONATHAN VINCENT HORNE AND JANET MANNING HORNE...

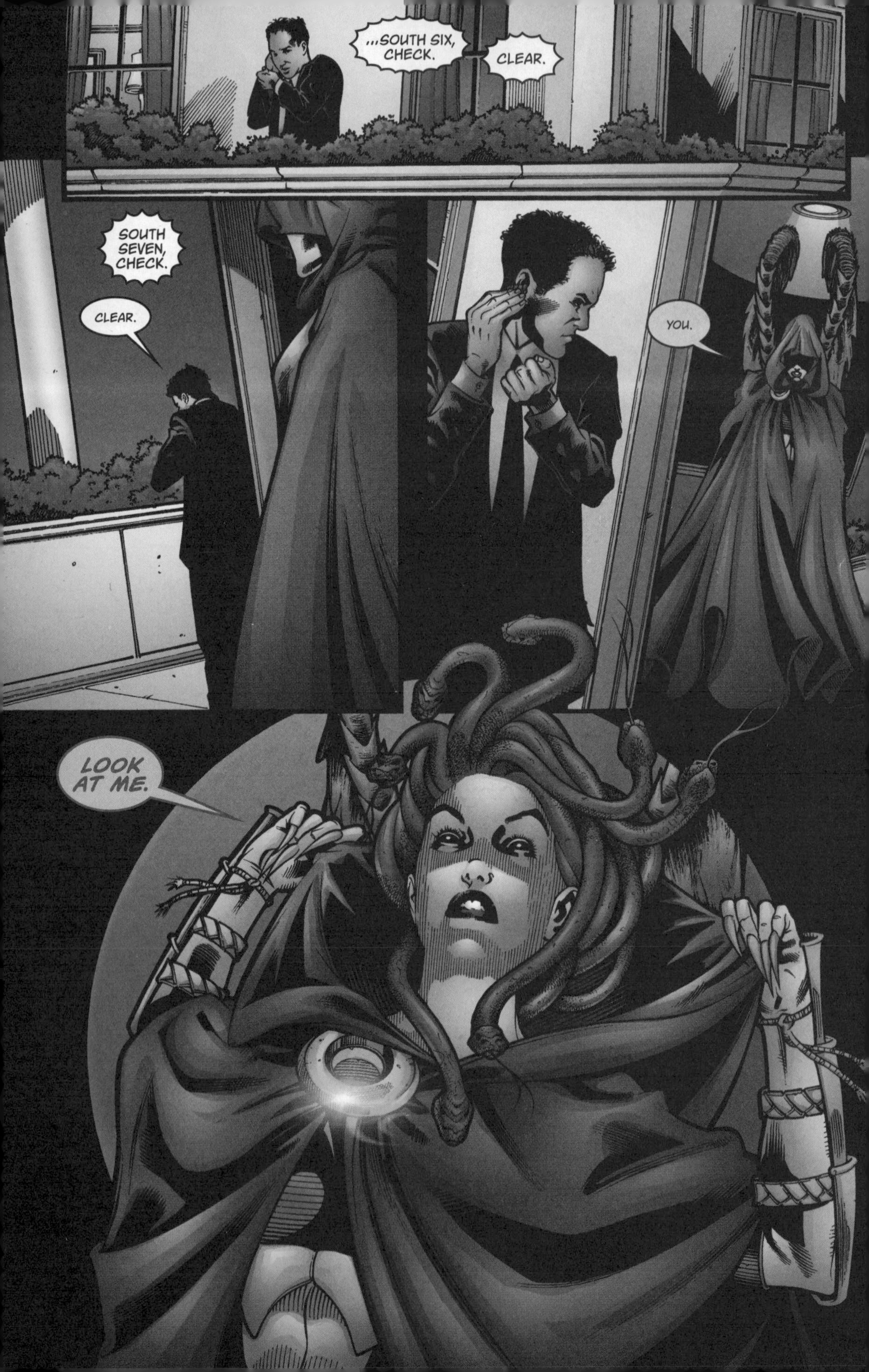
...SOUTH SIX, CHECK.
CLEAR.
SOUTH SEVEN, CHECK.
CLEAR.
YOU.
LOOK AT ME.

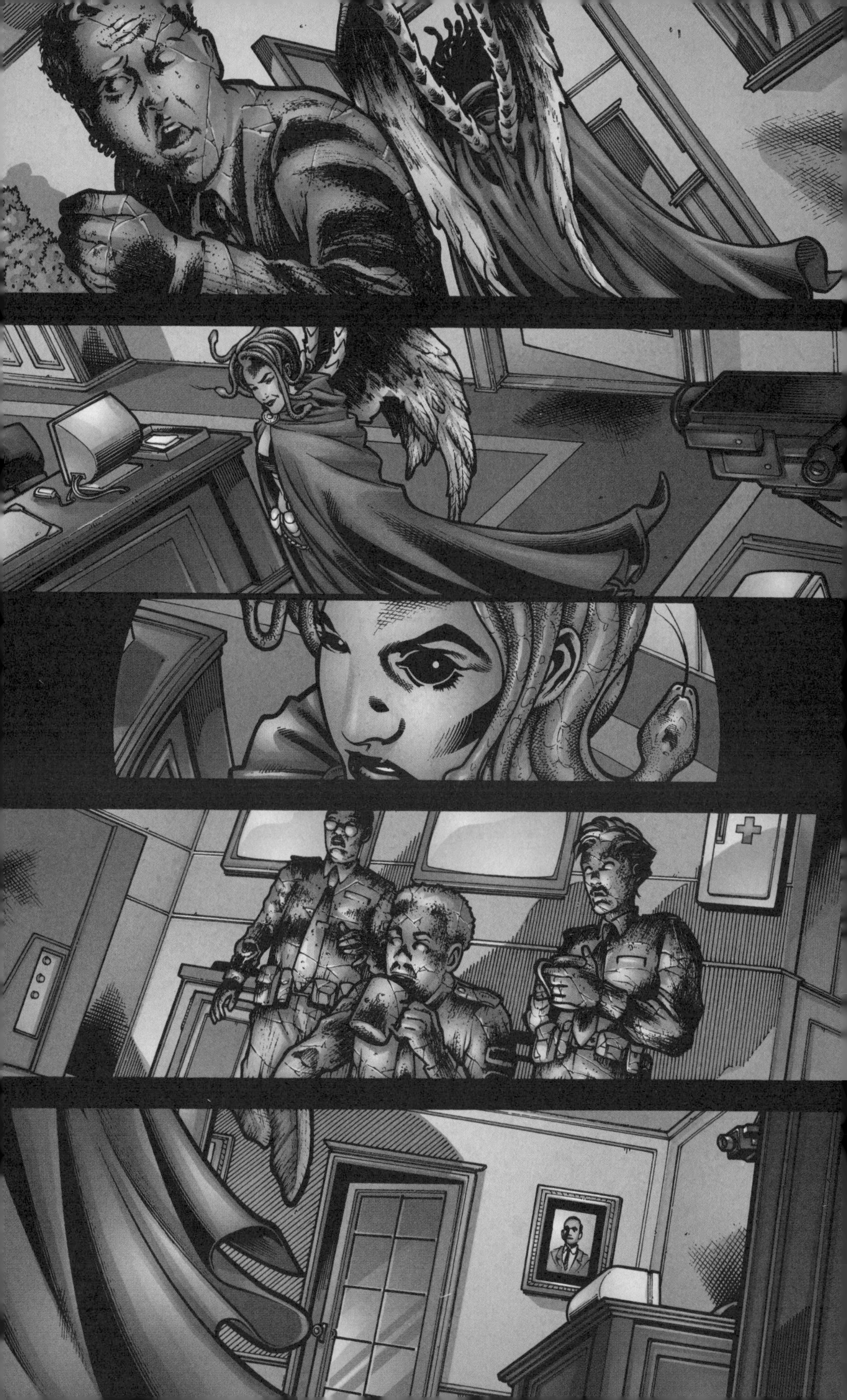

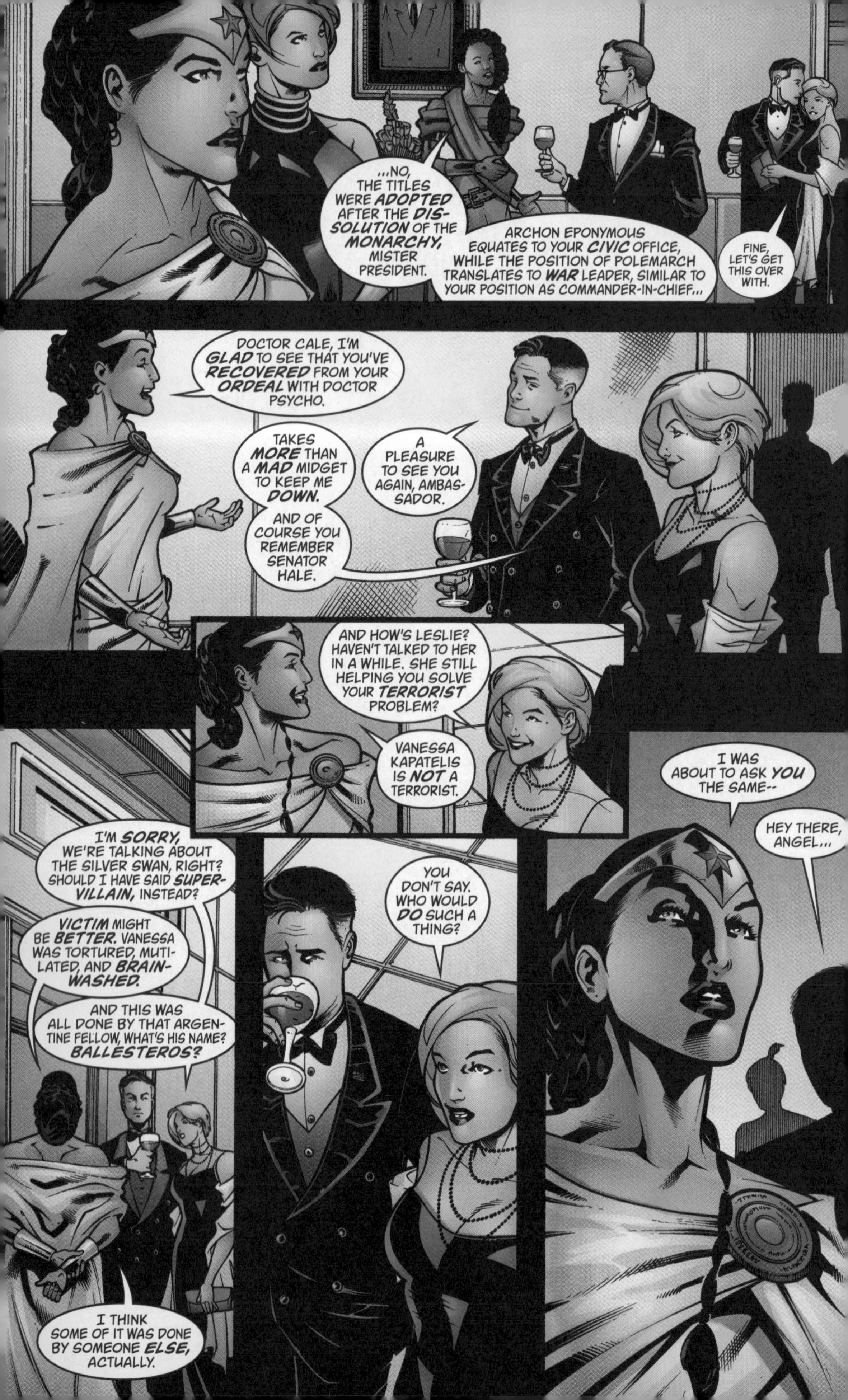
...NO, THE TITLES WERE ADOPTED AFTER THE DIS-SOLUTION OF THE MONARCHY, MISTER PRESIDENT.
ARCHON EPONYMOUS EQUATES TO YOUR CIVIC OFFICE, WHILE THE POSITION OF POLEMARCH TRANSLATES TO WAR LEADER, SIMILAR TO YOUR POSITION AS COMMANDER-IN-CHIEF...
FINE, LET'S GET THIS OVER WITH.
DOCTOR CALE, I'M GLAD TO SEE THAT YOU'VE RECOVERED FROM YOUR ORDEAL WITH DOCTOR PSYCHO.
A PLEASURE TO SEE YOU AGAIN, AMBAS-SADOR.
TAKES MORE THAN A MAD MIDGET TO KEEP ME DOWN.
AND OF COURSE YOU REMEMBER SENATOR HALE.
AND HOW'S LESLIE? HAVEN'T TALKED TO HER IN A WHILE. SHE STILL HELPING YOU SOLVE YOUR TERRORIST PROBLEM?
VANESSA KAPATELIS IS NOT A TERRORIST.
I'M SORRY, WE'RE TALKING ABOUT THE SILVER SWAN, RIGHT? SHOULD I HAVE SAID SUPER-VILLAIN, INSTEAD?
VICTIM MIGHT BE BETTER. VANESSA WAS TORTURED, MUTI-LATED, AND BRAIN-WASHED.
AND THIS WAS ALL DONE BY THAT ARGEN-TINE FELLOW, WHAT'S HIS NAME? BALLESTEROS?
I THINK SOME OF IT WAS DONE BY SOMEONE ELSE, ACTUALLY.
YOU DON'T SAY. WHO WOULD DO SUCH A THING?
I WAS ABOUT TO ASK YOU THE SAME--
HEY THERE, ANGEL...

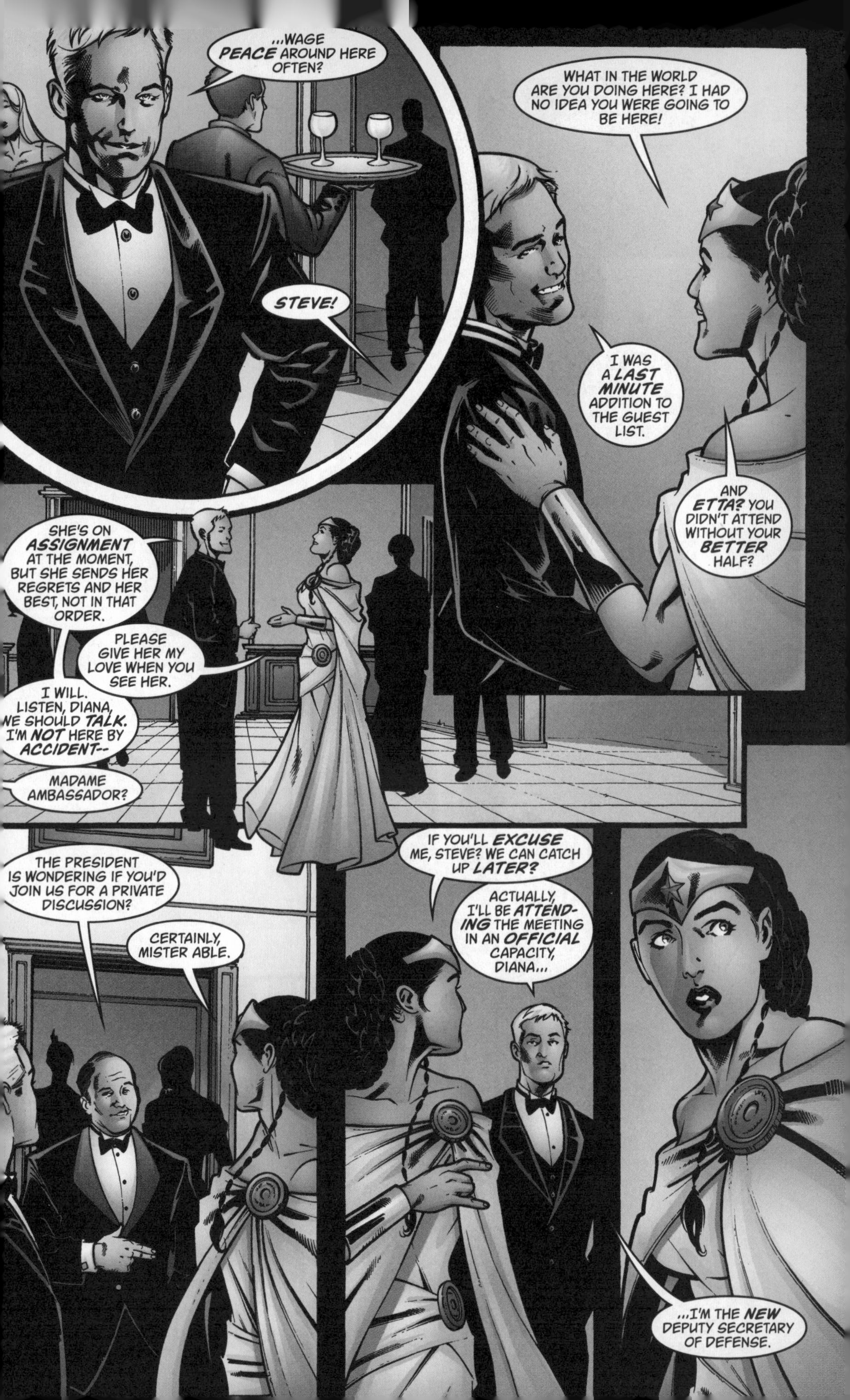

...WAGE PEACE AROUND HERE OFTEN?
STEVE!
WHAT IN THE WORLD ARE YOU DOING HERE? I HAD NO IDEA YOU WERE GOING TO BE HERE!
I WAS A LAST MINUTE ADDITION TO THE GUEST LIST.
AND ETTA? YOU DIDN'T ATTEND WITHOUT YOUR BETTER HALF?
SHE'S ON ASSIGNMENT AT THE MOMENT, BUT SHE SENDS HER REGRETS AND HER BEST, NOT IN THAT ORDER.
PLEASE GIVE HER MY LOVE WHEN YOU SEE HER.
I WILL. LISTEN, DIANA, WE SHOULD TALK. I'M NOT HERE BY ACCIDENT--
MADAME AMBASSADOR?
THE PRESIDENT IS WONDERING IF YOU'D JOIN US FOR A PRIVATE DISCUSSION?
CERTAINLY, MISTER ABLE.
IF YOU'LL EXCUSE ME, STEVE? WE CAN CATCH UP LATER?
ACTUALLY, I'LL BE ATTENDING THE MEETING IN AN OFFICIAL CAPACITY, DIANA...
...I'M THE NEW DEPUTY SECRETARY OF DEFENSE.

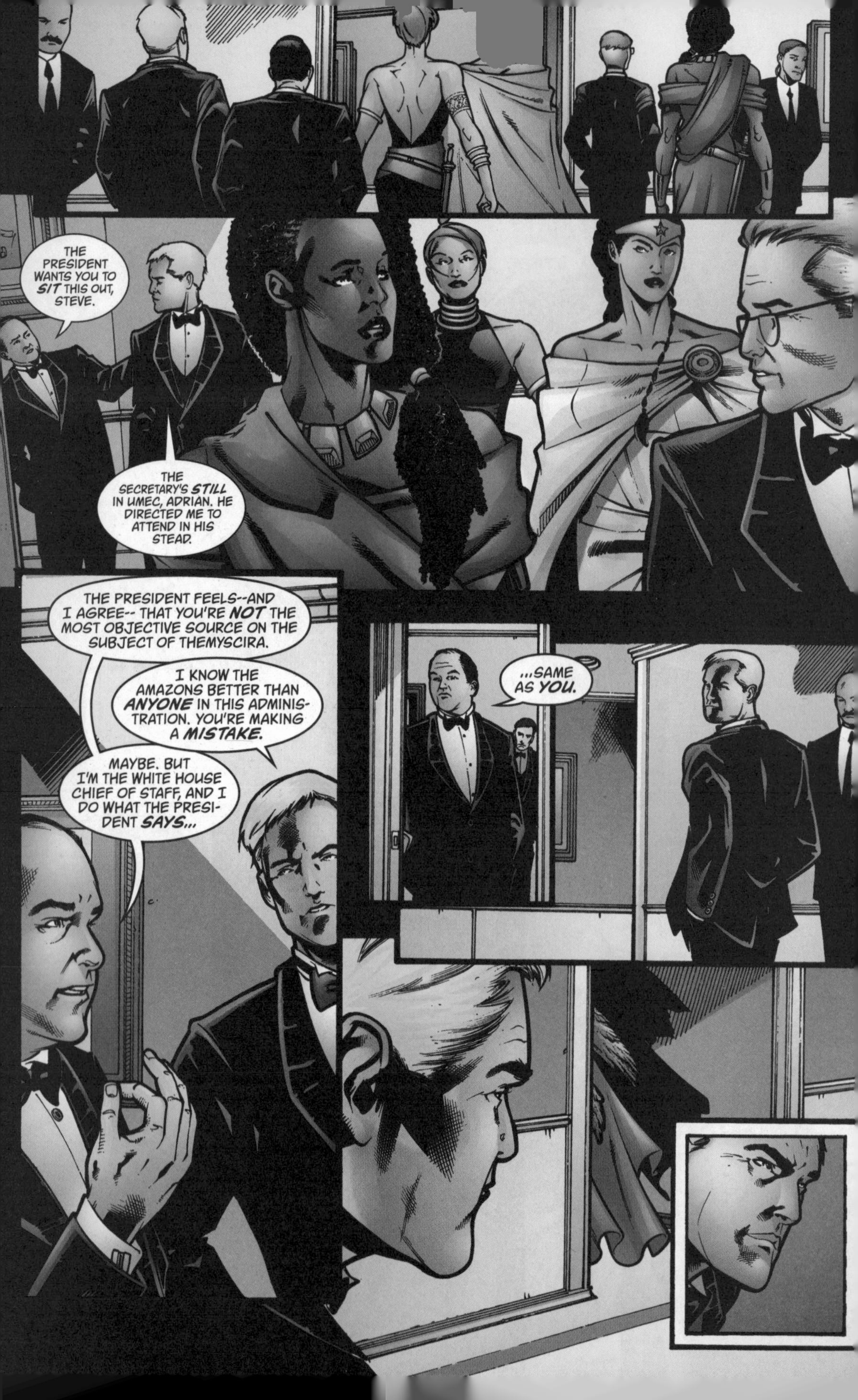
THE PRESIDENT WANTS YOU TO SIT THIS OUT, STEVE.
THE SECRETARY'S STILL IN UMEC, ADRIAN. HE DIRECTED ME TO ATTEND IN HIS STEAD.
THE PRESIDENT FEELS--AND I AGREE-- THAT YOU'RE NOT THE MOST OBJECTIVE SOURCE ON THE SUBJECT OF THEMYSCIRA.
I KNOW THE AMAZONS BETTER THAN ANYONE IN THIS ADMINISTRATION. YOU'RE MAKING A MISTAKE.
MAYBE. BUT I'M THE WHITE HOUSE CHIEF OF STAFF, AND I DO WHAT THE PRESIDENT SAYS...
...SAME AS YOU.

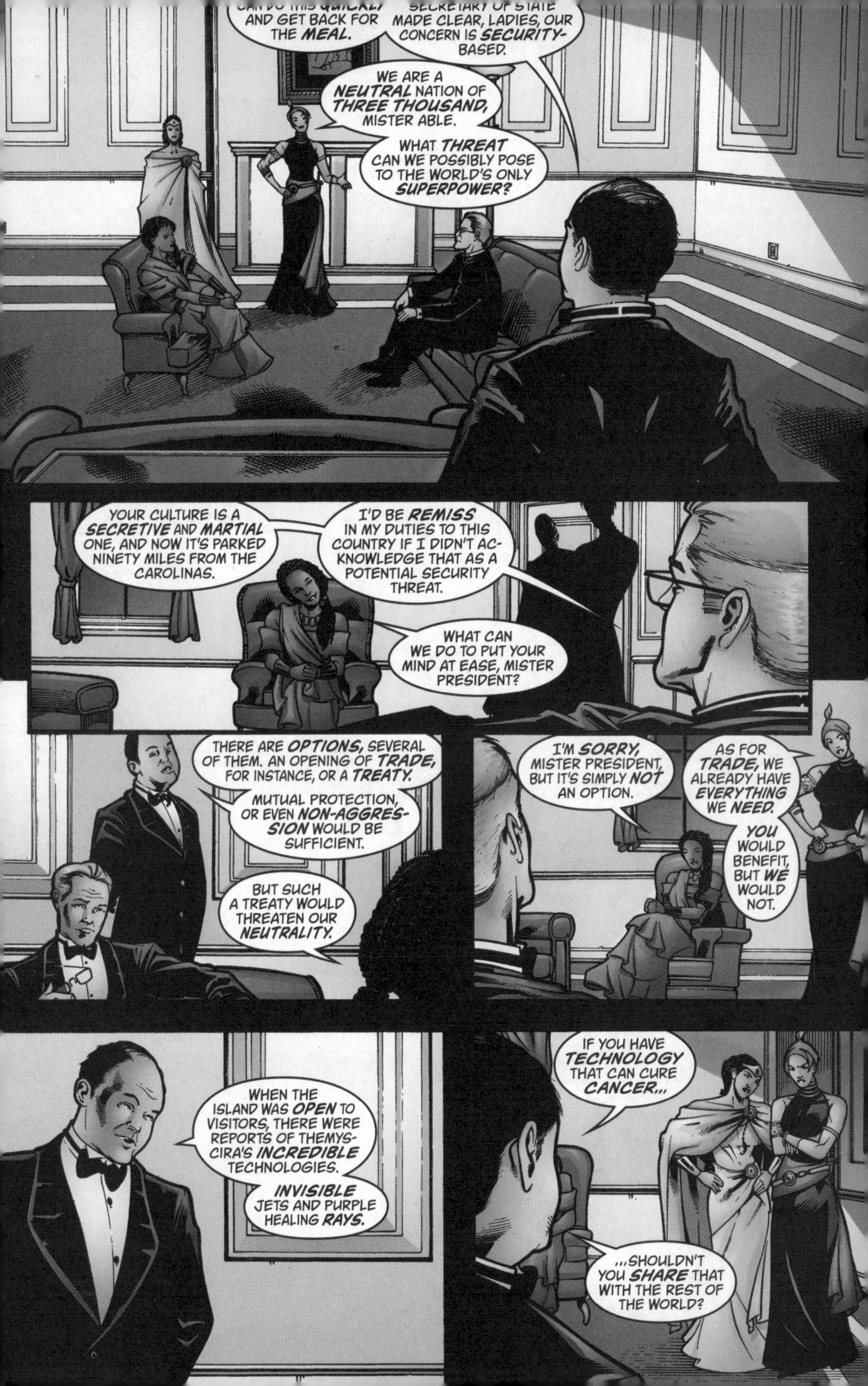

AND GET BACK FOR THE MEAL.
MADE CLEAR, LADIES, OUR CONCERN IS SECURITY-BASED.
WE ARE A NEUTRAL NATION OF THREE THOUSAND, MISTER ABLE.
WHAT THREAT CAN WE POSSIBLY POSE TO THE WORLD'S ONLY SUPERPOWER?
YOUR CULTURE IS A SECRETIVE AND MARTIAL ONE, AND NOW IT'S PARKED NINETY MILES FROM THE CAROLINAS.
I'D BE REMISS IN MY DUTIES TO THIS COUNTRY IF I DIDN'T ACKNOWLEDGE THAT AS A POTENTIAL SECURITY THREAT.
WHAT CAN WE DO TO PUT YOUR MIND AT EASE, MISTER PRESIDENT?
THERE ARE OPTIONS, SEVERAL OF THEM. AN OPENING OF TRADE, FOR INSTANCE, OR A TREATY.
MUTUAL PROTECTION, OR EVEN NON-AGGRESSION WOULD BE SUFFICIENT.
BUT SUCH A TREATY WOULD THREATEN OUR NEUTRALITY.
I'M SORRY, MISTER PRESIDENT, BUT IT'S SIMPLY NOT AN OPTION.
AS FOR TRADE, WE ALREADY HAVE EVERYTHING WE NEED.
YOU WOULD BENEFIT, BUT WE WOULD NOT.
WHEN THE ISLAND WAS OPEN TO VISITORS, THERE WERE REPORTS OF THEMYSCIRA'S INCREDIBLE TECHNOLOGIES.
INVISIBLE JETS AND PURPLE HEALING RAYS.
IF YOU HAVE TECHNOLOGY THAT CAN CURE CANCER...
...SHOULDN'T YOU SHARE THAT WITH THE REST OF THE WORLD?

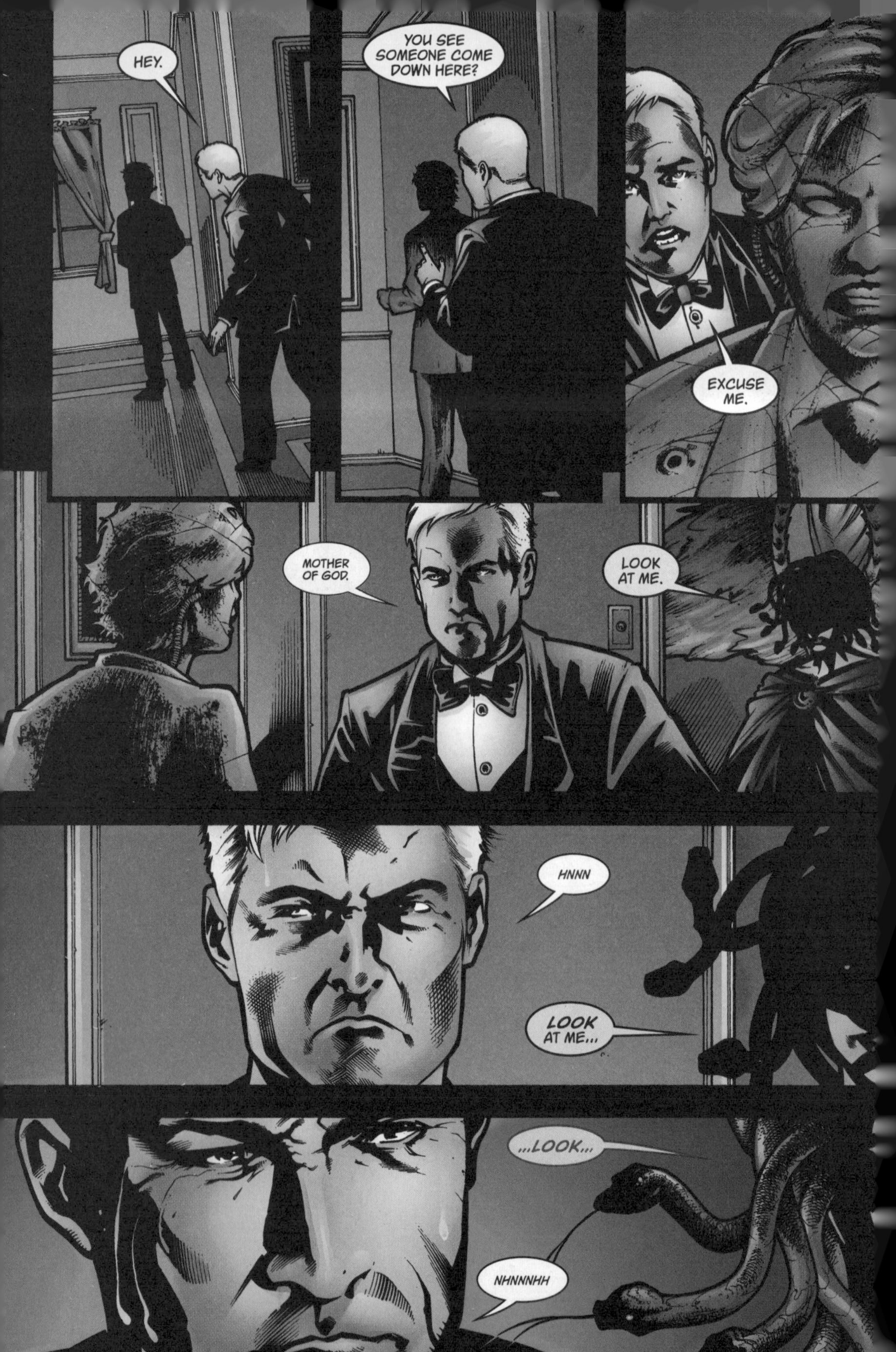
HEY.
YOU SEE SOMEONE COME DOWN HERE?
EXCUSE ME.
MOTHER OF GOD.
LOOK AT ME.
HNNN
LOOK AT ME...
...LOOK...
NHNNNHH

GHAA!
<AWAY FROM ME, BEAST!>
HFFF
<WHAT IS THIS MORTAL TO YOU, THAT YOU WOULD SAVE HIM?>
YOU'RE IN THE WRONG HOUSE, LADY.
WHOOOOP WHOOOO

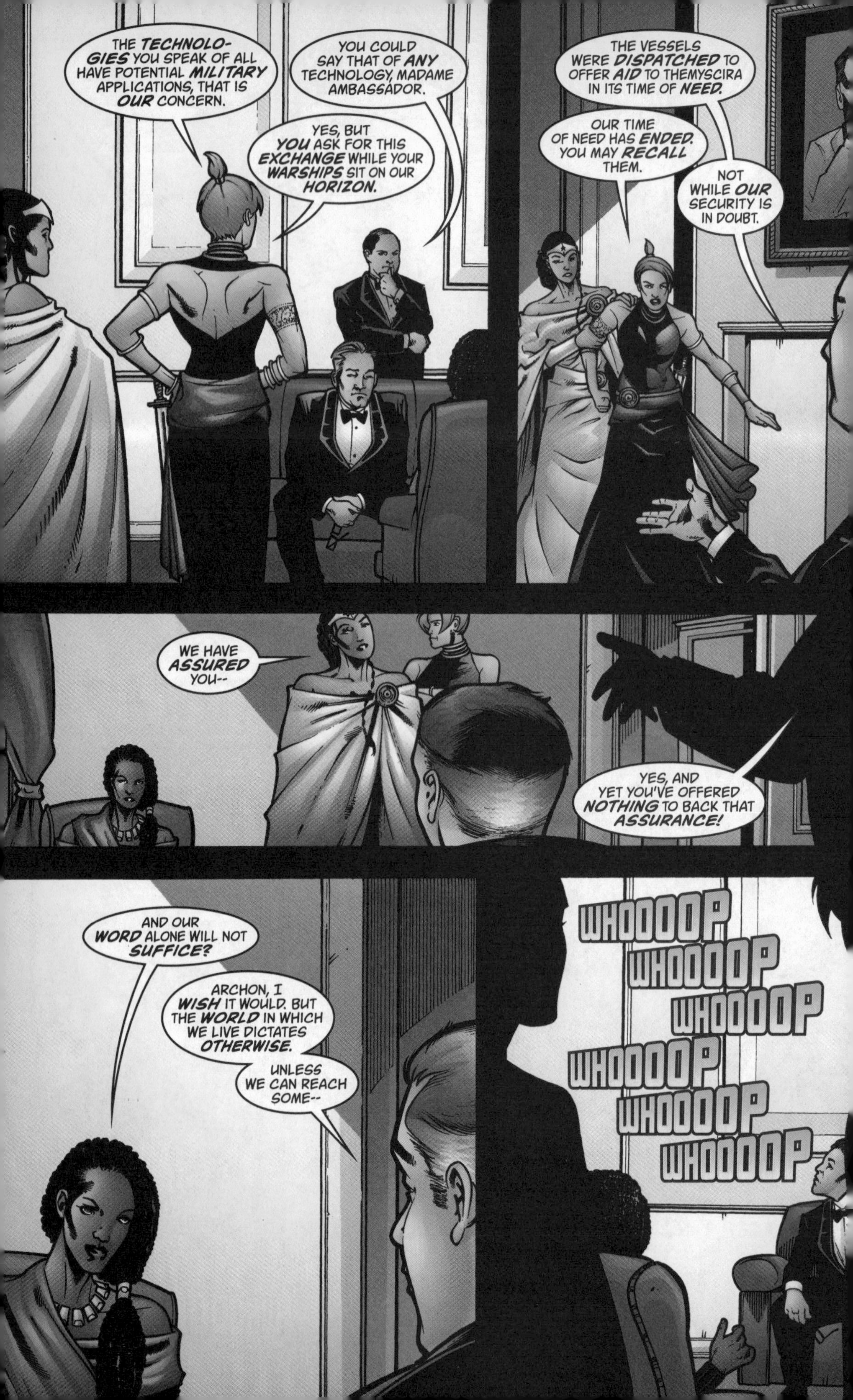
THE TECHNOLOGIES YOU SPEAK OF ALL HAVE POTENTIAL MILITARY APPLICATIONS, THAT IS OUR CONCERN.
YOU COULD SAY THAT OF ANY TECHNOLOGY, MADAME AMBASSADOR.
YES, BUT YOU ASK FOR THIS EXCHANGE WHILE YOUR WARSHIPS SIT ON OUR HORIZON.
THE VESSELS WERE DISPATCHED TO OFFER AID TO THEMYSCIRA IN ITS TIME OF NEED.
OUR TIME OF NEED HAS ENDED. YOU MAY RECALL THEM.
NOT WHILE OUR SECURITY IS IN DOUBT.
WE HAVE ASSURED YOU--
YES, AND YET YOU'VE OFFERED NOTHING TO BACK THAT ASSURANCE!
AND OUR WORD ALONE WILL NOT SUFFICE?
ARCHON, I WISH IT WOULD. BUT THE WORLD IN WHICH WE LIVE DICTATES OTHERWISE.
UNLESS WE CAN REACH SOME--
WHOOOOP
WHOOOOP
WHOOOOP
WHOOOOP
WHOOOOP
WHOOOOP

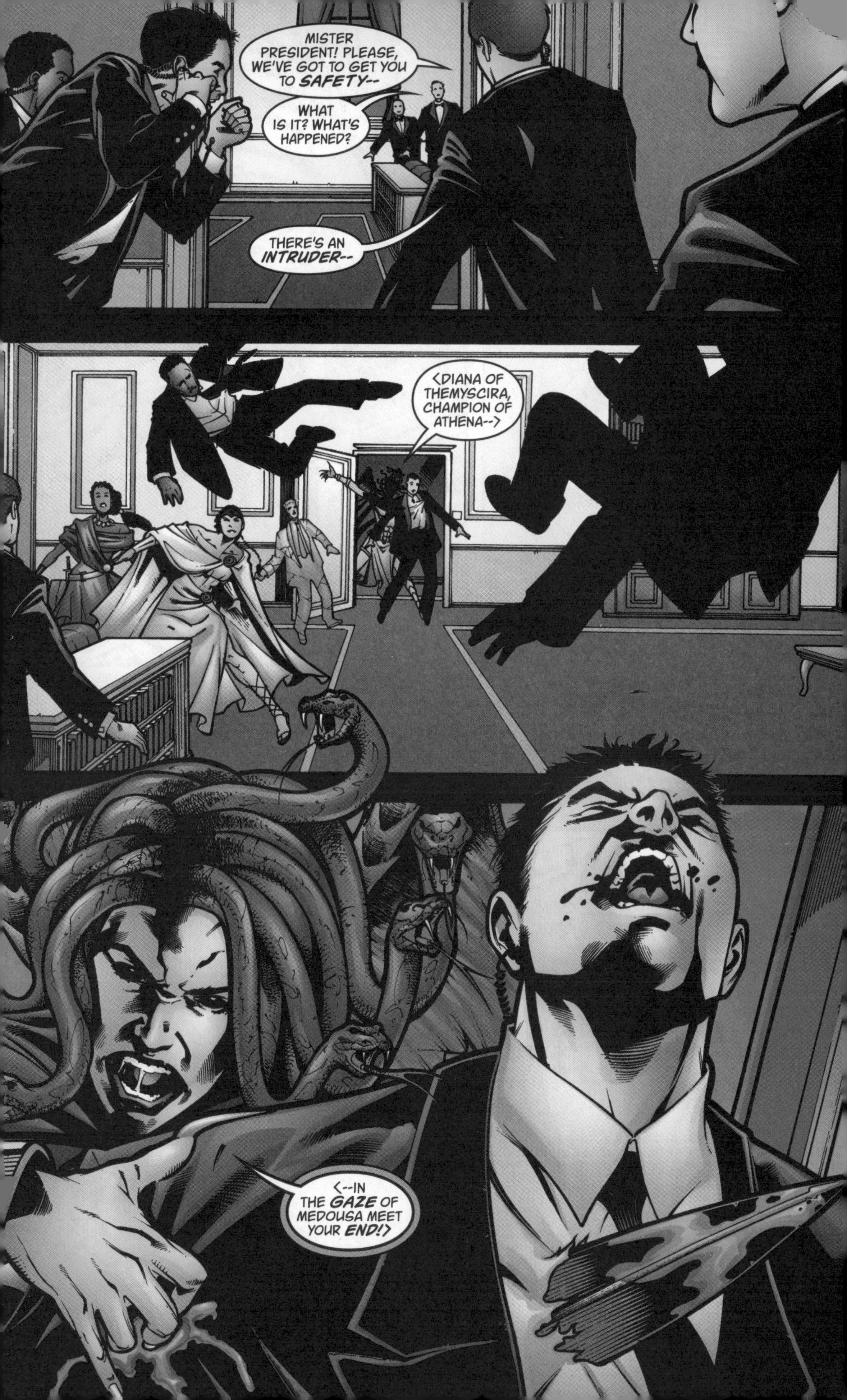
MISTER PRESIDENT! PLEASE, WE'VE GOT TO GET YOU TO SAFETY--
WHAT IS IT? WHAT'S HAPPENED?
THERE'S AN INTRUDER--
<DIANA OF THEMYSCIRA, CHAMPION OF ATHENA-->
<--IN THE GAZE OF MEDOUSA MEET YOUR END!>

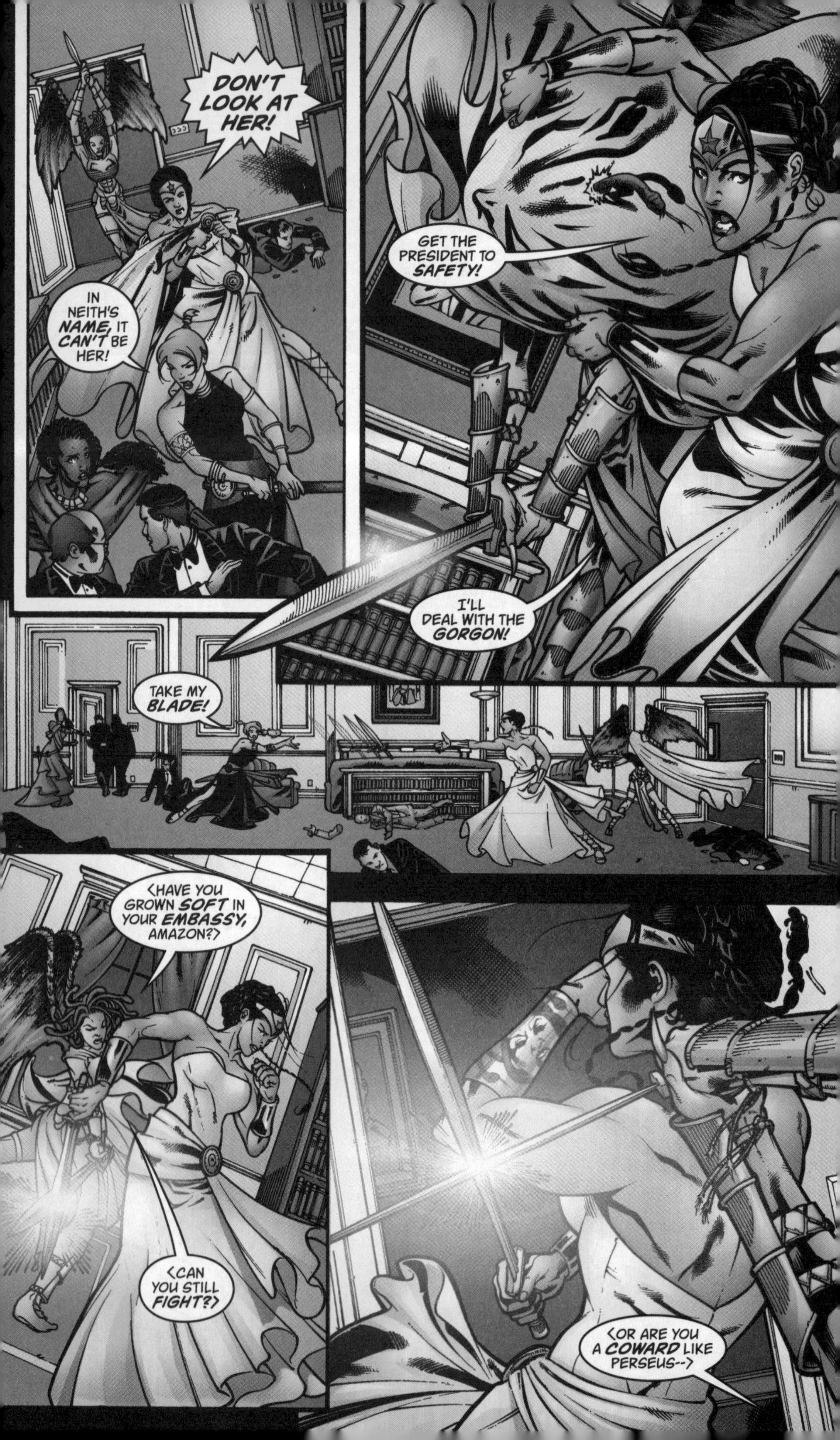
DON'T LOOK AT HER!
IN NEITH'S NAME, IT CAN'T BE HER!
GET THE PRESIDENT TO SAFETY!
I'LL DEAL WITH THE GORGON!
TAKE MY BLADE!
<HAVE YOU GROWN SOFT IN YOUR EMBASSY, AMAZON?>
<CAN YOU STILL FIGHT?>
<OR ARE YOU A COWARD LIKE PERSEUS-->

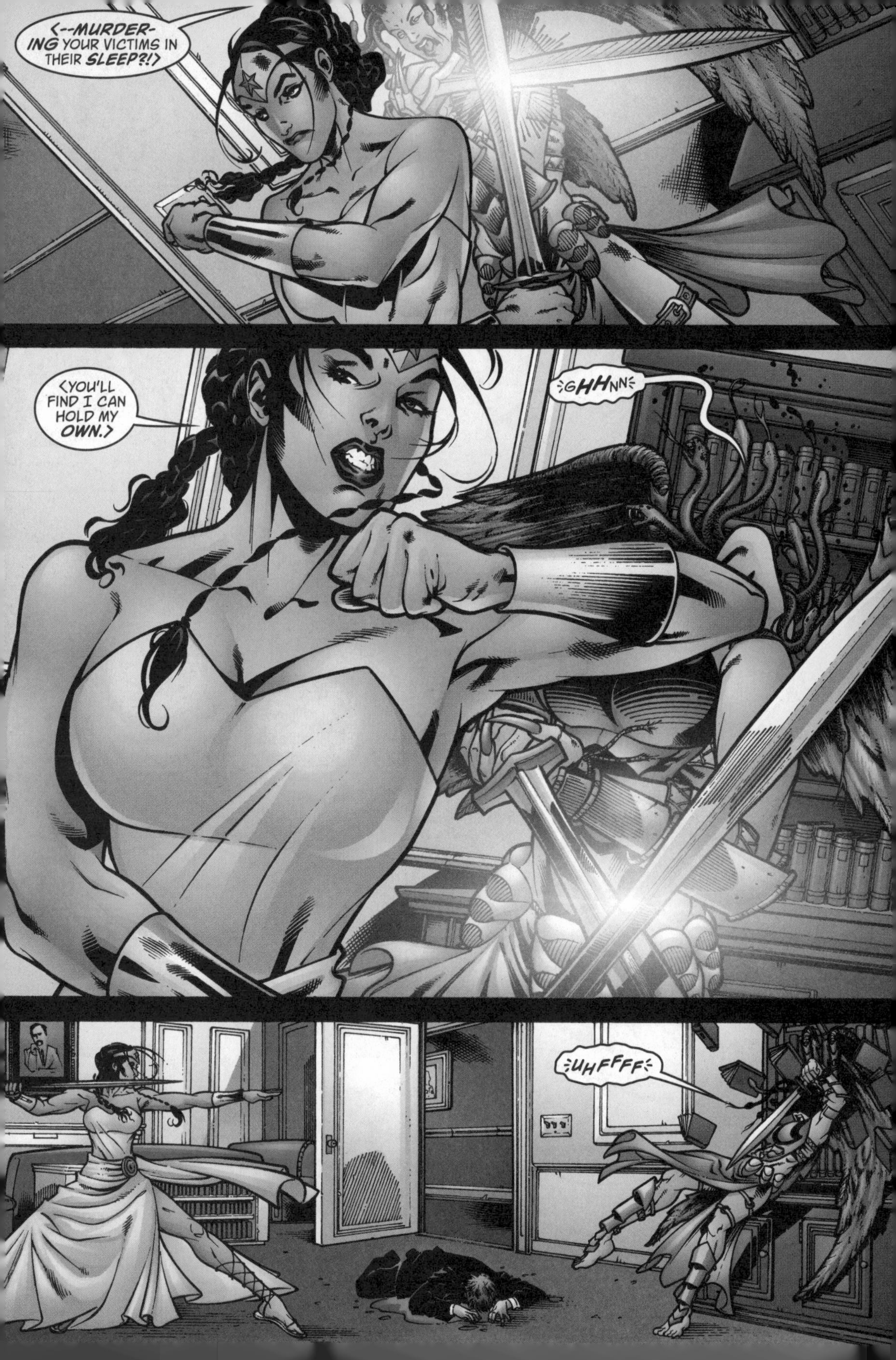

<--MURDER-ING YOUR VICTIMS IN THEIR SLEEP?!>
<YOU'LL FIND I CAN HOLD MY OWN.>
GHHNN
UHFFFF

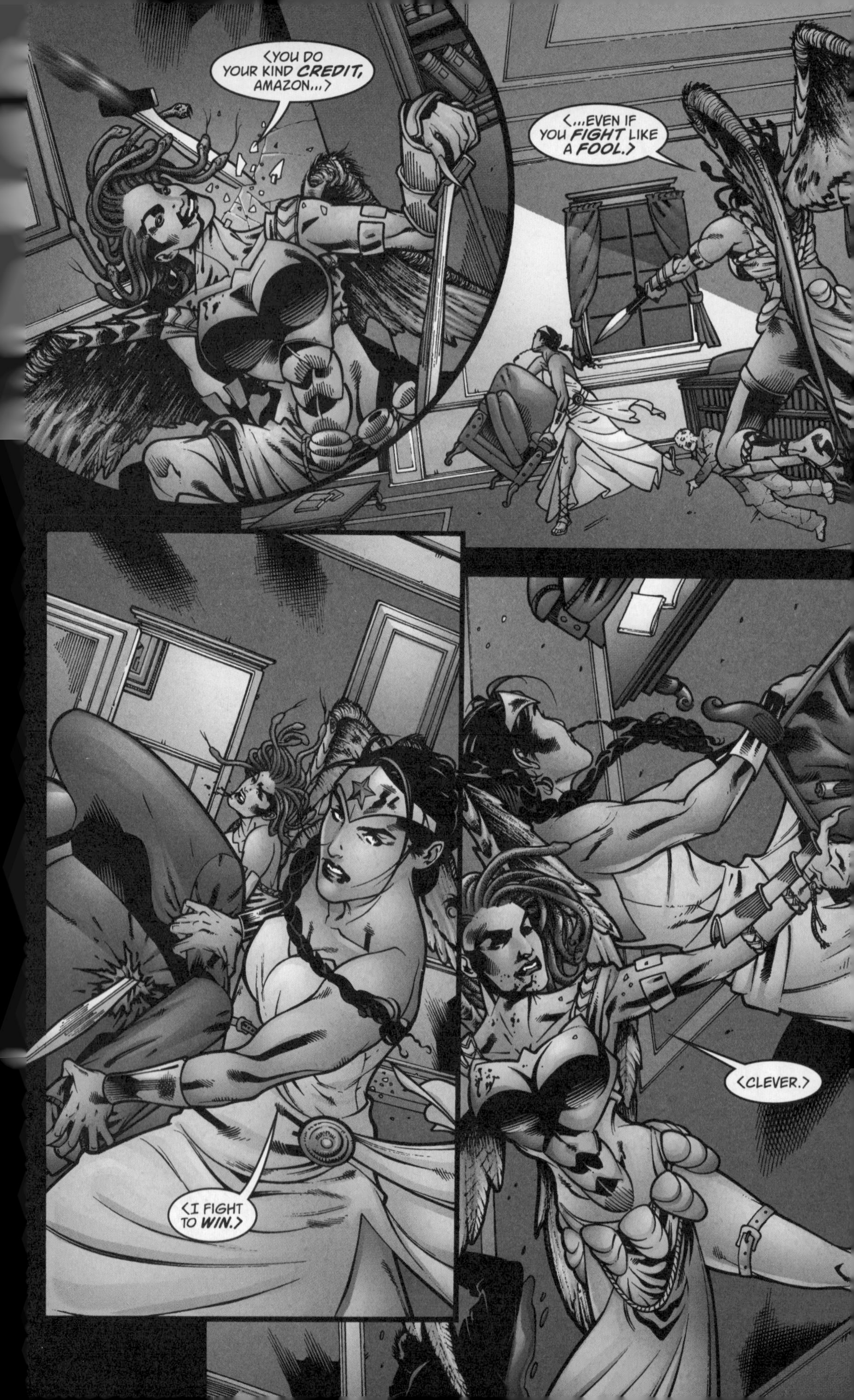
<YOU DO YOUR KIND CREDIT, AMAZON...>
<...EVEN IF YOU FIGHT LIKE A FOOL.>
<I FIGHT TO WIN.>
<CLEVER.>

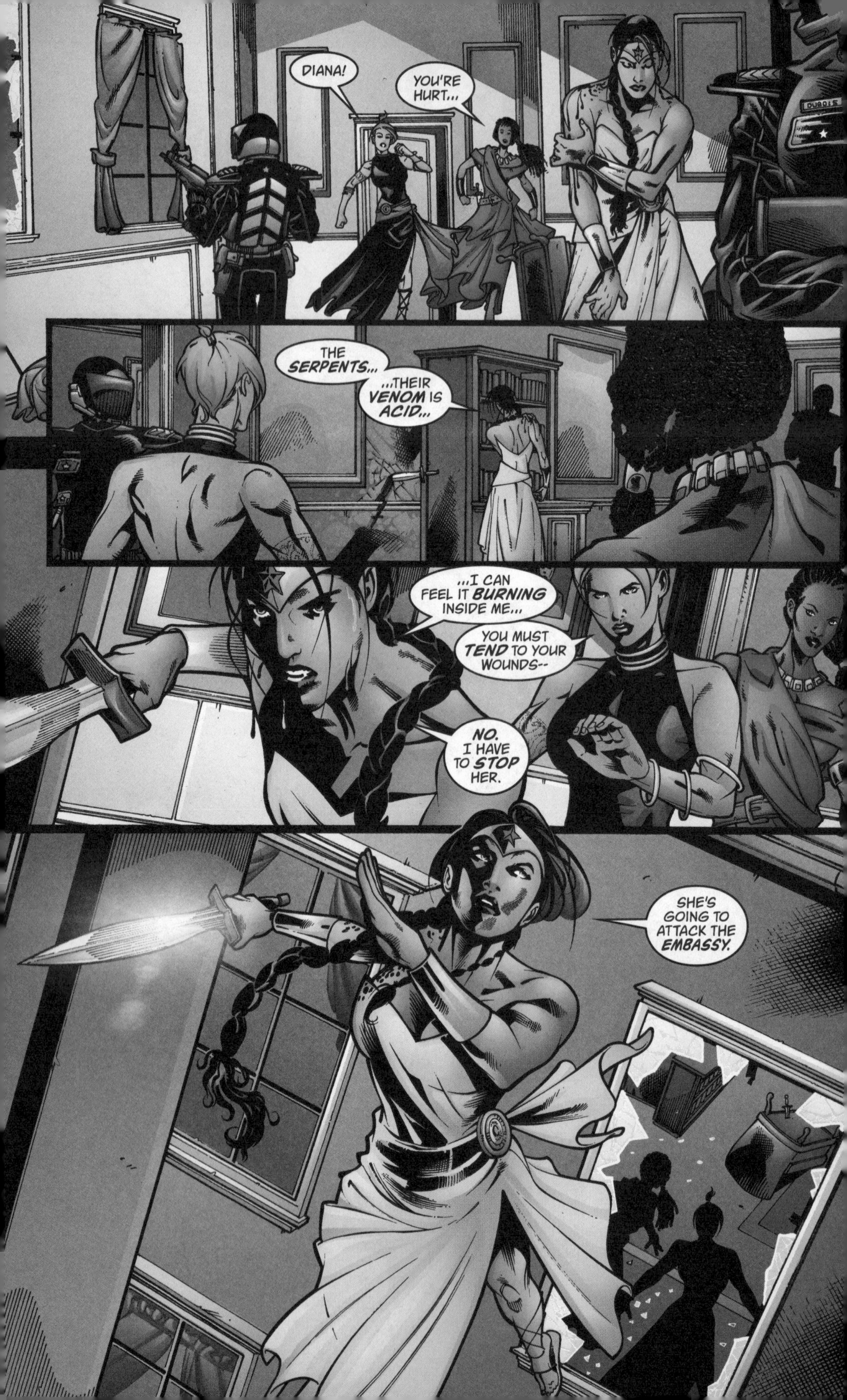
DIANA!
YOU'RE HURT...
THE SERPENTS...
...THEIR VENOM IS ACID...
...I CAN FEEL IT BURNING INSIDE ME...
YOU MUST TEND TO YOUR WOUNDS--
NO. I HAVE TO STOP HER.
SHE'S GOING TO ATTACK THE EMBASSY.

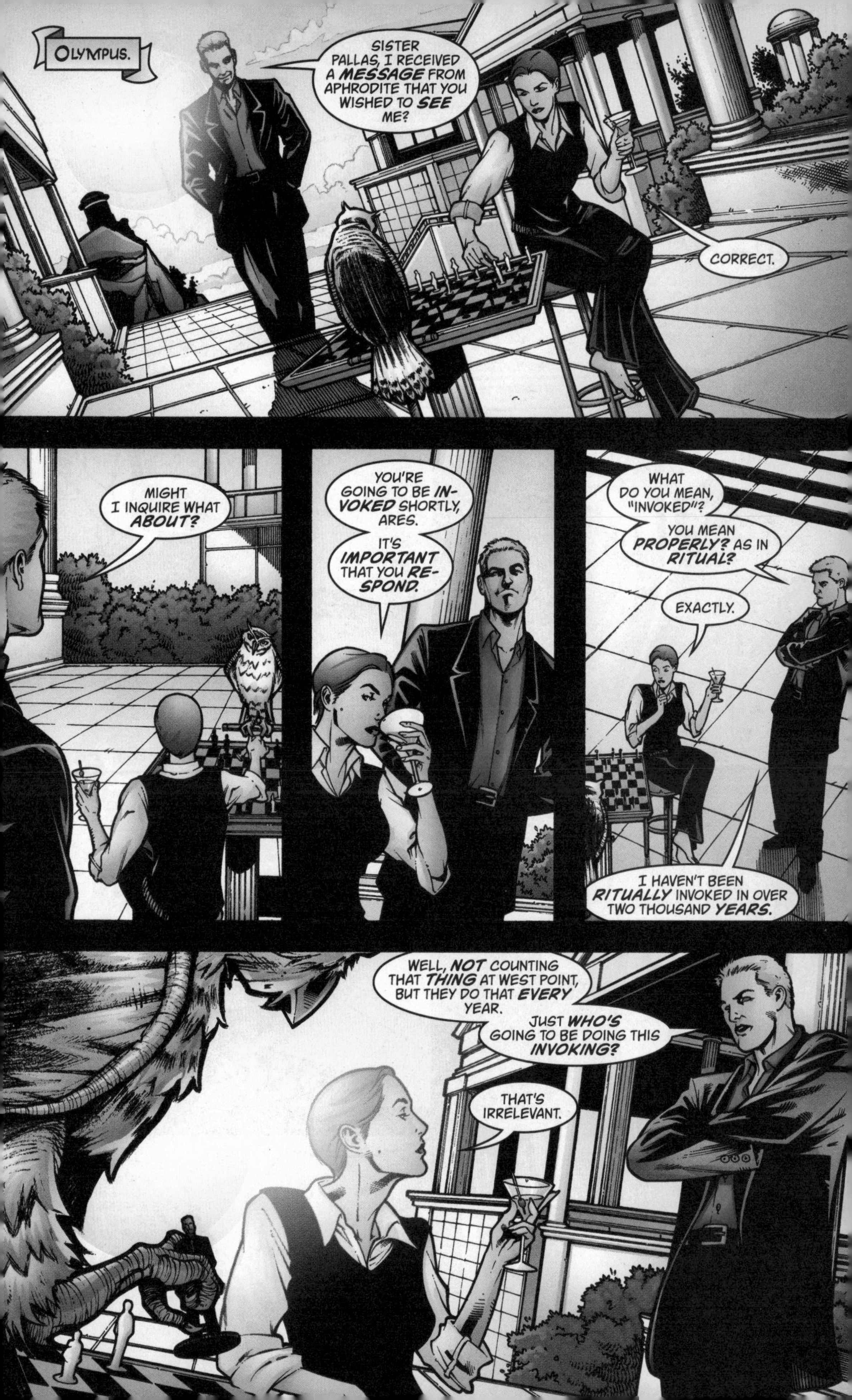

OLYMPUS.
SISTER PALLAS, I RECEIVED A MESSAGE FROM APHRODITE THAT YOU WISHED TO SEE ME?
CORRECT.
MIGHT I INQUIRE WHAT ABOUT?
YOU'RE GOING TO BE INVOKED SHORTLY, ARES.
IT'S IMPORTANT THAT YOU RESPOND.
WHAT DO YOU MEAN, "INVOKED"?
YOU MEAN PROPERLY? AS IN RITUAL?
EXACTLY.
I HAVEN'T BEEN RITUALLY INVOKED IN OVER TWO THOUSAND YEARS.
WELL, NOT COUNTING THAT THING AT WEST POINT, BUT THEY DO THAT EVERY YEAR.
JUST WHO'S GOING TO BE DOING THIS INVOKING?
THAT'S IRRELEVANT.

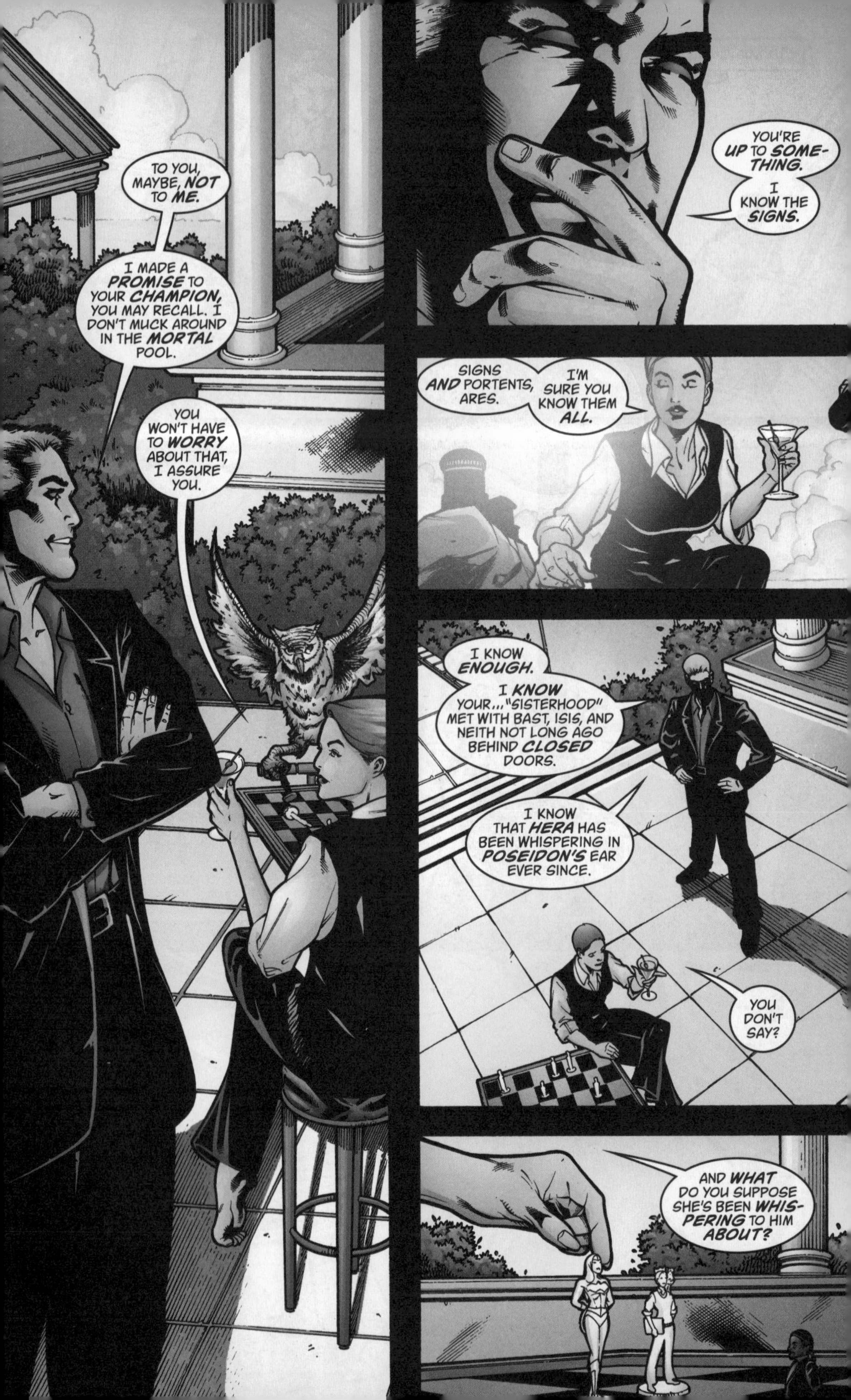
TO YOU, MAYBE, NOT TO ME.
I MADE A PROMISE TO YOUR CHAMPION, YOU MAY RECALL. I DON'T MUCK AROUND IN THE MORTAL POOL.
YOU WON'T HAVE TO WORRY ABOUT THAT, I ASSURE YOU.
YOU'RE UP TO SOME-THING.
I KNOW THE SIGNS.
SIGNS AND PORTENTS, ARES.
I'M SURE YOU KNOW THEM ALL.
I KNOW ENOUGH.
I KNOW YOUR... "SISTERHOOD" MET WITH BAST, ISIS, AND NEITH NOT LONG AGO BEHIND CLOSED DOORS.
I KNOW THAT HERA HAS BEEN WHISPERING IN POSEIDON'S EAR EVER SINCE.
YOU DON'T SAY?
AND WHAT DO YOU SUPPOSE SHE'S BEEN WHIS-PERING TO HIM ABOUT?

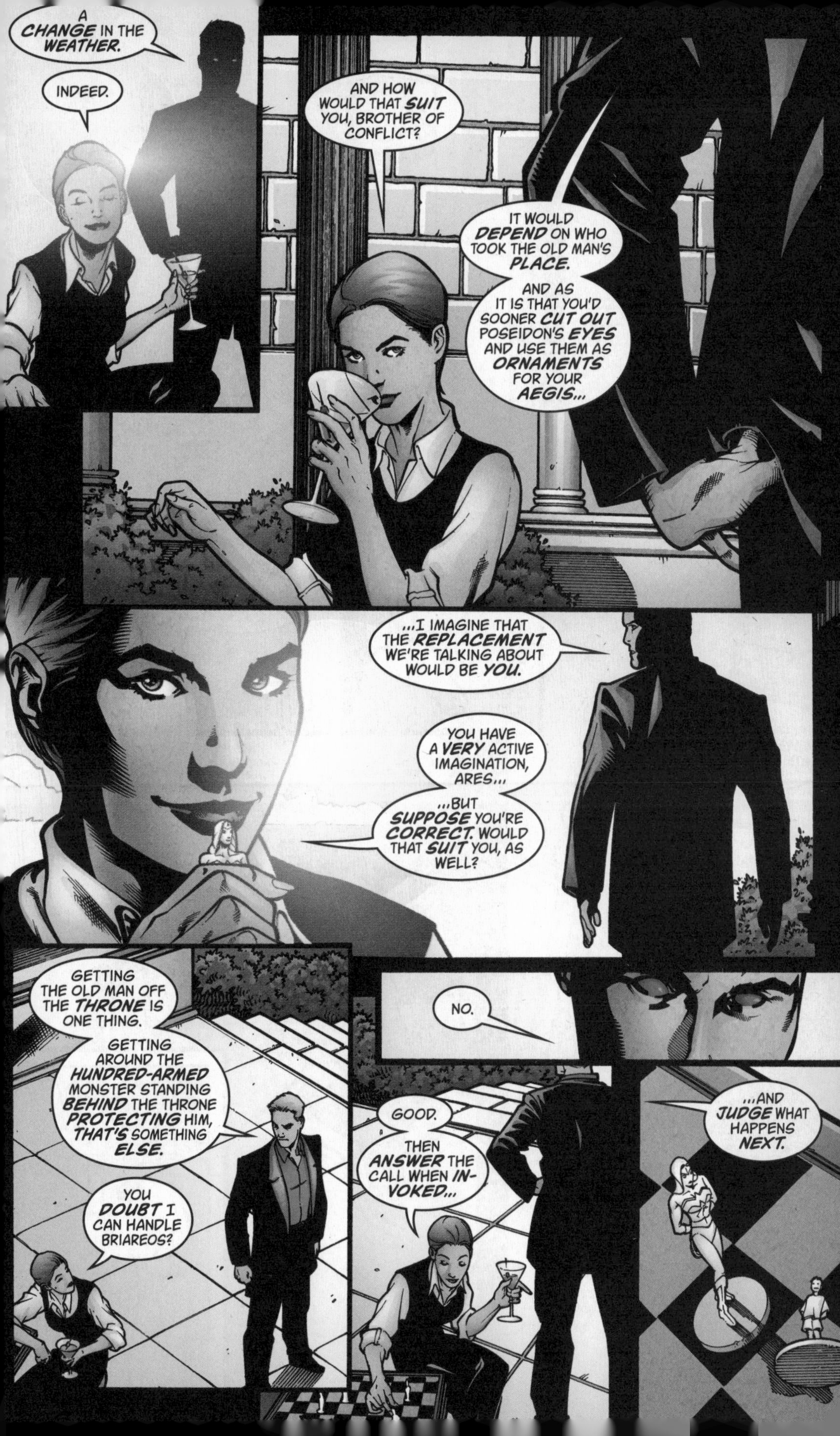
A CHANGE IN THE WEATHER.
INDEED.
AND HOW WOULD THAT SUIT YOU, BROTHER OF CONFLICT?
IT WOULD DEPEND ON WHO TOOK THE OLD MAN'S PLACE.
AND AS IT IS THAT YOU'D SOONER CUT OUT POSEIDON'S EYES AND USE THEM AS ORNAMENTS FOR YOUR AEGIS...
...I IMAGINE THAT THE REPLACEMENT WE'RE TALKING ABOUT WOULD BE YOU.
YOU HAVE A VERY ACTIVE IMAGINATION, ARES...
...BUT SUPPOSE YOU'RE CORRECT. WOULD THAT SUIT YOU, AS WELL?
GETTING THE OLD MAN OFF THE THRONE IS ONE THING.
GETTING AROUND THE HUNDRED-ARMED MONSTER STANDING BEHIND THE THRONE PROTECTING HIM, THAT'S SOMETHING ELSE.
YOU DOUBT I CAN HANDLE BRIAREOS?
NO.
GOOD.
THEN ANSWER THE CALL WHEN IN-VOKED...
...AND JUDGE WHAT HAPPENS NEXT.

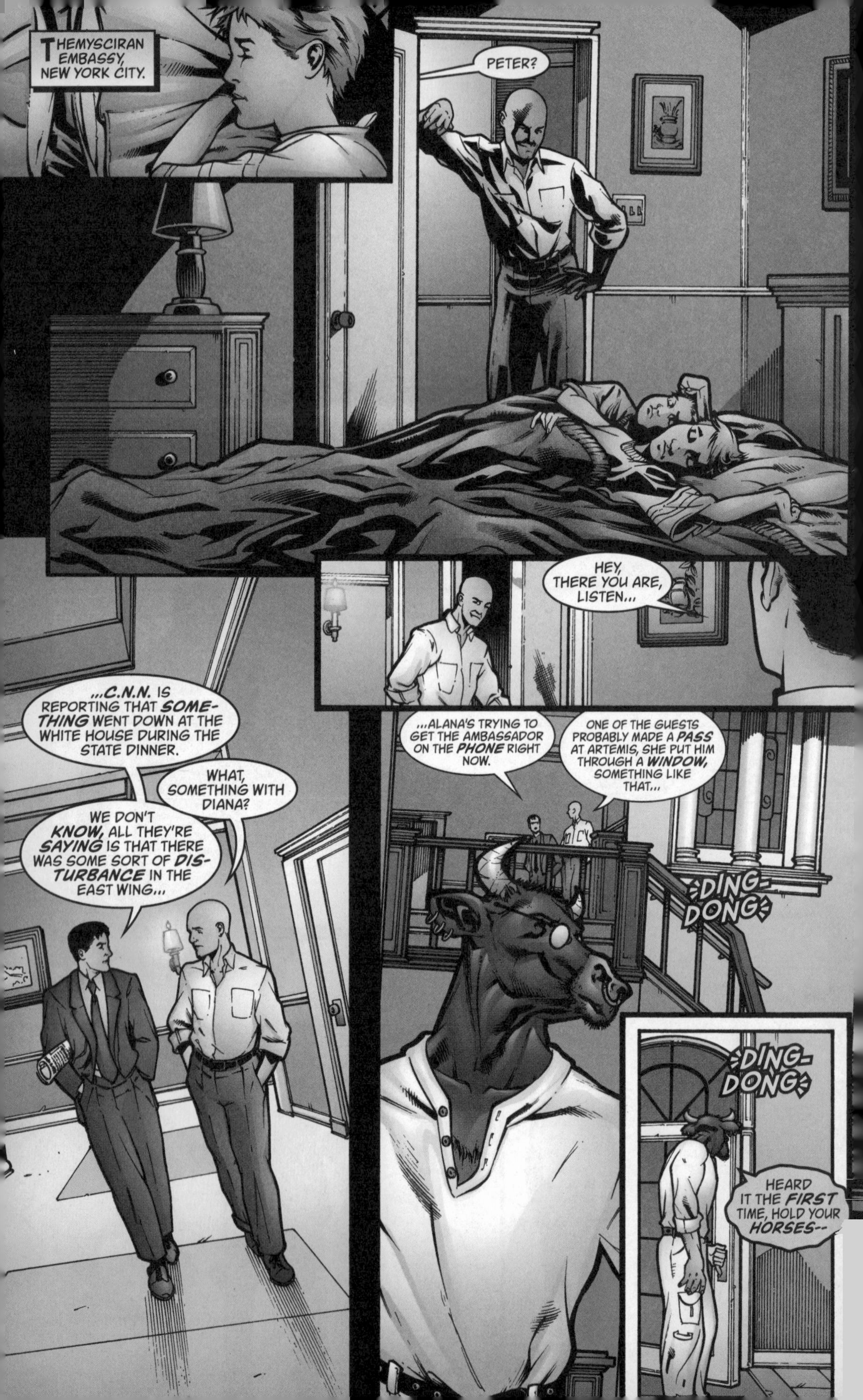
THEMYSCIRAN EMBASSY, NEW YORK CITY.
PETER?
HEY, THERE YOU ARE, LISTEN...
...C.N.N. IS REPORTING THAT SOMETHING WENT DOWN AT THE WHITE HOUSE DURING THE STATE DINNER.
WHAT, SOMETHING WITH DIANA?
WE DON'T KNOW, ALL THEY'RE SAYING IS THAT THERE WAS SOME SORT OF DISTURBANCE IN THE EAST WING...
...ALANA'S TRYING TO GET THE AMBASSADOR ON THE PHONE RIGHT NOW.
ONE OF THE GUESTS PROBABLY MADE A PASS AT ARTEMIS, SHE PUT HIM THROUGH A WINDOW, SOMETHING LIKE THAT...
DING-DONG
DING-DONG
HEARD IT THE FIRST TIME, HOLD YOUR HORSES--

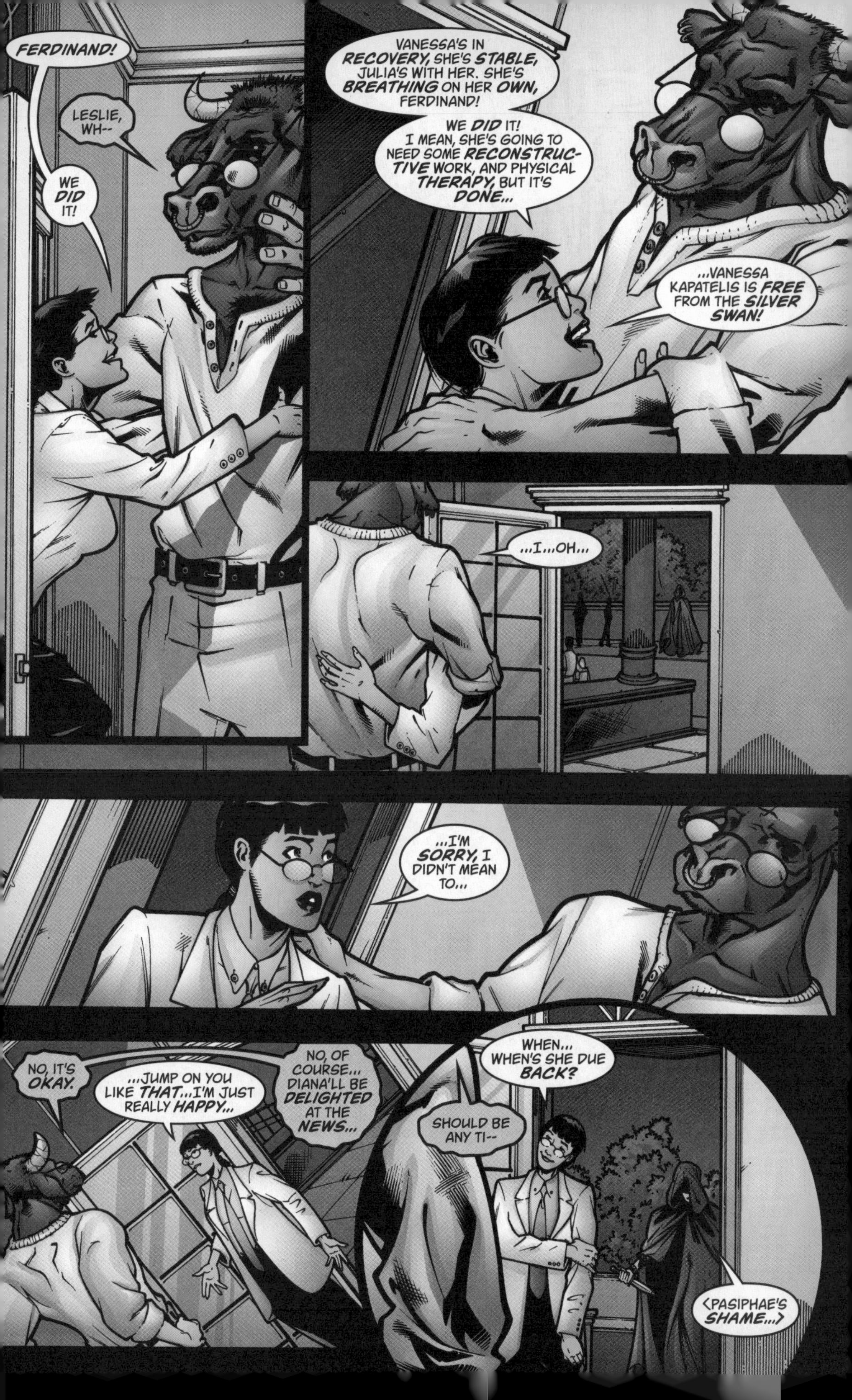

FERDINAND!
LESLIE, WH--
WE DID IT!
VANESSA'S IN RECOVERY, SHE'S STABLE, JULIA'S WITH HER. SHE'S BREATHING ON HER OWN, FERDINAND!
WE DID IT! I MEAN, SHE'S GOING TO NEED SOME RECONSTRUCTIVE WORK, AND PHYSICAL THERAPY, BUT IT'S DONE...
...VANESSA KAPATELIS IS FREE FROM THE SILVER SWAN!
...I...OH...
...I'M SORRY, I DIDN'T MEAN TO...
NO, IT'S OKAY.
...JUMP ON YOU LIKE THAT...I'M JUST REALLY HAPPY...
NO, OF COURSE... DIANA'LL BE DELIGHTED AT THE NEWS...
WHEN... WHEN'S SHE DUE BACK?
SHOULD BE ANY TI--
<PASIPHAE'S SHAME...>

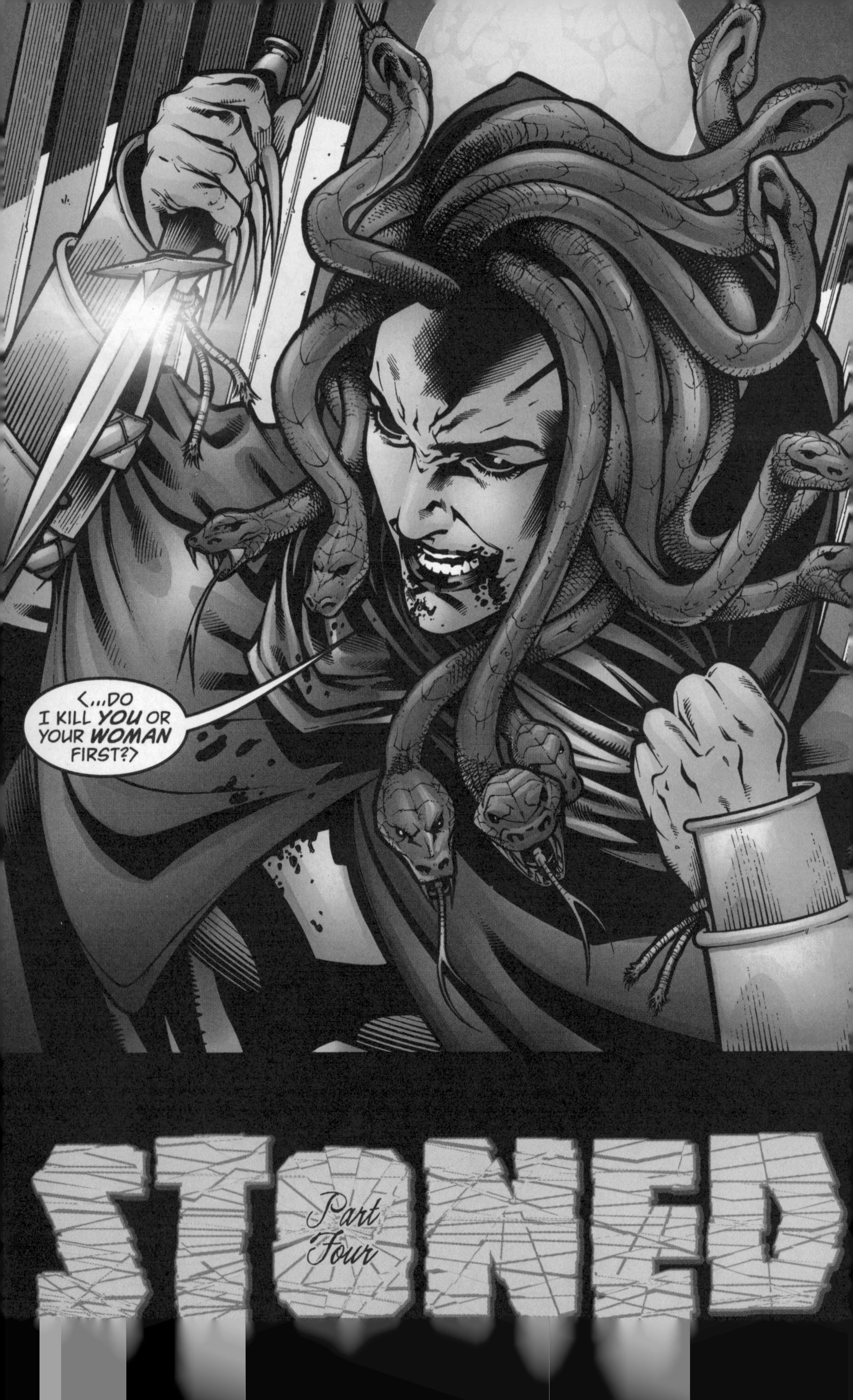
<...DO I KILL YOU OR YOUR WOMAN FIRST?>
STONED
Part Four

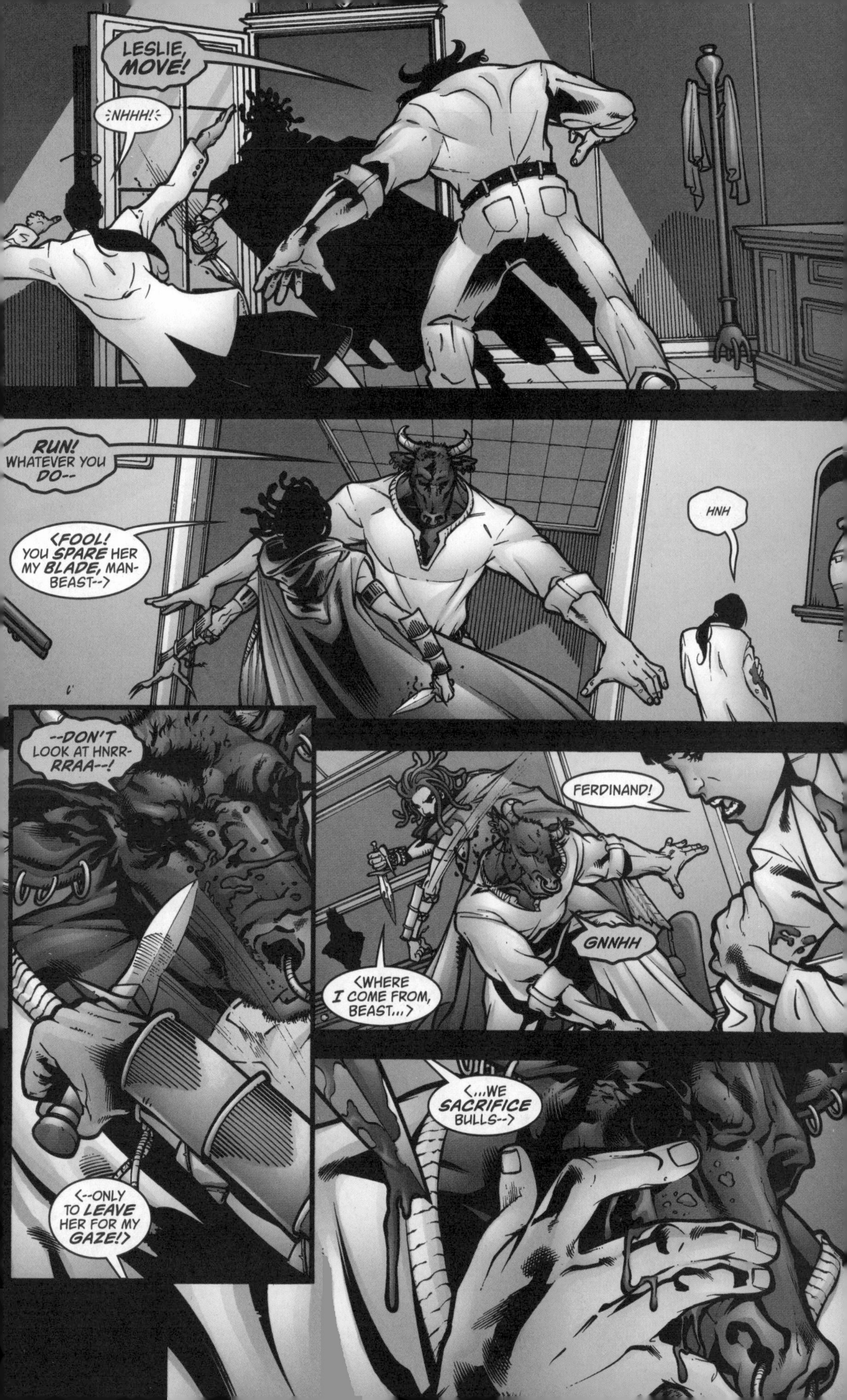
LESLIE, MOVE!
NHHH!
RUN! WHATEVER YOU DO--
<FOOL! YOU SPARE HER MY BLADE, MAN-BEAST-->
HNH
--DON'T LOOK AT HNRR-RRAA--!
<--ONLY TO LEAVE HER FOR MY GAZE!>
FERDINAND!
GNNHH
<WHERE I COME FROM, BEAST...>
<...WE SACRIFICE BULLS-->

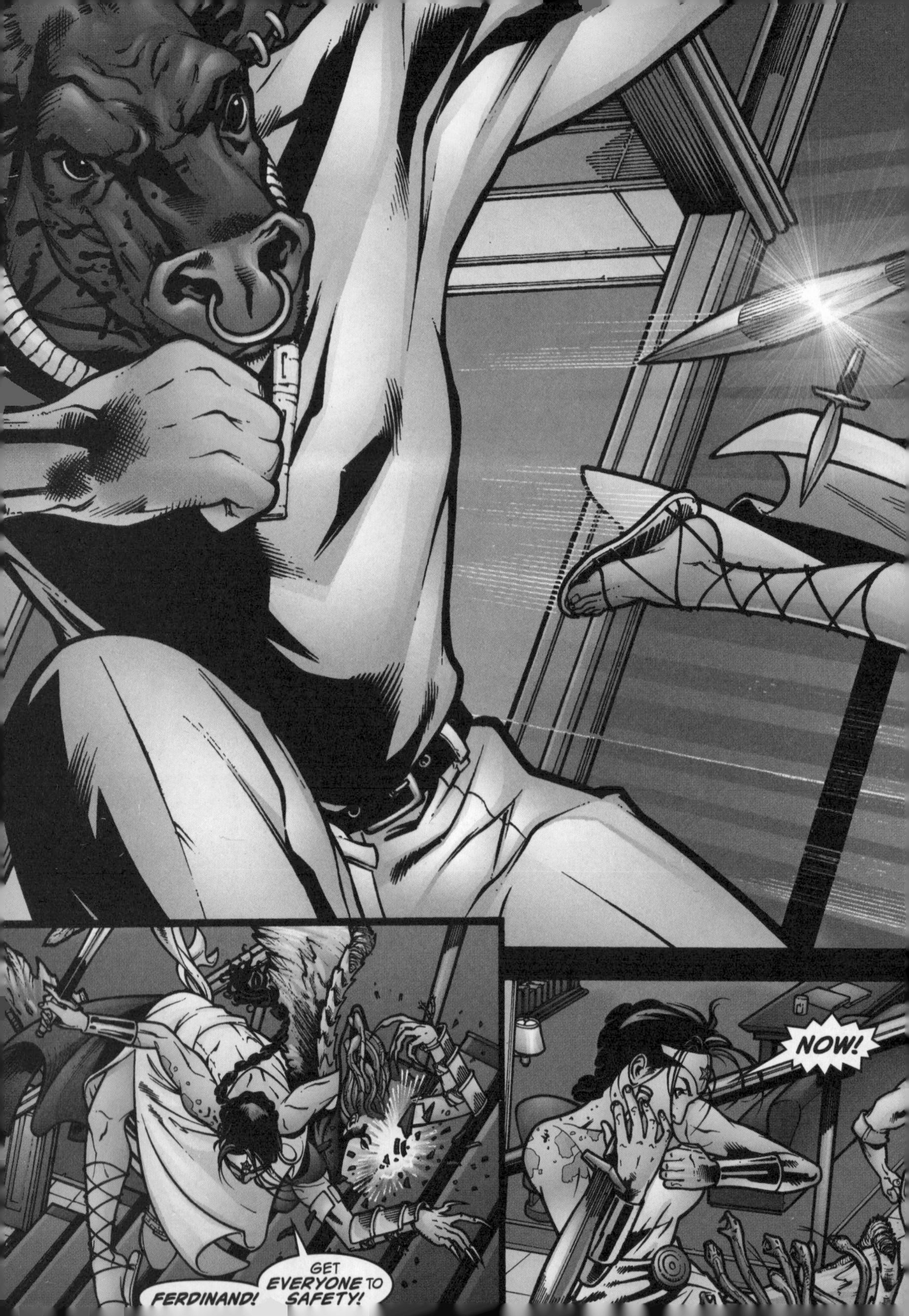

FERDINAND!
GET EVERYONE TO SAFETY!
NOW!

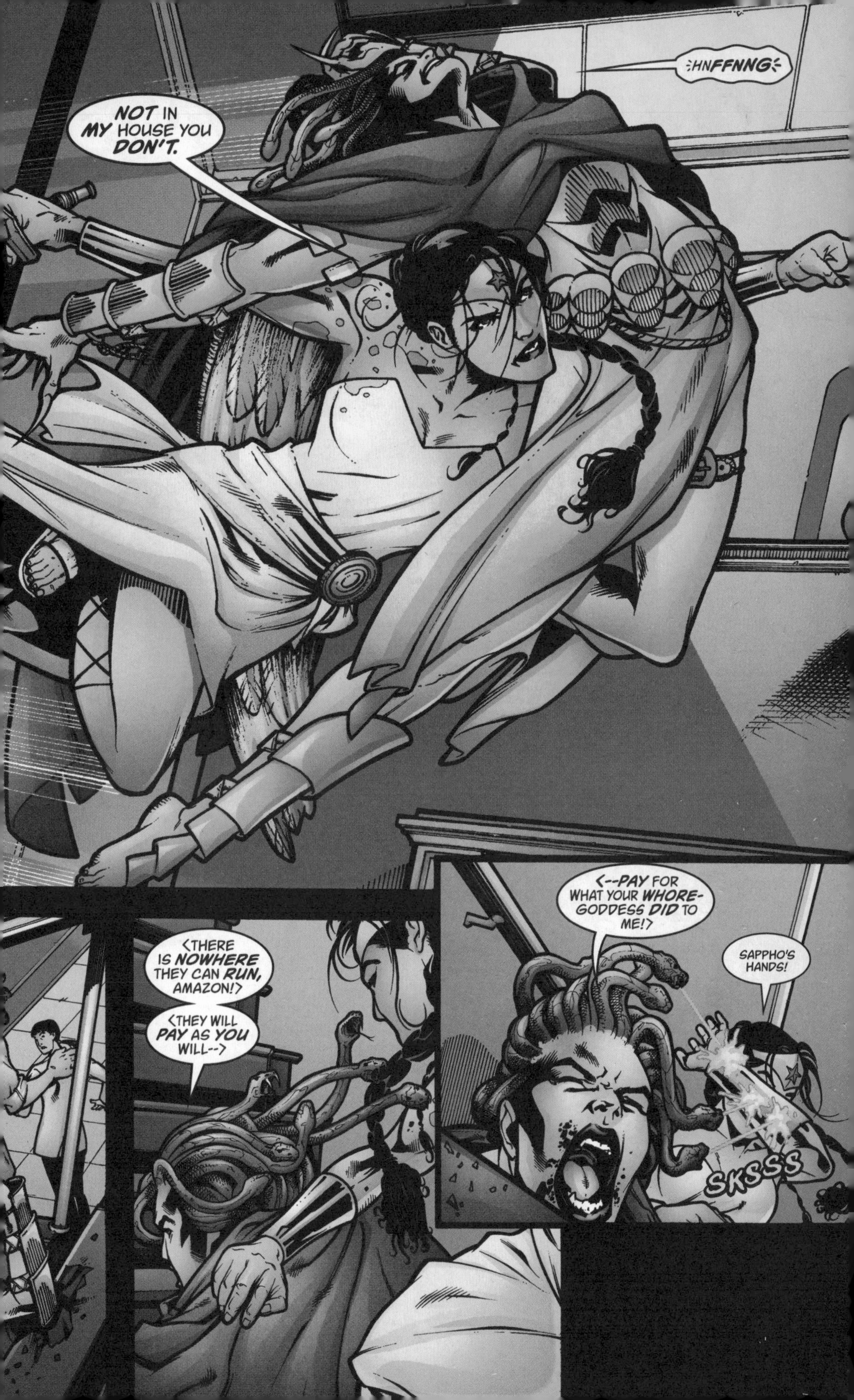

HNFFNNG
NOT IN MY HOUSE YOU DON'T.
<THERE IS NOWHERE THEY CAN RUN, AMAZON!>
<THEY WILL PAY AS YOU WILL-->
<--PAY FOR WHAT YOUR WHORE-GODDESS DID TO ME!>
SAPPHO'S HANDS!
SKSSS

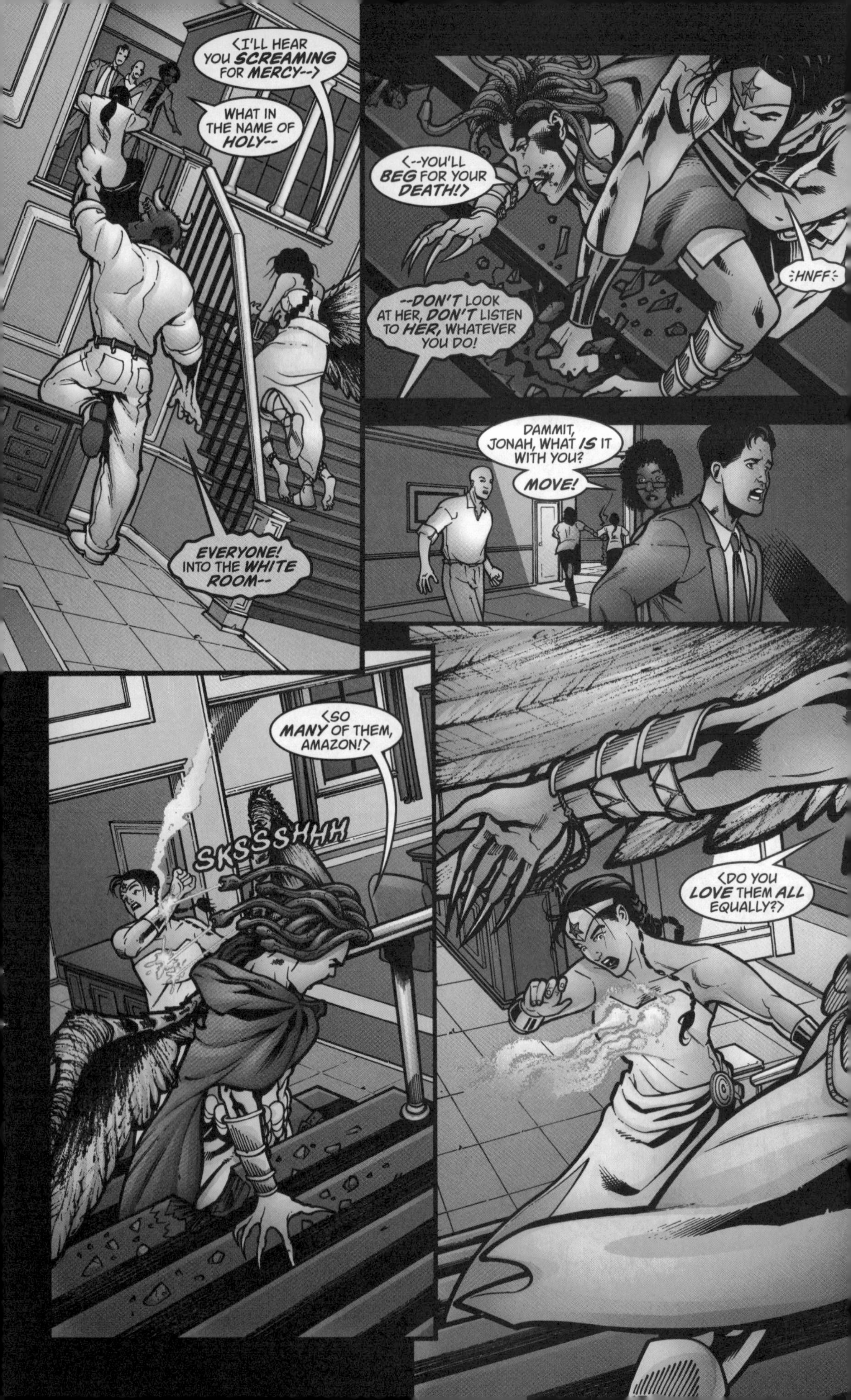

<I'LL HEAR YOU SCREAMING FOR MERCY-->
WHAT IN THE NAME OF HOLY--
EVERYONE! INTO THE WHITE ROOM--
<--YOU'LL BEG FOR YOUR DEATH!>
--DON'T LOOK AT HER, DON'T LISTEN TO HER, WHATEVER YOU DO!
HNFF
DAMMIT, JONAH, WHAT IS IT WITH YOU?
MOVE!
<SO MANY OF THEM, AMAZON!>
SKSSSHHH
<DO YOU LOVE THEM ALL EQUALLY?>

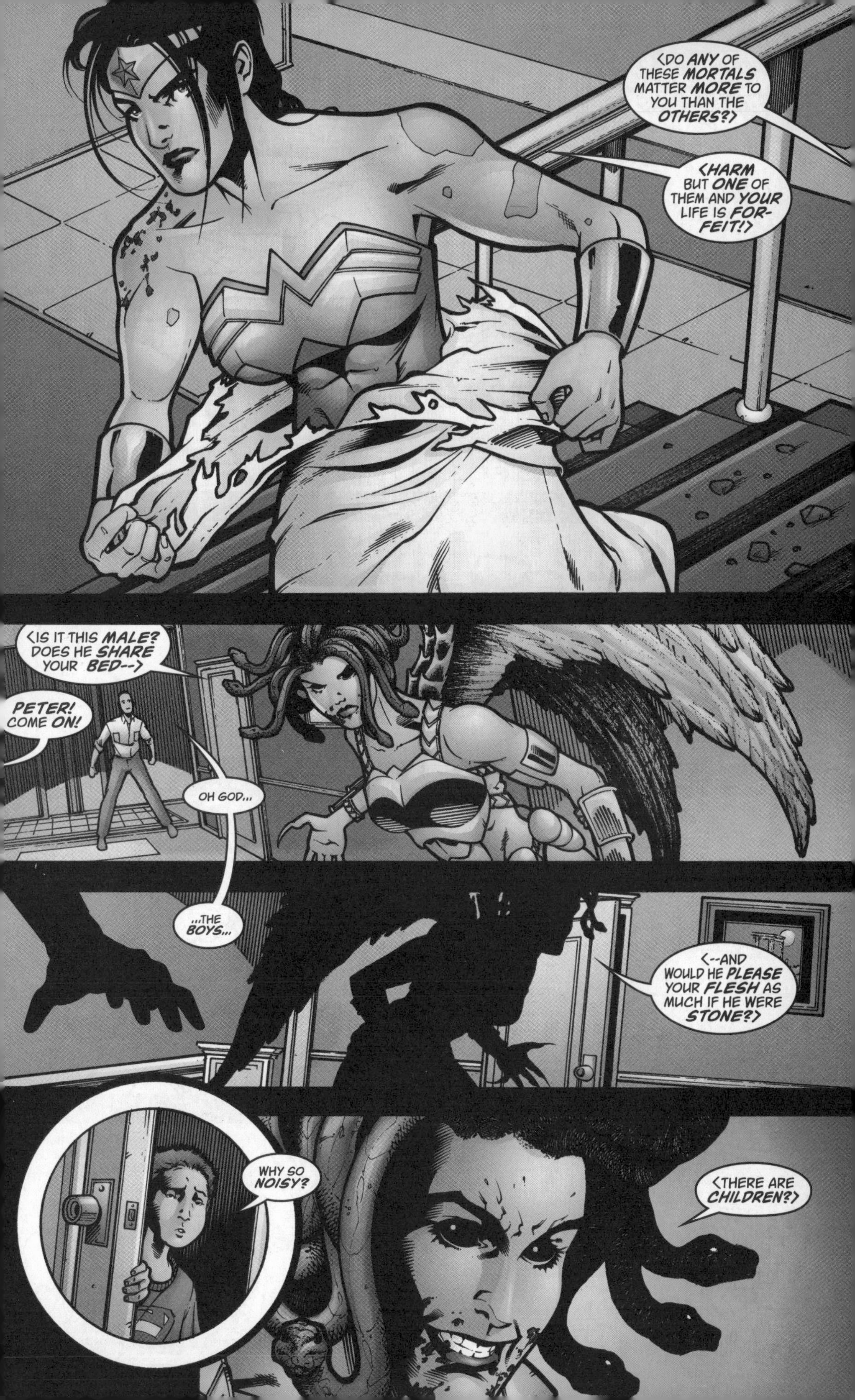

<DO ANY OF THESE MORTALS MATTER MORE TO YOU THAN THE OTHERS?>
<HARM BUT ONE OF THEM AND YOUR LIFE IS FOR-FEIT!>
<IS IT THIS MALE? DOES HE SHARE YOUR BED-->
PETER! COME ON!
OH GOD...
...THE BOYS...
<--AND WOULD HE PLEASE YOUR FLESH AS MUCH IF HE WERE STONE?>
WHY SO NOISY?
<THERE ARE CHILDREN?>

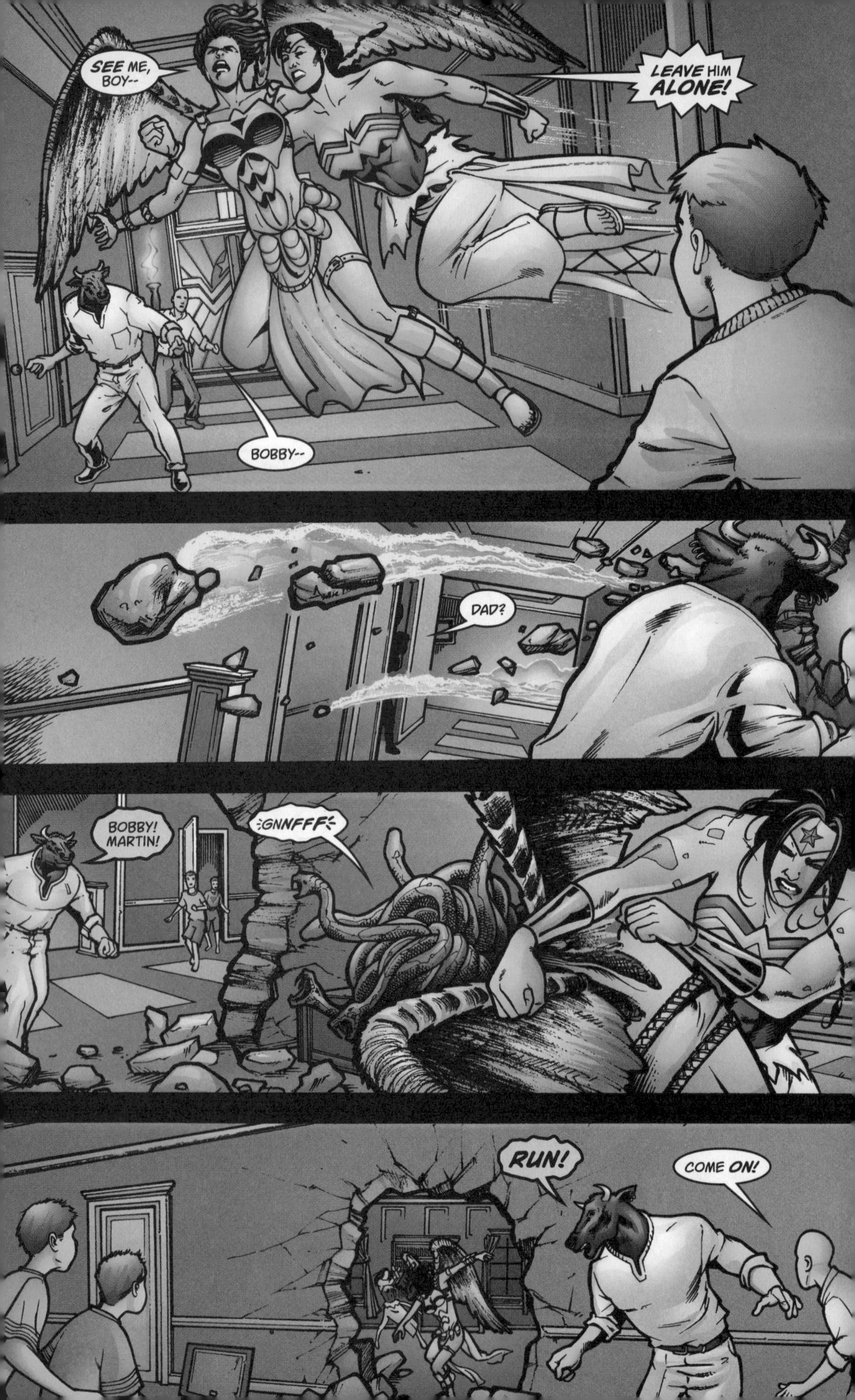
SEE ME, BOY--
LEAVE HIM ALONE!
BOBBY--
DAD?
BOBBY! MARTIN!
GNNFFF
RUN!
COME ON!

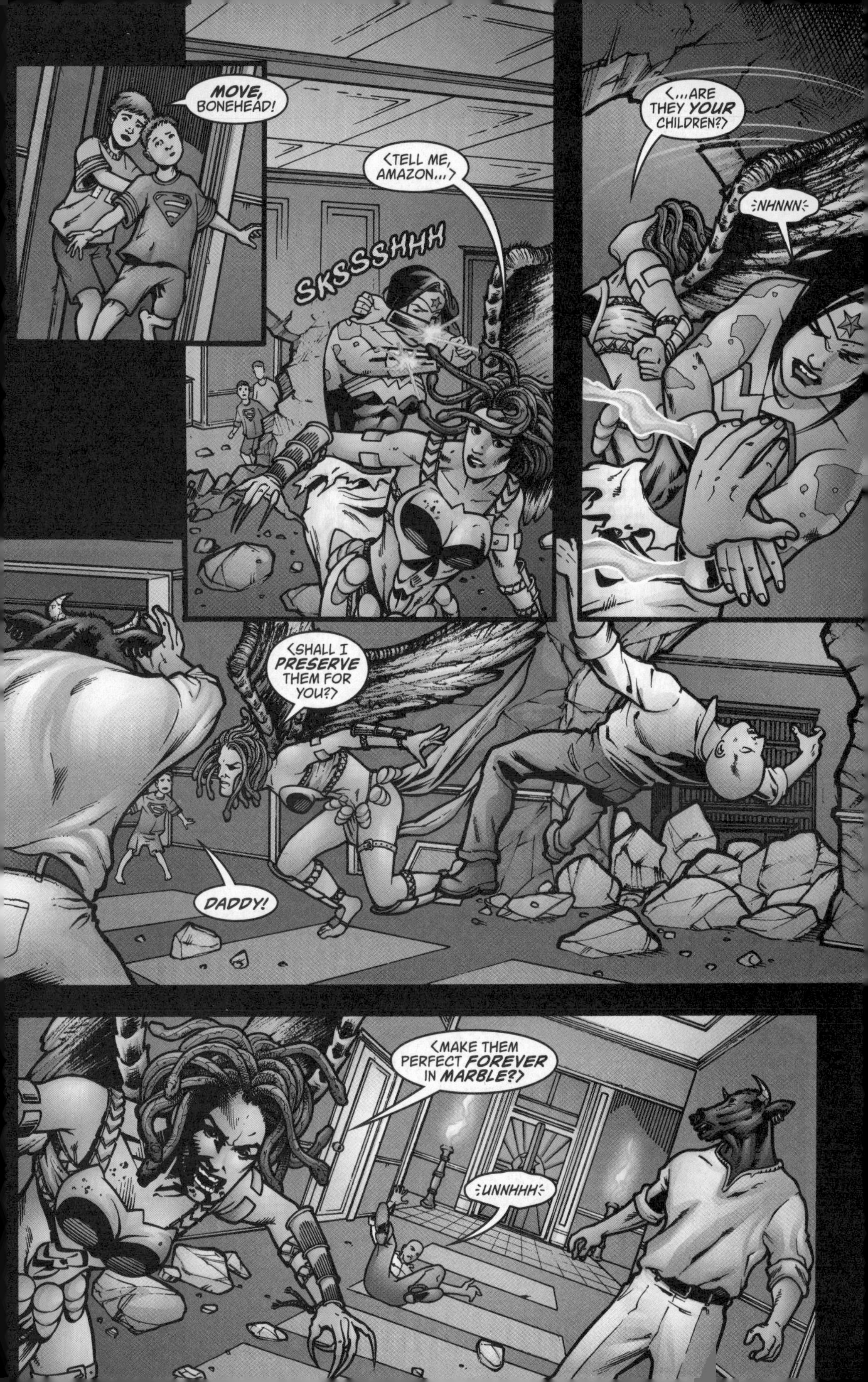
MOVE, BONEHEAD!
<TELL ME, AMAZON...>
SKSSSHHH
<...ARE THEY YOUR CHILDREN?>
NHNNN
<SHALL I PRESERVE THEM FOR YOU?>
DADDY!
<MAKE THEM PERFECT FOREVER IN MARBLE?>
UNNHHH

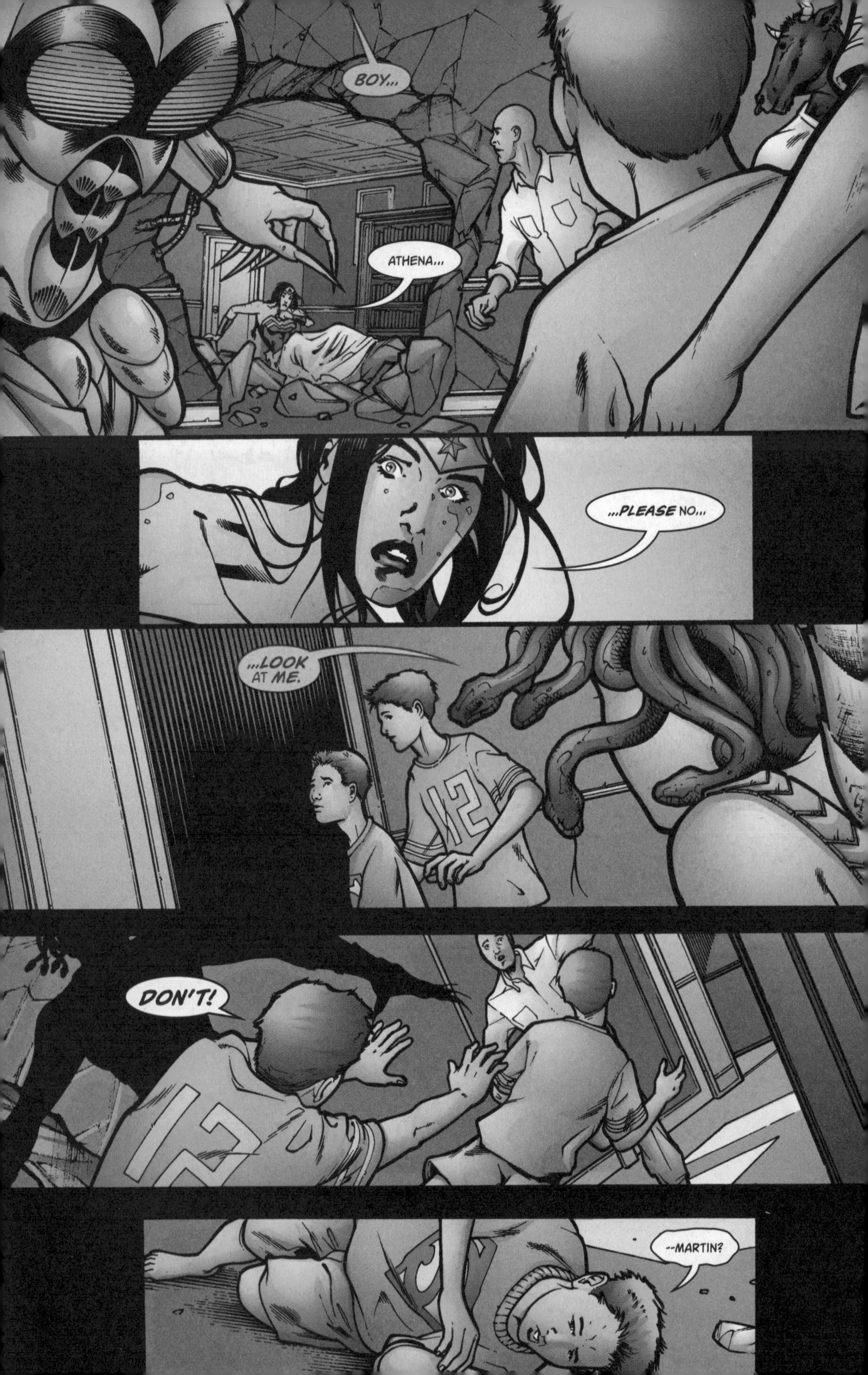
BOY...
ATHENA...
...PLEASE NO...
...LOOK AT ME.
DON'T!
--MARTIN?

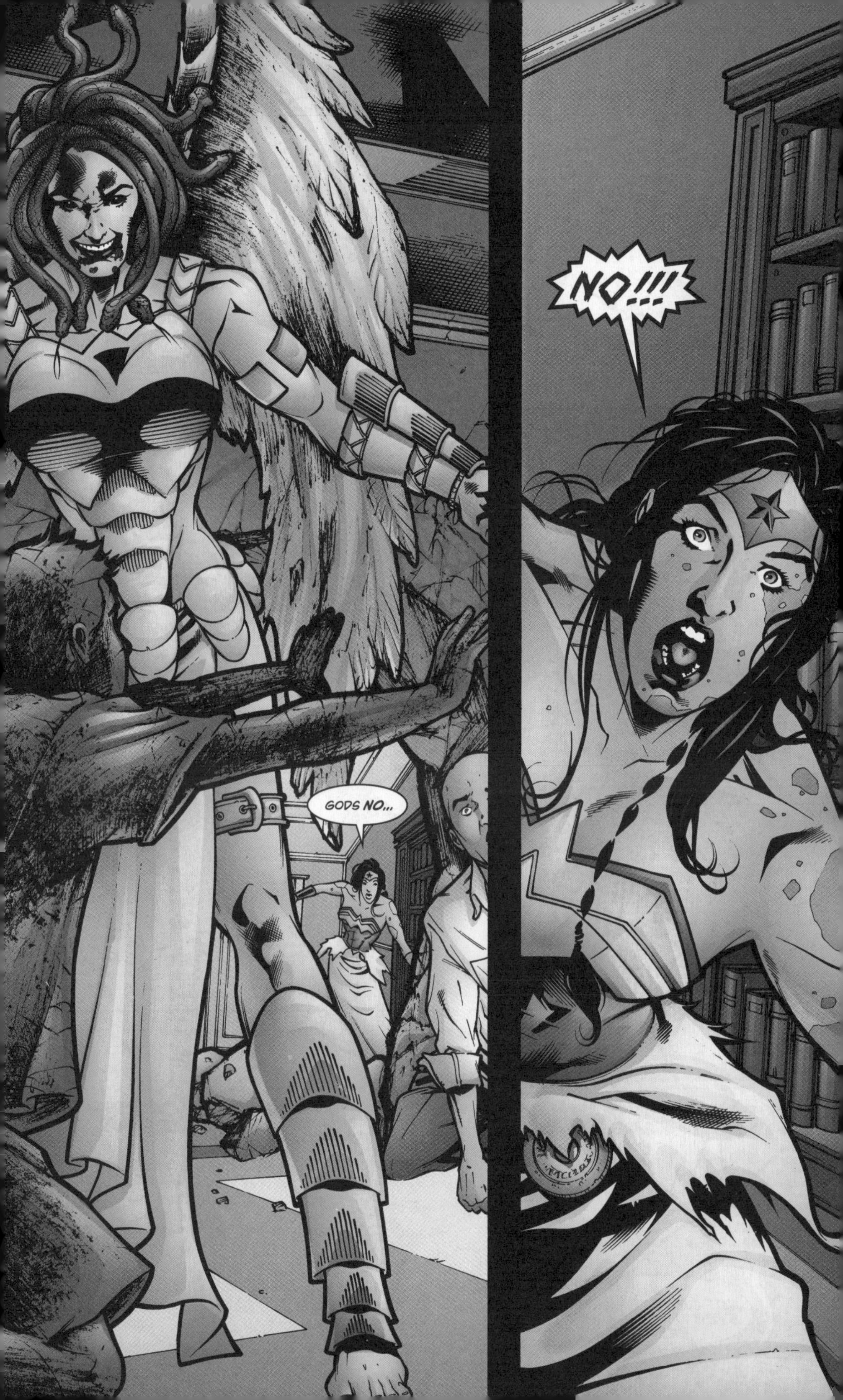
GODS NO...
NO!!!

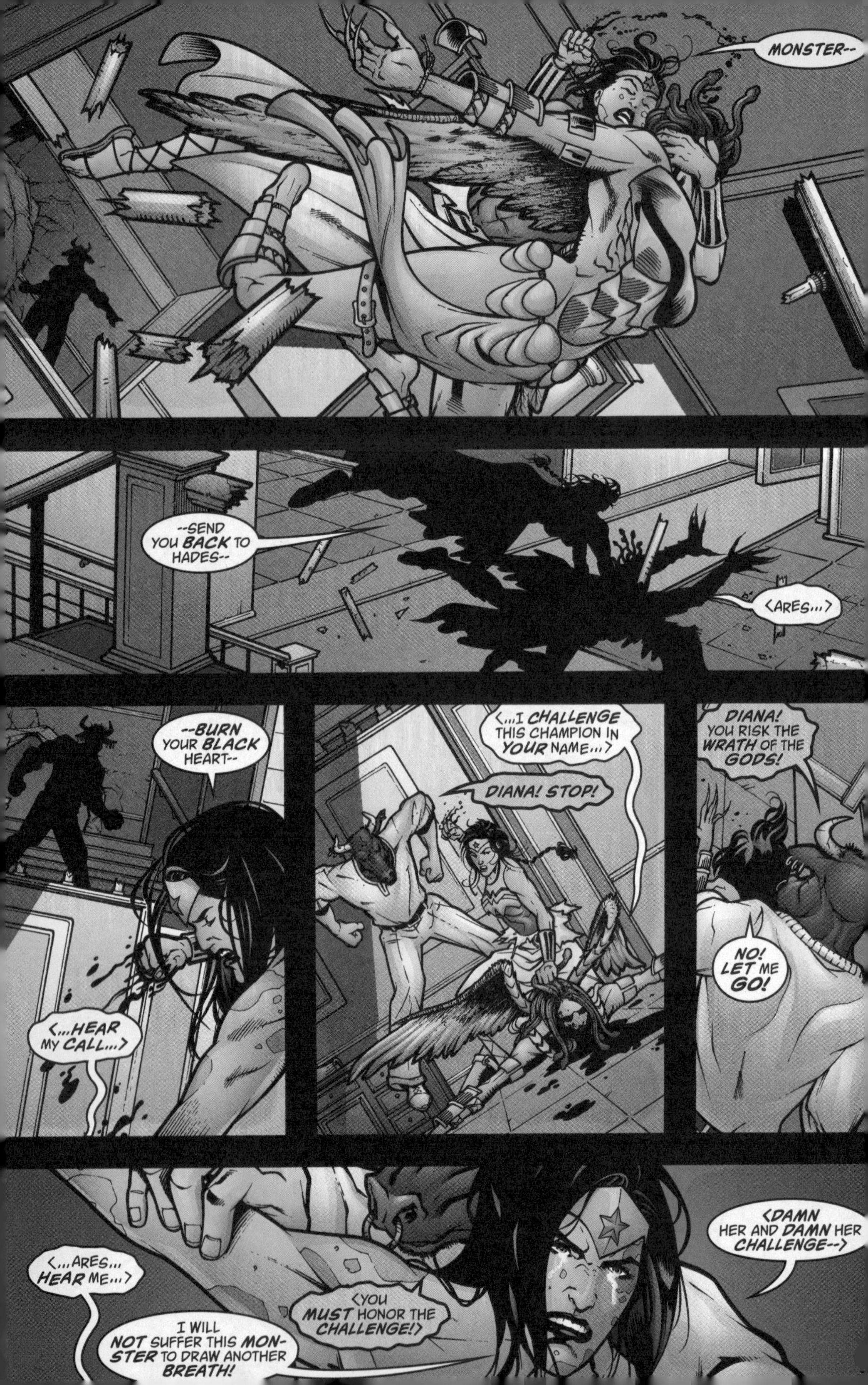
MONSTER--
--SEND YOU BACK TO HADES--
<ARES...>
--BURN YOUR BLACK HEART--
<...HEAR MY CALL...>
<...I CHALLENGE THIS CHAMPION IN YOUR NAME...>
DIANA! STOP!
DIANA! YOU RISK THE WRATH OF THE GODS!
NO! LET ME GO!
<...ARES... HEAR ME...>
I WILL NOT SUFFER THIS MON-STER TO DRAW ANOTHER BREATH!
<YOU MUST HONOR THE CHALLENGE!>
<DAMN HER AND DAMN HER CHALLENGE-->

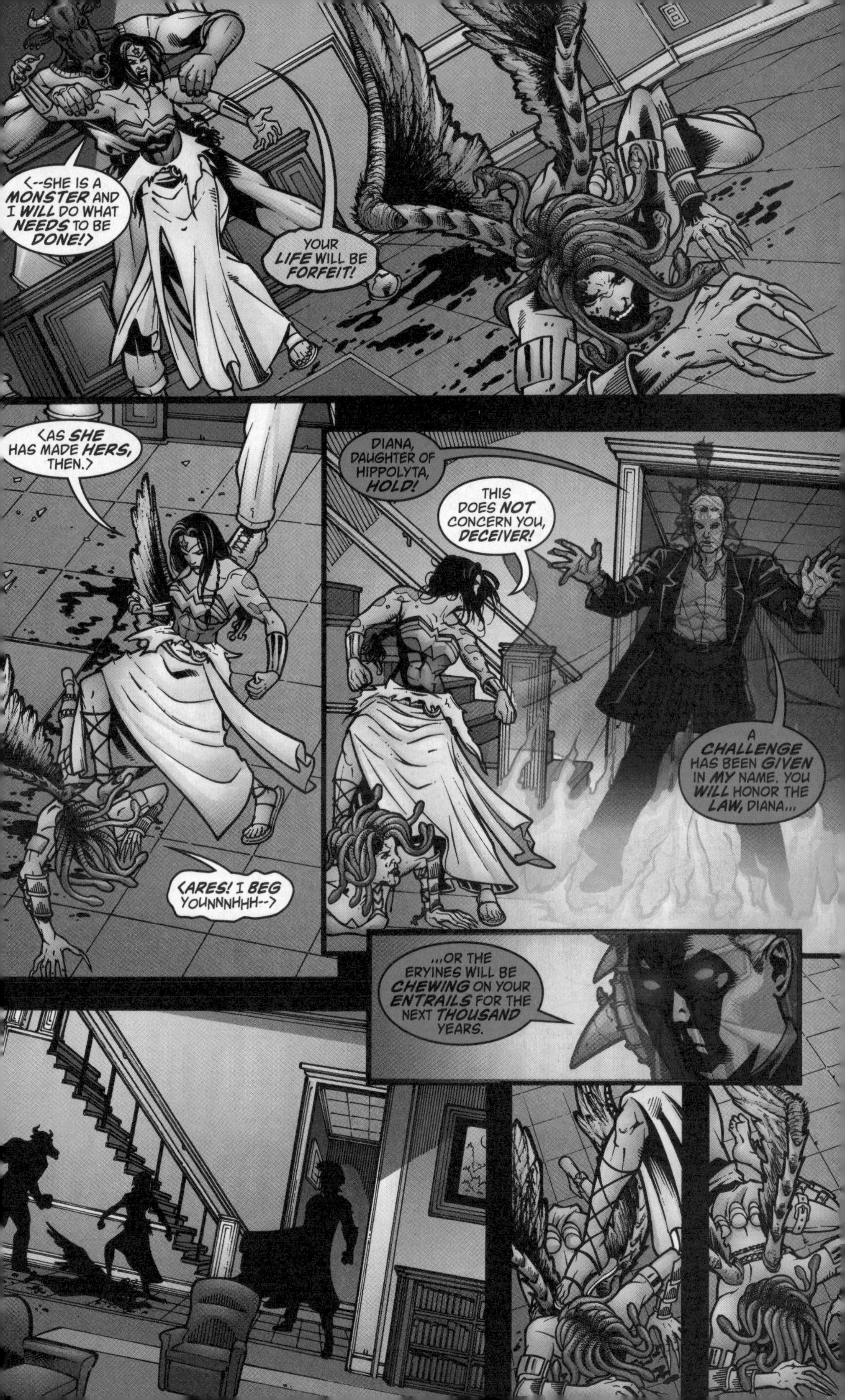

<--SHE IS A MONSTER AND I WILL DO WHAT NEEDS TO BE DONE!>
YOUR LIFE WILL BE FORFEIT!
<AS SHE HAS MADE HERS, THEN.>
<ARES! I BEG YOUNNNHHH-->
DIANA, DAUGHTER OF HIPPOLYTA, HOLD!
THIS DOES NOT CONCERN YOU, DECEIVER!
A CHALLENGE HAS BEEN GIVEN IN MY NAME. YOU WILL HONOR THE LAW, DIANA...
...OR THE ERYINES WILL BE CHEWING ON YOUR ENTRAILS FOR THE NEXT THOUSAND YEARS.

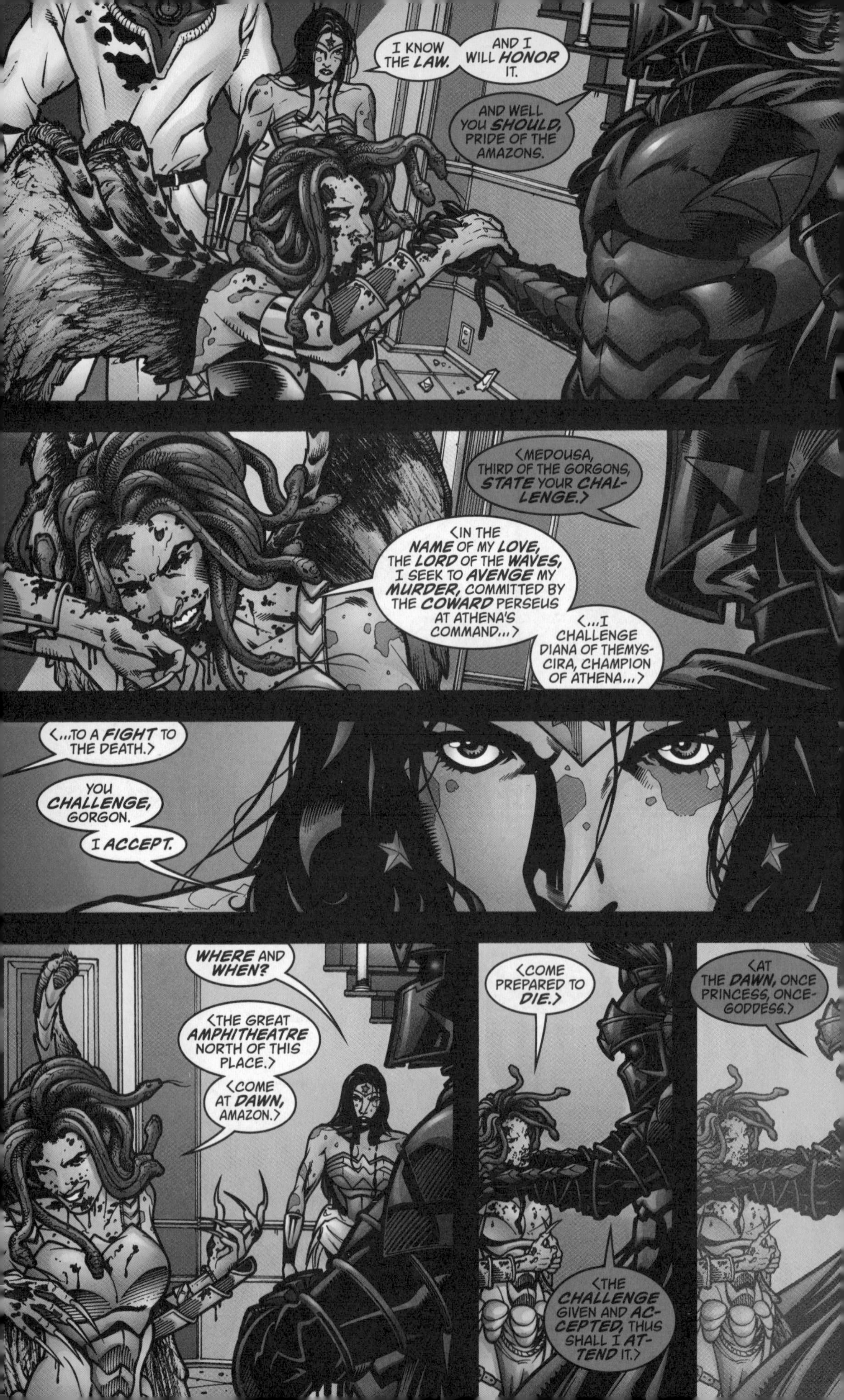
I KNOW THE LAW.
AND I WILL HONOR IT.
AND WELL YOU SHOULD, PRIDE OF THE AMAZONS.
<MEDOUSA, THIRD OF THE GORGONS, STATE YOUR CHAL-LENGE.>
<IN THE NAME OF MY LOVE, THE LORD OF THE WAVES, I SEEK TO AVENGE MY MURDER, COMMITTED BY THE COWARD PERSEUS AT ATHENA'S COMMAND...>
<...I CHALLENGE DIANA OF THEMYS-CIRA, CHAMPION OF ATHENA...>
<...TO A FIGHT TO THE DEATH.>
YOU CHALLENGE, GORGON.
I ACCEPT.
WHERE AND WHEN?
<THE GREAT AMPHITHEATRE NORTH OF THIS PLACE.>
<COME AT DAWN, AMAZON.>
<COME PREPARED TO DIE.>
<THE CHALLENGE GIVEN AND AC-CEPTED, THUS SHALL I AT-TEND IT.>
<AT THE DAWN, ONCE PRINCESS, ONCE-GODDESS.>

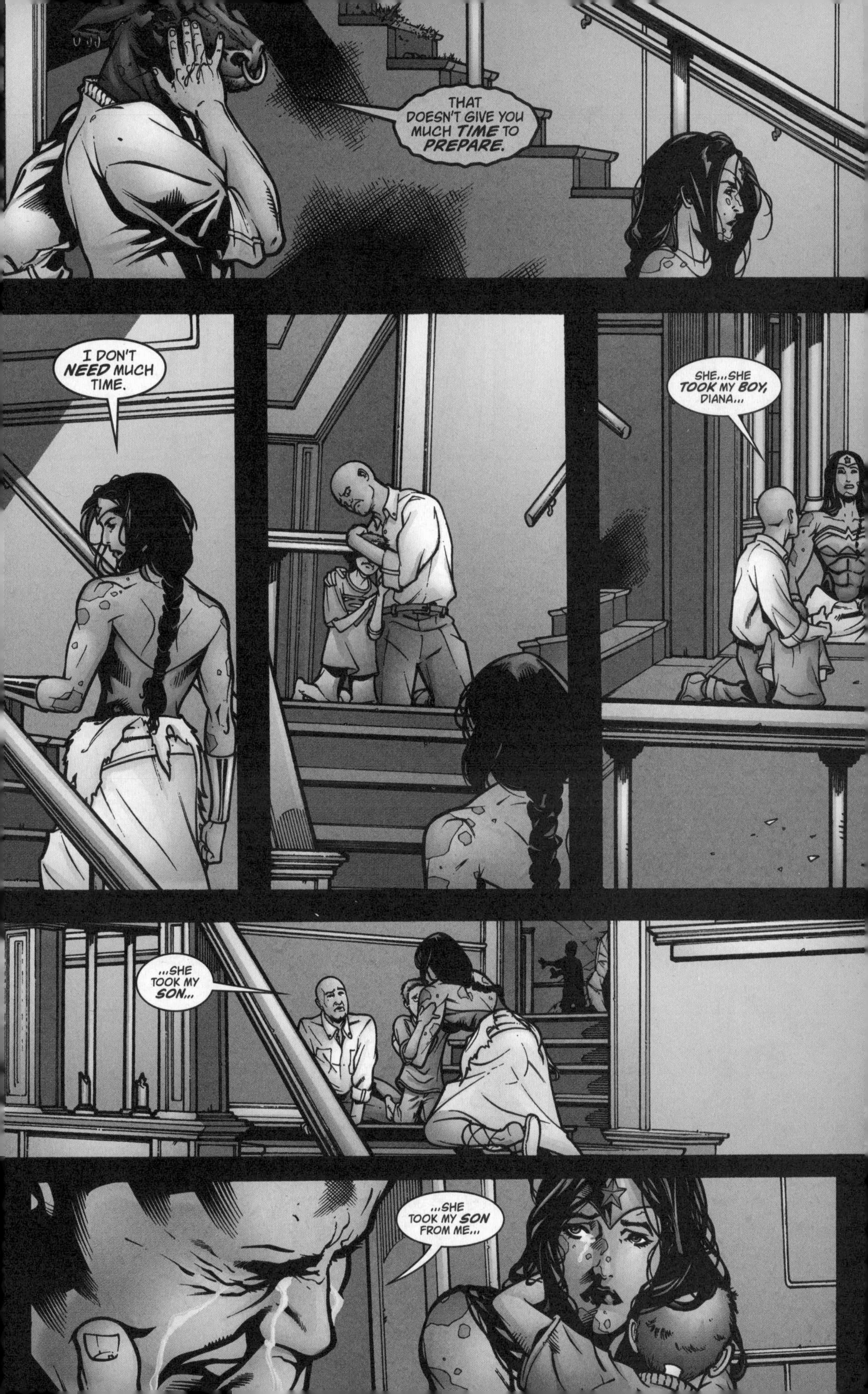
THAT DOESN'T GIVE YOU MUCH TIME TO PREPARE.
I DON'T NEED MUCH TIME.
SHE...SHE TOOK MY BOY, DIANA...
...SHE TOOK MY SON...
...SHE TOOK MY SON FROM ME...

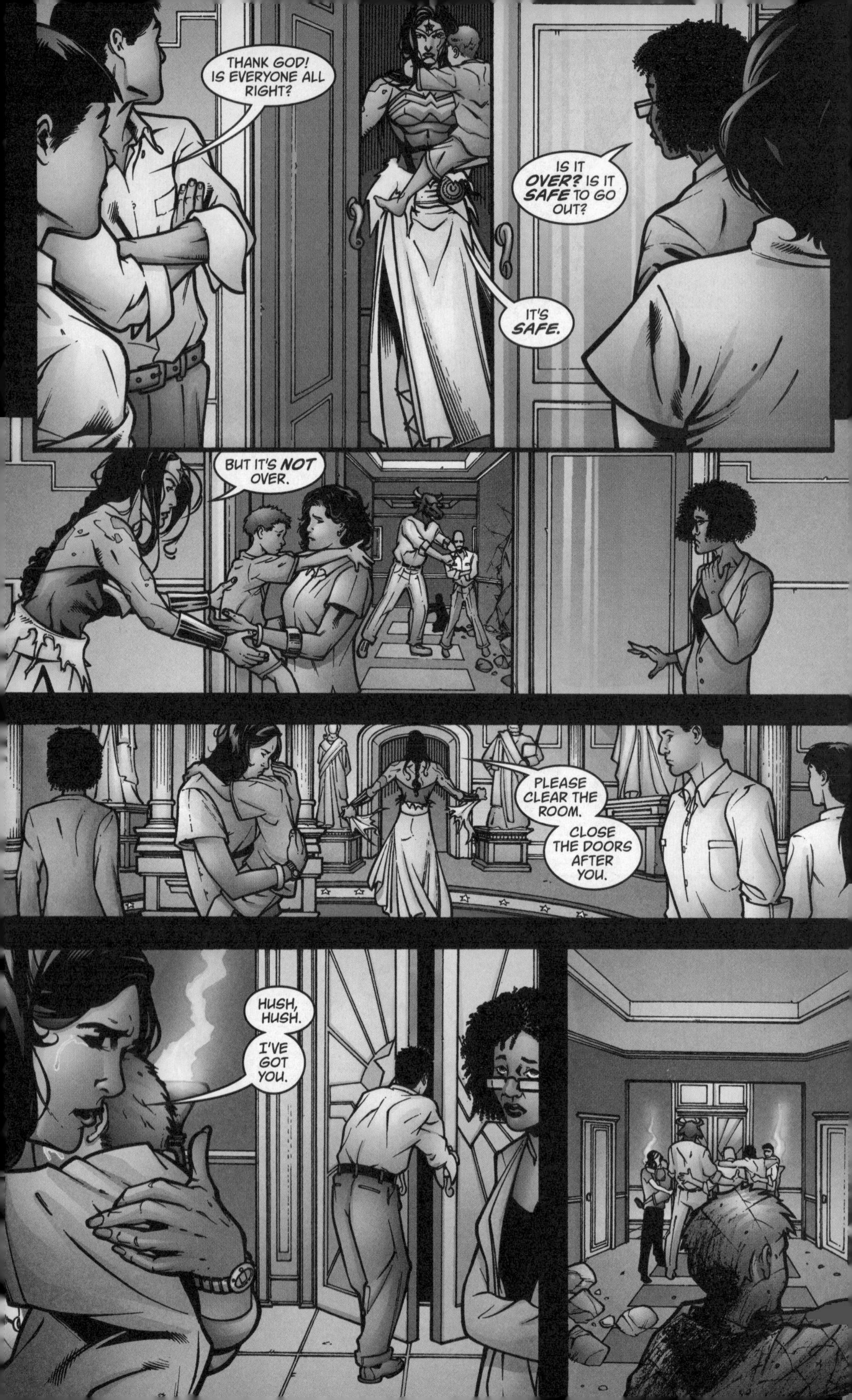
THANK GOD! IS EVERYONE ALL RIGHT?
IS IT OVER? IS IT SAFE TO GO OUT?
IT'S SAFE.
BUT IT'S NOT OVER.
PLEASE CLEAR THE ROOM.
CLOSE THE DOORS AFTER YOU.
HUSH, HUSH.
I'VE GOT YOU.

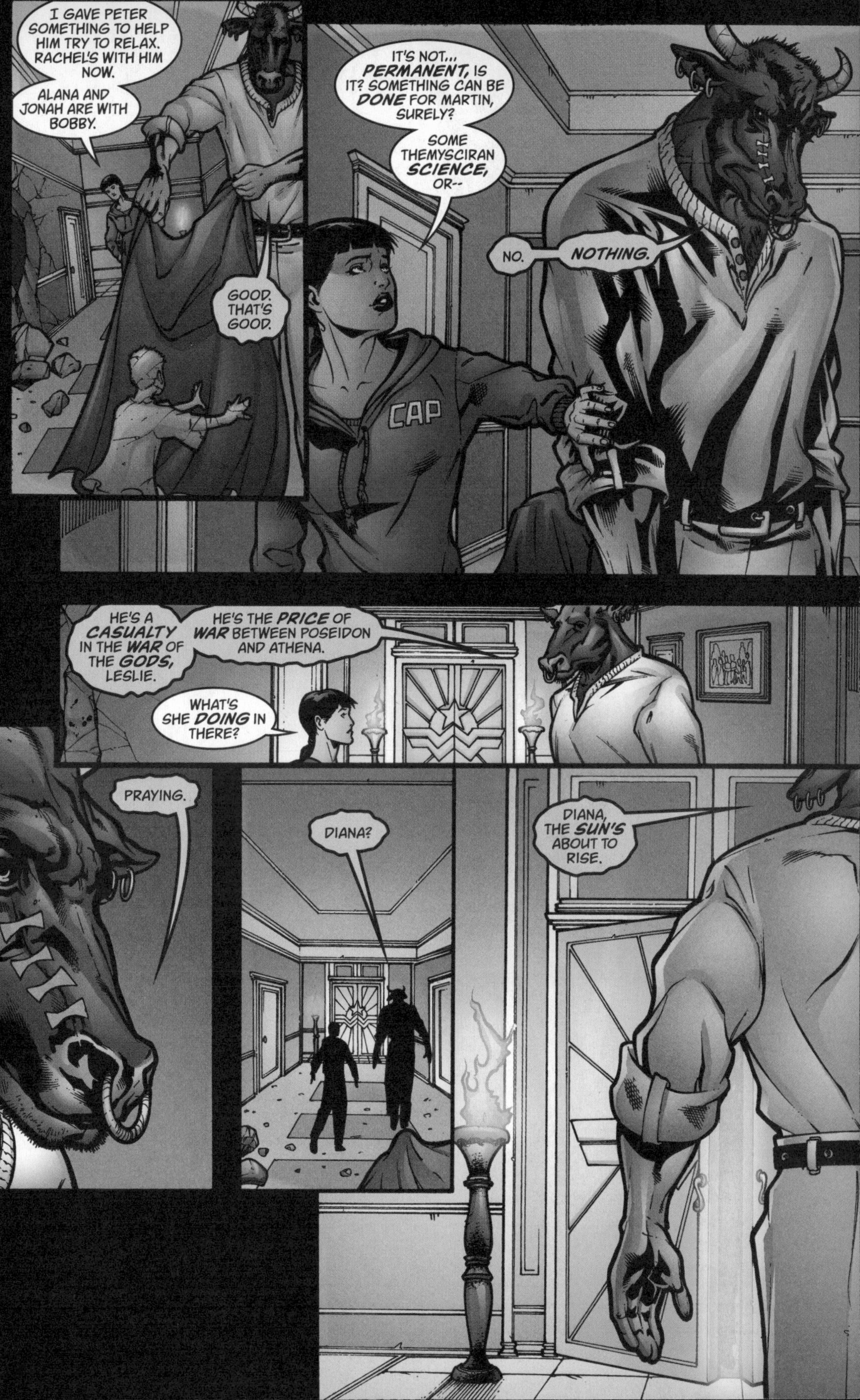
I GAVE PETER SOMETHING TO HELP HIM TRY TO RELAX. RACHEL'S WITH HIM NOW.
ALANA AND JONAH ARE WITH BOBBY.
GOOD. THAT'S GOOD.
IT'S NOT... PERMANENT, IS IT? SOMETHING CAN BE DONE FOR MARTIN, SURELY?
SOME THEMYSCIRAN SCIENCE, OR--
NO.
NOTHING.
HE'S A CASUALTY IN THE WAR OF THE GODS, LESLIE.
HE'S THE PRICE OF WAR BETWEEN POSEIDON AND ATHENA.
WHAT'S SHE DOING IN THERE?
PRAYING.
DIANA?
DIANA, THE SUN'S ABOUT TO RISE.
CAP

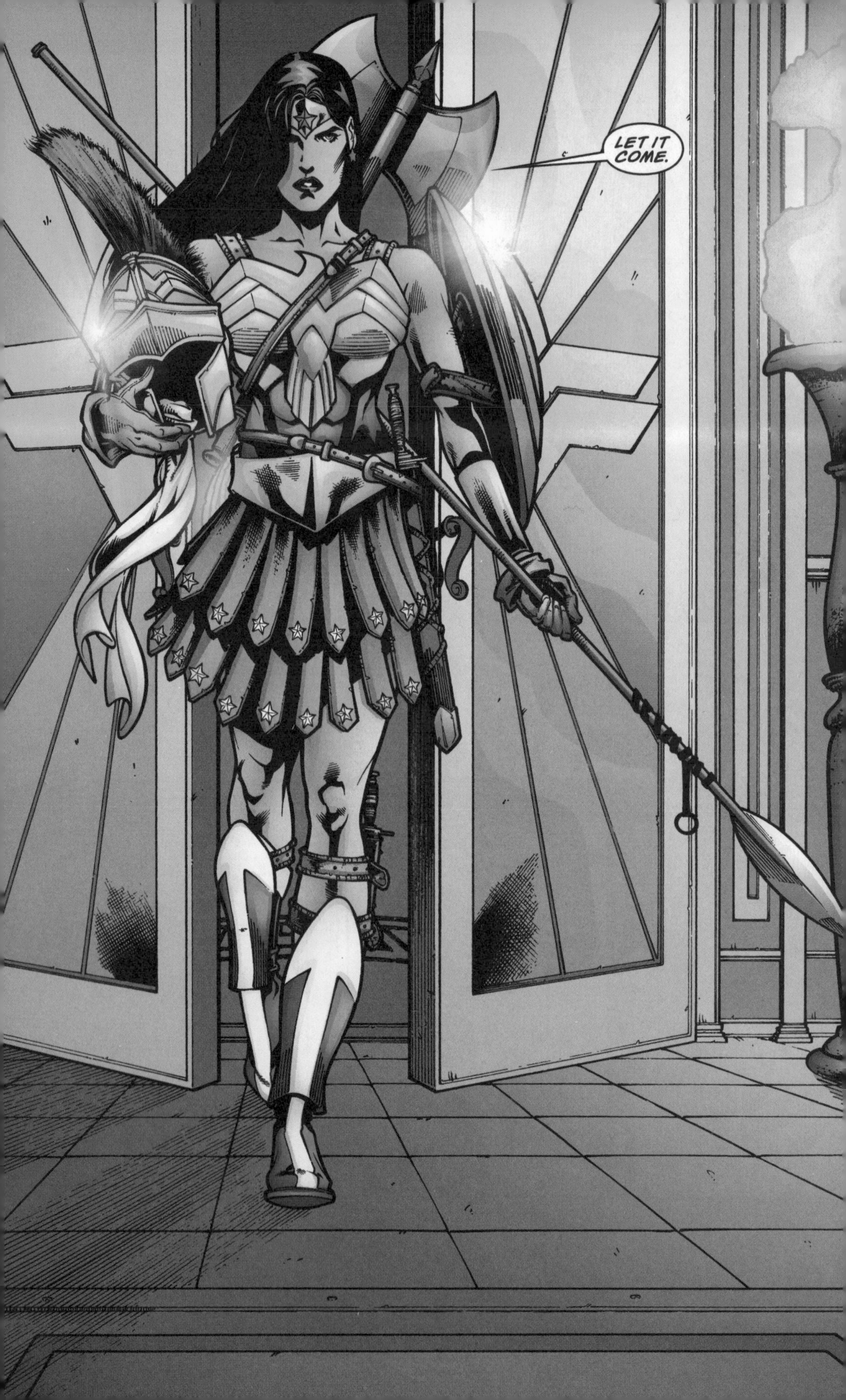
LET IT COME.

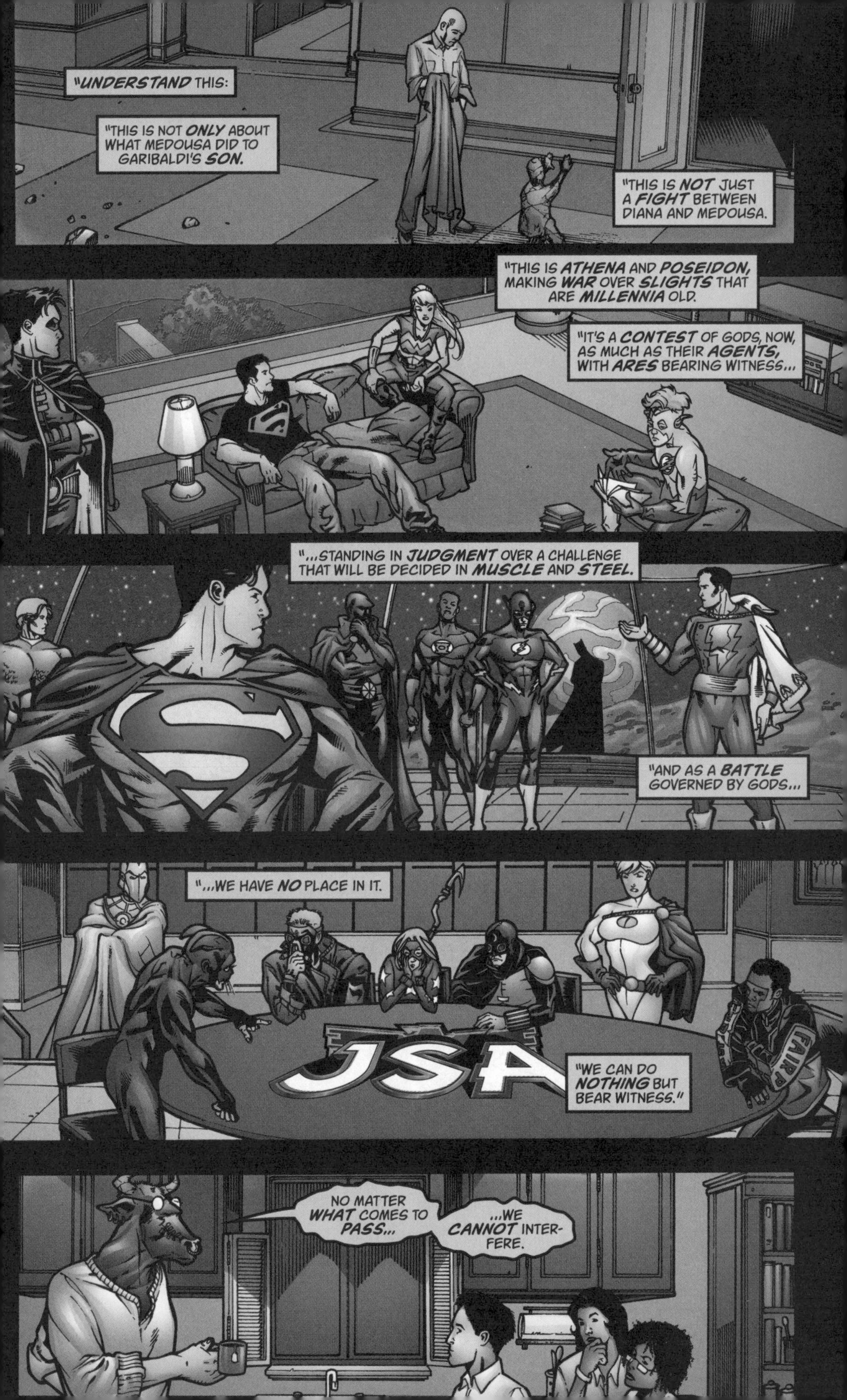
"UNDERSTAND THIS:
"THIS IS NOT ONLY ABOUT WHAT MEDOUSA DID TO GARIBALDI'S SON.
"THIS IS NOT JUST A FIGHT BETWEEN DIANA AND MEDOUSA.
"THIS IS ATHENA AND POSEIDON, MAKING WAR OVER SLIGHTS THAT ARE MILLENNIA OLD.
"IT'S A CONTEST OF GODS, NOW, AS MUCH AS THEIR AGENTS, WITH ARES BEARING WITNESS...
"...STANDING IN JUDGMENT OVER A CHALLENGE THAT WILL BE DECIDED IN MUSCLE AND STEEL.
"AND AS A BATTLE GOVERNED BY GODS...
"...WE HAVE NO PLACE IN IT.
JSA
"WE CAN DO NOTHING BUT BEAR WITNESS."
NO MATTER WHAT COMES TO PASS...
...WE CANNOT INTER-FERE.

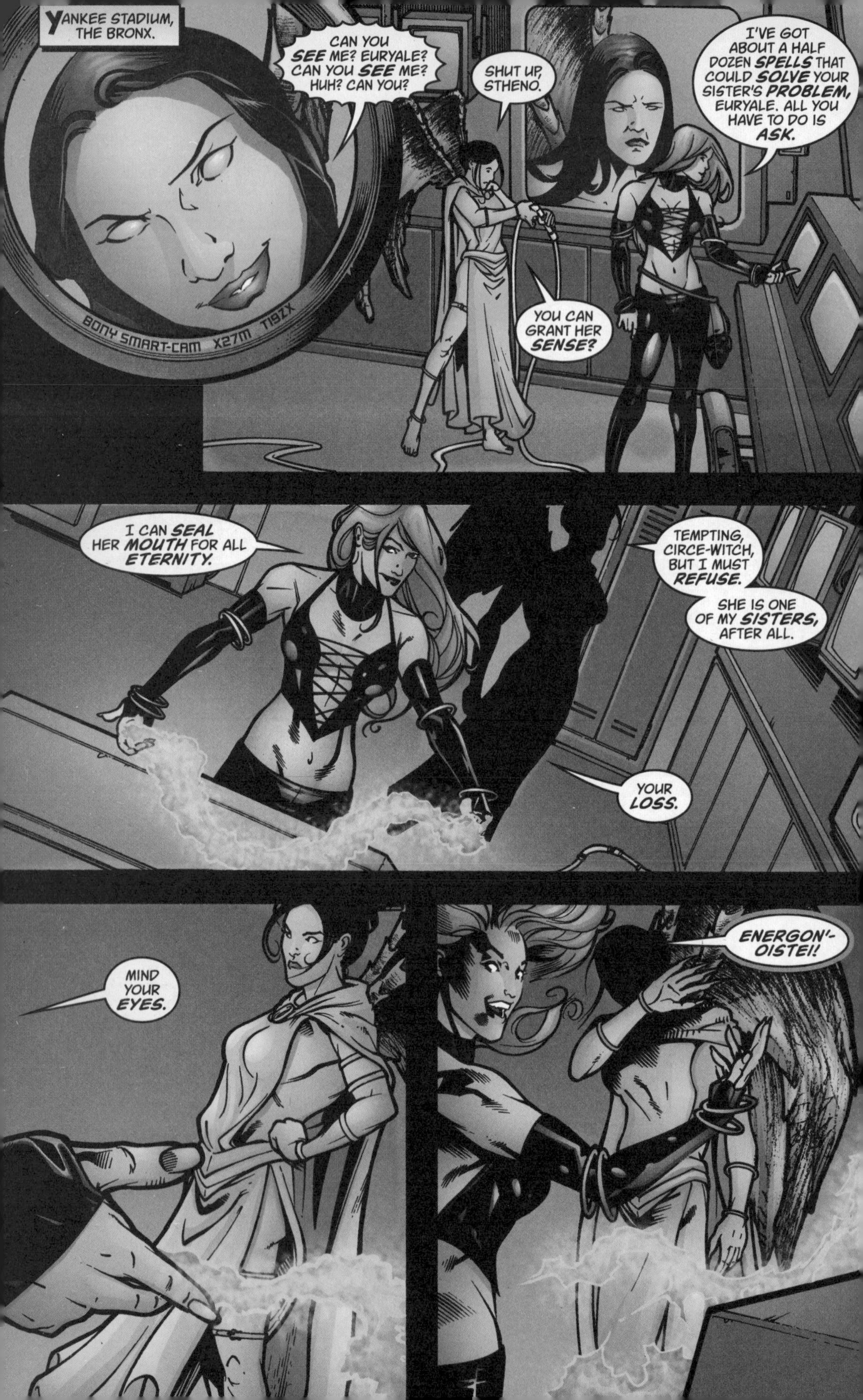
YANKEE STADIUM, THE BRONX.
CAN YOU SEE ME? EURYALE? CAN YOU SEE ME? HUH? CAN YOU?
SHUT UP, STHENO.
I'VE GOT ABOUT A HALF DOZEN SPELLS THAT COULD SOLVE YOUR SISTER'S PROBLEM, EURYALE. ALL YOU HAVE TO DO IS ASK.
BONY SMART-CAM X27M T192X
YOU CAN GRANT HER SENSE?
I CAN SEAL HER MOUTH FOR ALL ETERNITY.
TEMPTING, CIRCE-WITCH, BUT I MUST REFUSE.
SHE IS ONE OF MY SISTERS, AFTER ALL.
YOUR LOSS.
MIND YOUR EYES.
ENERGON'-OISTEI!

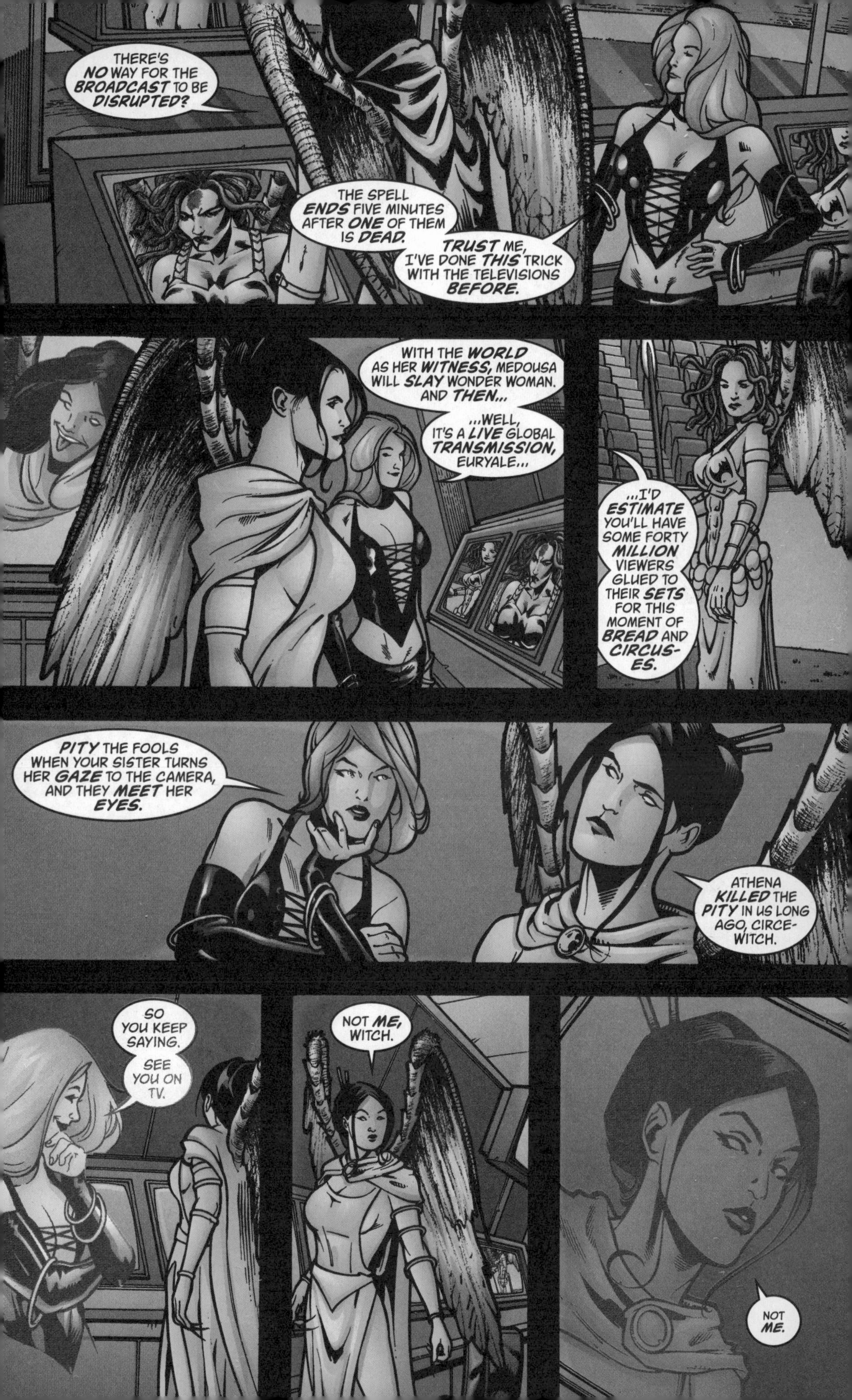

THERE'S NO WAY FOR THE BROADCAST TO BE DISRUPTED?
THE SPELL ENDS FIVE MINUTES AFTER ONE OF THEM IS DEAD.
TRUST ME, I'VE DONE THIS TRICK WITH THE TELEVISIONS BEFORE.
WITH THE WORLD AS HER WITNESS, MEDOUSA WILL SLAY WONDER WOMAN. AND THEN...
...WELL, IT'S A LIVE GLOBAL TRANSMISSION, EURYALE...
...I'D ESTIMATE YOU'LL HAVE SOME FORTY MILLION VIEWERS GLUED TO THEIR SETS FOR THIS MOMENT OF BREAD AND CIRCUS-ES.
PITY THE FOOLS WHEN YOUR SISTER TURNS HER GAZE TO THE CAMERA, AND THEY MEET HER EYES.
ATHENA KILLED THE PITY IN US LONG AGO, CIRCE-WITCH.
SO YOU KEEP SAYING.
SEE YOU ON TV.
NOT ME, WITCH.
NOT ME.

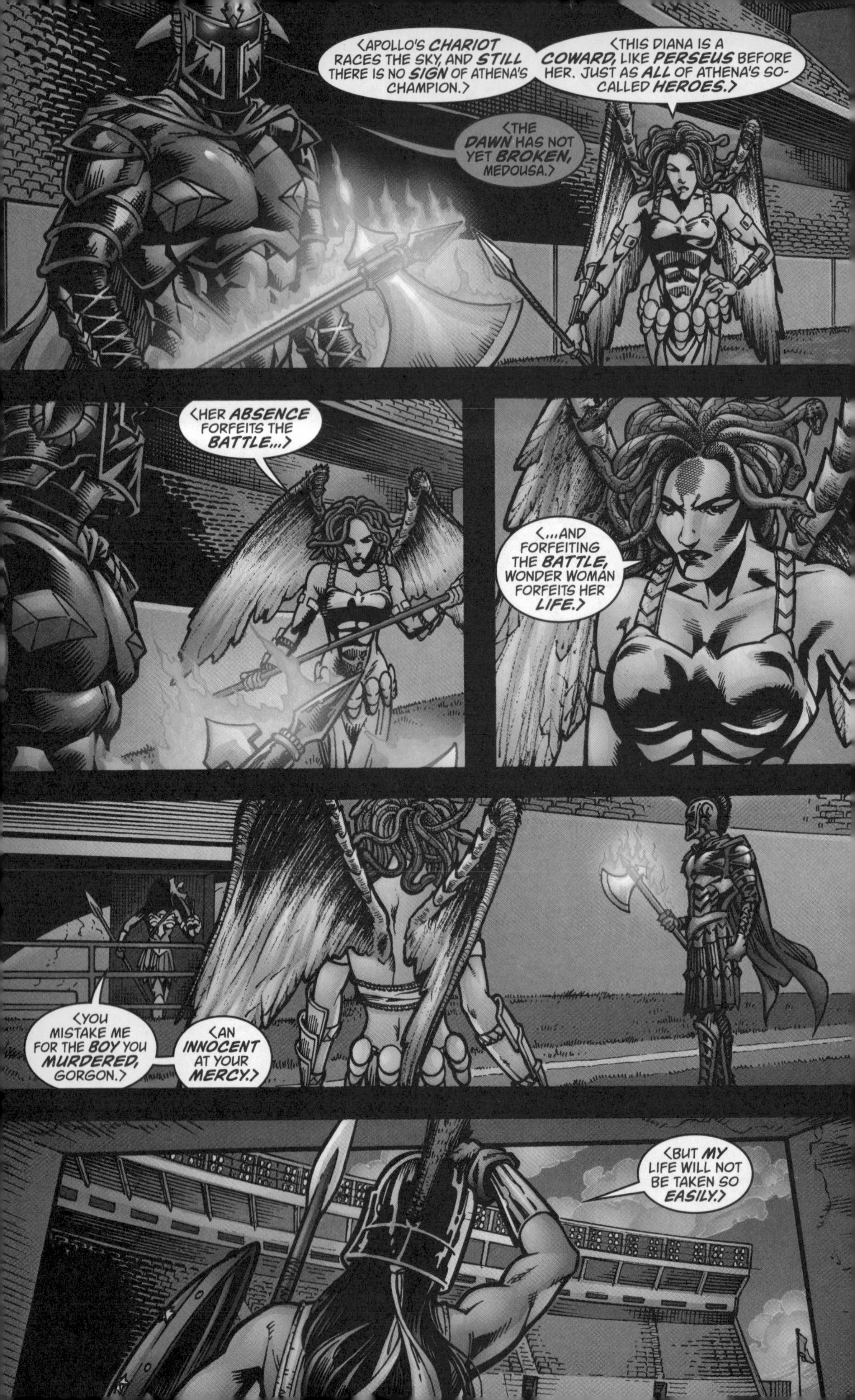

<APOLLO'S CHARIOT RACES THE SKY, AND STILL THERE IS NO SIGN OF ATHENA'S CHAMPION.>
<THIS DIANA IS A COWARD, LIKE PERSEUS BEFORE HER. JUST AS ALL OF ATHENA'S SO-CALLED HEROES.>
<THE DAWN HAS NOT YET BROKEN, MEDOUSA.>
<HER ABSENCE FORFEITS THE BATTLE...>
<...AND FORFEITING THE BATTLE, WONDER WOMAN FORFEITS HER LIFE.>
<YOU MISTAKE ME FOR THE BOY YOU MURDERED, GORGON.>
<AN INNOCENT AT YOUR MERCY.>
<BUT MY LIFE WILL NOT BE TAKEN SO EASILY.>

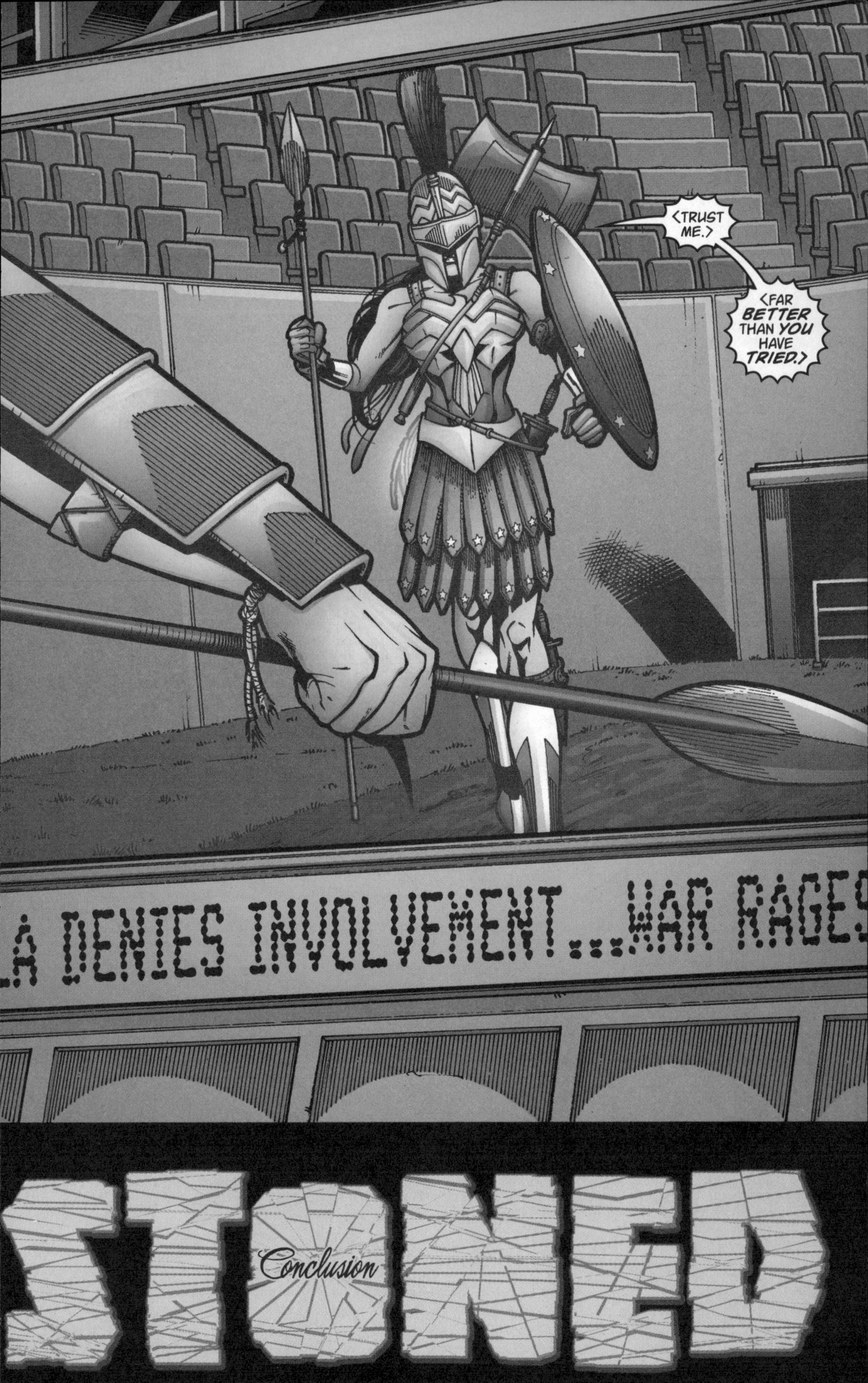

<TRUST ME.>
<FAR BETTER THAN YOU HAVE TRIED.>
..A DENIES INVOLVEMENT...WAR RAGES
STONED
Conclusion

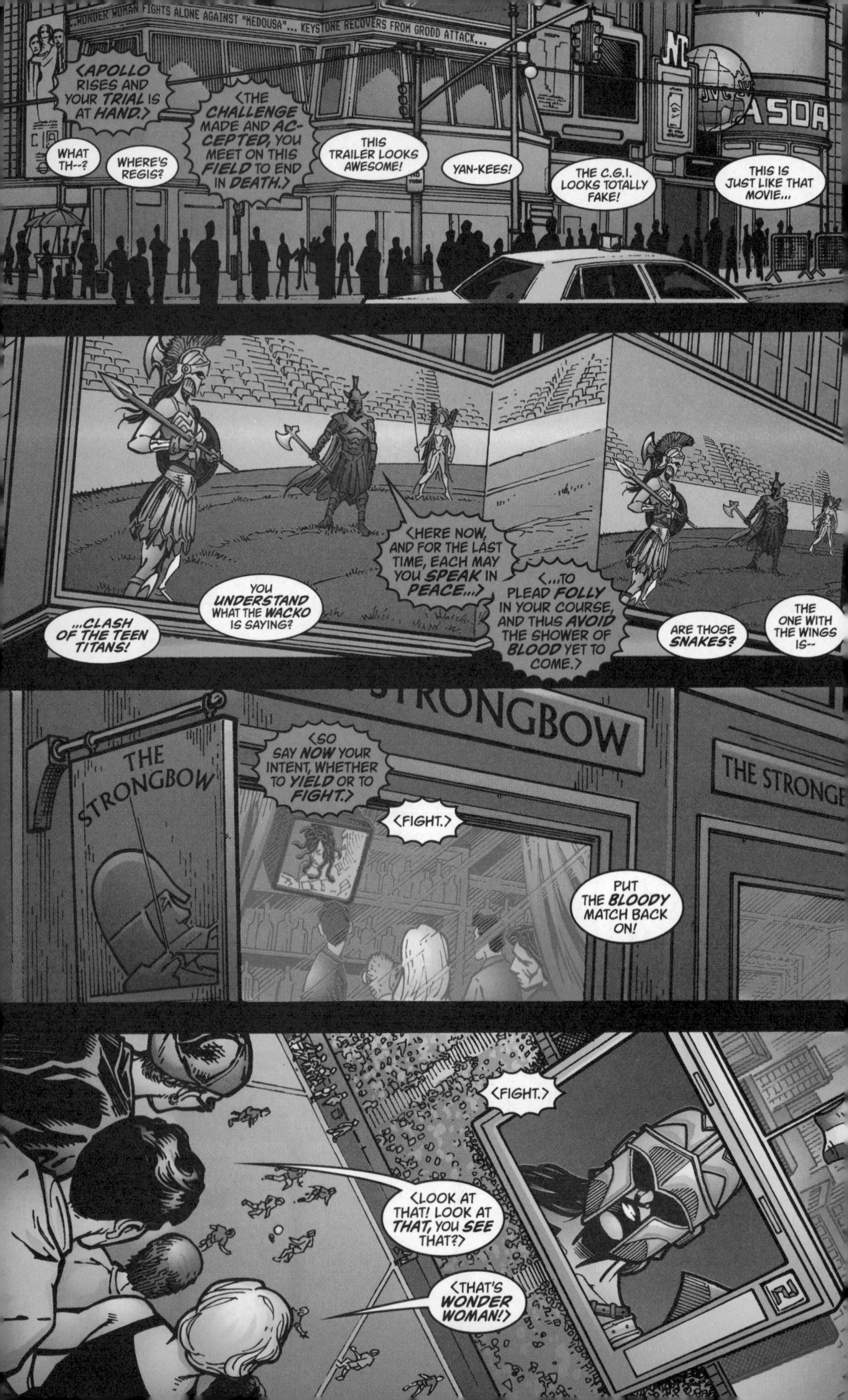
...WONDER WOMAN FIGHTS ALONE AGAINST "MEDOUSA"... KEYSTONE RECOVERS FROM GRODD ATTACK...
<APOLLO RISES AND YOUR TRIAL IS AT HAND.>
<THE CHALLENGE MADE AND ACCEPTED, YOU MEET ON THIS FIELD TO END IN DEATH.>
WHAT TH--?
WHERE'S REGIS?
THIS TRAILER LOOKS AWESOME!
YAN-KEES!
THE C.G.I. LOOKS TOTALLY FAKE!
THIS IS JUST LIKE THAT MOVIE...
<HERE NOW, AND FOR THE LAST TIME, EACH MAY YOU SPEAK IN PEACE...>
<...TO PLEAD FOLLY IN YOUR COURSE, AND THUS AVOID THE SHOWER OF BLOOD YET TO COME.>
...CLASH OF THE TEEN TITANS!
YOU UNDERSTAND WHAT THE WACKO IS SAYING?
ARE THOSE SNAKES?
THE ONE WITH THE WINGS IS--
STRONGBOW
THE STRONGBOW
THE STRONGB
<SO SAY NOW YOUR INTENT, WHETHER TO YIELD OR TO FIGHT.>
<FIGHT.>
PUT THE BLOODY MATCH BACK ON!
<FIGHT.>
<LOOK AT THAT! LOOK AT THAT, YOU SEE THAT?>
<THAT'S WONDER WOMAN!>

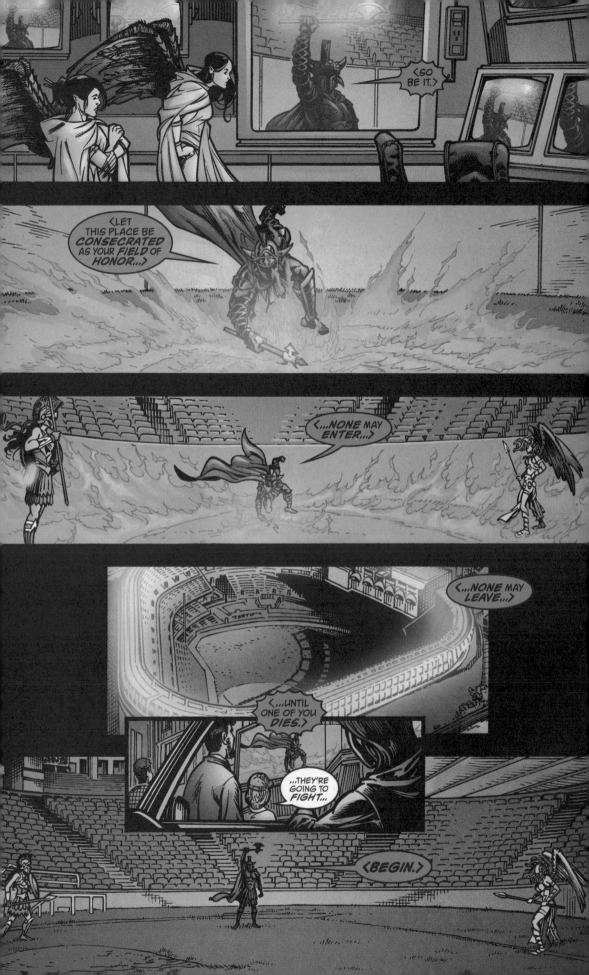

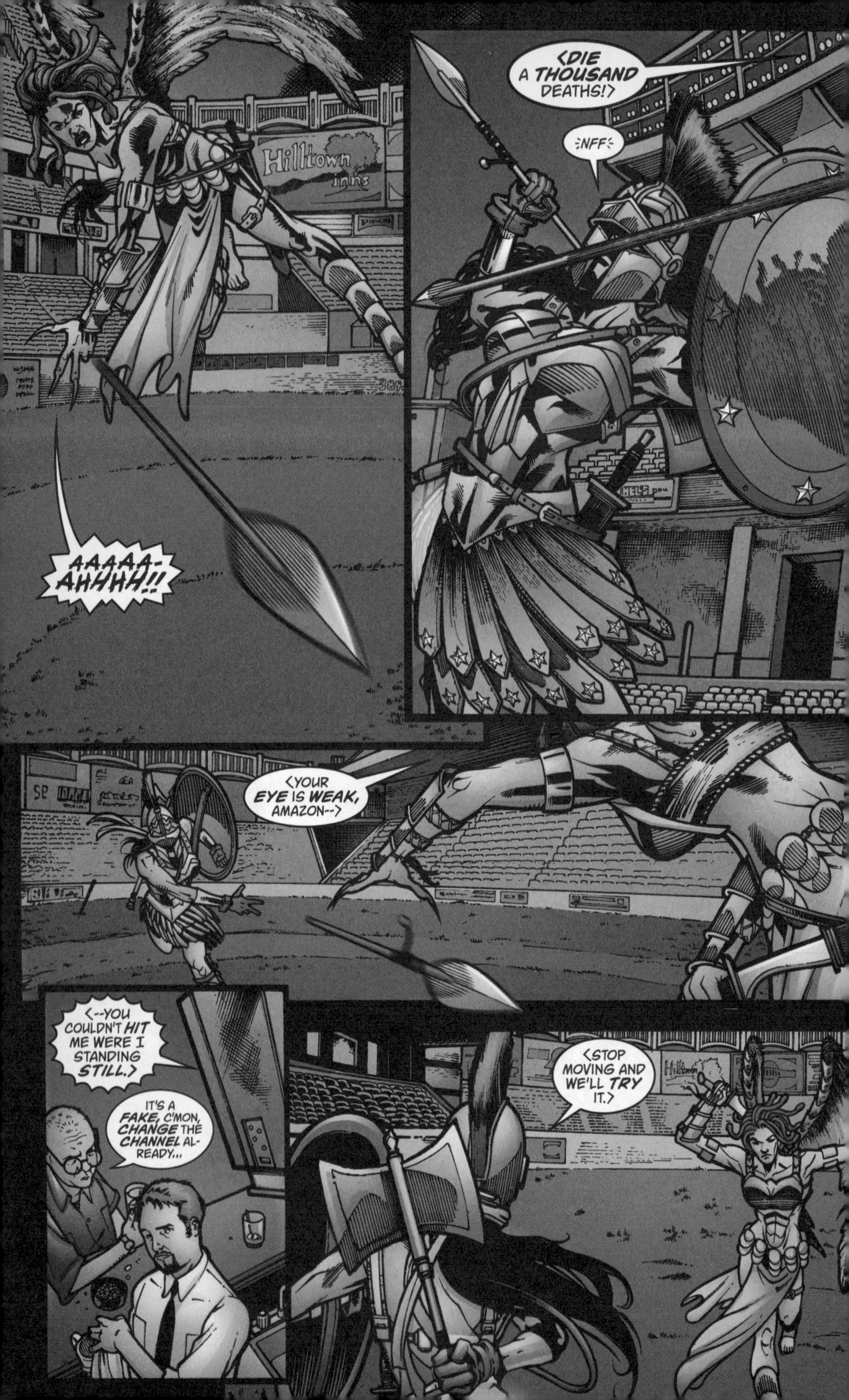
Hilltown
inns
AAAAA-AHHHH!!
<DIE A THOUSAND DEATHS!>
NFF
<YOUR EYE IS WEAK, AMAZON-->
<--YOU COULDN'T HIT ME WERE I STANDING STILL.>
IT'S A FAKE, C'MON, CHANGE THE CHANNEL ALREADY...
<STOP MOVING AND WE'LL TRY IT.>

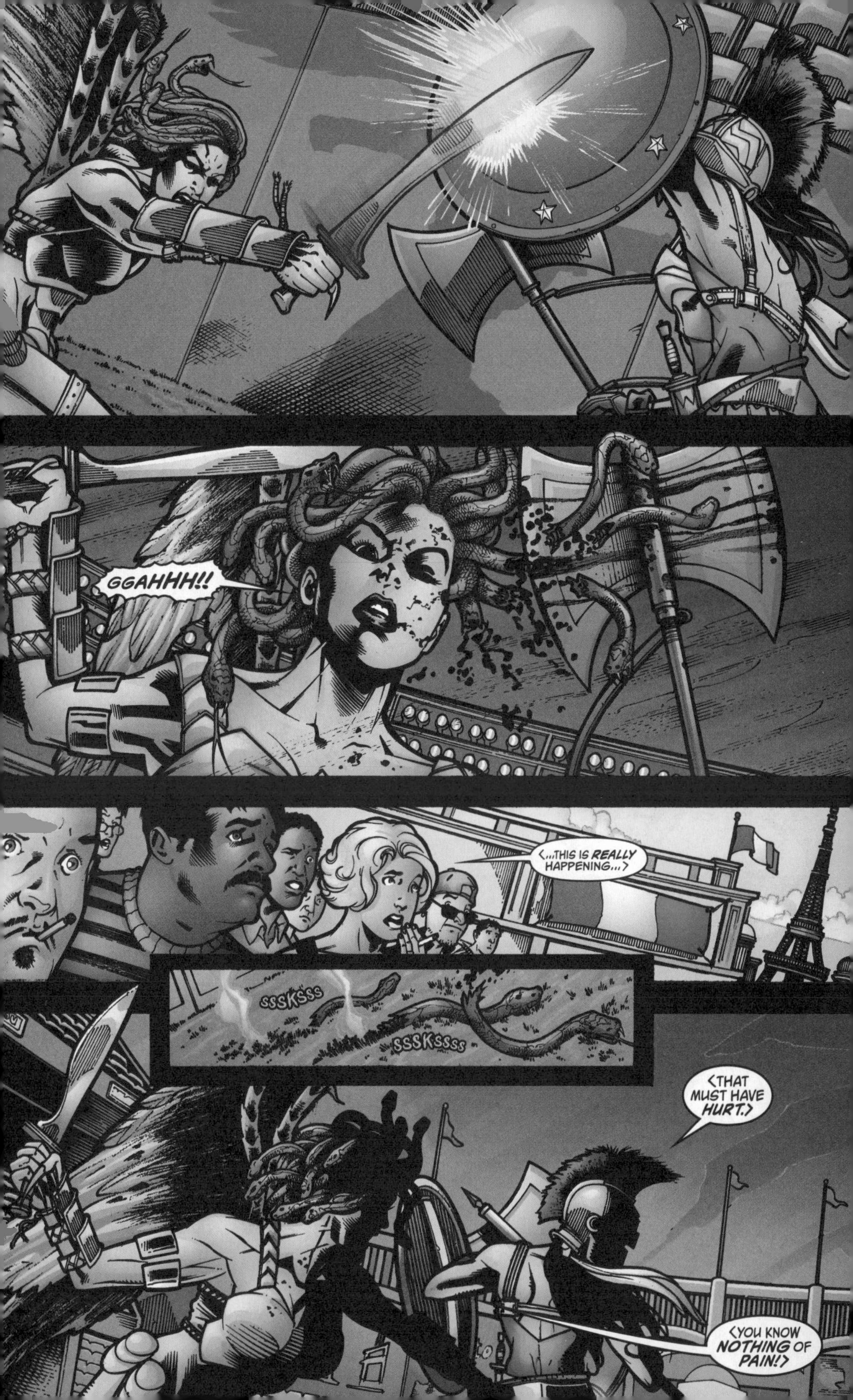
GGAHHH!!
<...THIS IS REALLY HAPPENING...>
SSSKSSS
SSSKSSSS
<THAT MUST HAVE HURT.>
<YOU KNOW NOTHING OF PAIN!>

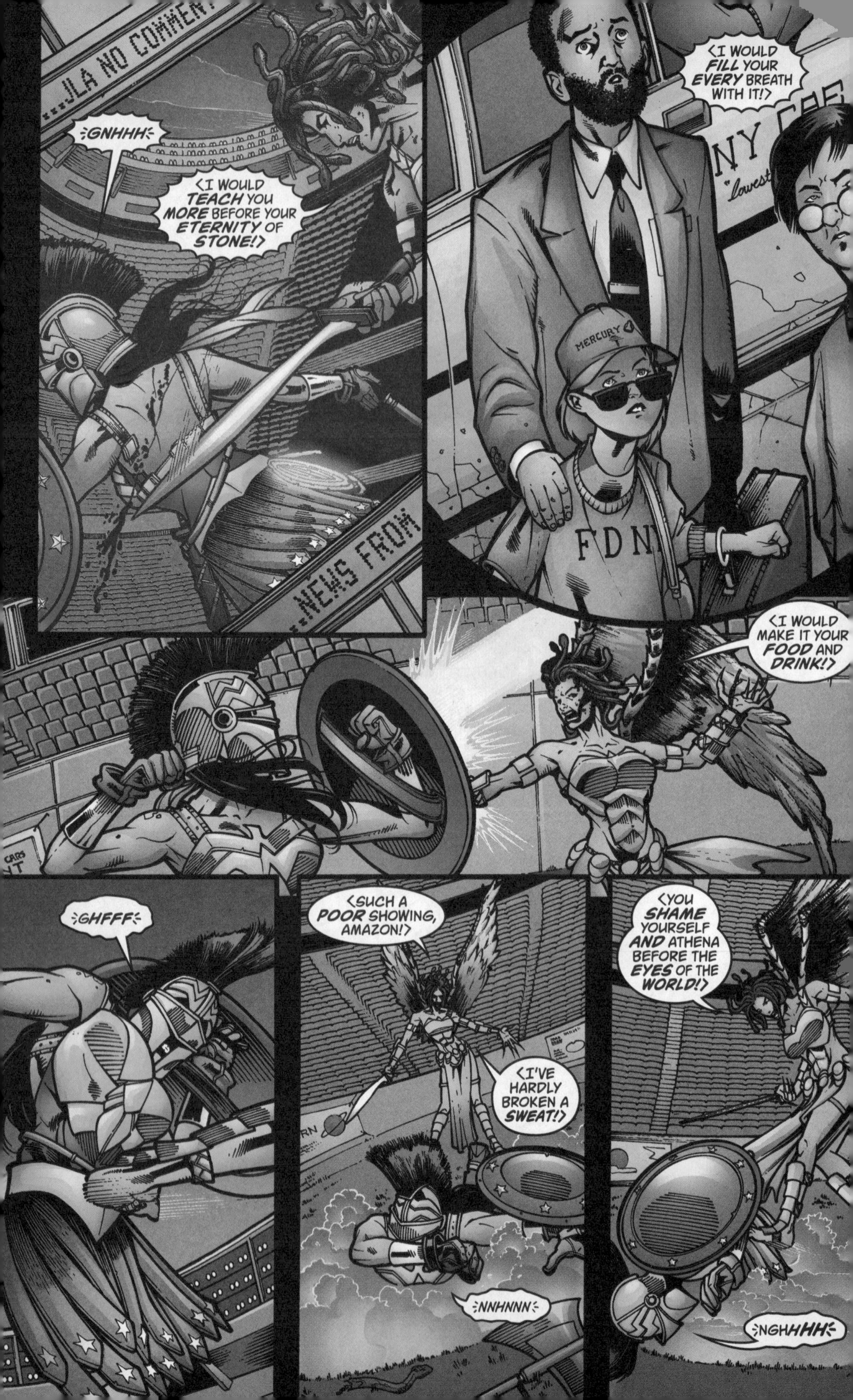
...JLA NO COMMER
GNHHH
<I WOULD TEACH YOU MORE BEFORE YOUR ETERNITY OF STONE!>
NEWS FROM
<I WOULD FILL YOUR EVERY BREATH WITH IT!>
NY CAB
MERCURY
FDN
<I WOULD MAKE IT YOUR FOOD AND DRINK!>
GHFFF
<SUCH A POOR SHOWING, AMAZON!>
<I'VE HARDLY BROKEN A SWEAT!>
NNHNNN
<YOU SHAME YOURSELF AND ATHENA BEFORE THE EYES OF THE WORLD!>
NGHHHH

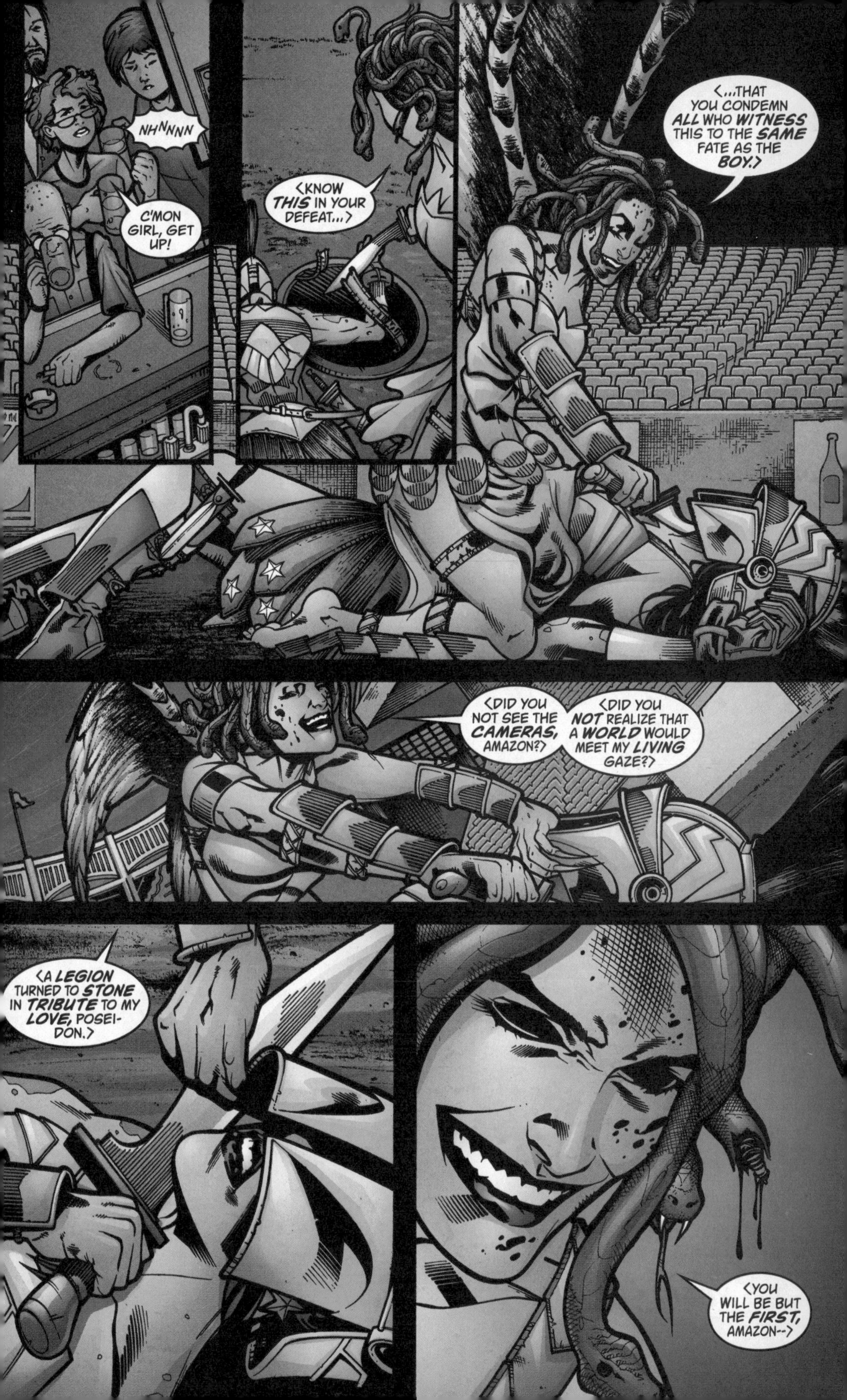
NHNNNN
C'MON GIRL, GET UP!
<KNOW THIS IN YOUR DEFEAT...>
<...THAT YOU CONDEMN ALL WHO WITNESS THIS TO THE SAME FATE AS THE BOY.>
<DID YOU NOT SEE THE CAMERAS, AMAZON?>
<DID YOU NOT REALIZE THAT A WORLD WOULD MEET MY LIVING GAZE?>
<A LEGION TURNED TO STONE IN TRIBUTE TO MY LOVE, POSEI-DON.>
<YOU WILL BE BUT THE FIRST, AMAZON-->

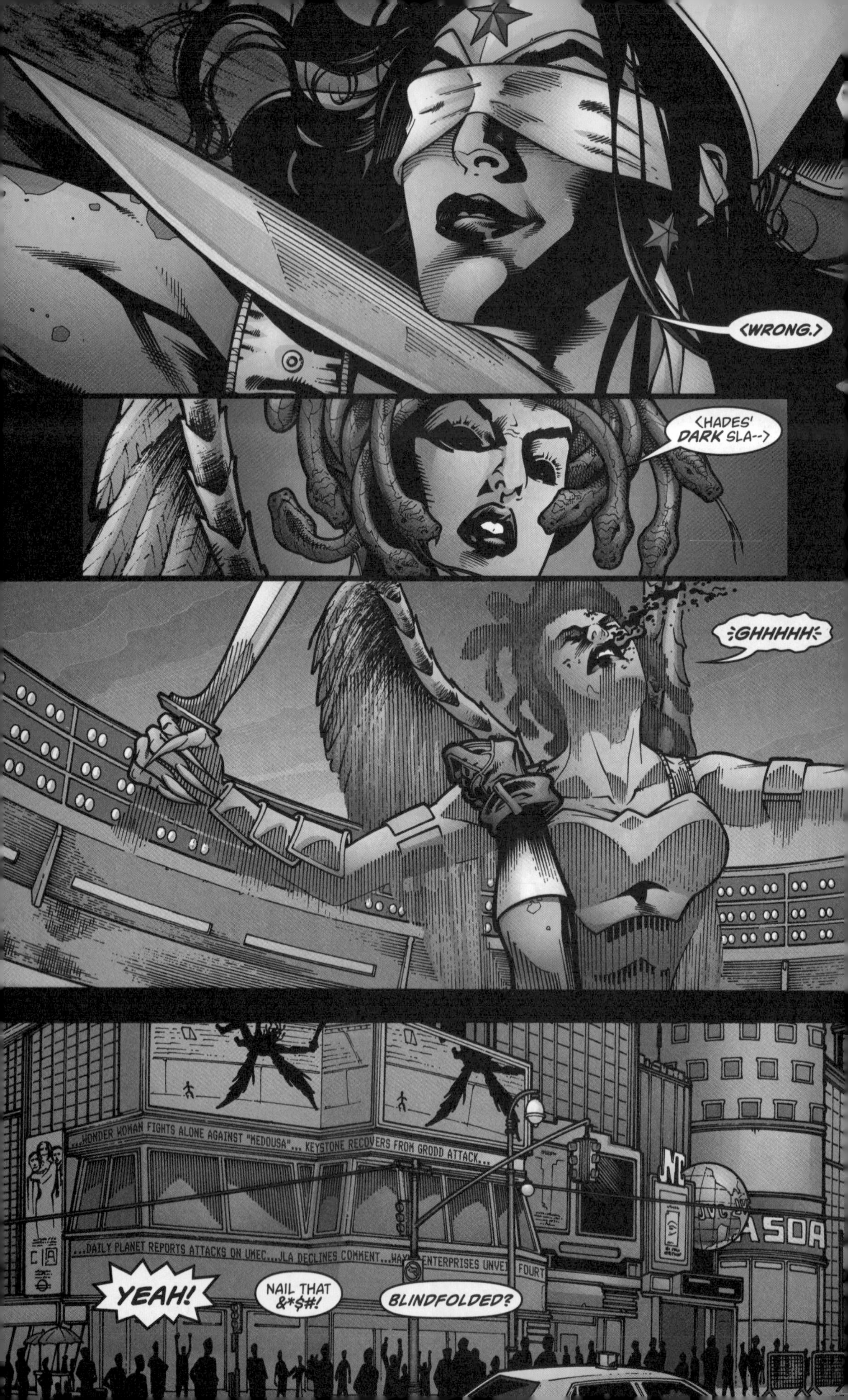

⟨WRONG.⟩
⟨HADES' DARK SLA--⟩
GHHHHH
...WONDER WOMAN FIGHTS ALONE AGAINST "MEDOUSA"... KEYSTONE RECOVERS FROM GRODD ATTACK...
...DAILY PLANET REPORTS ATTACKS ON UMEC...JLA DECLINES COMMENT...WAY ENTERPRISES UNVE FOURT
YEAH!
NAIL THAT &*$#!
BLINDFOLDED?

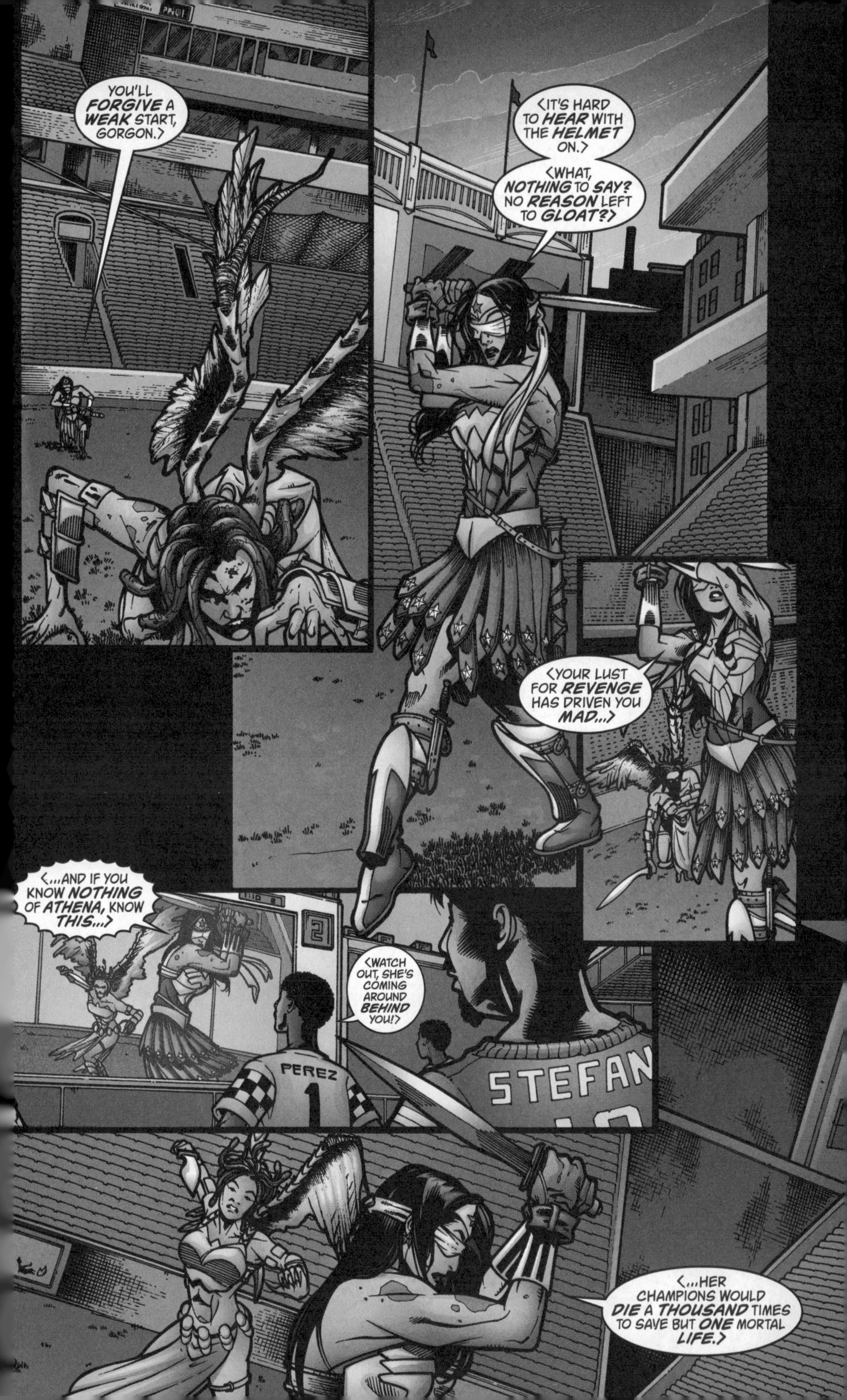
<YOU'LL FORGIVE A WEAK START, GORGON.>
<IT'S HARD TO HEAR WITH THE HELMET ON.>
<WHAT, NOTHING TO SAY? NO REASON LEFT TO GLOAT?>
<YOUR LUST FOR REVENGE HAS DRIVEN YOU MAD...>
<...AND IF YOU KNOW NOTHING OF ATHENA, KNOW THIS...>
<WATCH OUT, SHE'S COMING AROUND BEHIND YOU!>
PEREZ
1
STEFAN
<...HER CHAMPIONS WOULD DIE A THOUSAND TIMES TO SAVE BUT ONE MORTAL LIFE.>

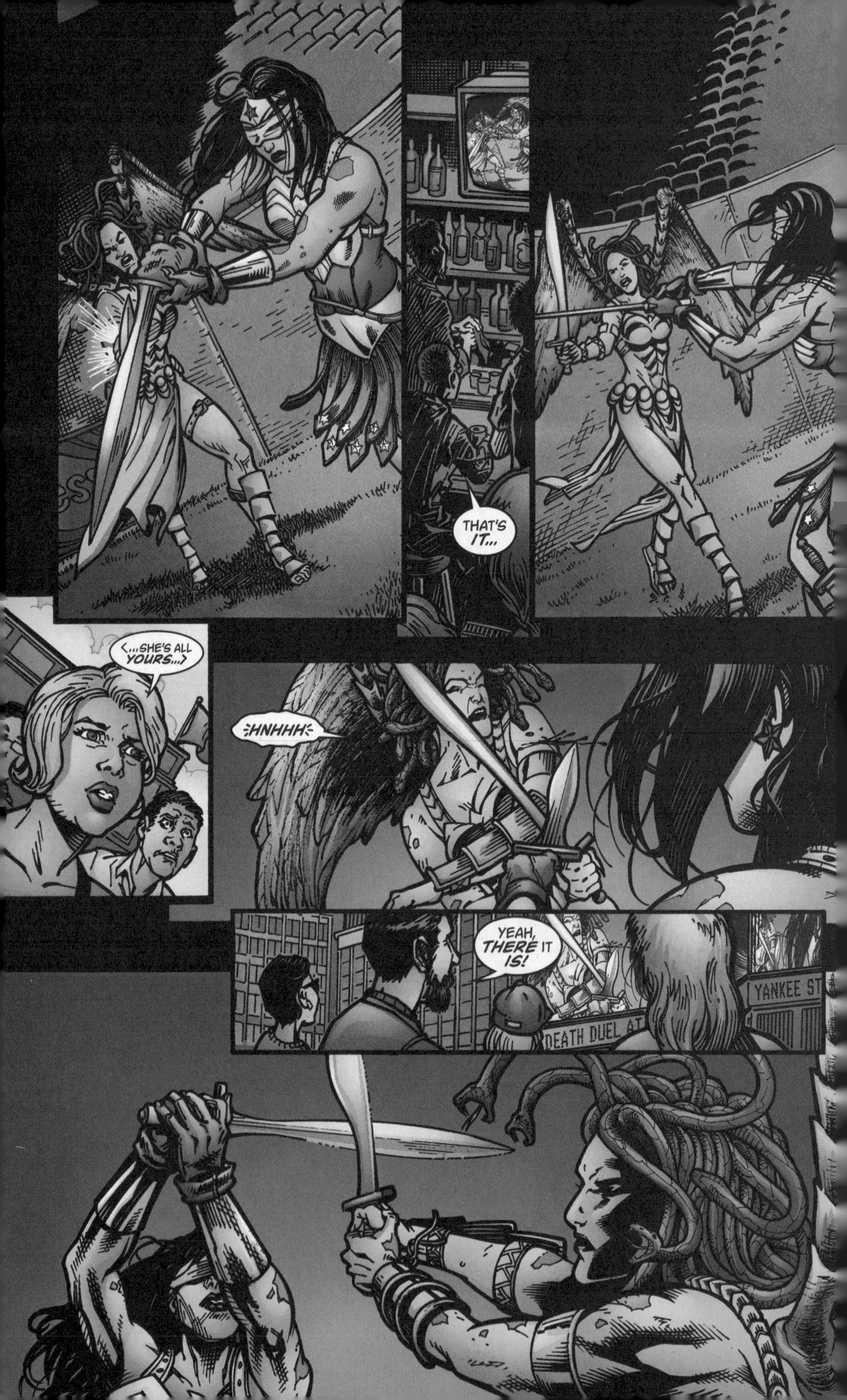

THAT'S IT...
<...SHE'S ALL YOURS...>
HNHHH
YEAH, THERE IT IS!
YANKEE ST
DEATH DUEL AT

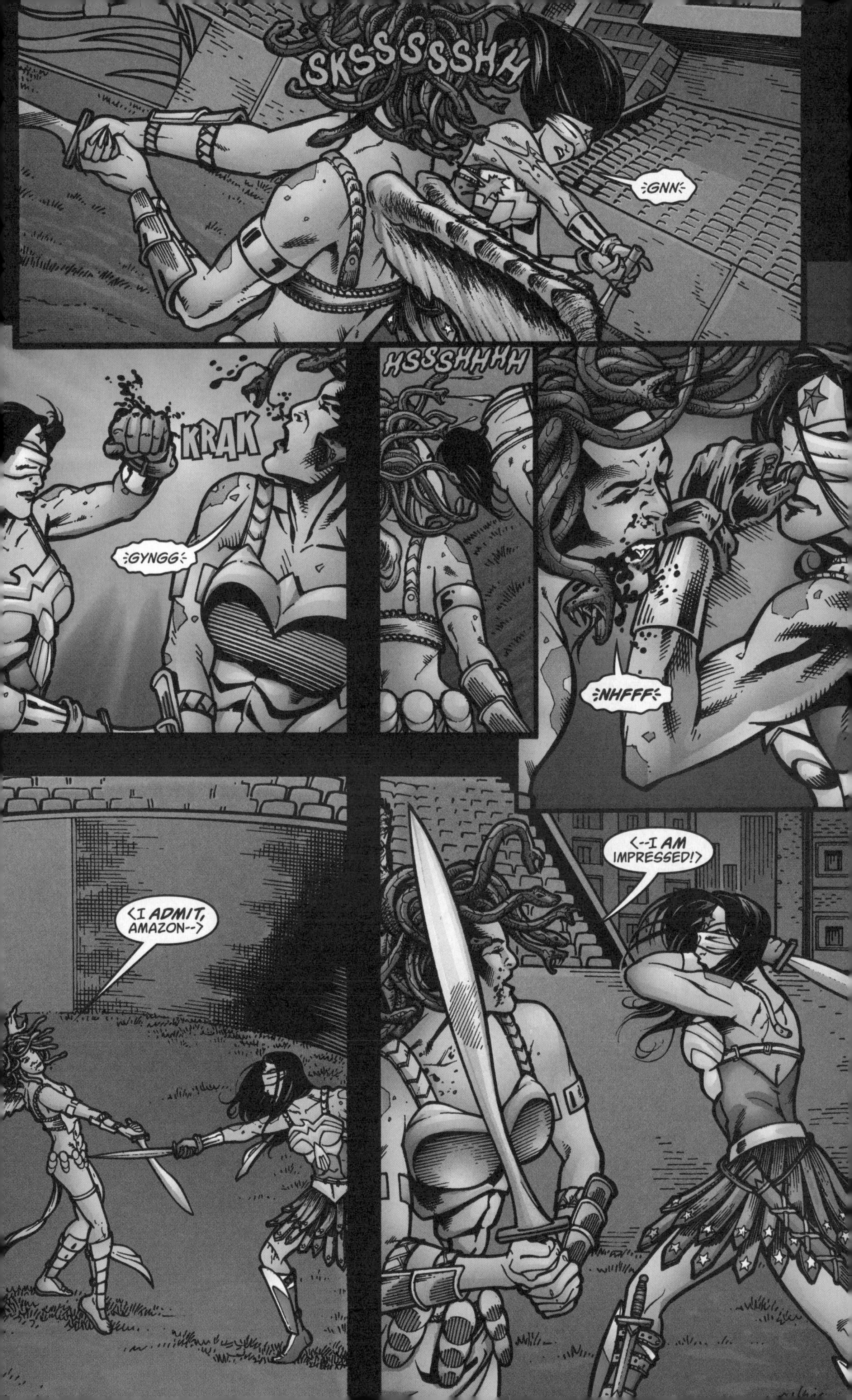
SKSSSSSHH
GNN
KRAK
GYNGG
HSSSHHHH
NHFFF
<I ADMIT, AMAZON-->
<--I AM IMPRESSED!>

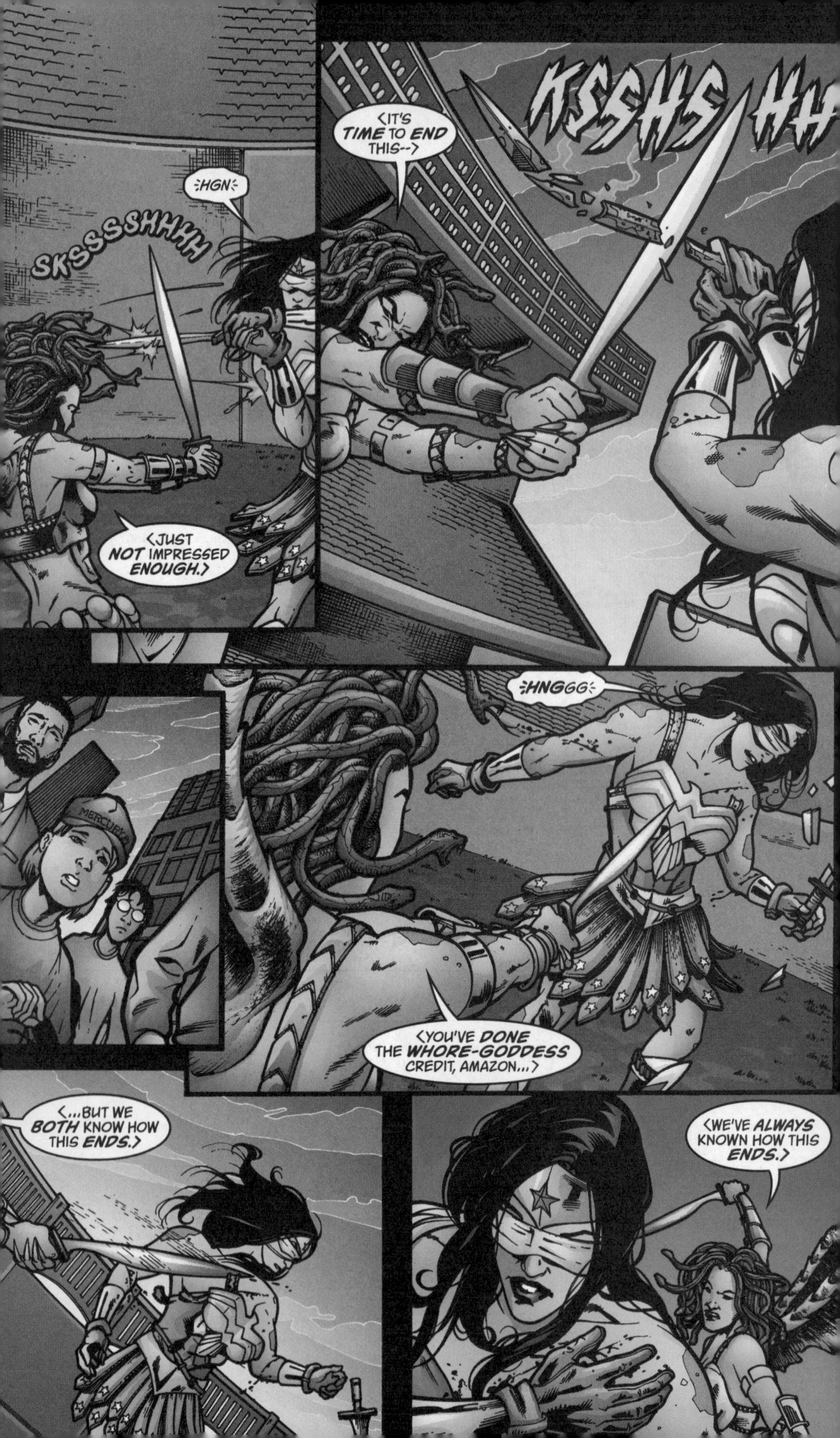

HGN
SKSSSSHHHH
<JUST NOT IMPRESSED ENOUGH.>
<IT'S TIME TO END THIS-->
KSSHS HH
HNGGG
MERCURY
<YOU'VE DONE THE WHORE-GODDESS CREDIT, AMAZON...>
<...BUT WE BOTH KNOW HOW THIS ENDS.>
<WE'VE ALWAYS KNOWN HOW THIS ENDS.>

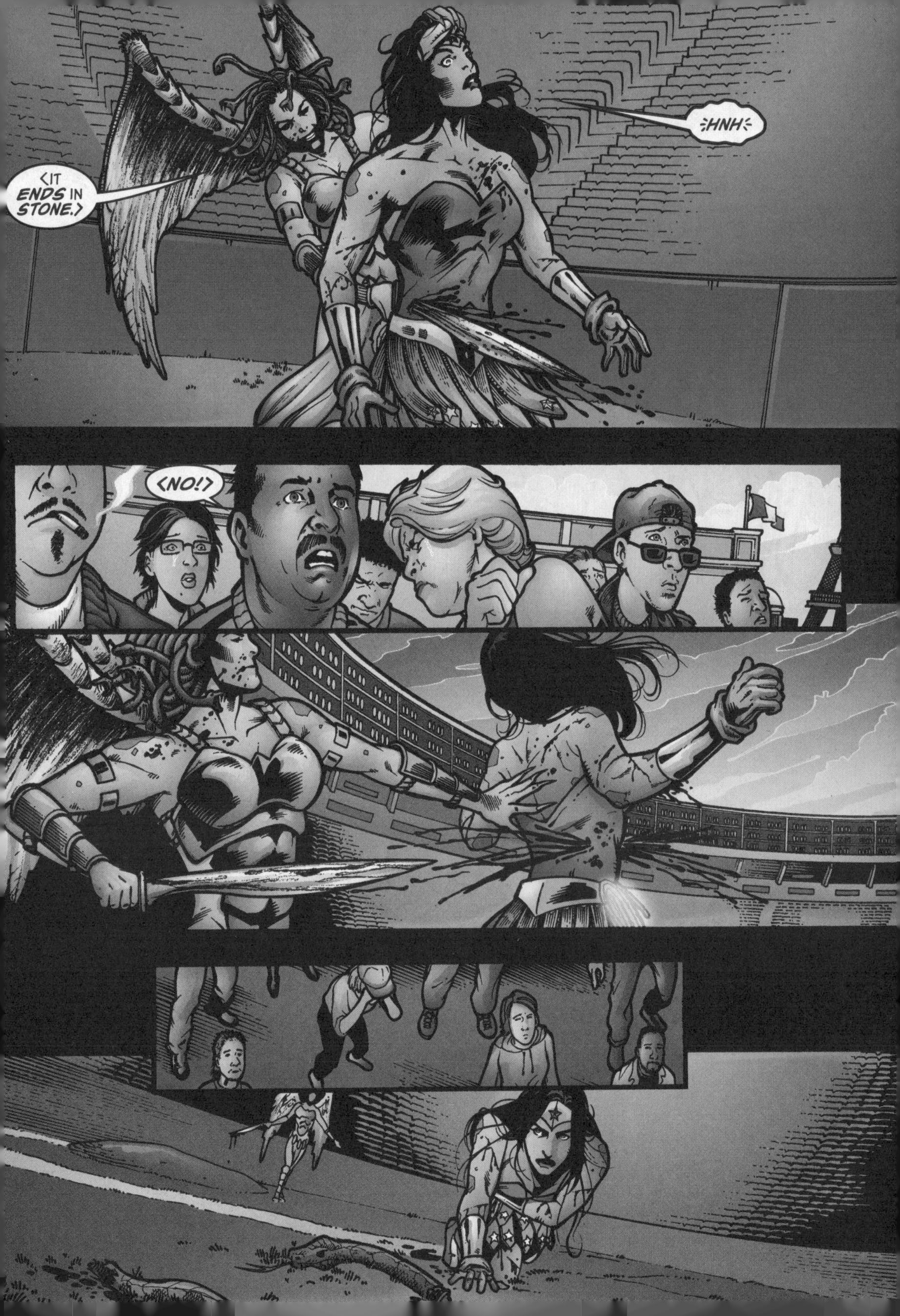
<IT ENDS IN STONE.>
HNH
<NO!>

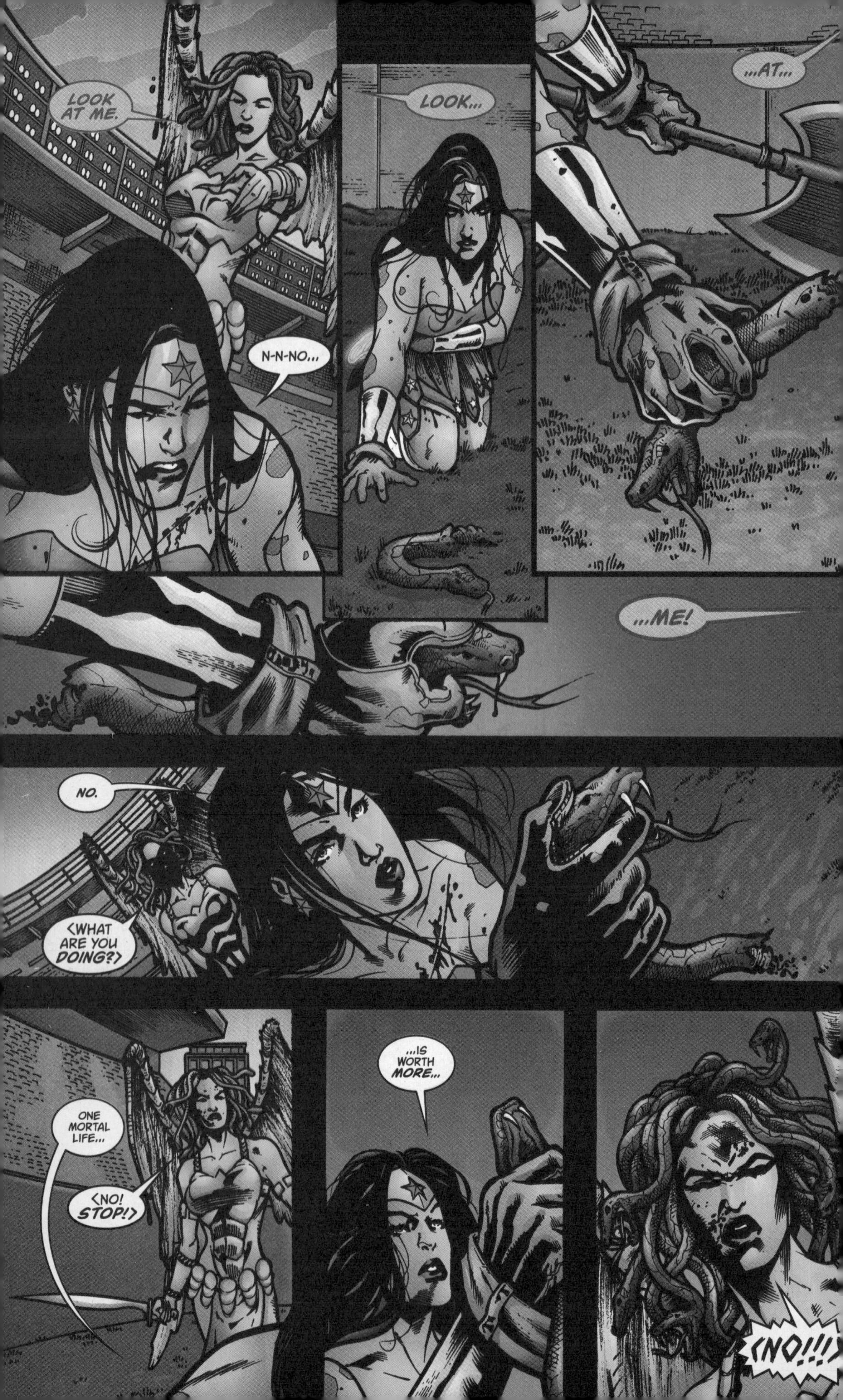
LOOK AT ME.
N-N-NO...
LOOK...
...AT...
...ME!
NO.
<WHAT ARE YOU DOING?>
ONE MORTAL LIFE...
<NO! STOP!>
...IS WORTH MORE...
<NO!!!>

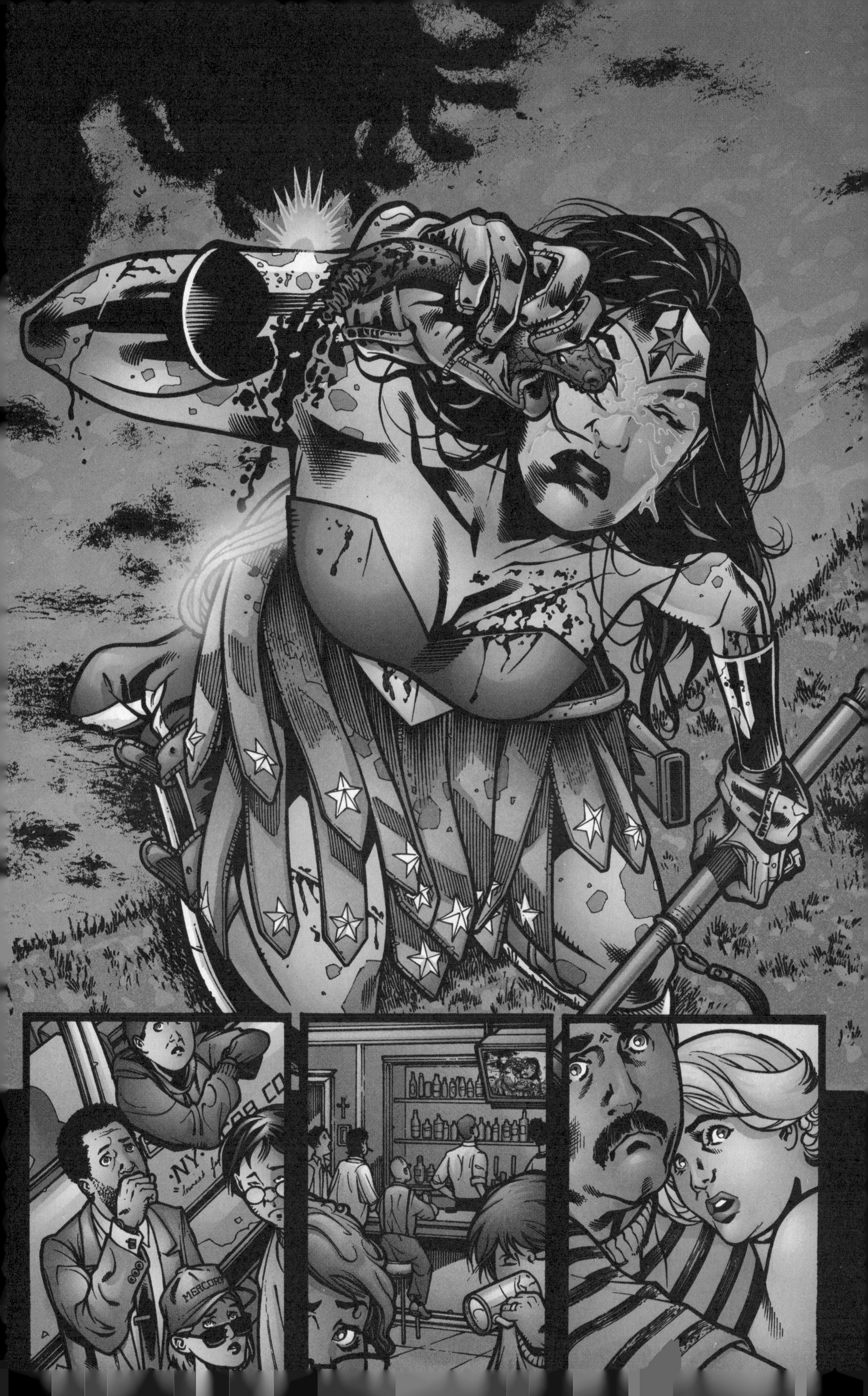

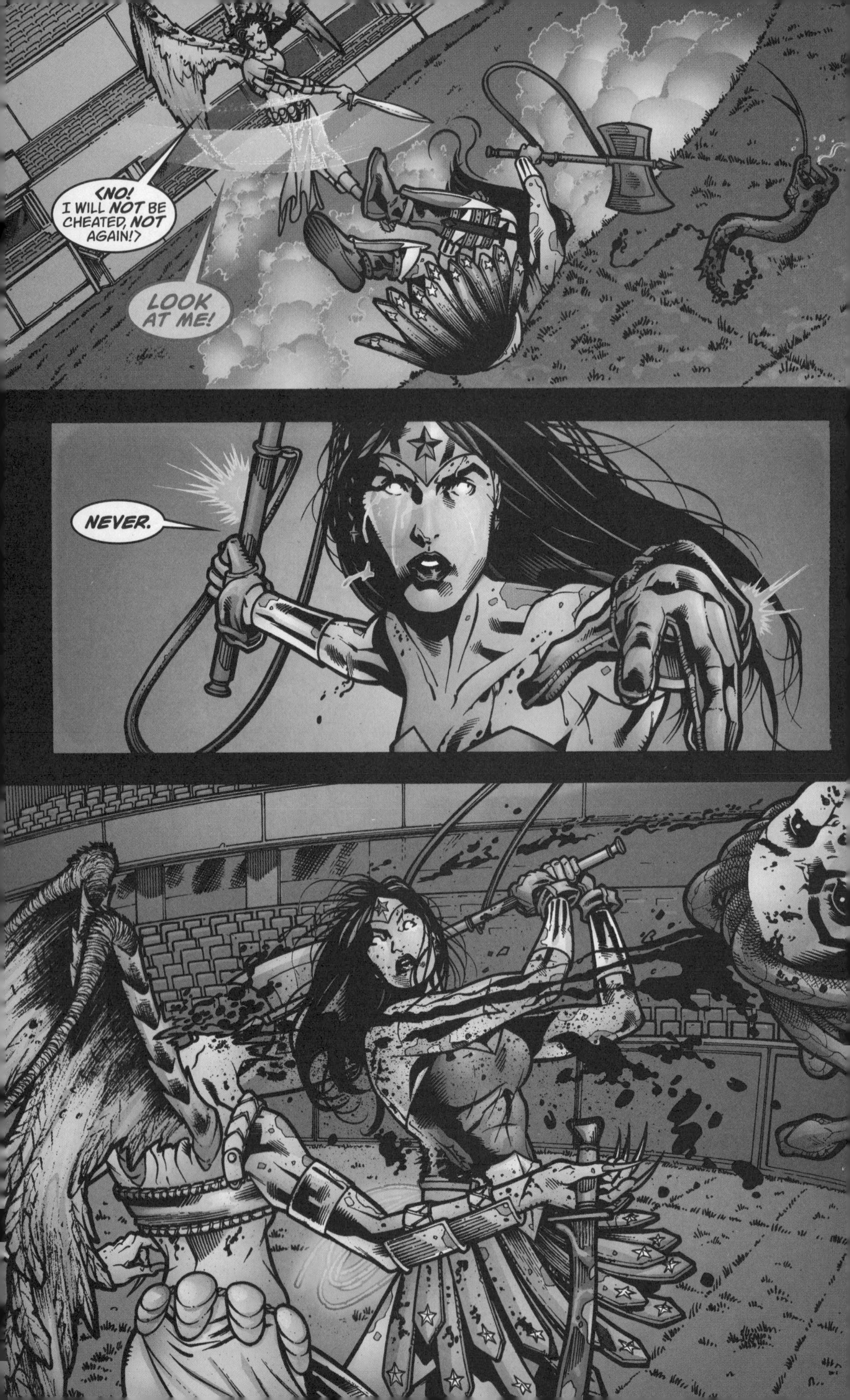
<NO! I WILL NOT BE CHEATED, NOT AGAIN!>
LOOK AT ME!
NEVER.

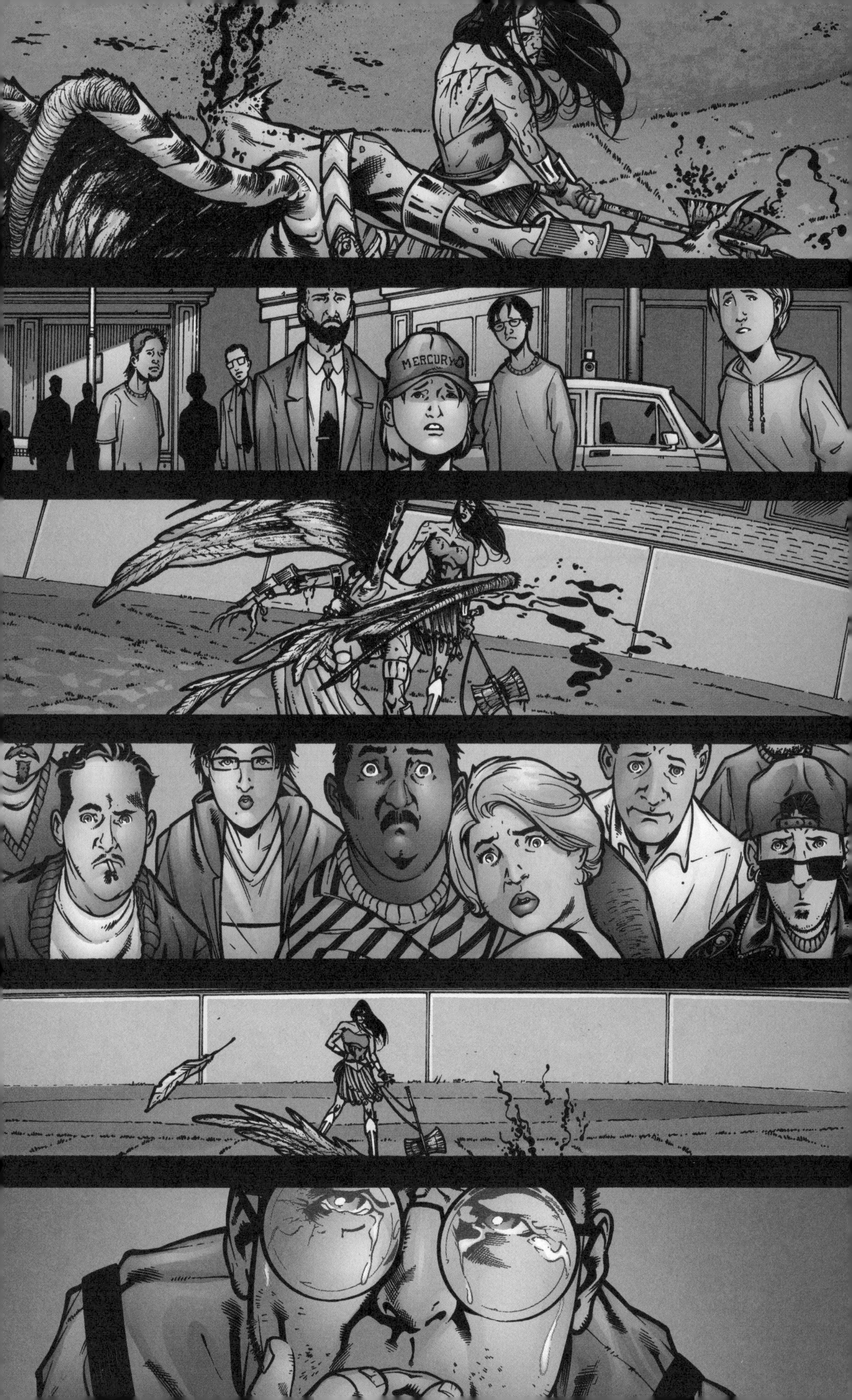
MERCURY

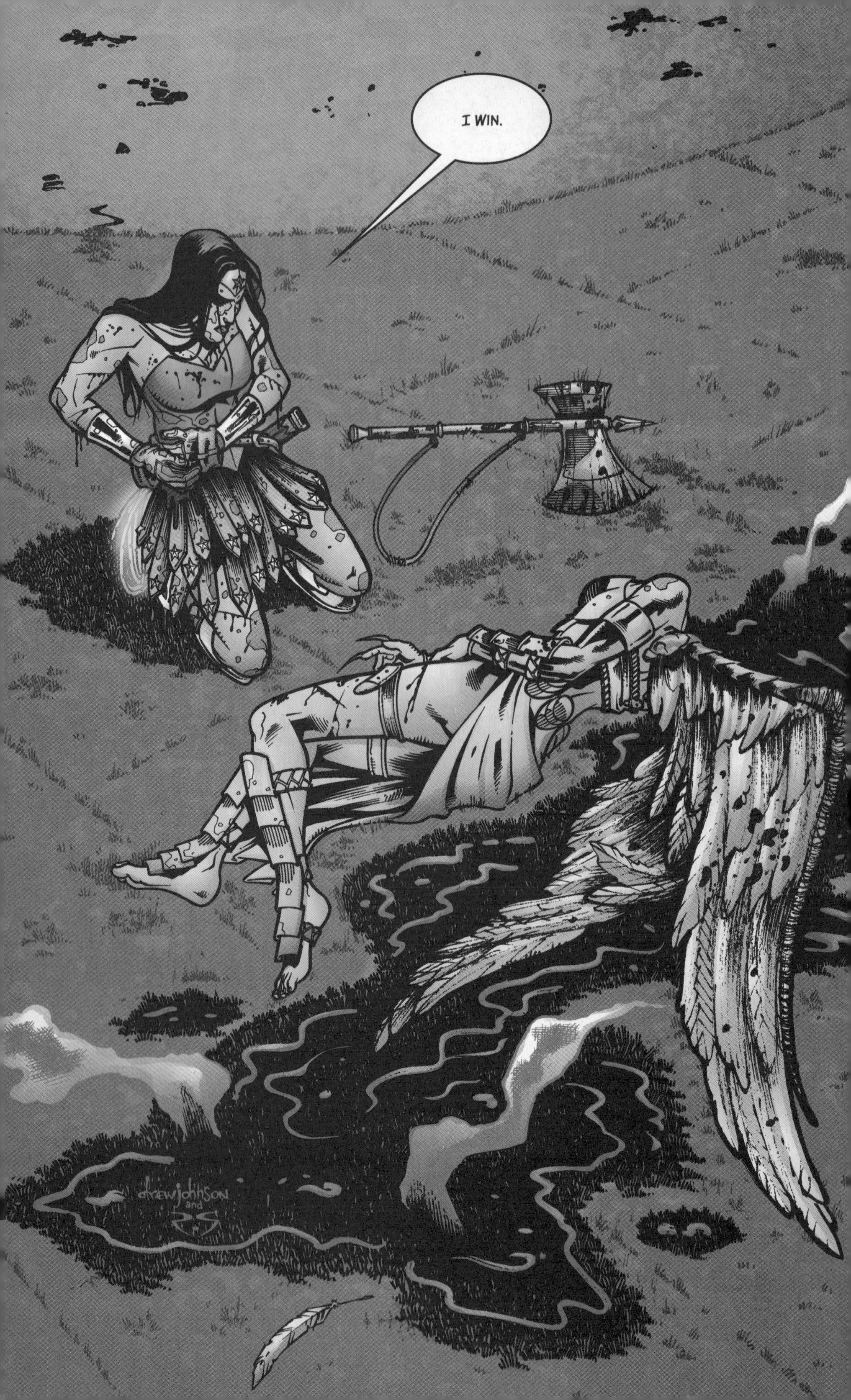
I WIN.
drew johnson and RS

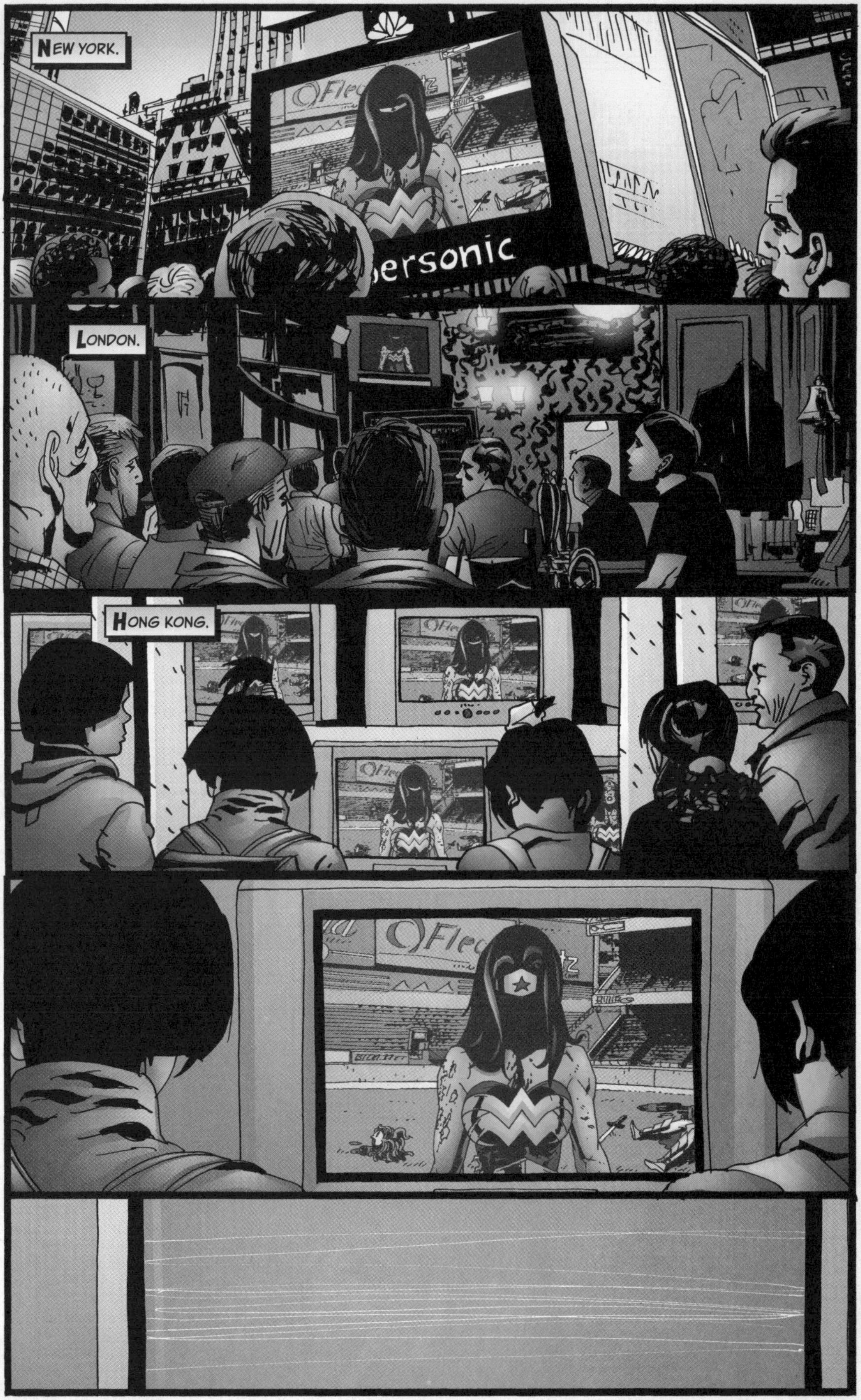
NEW YORK.
LONDON.
HONG KONG.
ersonic

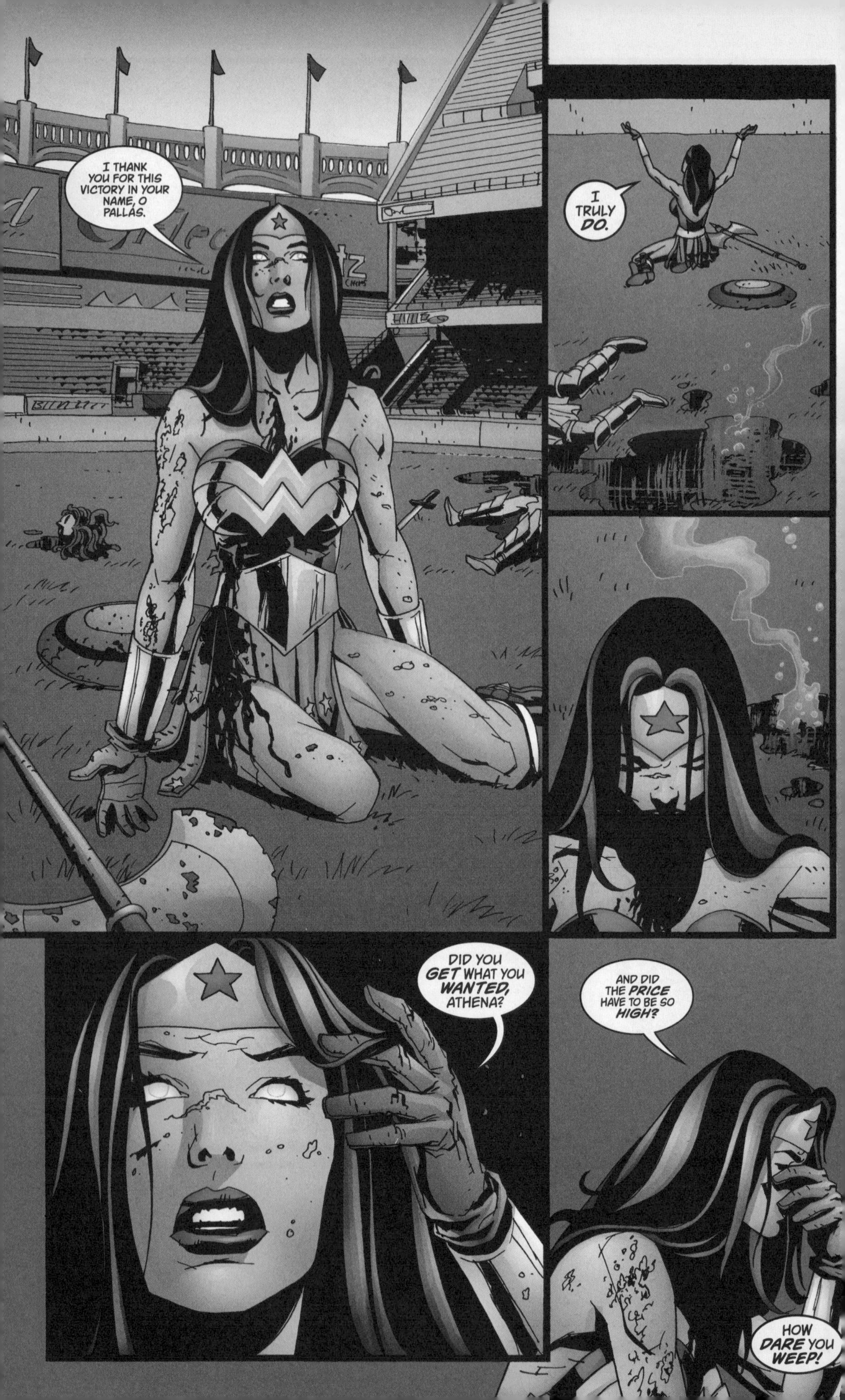
I THANK YOU FOR THIS VICTORY IN YOUR NAME, O PALLAS.
I TRULY DO.
DID YOU GET WHAT YOU WANTED, ATHENA?
AND DID THE PRICE HAVE TO BE SO HIGH?
HOW DARE YOU WEEP!

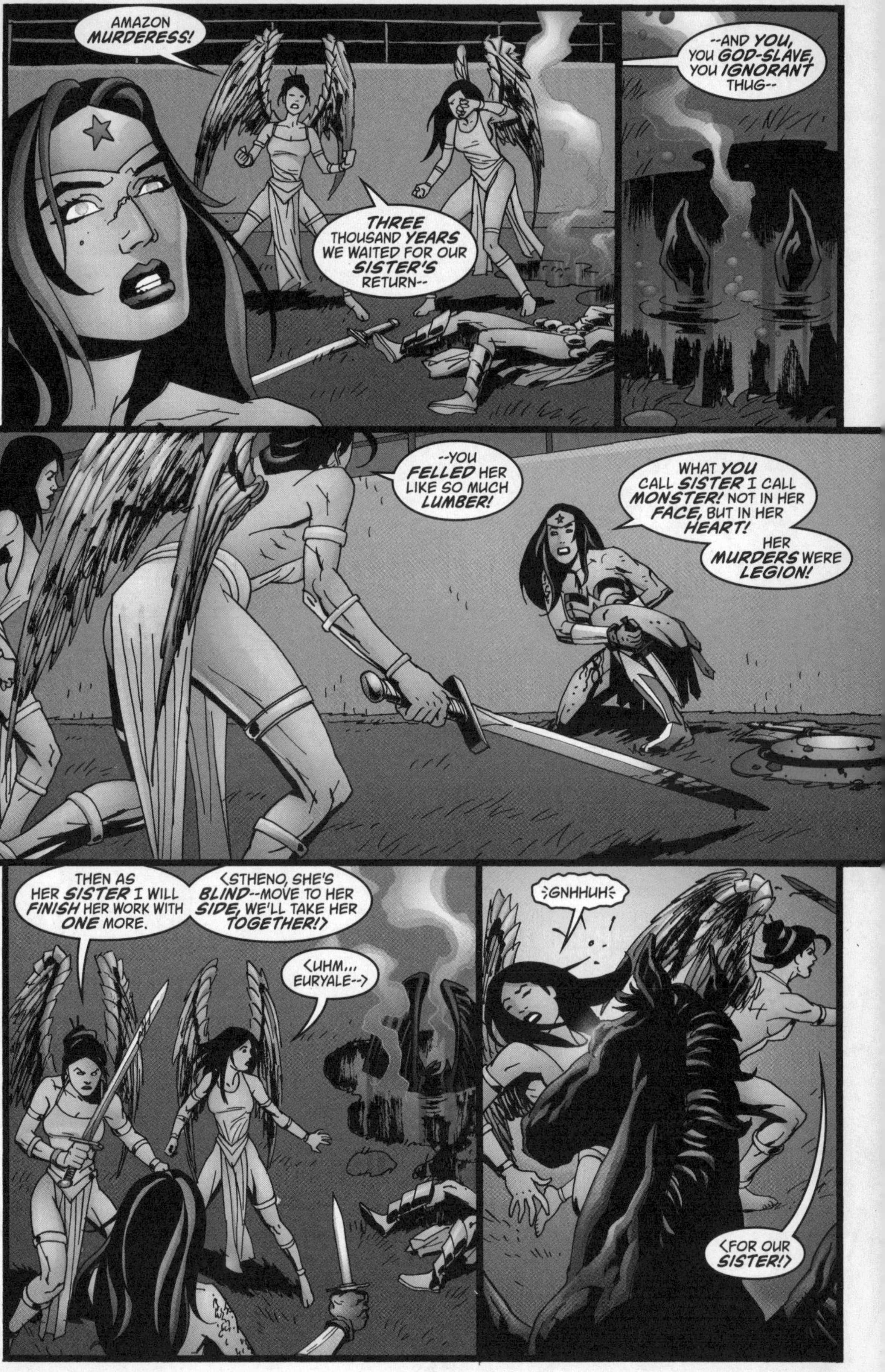
AMAZON MURDERESS!
THREE THOUSAND YEARS WE WAITED FOR OUR SISTER'S RETURN--
--AND YOU, YOU GOD-SLAVE, YOU IGNORANT THUG--
--YOU FELLED HER LIKE SO MUCH LUMBER!
WHAT YOU CALL SISTER I CALL MONSTER! NOT IN HER FACE, BUT IN HER HEART!
HER MURDERS WERE LEGION!
THEN AS HER SISTER I WILL FINISH HER WORK WITH ONE MORE.
<STHENO, SHE'S BLIND--MOVE TO HER SIDE, WE'LL TAKE HER TOGETHER!>
<UHM... EURYALE-->
GNHHUH
<FOR OUR SISTER!>

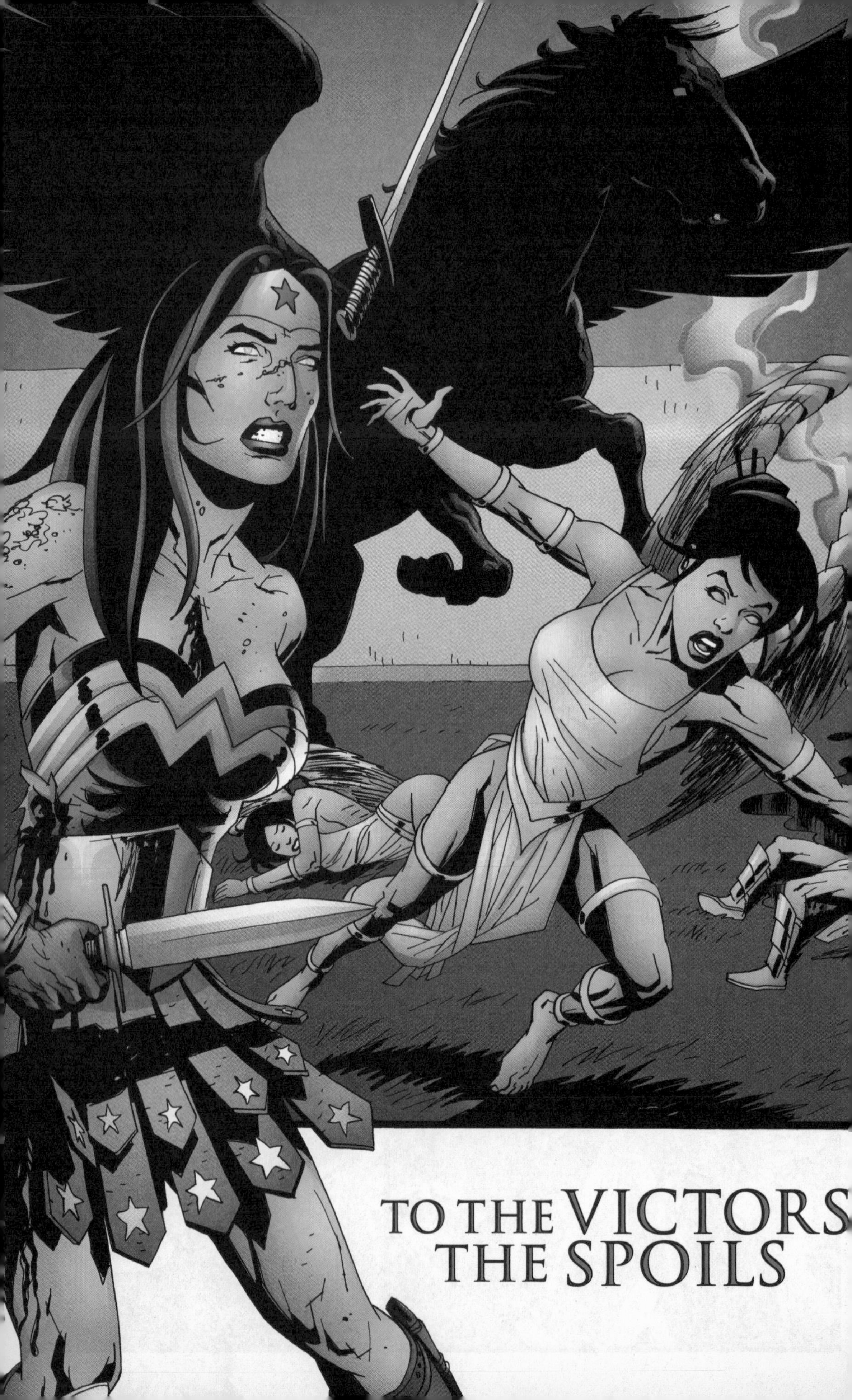

TO THE VICTORS THE SPOILS

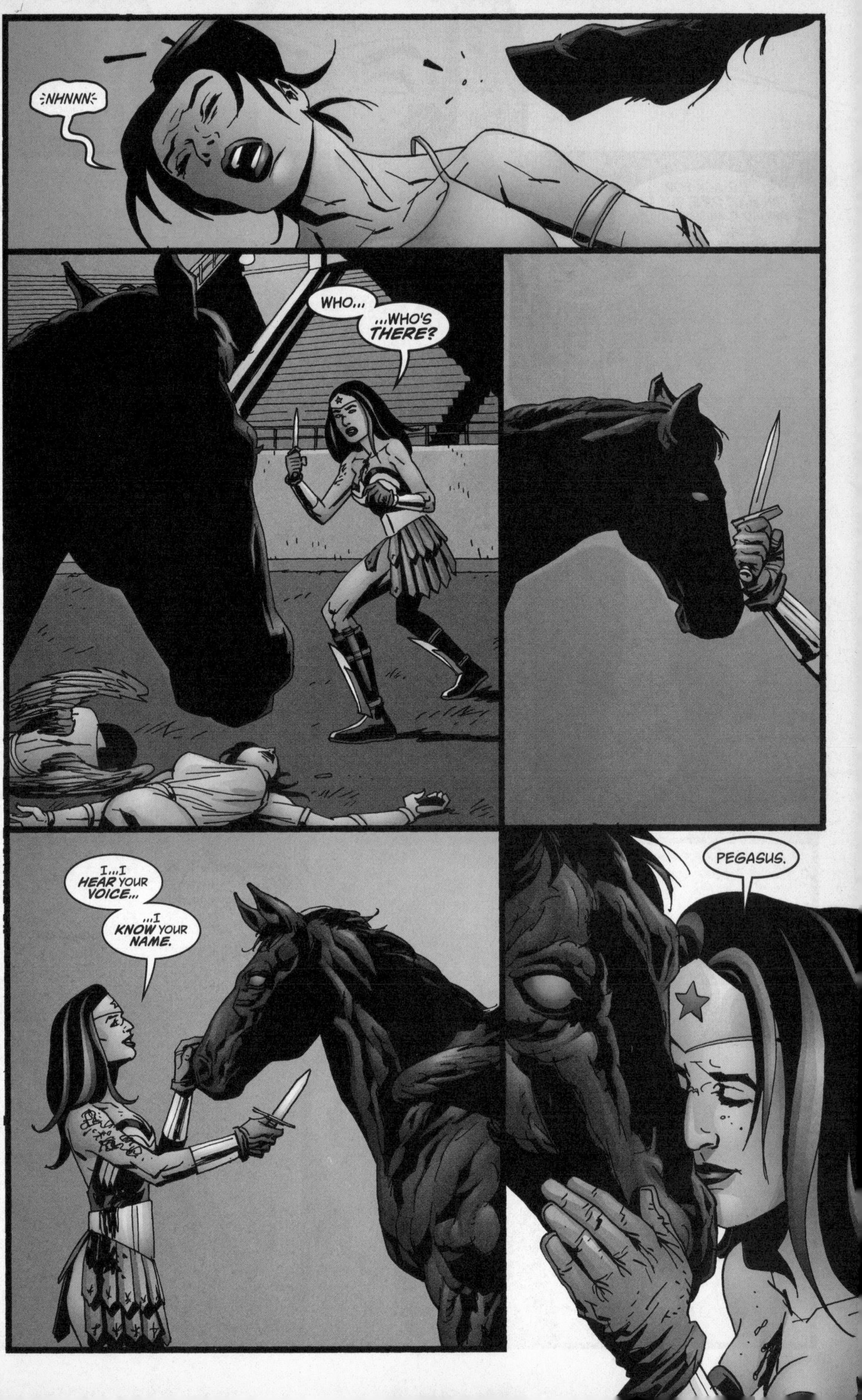
NHNNN
WHO...
...WHO'S THERE?
I...I HEAR YOUR VOICE...
...I KNOW YOUR NAME.
PEGASUS.

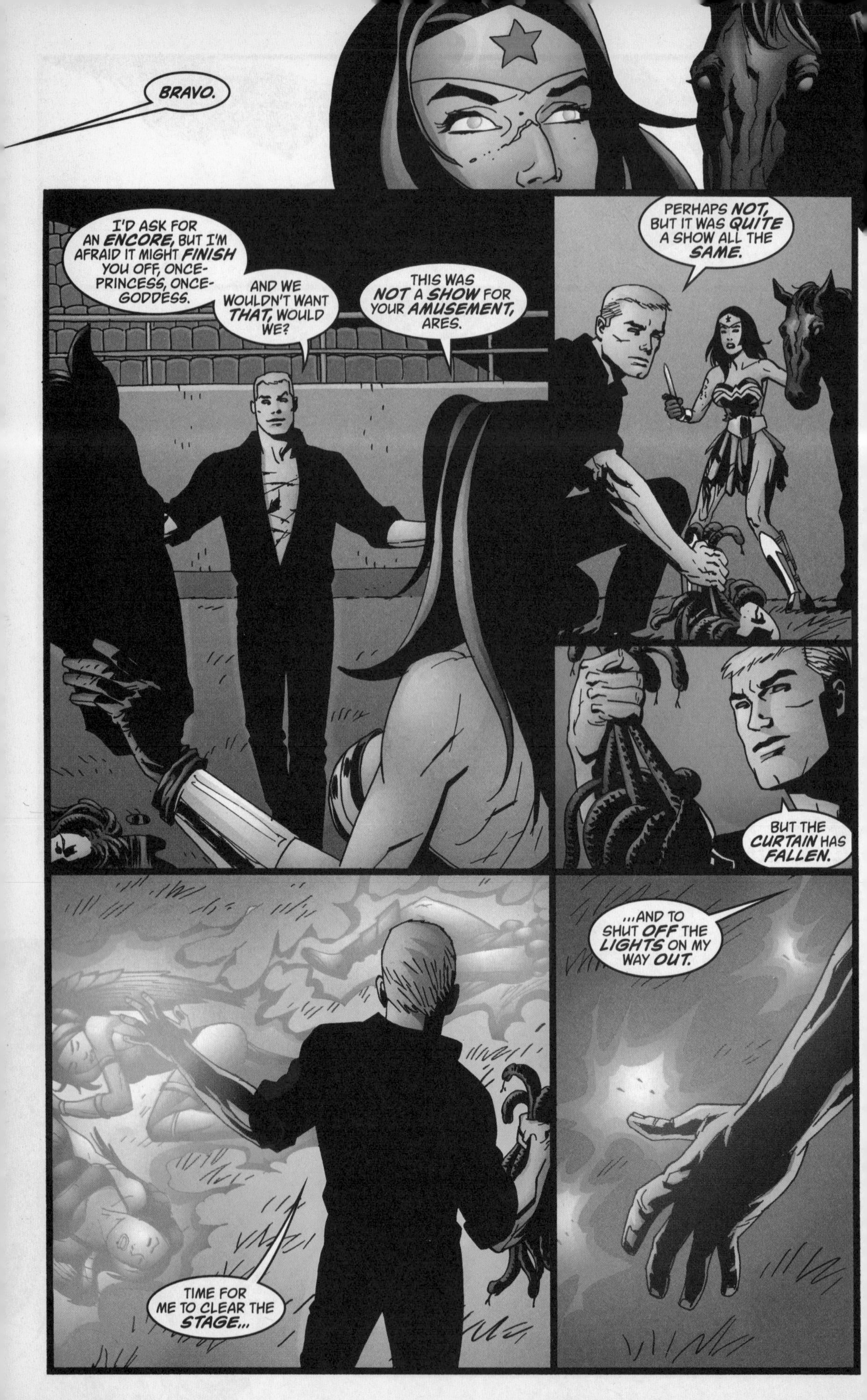
BRAVO.
I'D ASK FOR AN ENCORE, BUT I'M AFRAID IT MIGHT FINISH YOU OFF, ONCE-PRINCESS, ONCE-GODDESS.
AND WE WOULDN'T WANT THAT, WOULD WE?
THIS WAS NOT A SHOW FOR YOUR AMUSEMENT, ARES.
PERHAPS NOT, BUT IT WAS QUITE A SHOW ALL THE SAME.
BUT THE CURTAIN HAS FALLEN.
TIME FOR ME TO CLEAR THE STAGE...
...AND TO SHUT OFF THE LIGHTS ON MY WAY OUT.

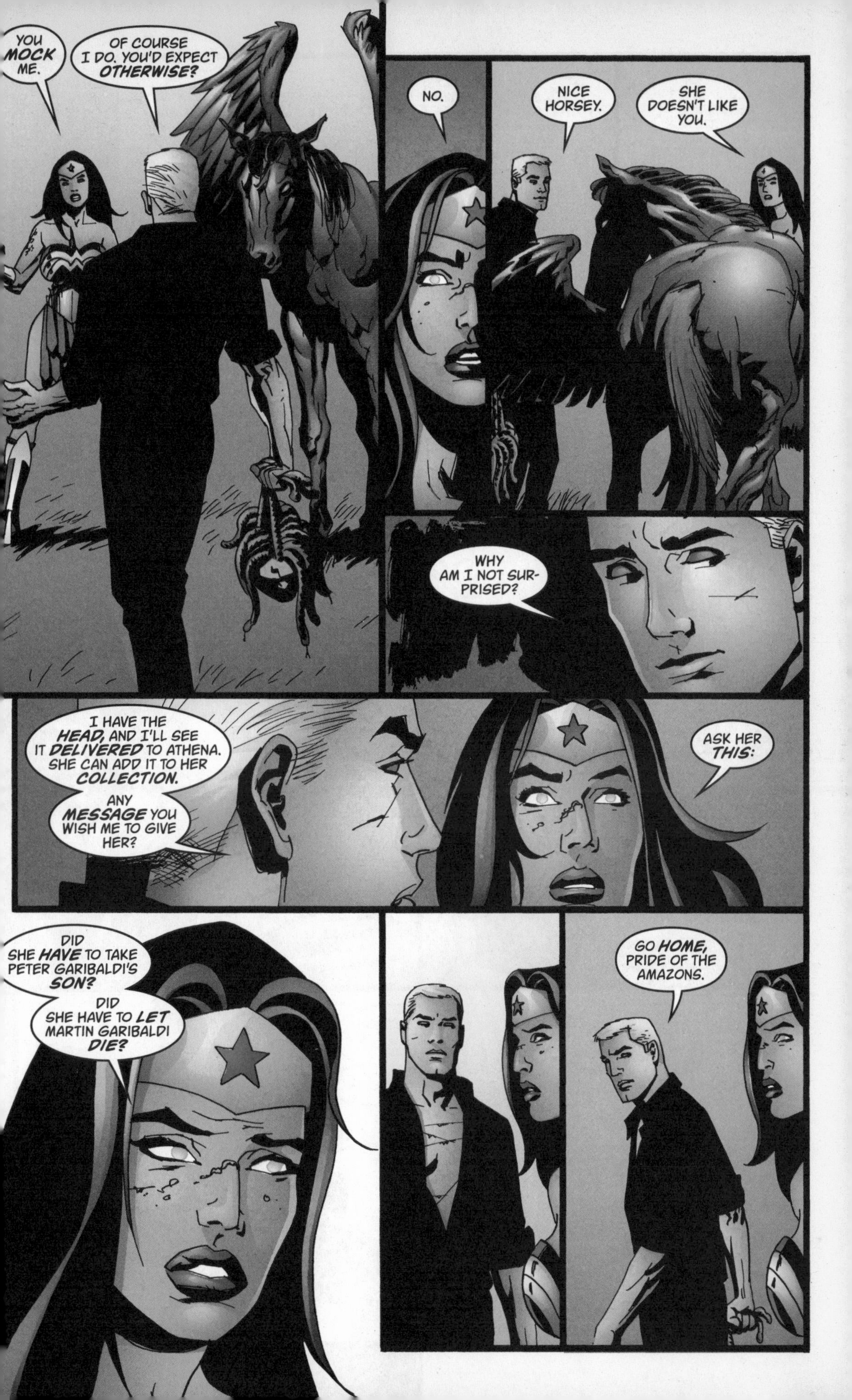
YOU MOCK ME.
OF COURSE I DO. YOU'D EXPECT OTHERWISE?
NO.
NICE HORSEY.
SHE DOESN'T LIKE YOU.
WHY AM I NOT SURPRISED?
I HAVE THE HEAD, AND I'LL SEE IT DELIVERED TO ATHENA. SHE CAN ADD IT TO HER COLLECTION.
ANY MESSAGE YOU WISH ME TO GIVE HER?
ASK HER THIS:
DID SHE HAVE TO TAKE PETER GARIBALDI'S SON?
DID SHE HAVE TO LET MARTIN GARIBALDI DIE?
GO HOME, PRIDE OF THE AMAZONS.

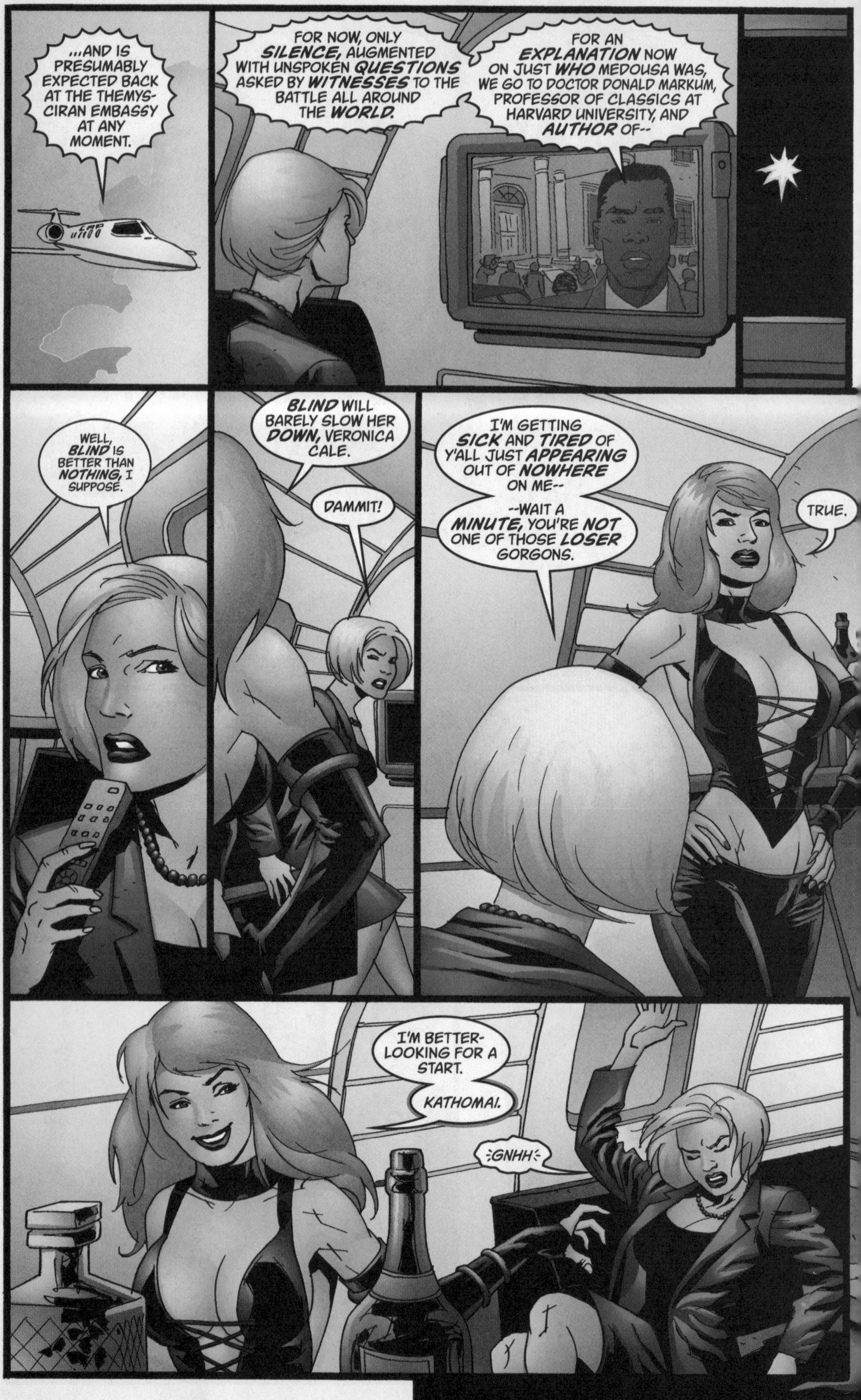
...AND IS PRESUMABLY EXPECTED BACK AT THE THEMYSCIRAN EMBASSY AT ANY MOMENT.
FOR NOW, ONLY SILENCE, AUGMENTED WITH UNSPOKEN QUESTIONS ASKED BY WITNESSES TO THE BATTLE ALL AROUND THE WORLD.
FOR AN EXPLANATION NOW ON JUST WHO MEDOUSA WAS, WE GO TO DOCTOR DONALD MARKUM, PROFESSOR OF CLASSICS AT HARVARD UNIVERSITY, AND AUTHOR OF--
WELL, BLIND IS BETTER THAN NOTHING, I SUPPOSE.
BLIND WILL BARELY SLOW HER DOWN, VERONICA CALE.
DAMMIT!
I'M GETTING SICK AND TIRED OF Y'ALL JUST APPEARING OUT OF NOWHERE ON ME--
--WAIT A MINUTE, YOU'RE NOT ONE OF THOSE LOSER GORGONS.
TRUE.
I'M BETTER-LOOKING FOR A START.
KATHOMAI.
GNHH

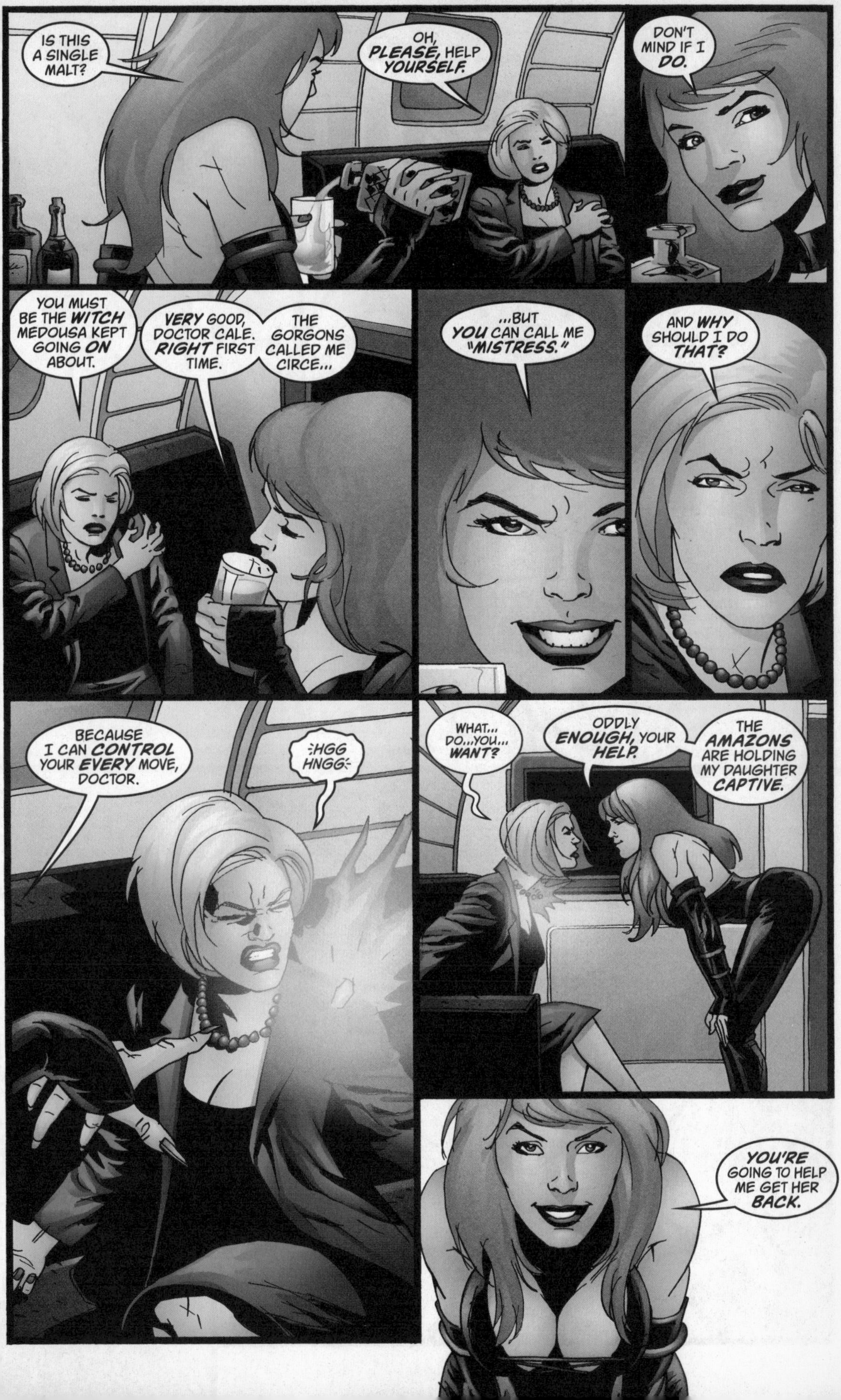
IS THIS A SINGLE MALT?
OH, PLEASE, HELP YOURSELF.
DON'T MIND IF I DO.
YOU MUST BE THE WITCH MEDOUSA KEPT GOING ON ABOUT.
VERY GOOD, DOCTOR CALE. RIGHT FIRST TIME.
THE GORGONS CALLED ME CIRCE...
...BUT YOU CAN CALL ME "MISTRESS."
AND WHY SHOULD I DO THAT?
BECAUSE I CAN CONTROL YOUR EVERY MOVE, DOCTOR.
HGG HNGG
WHAT... DO...YOU... WANT?
ODDLY ENOUGH, YOUR HELP.
THE AMAZONS ARE HOLDING MY DAUGHTER CAPTIVE.
YOU'RE GOING TO HELP ME GET HER BACK.

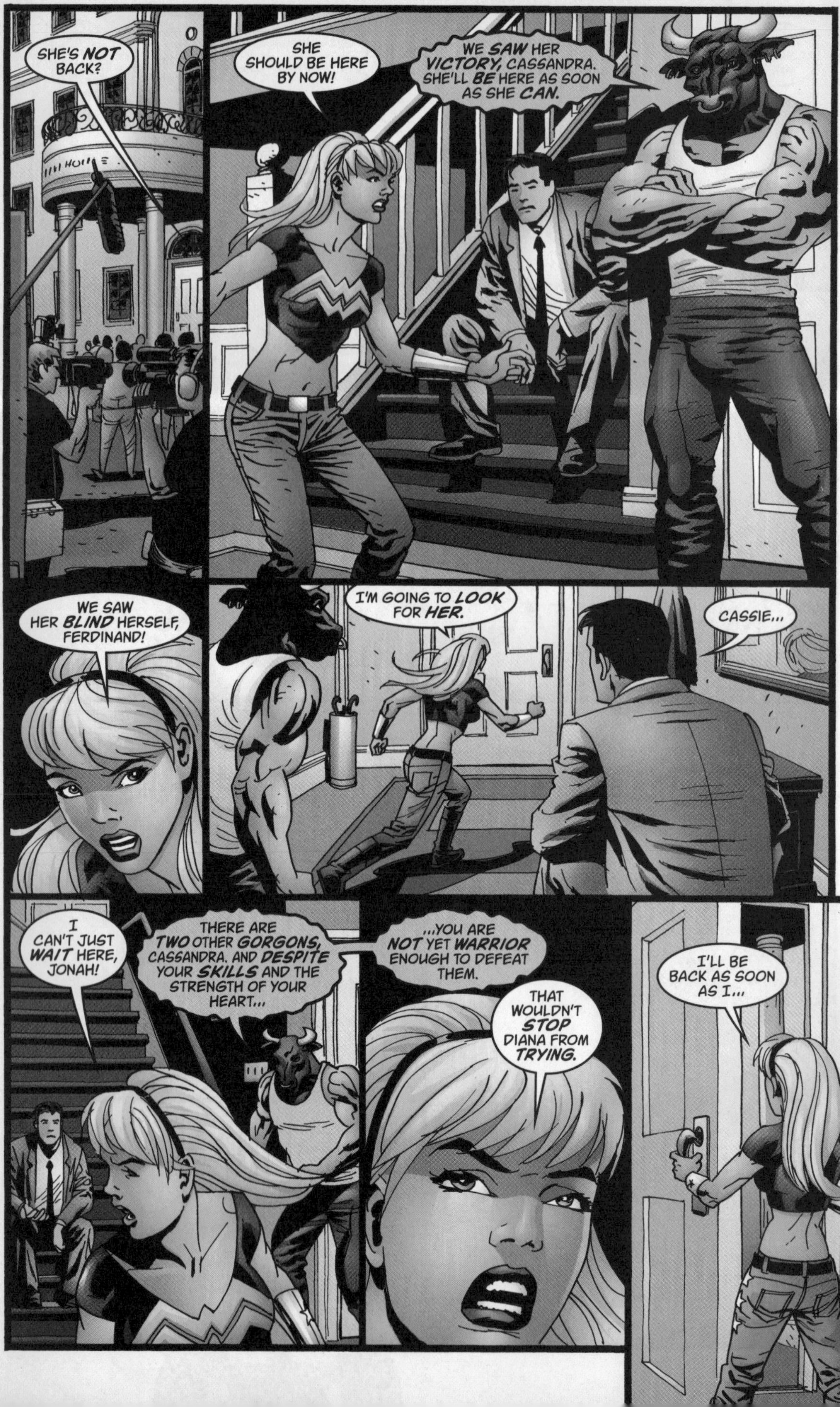

SHE'S NOT BACK?
SHE SHOULD BE HERE BY NOW!
WE SAW HER VICTORY, CASSANDRA. SHE'LL BE HERE AS SOON AS SHE CAN.
WE SAW HER BLIND HERSELF, FERDINAND!
I'M GOING TO LOOK FOR HER.
CASSIE...
I CAN'T JUST WAIT HERE, JONAH!
THERE ARE TWO OTHER GORGONS, CASSANDRA. AND DESPITE YOUR SKILLS AND THE STRENGTH OF YOUR HEART...
...YOU ARE NOT YET WARRIOR ENOUGH TO DEFEAT THEM.
THAT WOULDN'T STOP DIANA FROM TRYING.
I'LL BE BACK AS SOON AS I...

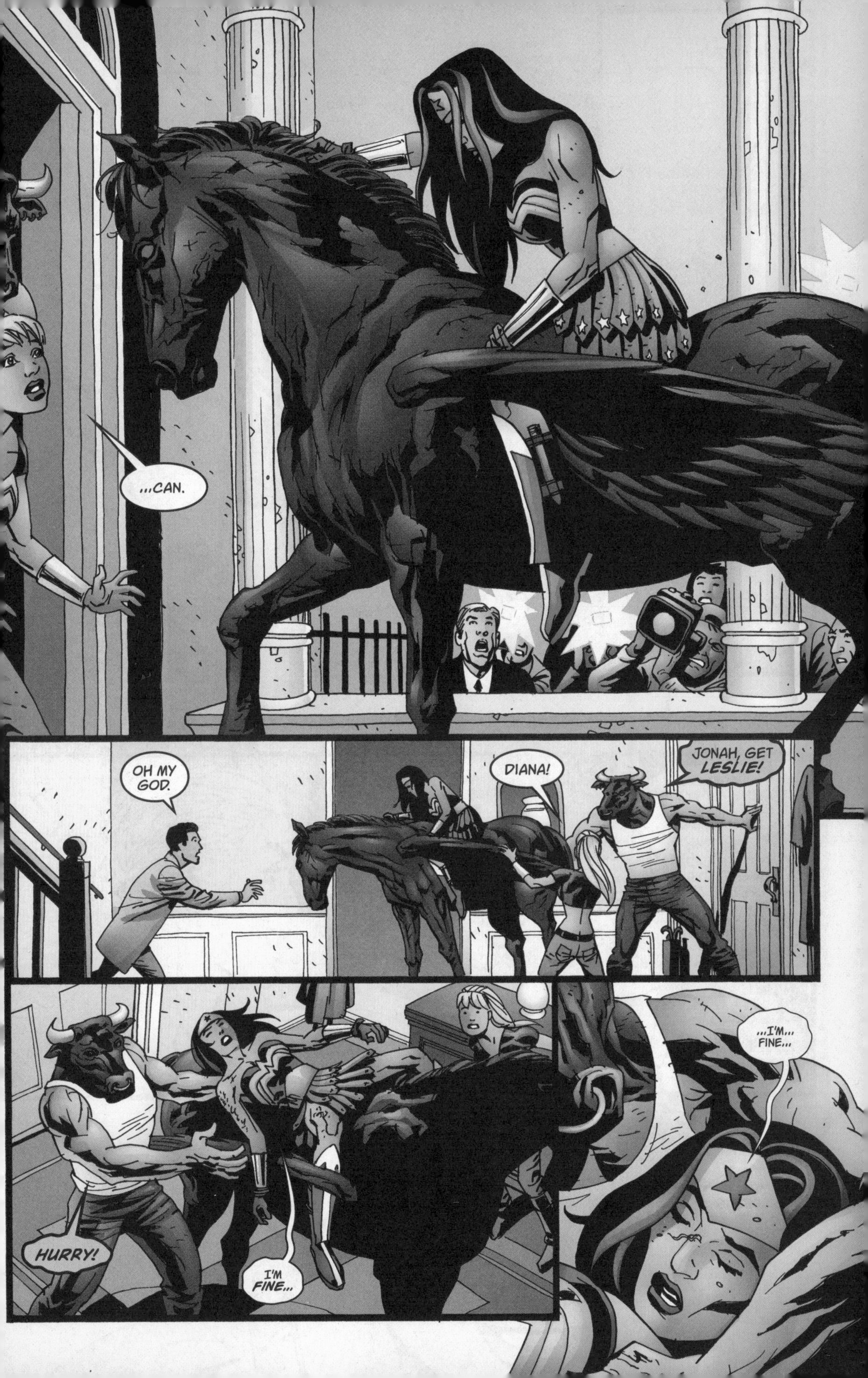
...CAN.
OH MY GOD.
DIANA!
JONAH, GET LESLIE!
HURRY!
I'M FINE...
...I'M... FINE...

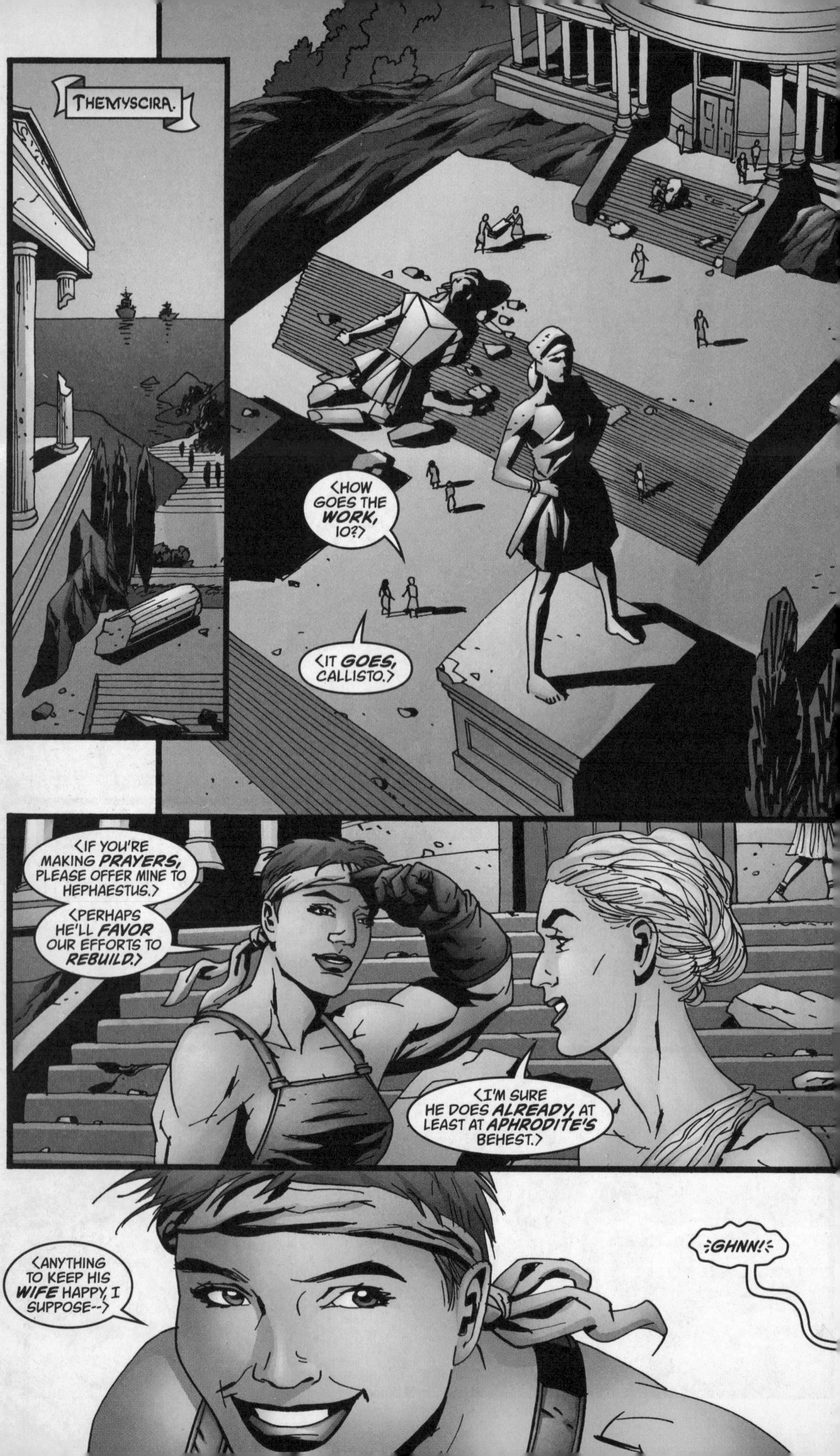
THEMYSCIRA.
<HOW GOES THE WORK, IO?>
<IT GOES, CALLISTO.>
<IF YOU'RE MAKING PRAYERS, PLEASE OFFER MINE TO HEPHAESTUS.>
<PERHAPS HE'LL FAVOR OUR EFFORTS TO REBUILD.>
<I'M SURE HE DOES ALREADY, AT LEAST AT APHRODITE'S BEHEST.>
<ANYTHING TO KEEP HIS WIFE HAPPY, I SUPPOSE-->
GHNN!

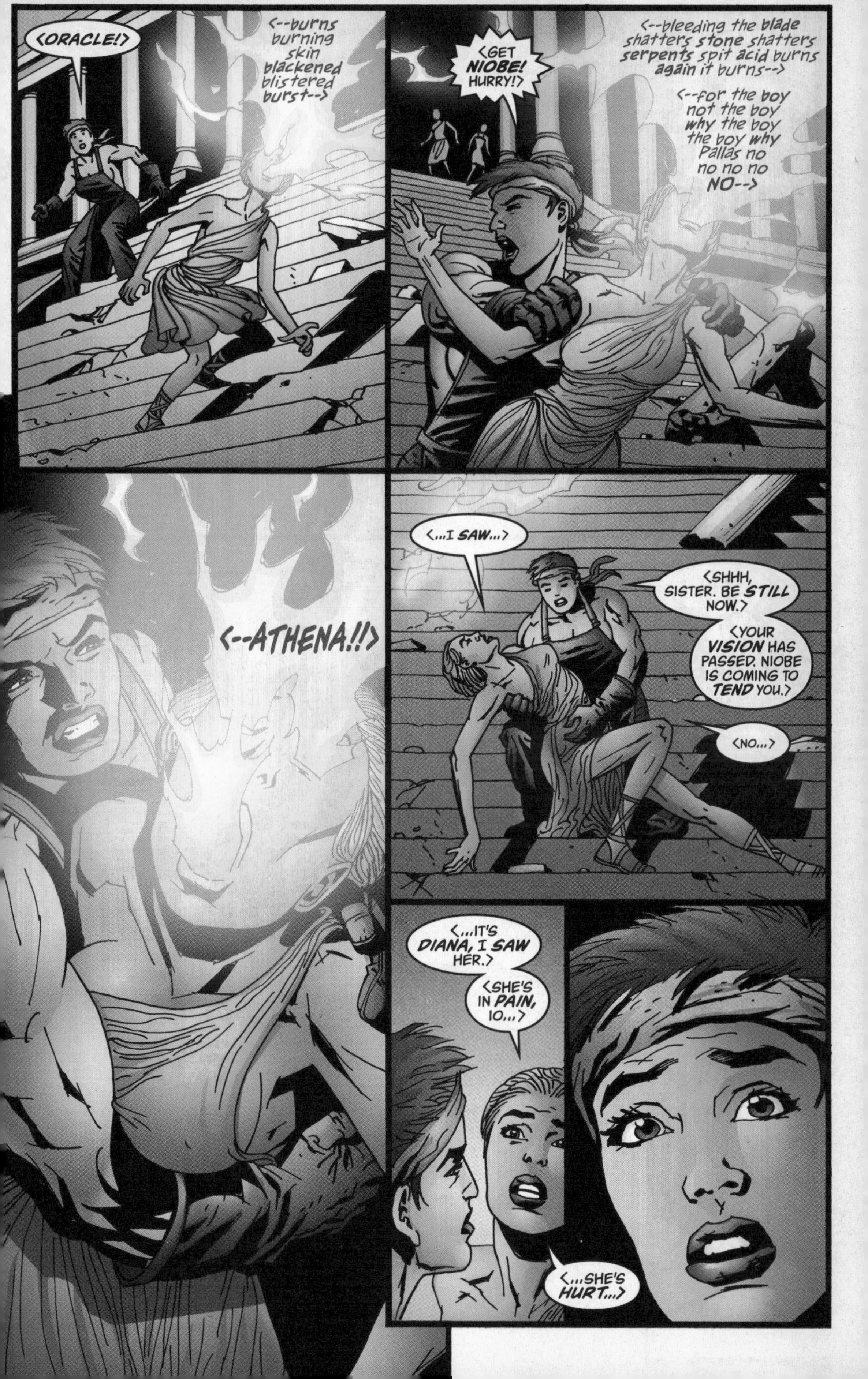

<ORACLE!>
<--burns burning skin blackened blistered burst-->
<GET NIOBE! HURRY!>
<--bleeding the blade shatters stone shatters serpents spit acid burns again it burns-->
<--for the boy not the boy why the boy the boy why Pallas no no no no NO-->
<--ATHENA!!>
<...I SAW...>
<SHHH, SISTER. BE STILL NOW.>
<YOUR VISION HAS PASSED. NIOBE IS COMING TO TEND YOU.>
<NO...>
<...IT'S DIANA, I SAW HER.>
<SHE'S IN PAIN, IO...>
<...SHE'S HURT...>

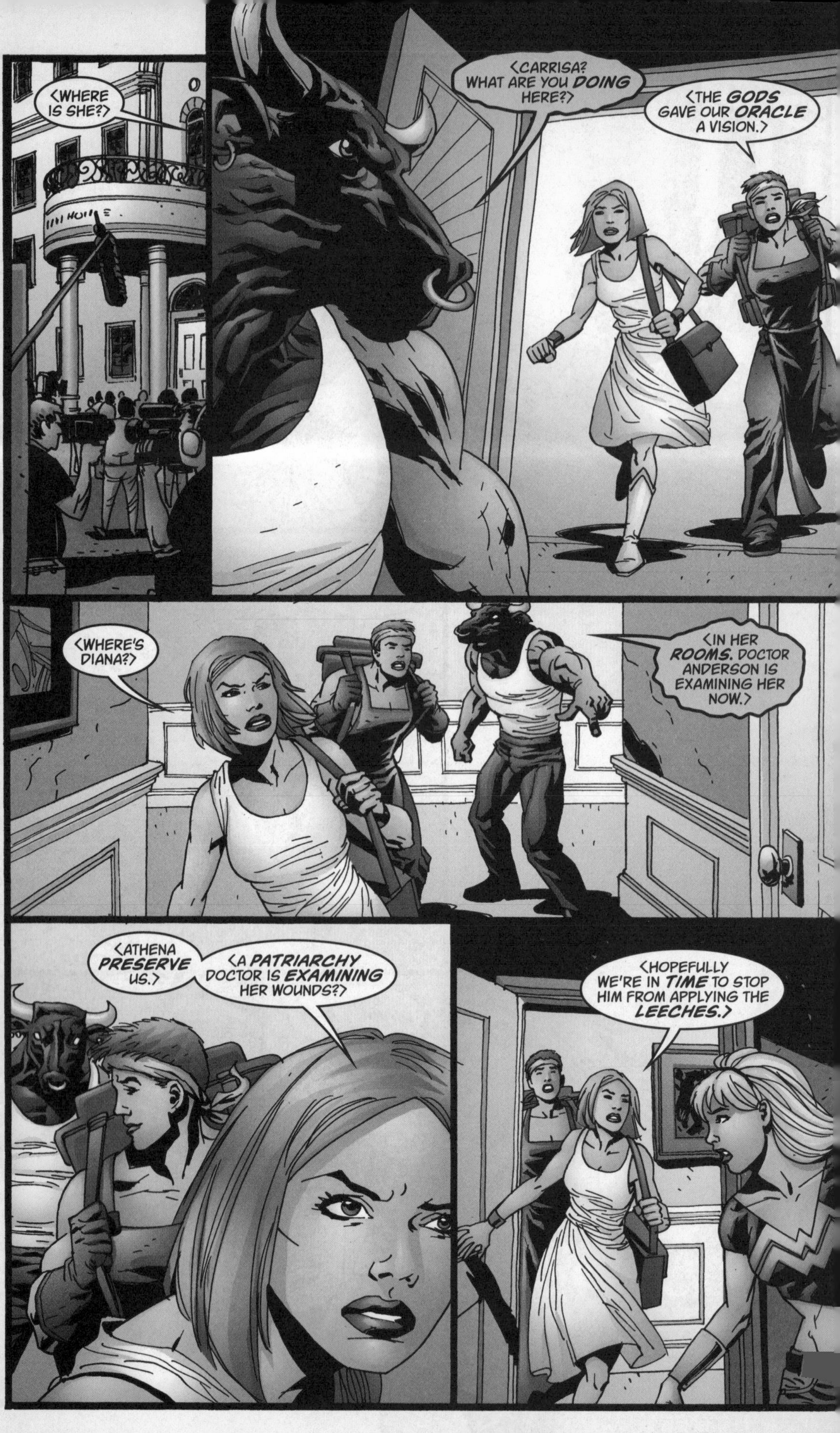

<WHERE IS SHE?>
<CARRISA? WHAT ARE YOU DOING HERE?>
<THE GODS GAVE OUR ORACLE A VISION.>
<WHERE'S DIANA?>
<IN HER ROOMS. DOCTOR ANDERSON IS EXAMINING HER NOW.>
<ATHENA PRESERVE US.>
<A PATRIARCHY DOCTOR IS EXAMINING HER WOUNDS?>
<HOPEFULLY WE'RE IN TIME TO STOP HIM FROM APPLYING THE LEECHES.>

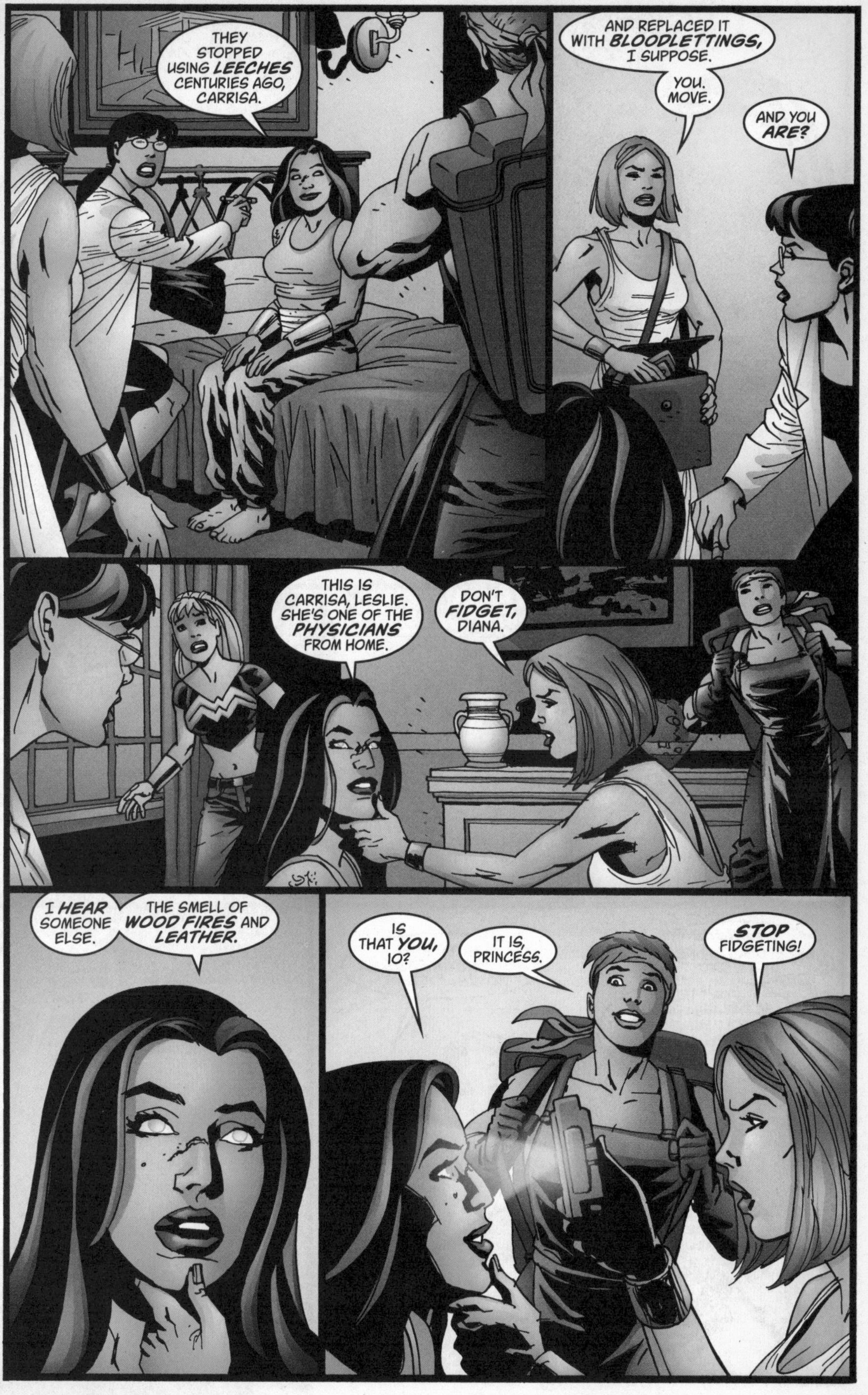
THEY STOPPED USING LEECHES CENTURIES AGO, CARRISA.
AND REPLACED IT WITH BLOODLETTINGS, I SUPPOSE.
YOU. MOVE.
AND YOU ARE?
THIS IS CARRISA, LESLIE. SHE'S ONE OF THE PHYSICIANS FROM HOME.
DON'T FIDGET, DIANA.
I HEAR SOMEONE ELSE.
THE SMELL OF WOOD FIRES AND LEATHER.
IS THAT YOU, IO?
IT IS, PRINCESS.
STOP FIDGETING!

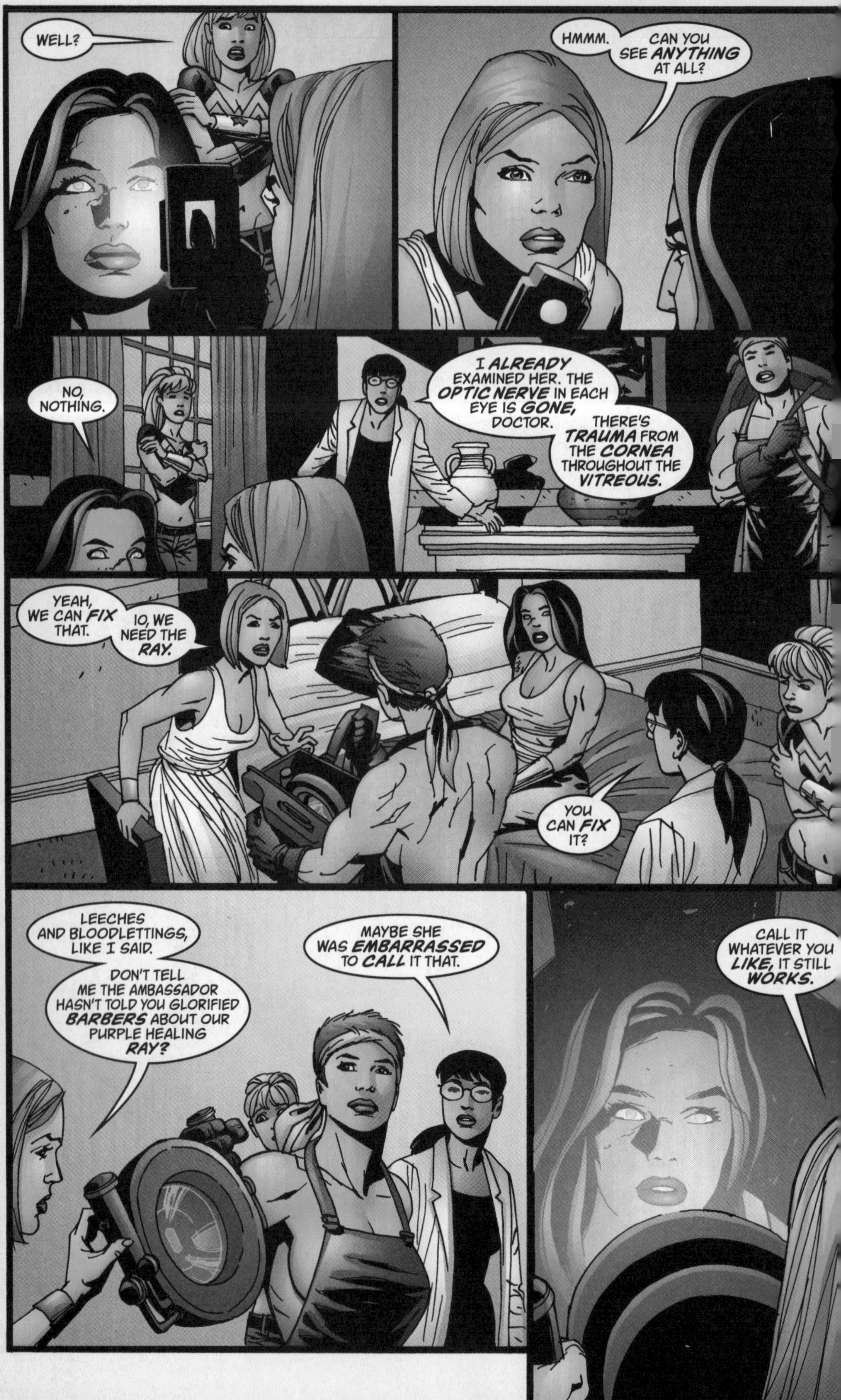

WELL?
HMMM.
CAN YOU SEE ANYTHING AT ALL?
NO, NOTHING.
I ALREADY EXAMINED HER. THE OPTIC NERVE IN EACH EYE IS GONE, DOCTOR.
THERE'S TRAUMA FROM THE CORNEA THROUGHOUT THE VITREOUS.
YEAH, WE CAN FIX THAT.
IO, WE NEED THE RAY.
YOU CAN FIX IT?
LEECHES AND BLOODLETTINGS, LIKE I SAID.
DON'T TELL ME THE AMBASSADOR HASN'T TOLD YOU GLORIFIED BARBERS ABOUT OUR PURPLE HEALING RAY?
MAYBE SHE WAS EMBARRASSED TO CALL IT THAT.
CALL IT WHATEVER YOU LIKE, IT STILL WORKS.

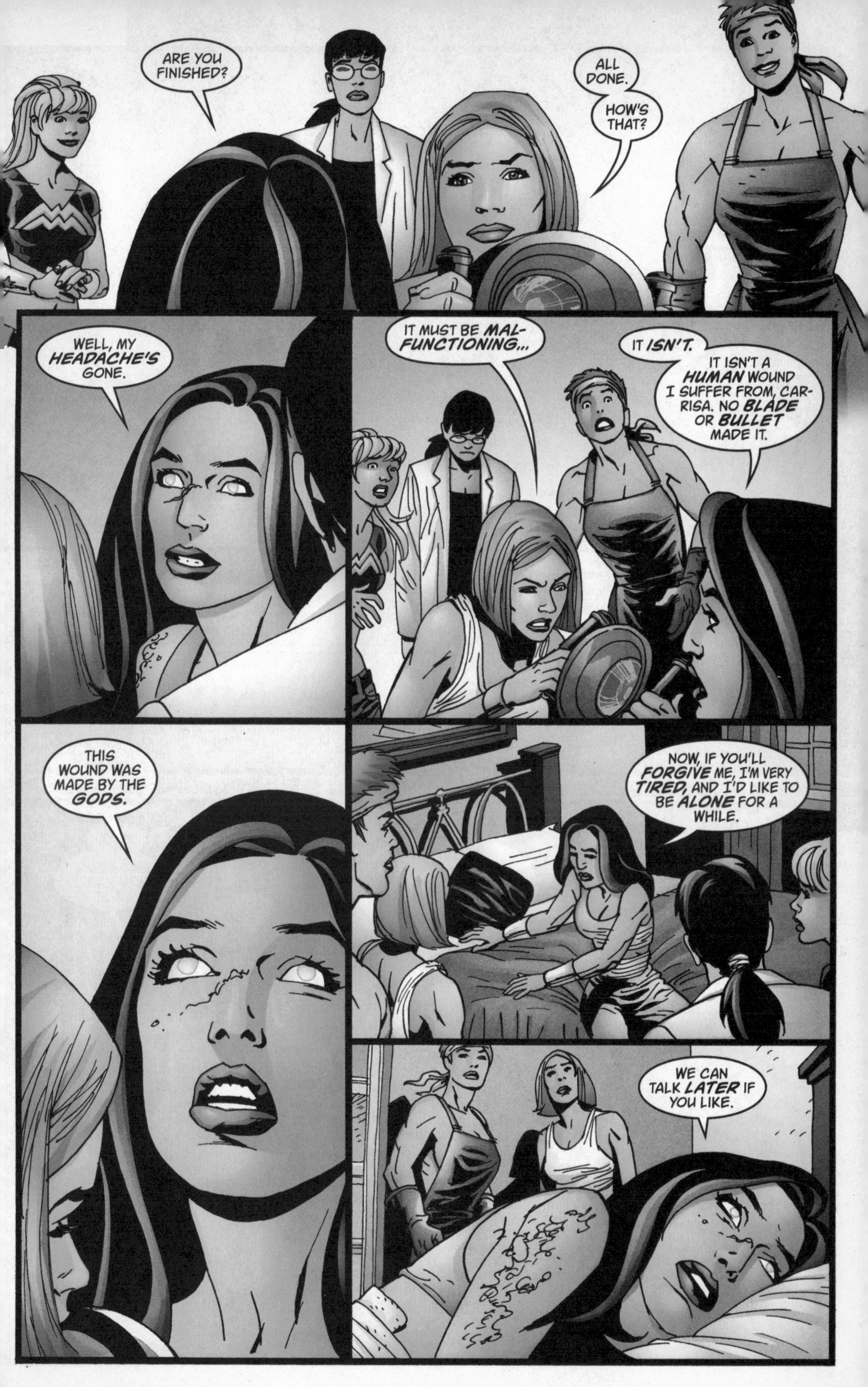

ARE YOU FINISHED?
ALL DONE.
HOW'S THAT?
WELL, MY HEADACHE'S GONE.
IT MUST BE MAL-FUNCTIONING...
IT ISN'T.
IT ISN'T A HUMAN WOUND I SUFFER FROM, CAR-RISA. NO BLADE OR BULLET MADE IT.
THIS WOUND WAS MADE BY THE GODS.
NOW, IF YOU'LL FORGIVE ME, I'M VERY TIRED, AND I'D LIKE TO BE ALONE FOR A WHILE.
WE CAN TALK LATER IF YOU LIKE.

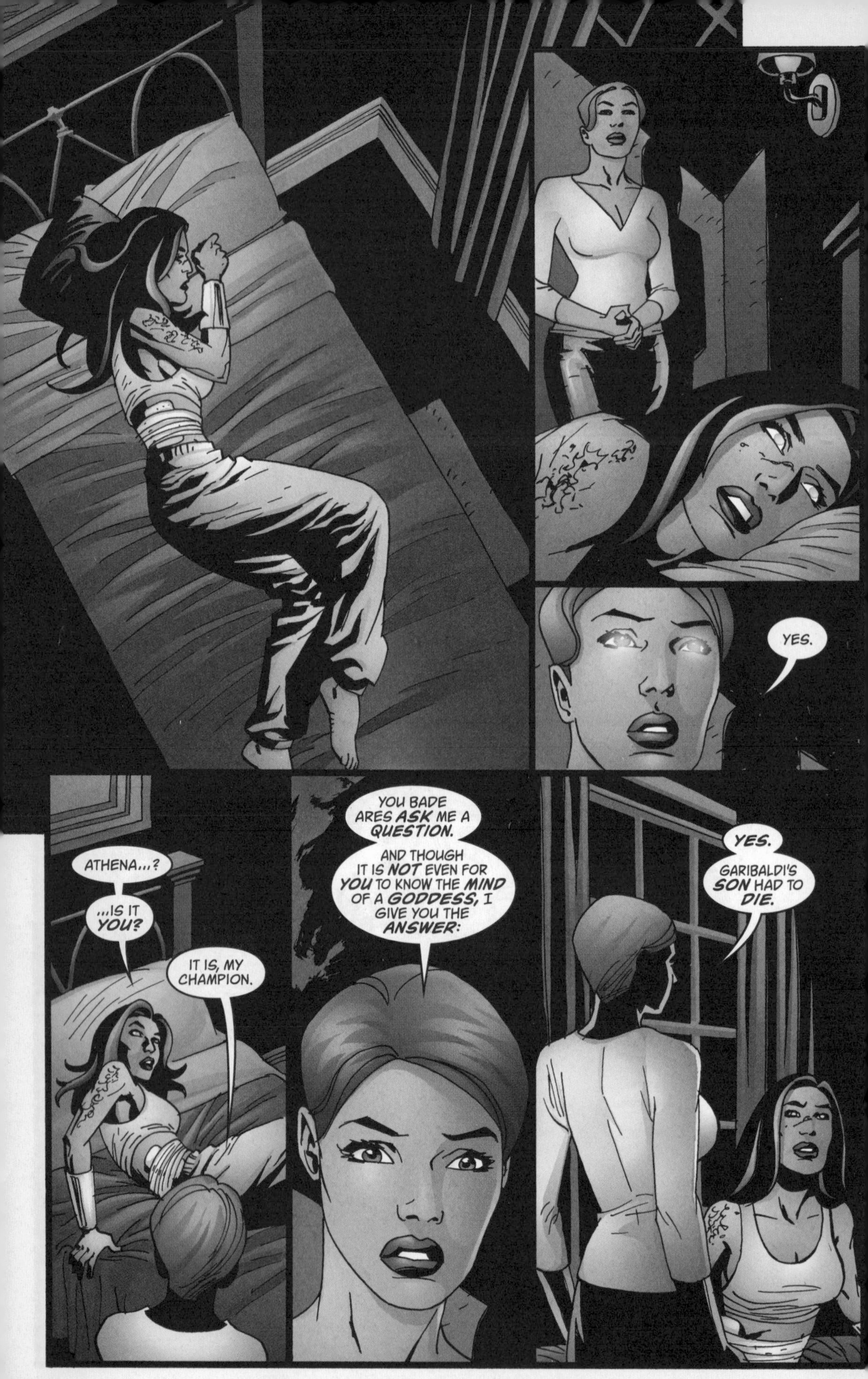
YES.
ATHENA...?
...IS IT YOU?
IT IS, MY CHAMPION.
YOU BADE ARES ASK ME A QUESTION.
AND THOUGH IT IS NOT EVEN FOR YOU TO KNOW THE MIND OF A GODDESS, I GIVE YOU THE ANSWER:
YES.
GARIBALDI'S SON HAD TO DIE.

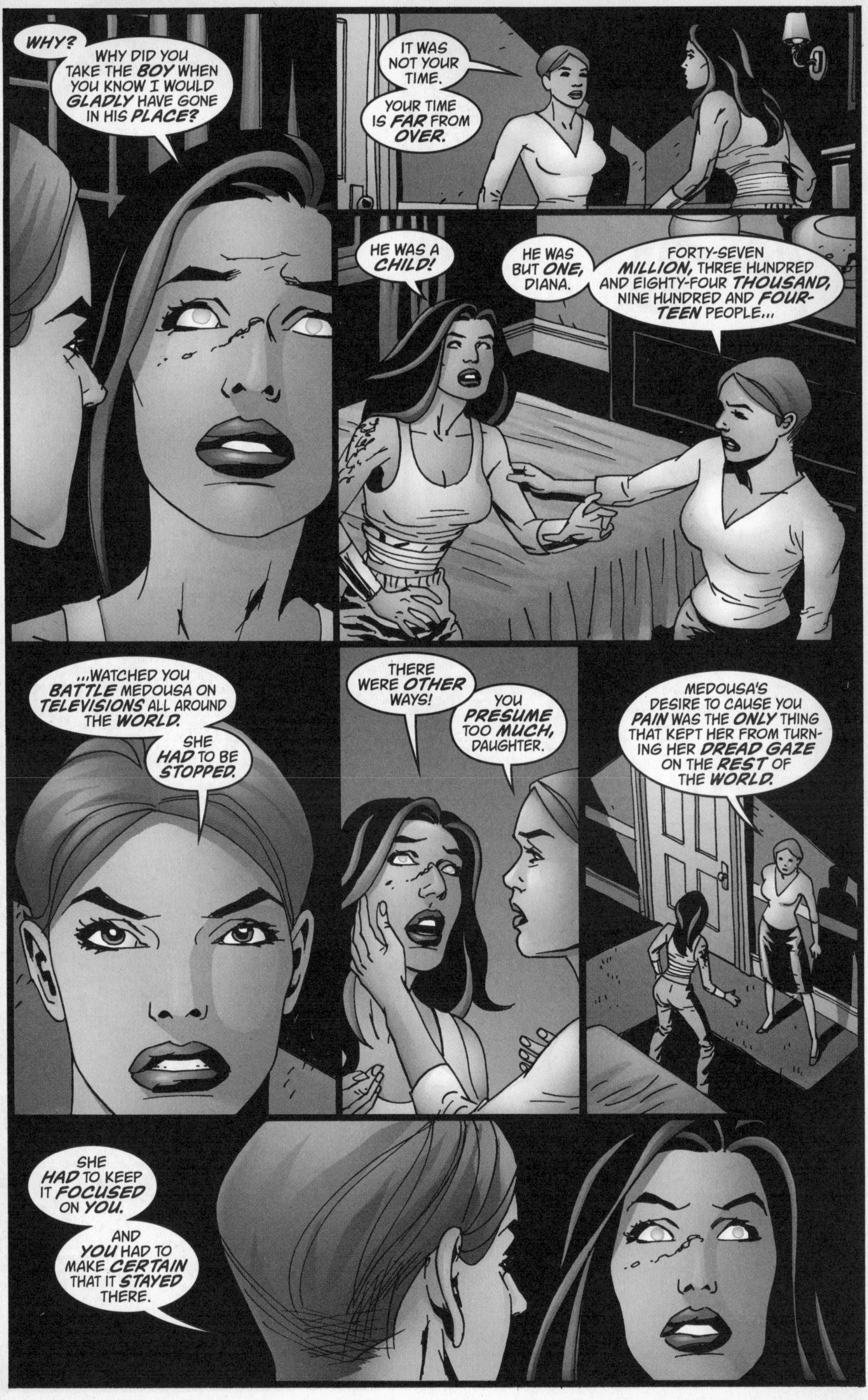
WHY?
WHY DID YOU TAKE THE BOY WHEN YOU KNOW I WOULD GLADLY HAVE GONE IN HIS PLACE?
IT WAS NOT YOUR TIME.
YOUR TIME IS FAR FROM OVER.
HE WAS A CHILD!
HE WAS BUT ONE, DIANA.
FORTY-SEVEN MILLION, THREE HUNDRED AND EIGHTY-FOUR THOUSAND, NINE HUNDRED AND FOURTEEN PEOPLE...
...WATCHED YOU BATTLE MEDOUSA ON TELEVISIONS ALL AROUND THE WORLD.
SHE HAD TO BE STOPPED.
THERE WERE OTHER WAYS!
YOU PRESUME TOO MUCH, DAUGHTER.
MEDOUSA'S DESIRE TO CAUSE YOU PAIN WAS THE ONLY THING THAT KEPT HER FROM TURNING HER DREAD GAZE ON THE REST OF THE WORLD.
SHE HAD TO KEEP IT FOCUSED ON YOU.
AND YOU HAD TO MAKE CERTAIN THAT IT STAYED THERE.

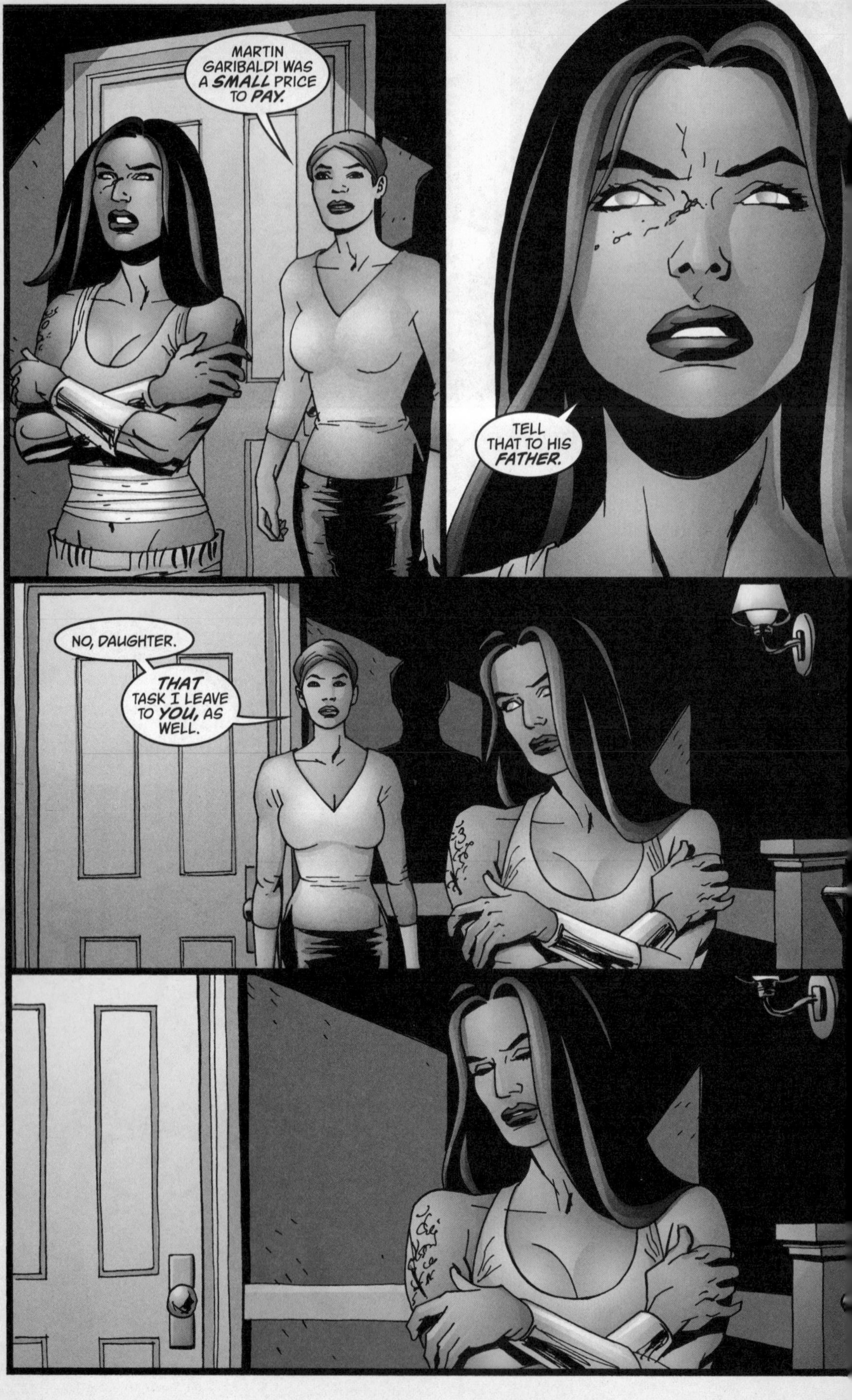
MARTIN GARIBALDI WAS A SMALL PRICE TO PAY.
TELL THAT TO HIS FATHER.
NO, DAUGHTER.
THAT TASK I LEAVE TO YOU, AS WELL.

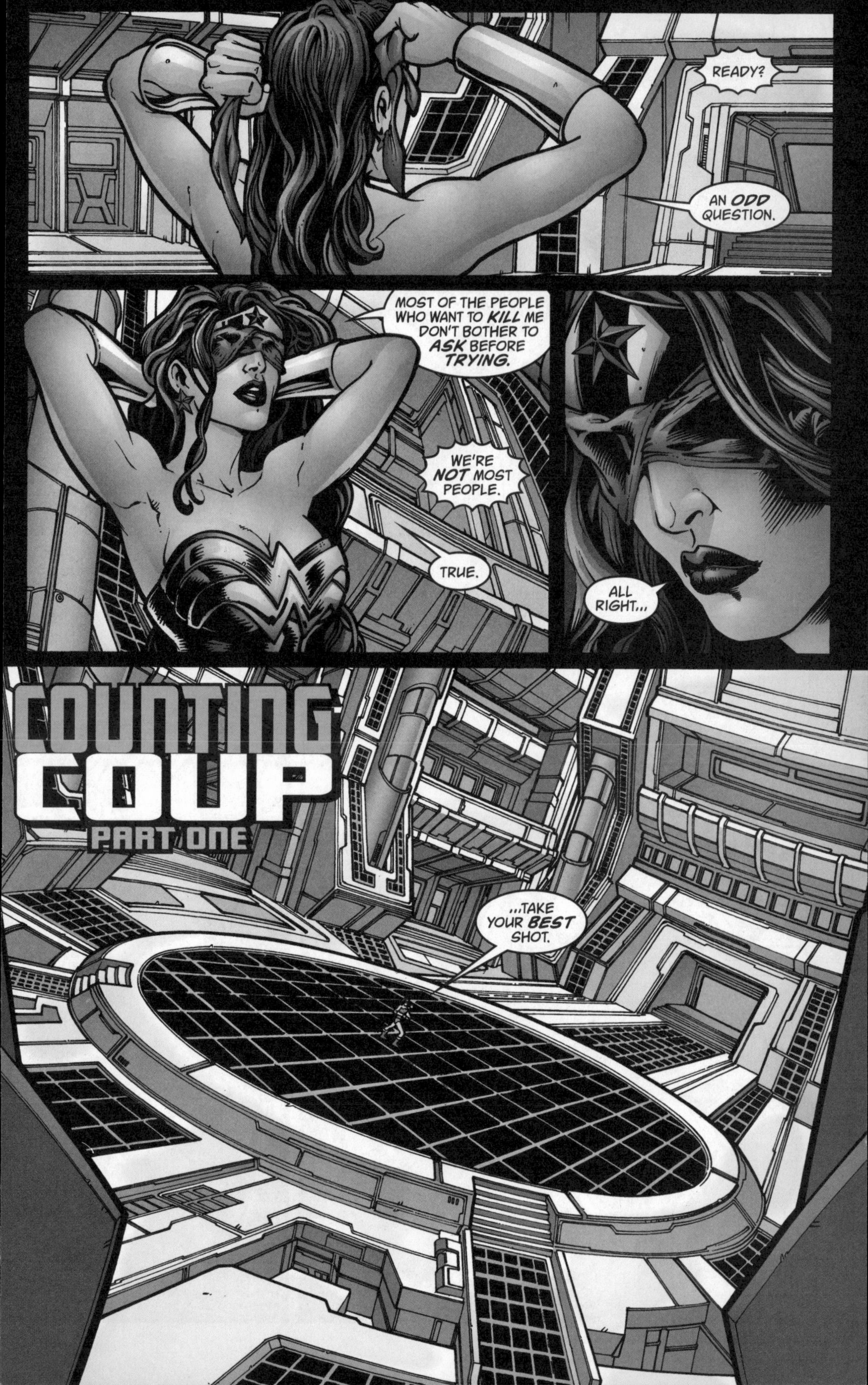
READY?
AN ODD QUESTION.
MOST OF THE PEOPLE WHO WANT TO KILL ME DON'T BOTHER TO ASK BEFORE TRYING.
WE'RE NOT MOST PEOPLE.
TRUE.
ALL RIGHT...
COUNTING COUP
PART ONE
...TAKE YOUR BEST SHOT.

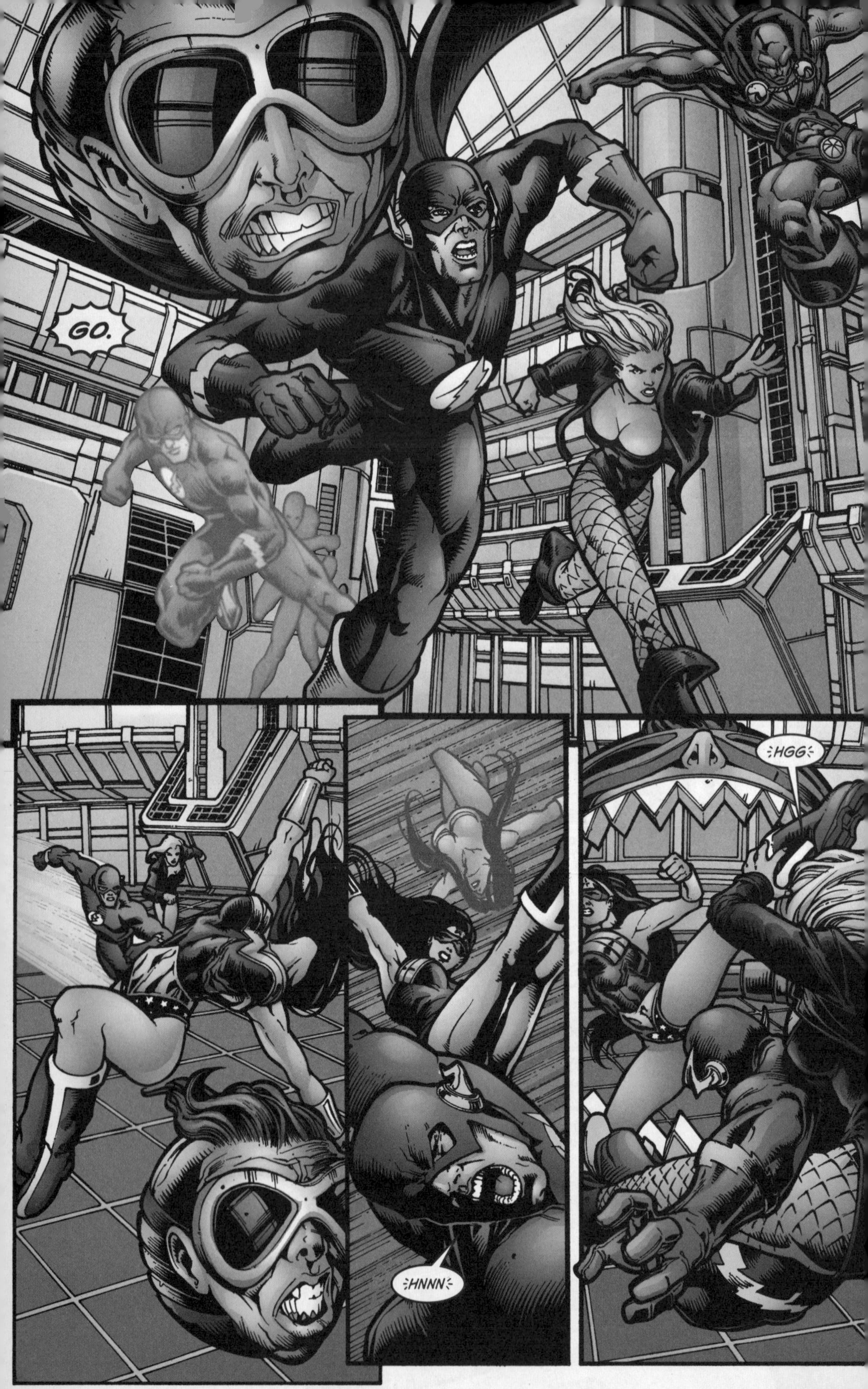
GO.
HNNN
HGG

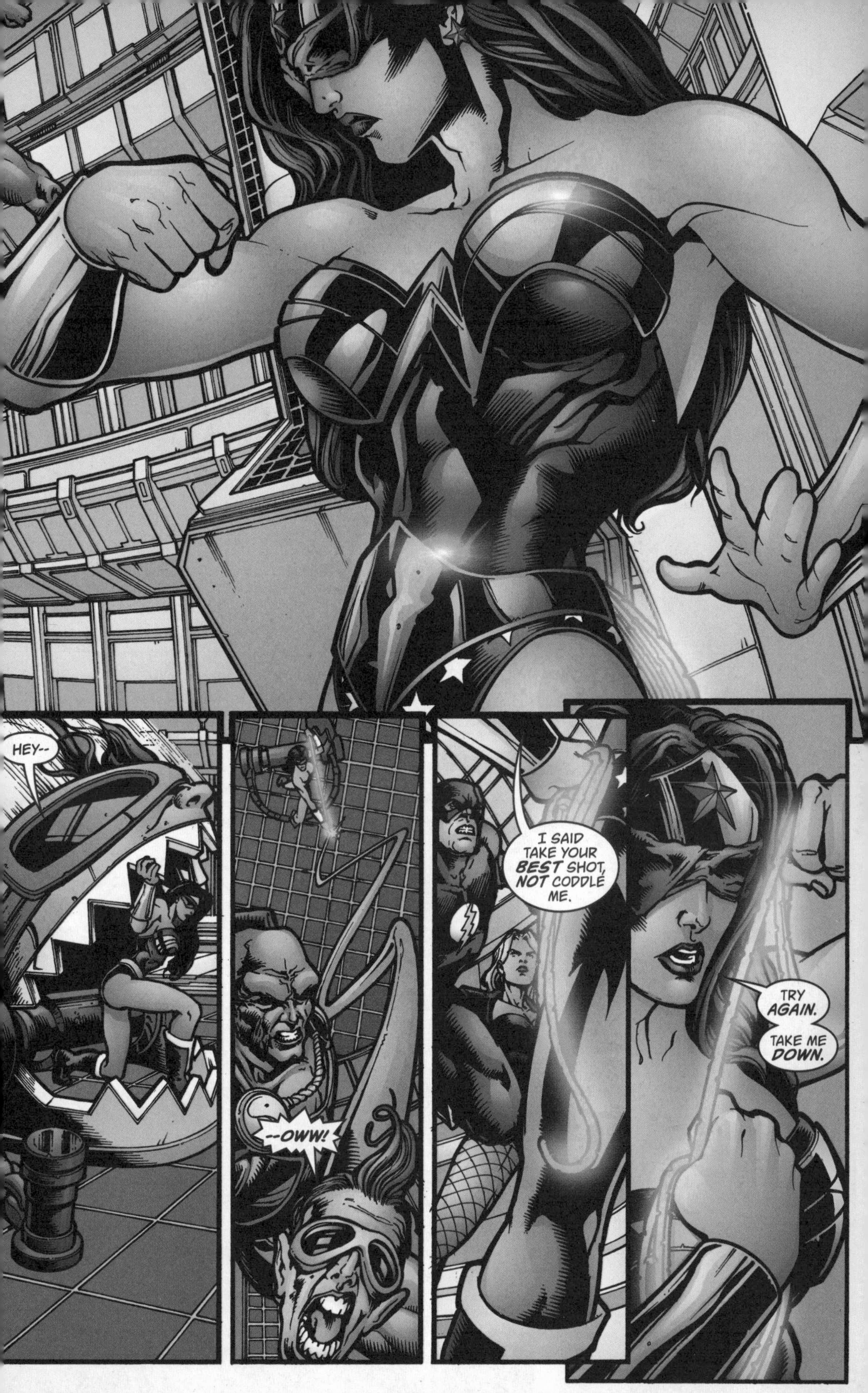
HEY--
--OWW!
I SAID TAKE YOUR BEST SHOT, NOT CODDLE ME.
TRY AGAIN.
TAKE ME DOWN.

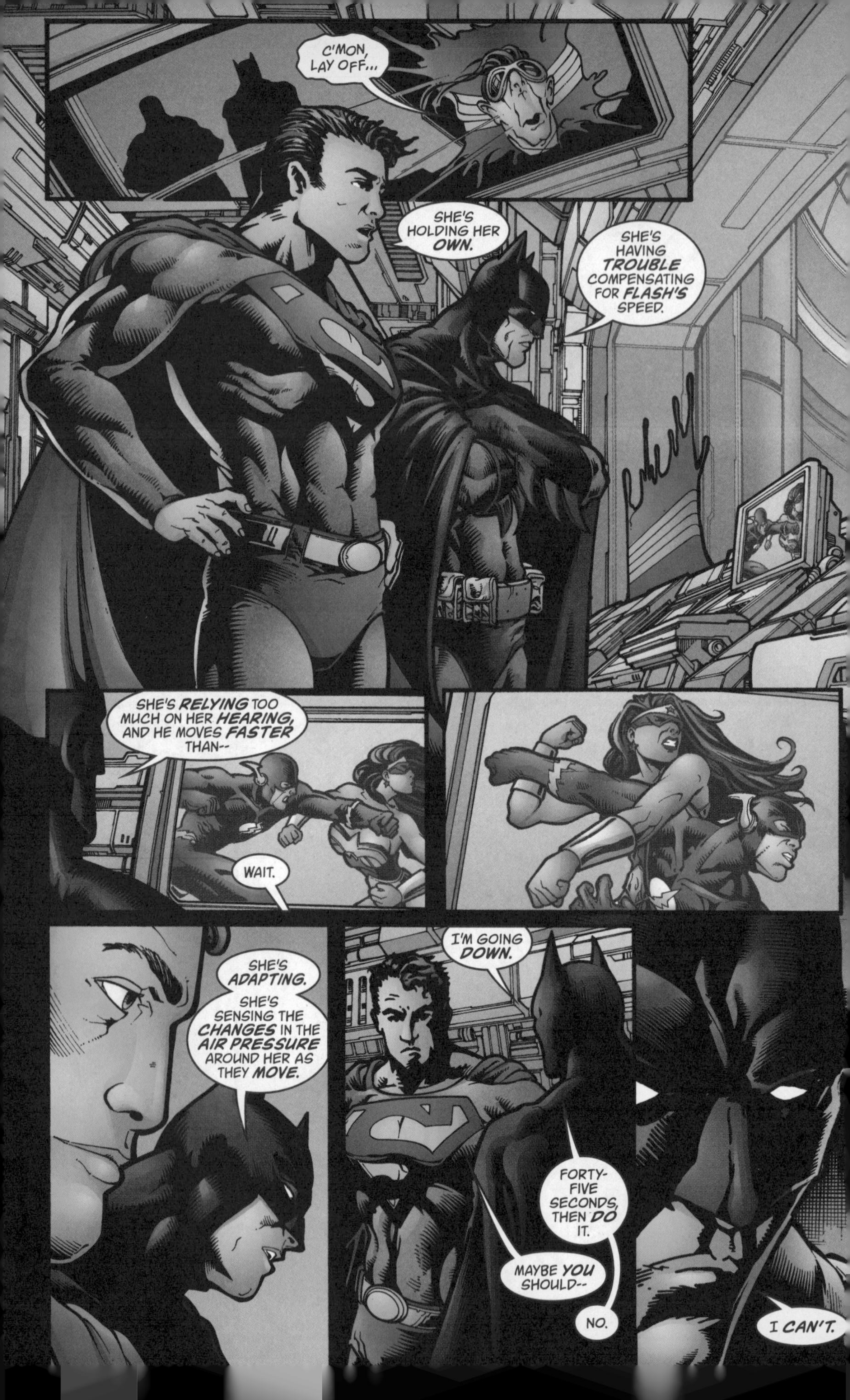
C'MON, LAY OFF...
SHE'S HOLDING HER OWN.
SHE'S HAVING TROUBLE COMPENSATING FOR FLASH'S SPEED.
SHE'S RELYING TOO MUCH ON HER HEARING, AND HE MOVES FASTER THAN--
WAIT.
SHE'S ADAPTING.
SHE'S SENSING THE CHANGES IN THE AIR PRESSURE AROUND HER AS THEY MOVE.
I'M GOING DOWN.
FORTY-FIVE SECONDS, THEN DO IT.
MAYBE YOU SHOULD--
NO.
I CAN'T.

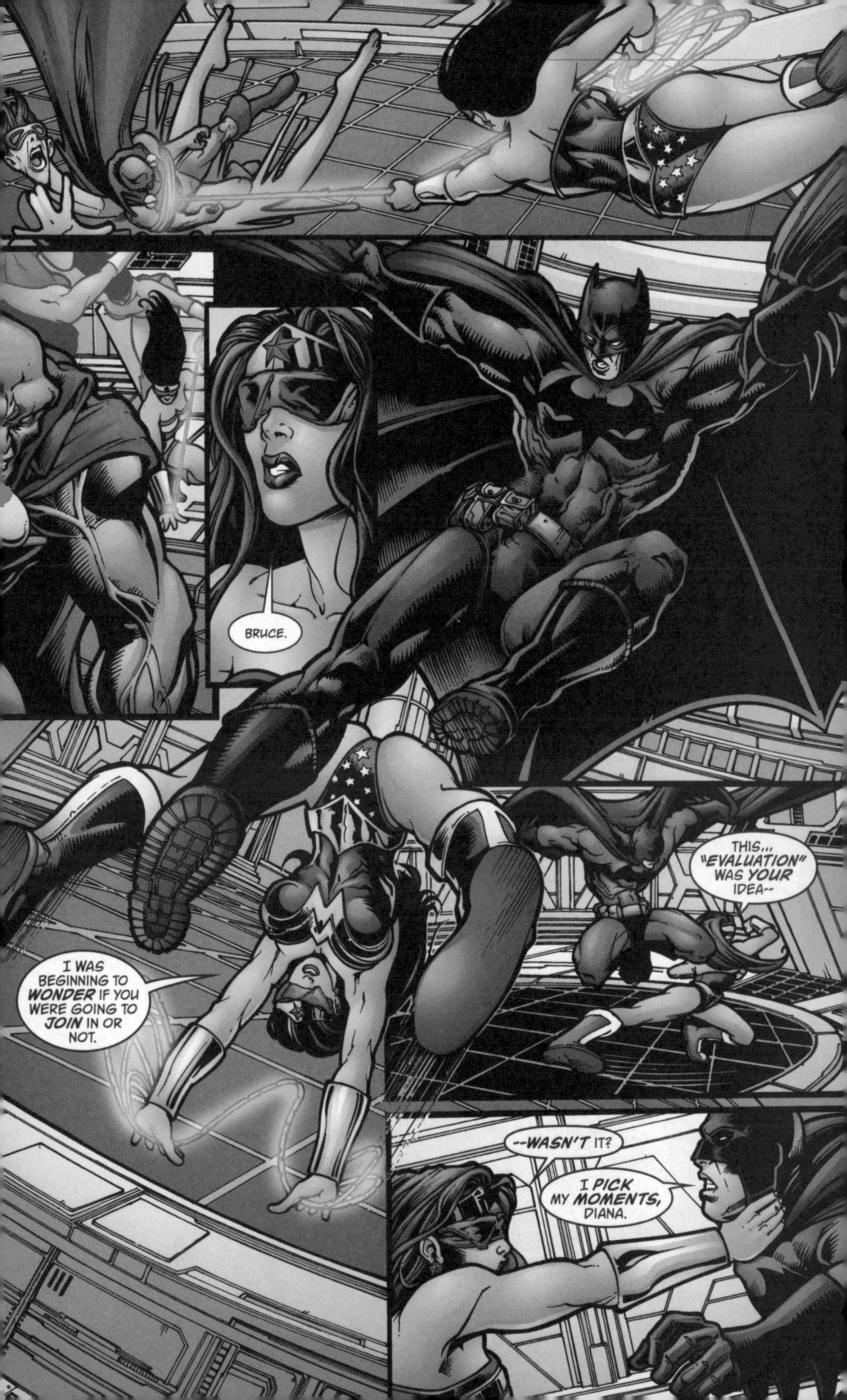

BRUCE.
I WAS BEGINNING TO WONDER IF YOU WERE GOING TO JOIN IN OR NOT.
THIS... "EVALUATION" WAS YOUR IDEA--
--WASN'T IT?
I PICK MY MOMENTS, DIANA.

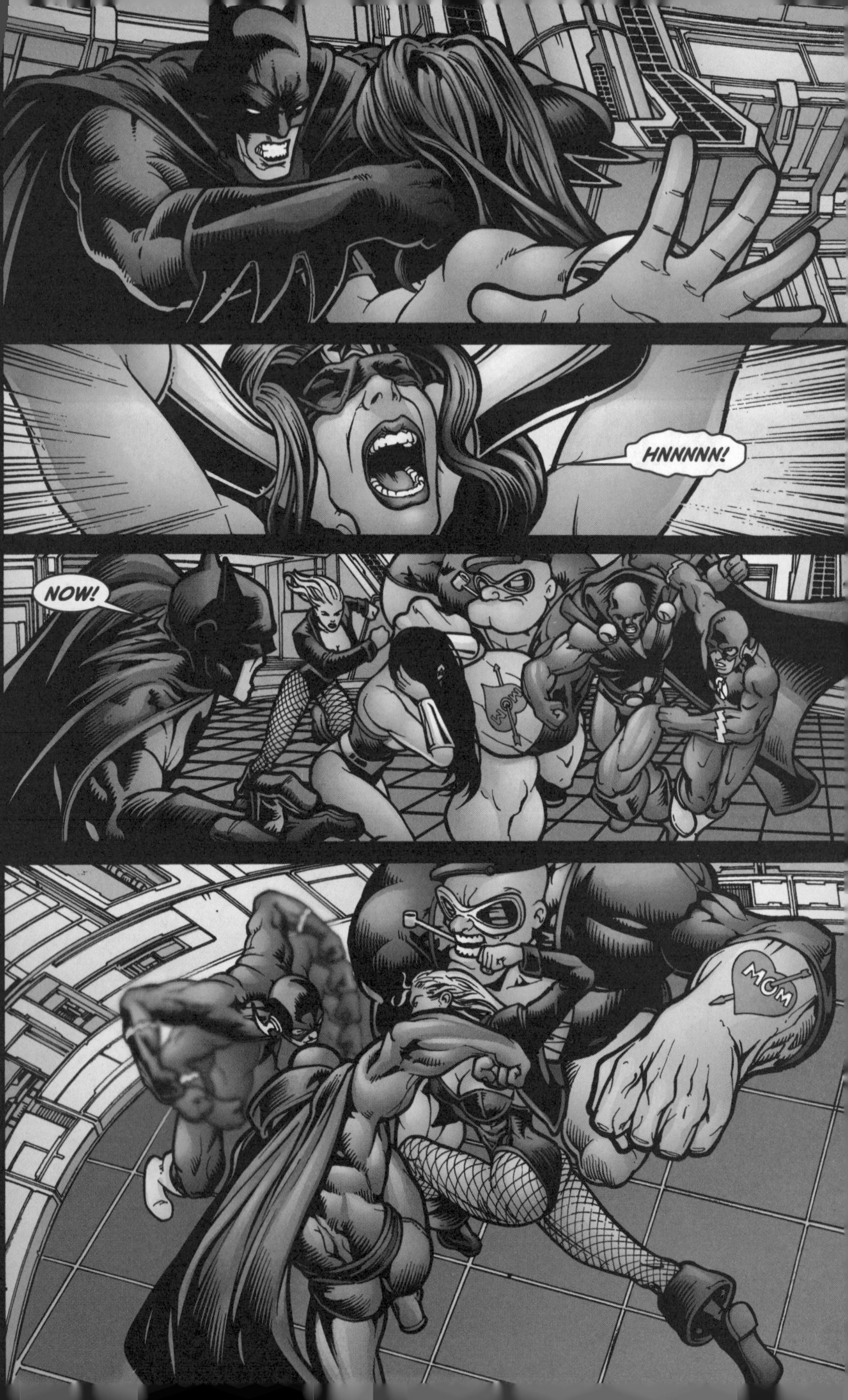
HNNNNN!
NOW!
MOM
MOM

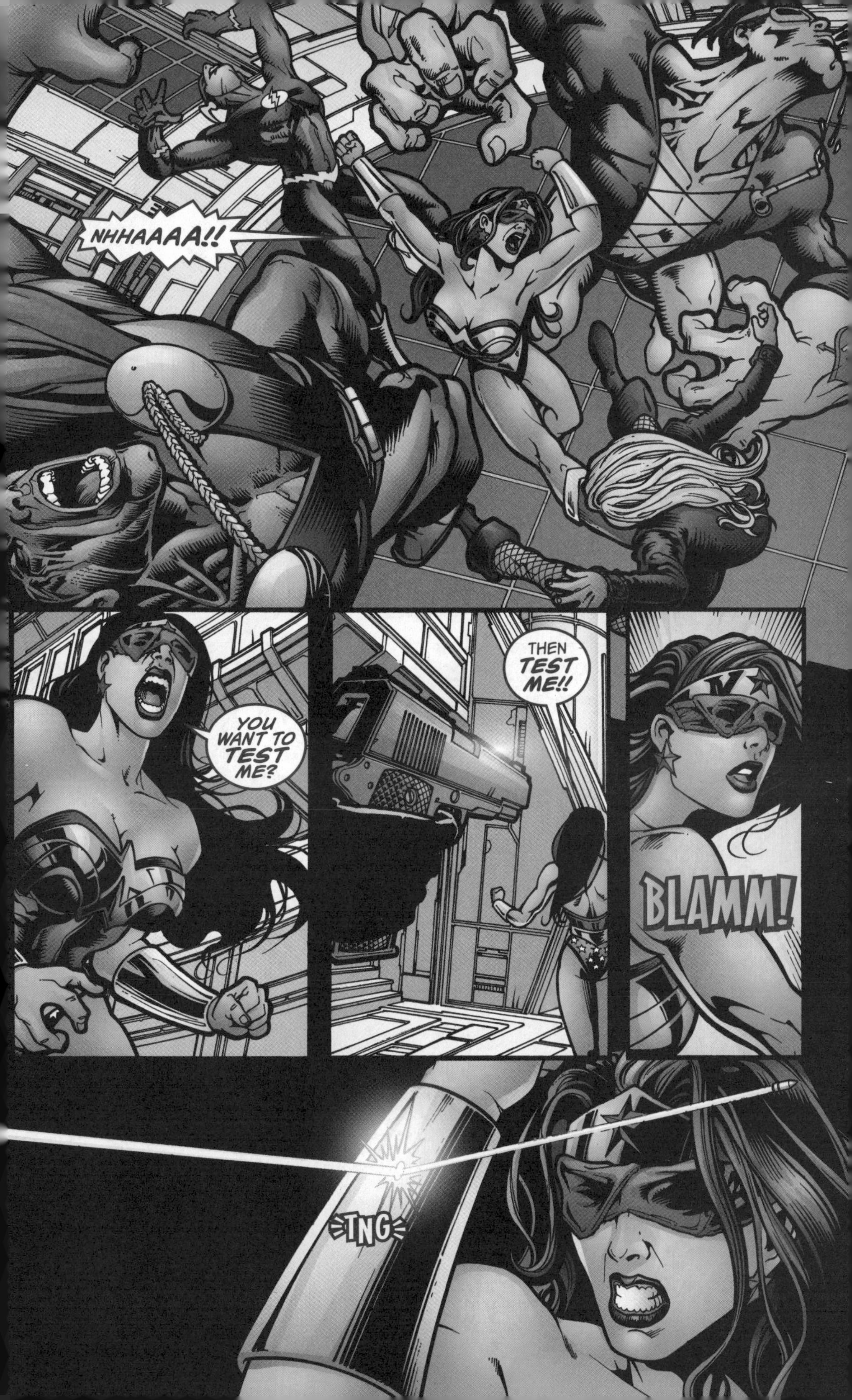
NHHAAAA!!
YOU WANT TO TEST ME?
THEN TEST ME!!
BLAMM!
TNG

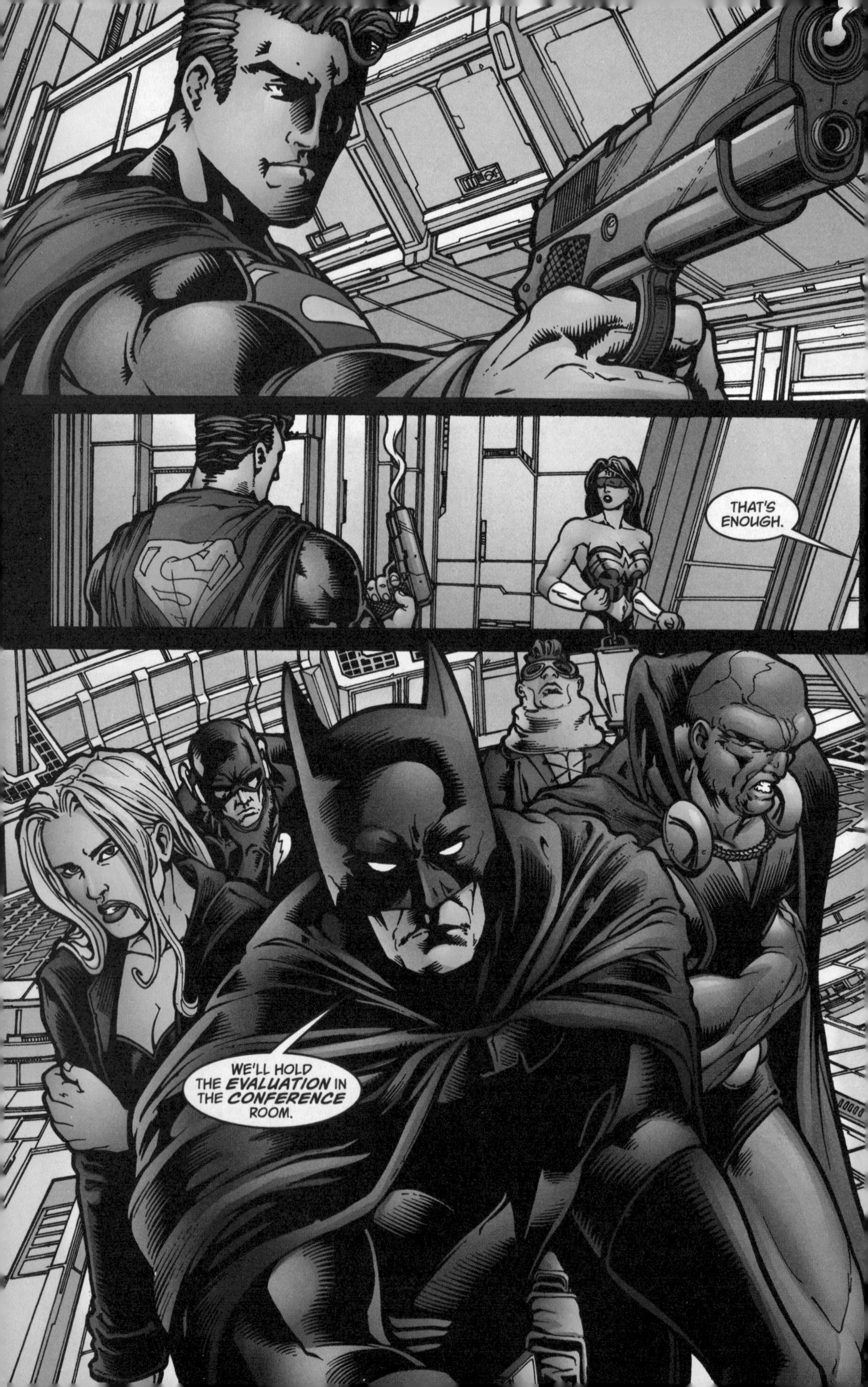
THAT'S ENOUGH.
WE'LL HOLD THE *EVALUATION* IN THE *CONFERENCE* ROOM.

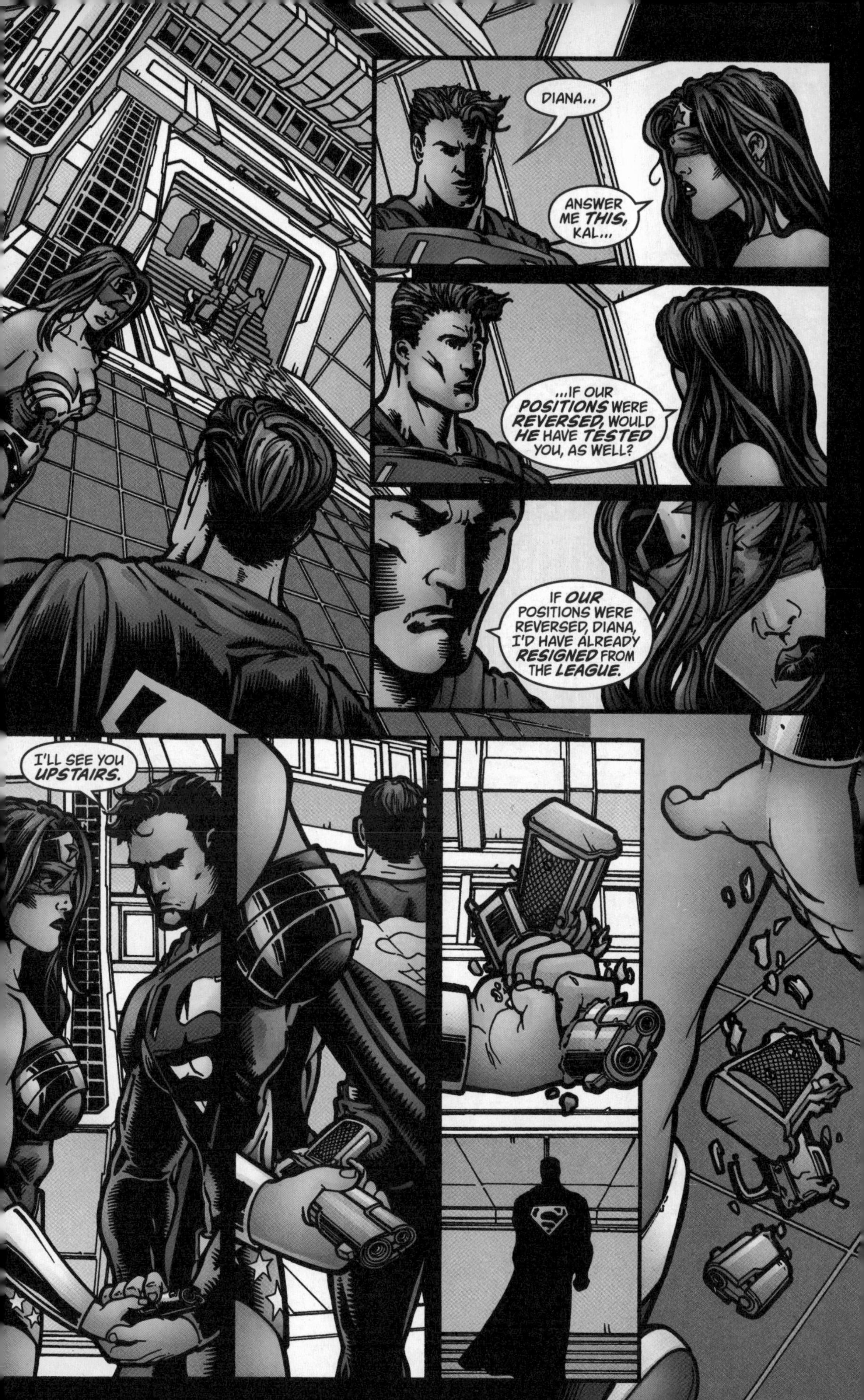
DIANA...
ANSWER ME THIS, KAL...
...IF OUR POSITIONS WERE REVERSED, WOULD HE HAVE TESTED YOU, AS WELL?
IF OUR POSITIONS WERE REVERSED, DIANA, I'D HAVE ALREADY RESIGNED FROM THE LEAGUE.
I'LL SEE YOU UPSTAIRS.

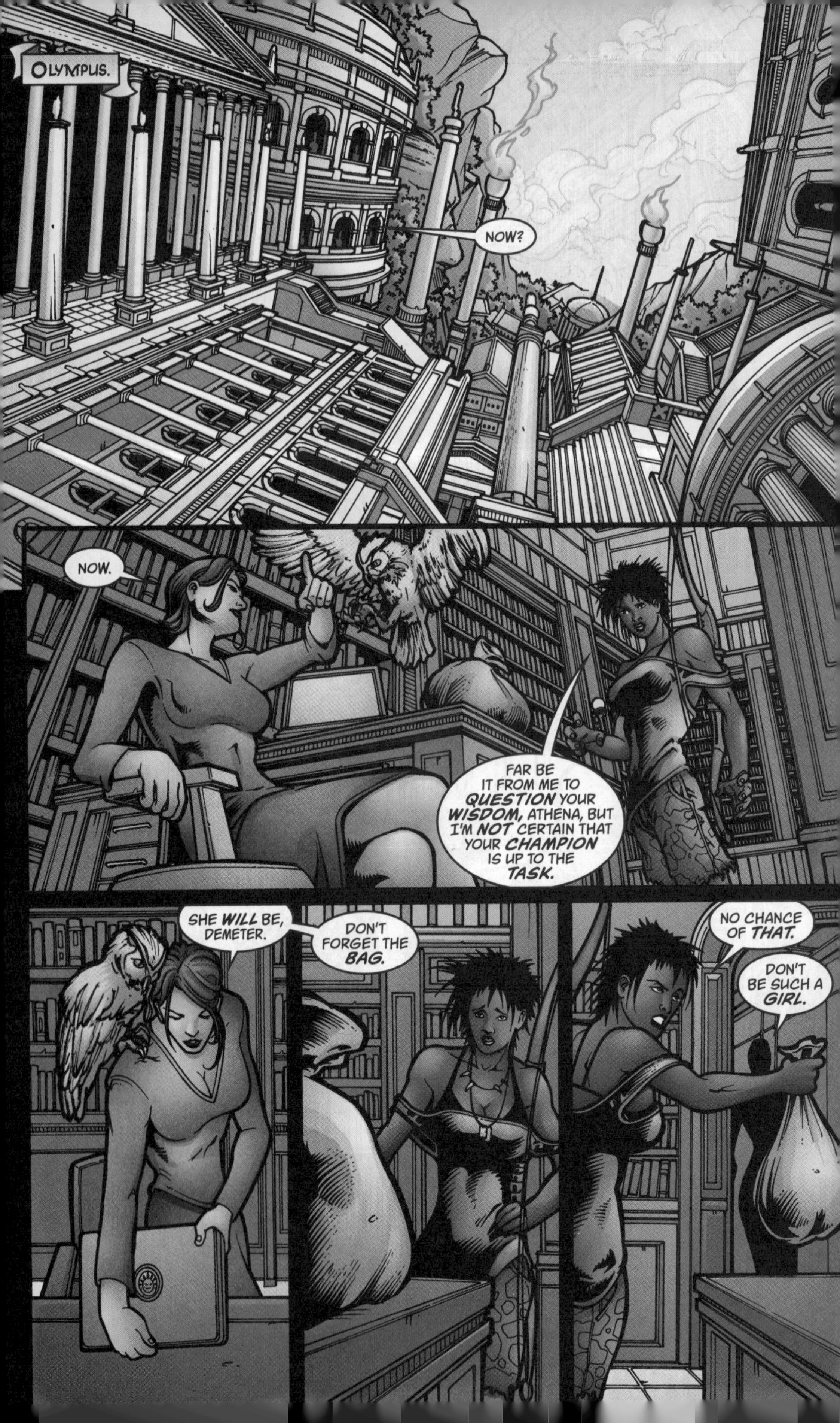
OLYMPUS.
NOW?
NOW.
FAR BE IT FROM ME TO QUESTION YOUR WISDOM, ATHENA, BUT I'M NOT CERTAIN THAT YOUR CHAMPION IS UP TO THE TASK.
SHE WILL BE, DEMETER.
DON'T FORGET THE BAG.
NO CHANCE OF THAT.
DON'T BE SUCH A GIRL.

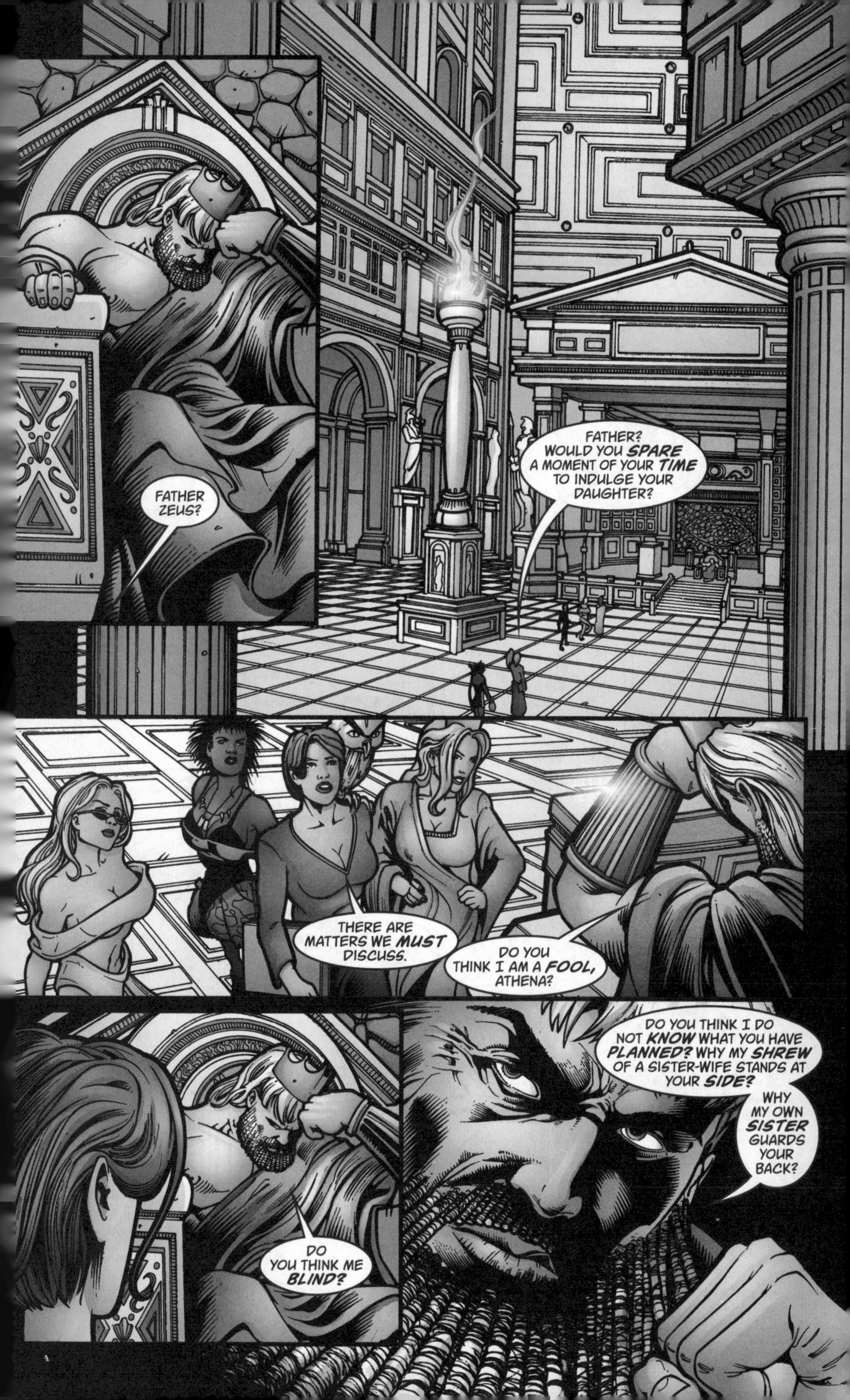
FATHER ZEUS?
FATHER? WOULD YOU SPARE A MOMENT OF YOUR TIME TO INDULGE YOUR DAUGHTER?
THERE ARE MATTERS WE MUST DISCUSS.
DO YOU THINK I AM A FOOL, ATHENA?
DO YOU THINK ME BLIND?
DO YOU THINK I DO NOT KNOW WHAT YOU HAVE PLANNED? WHY MY SHREW OF A SISTER-WIFE STANDS AT YOUR SIDE?
WHY MY OWN SISTER GUARDS YOUR BACK?

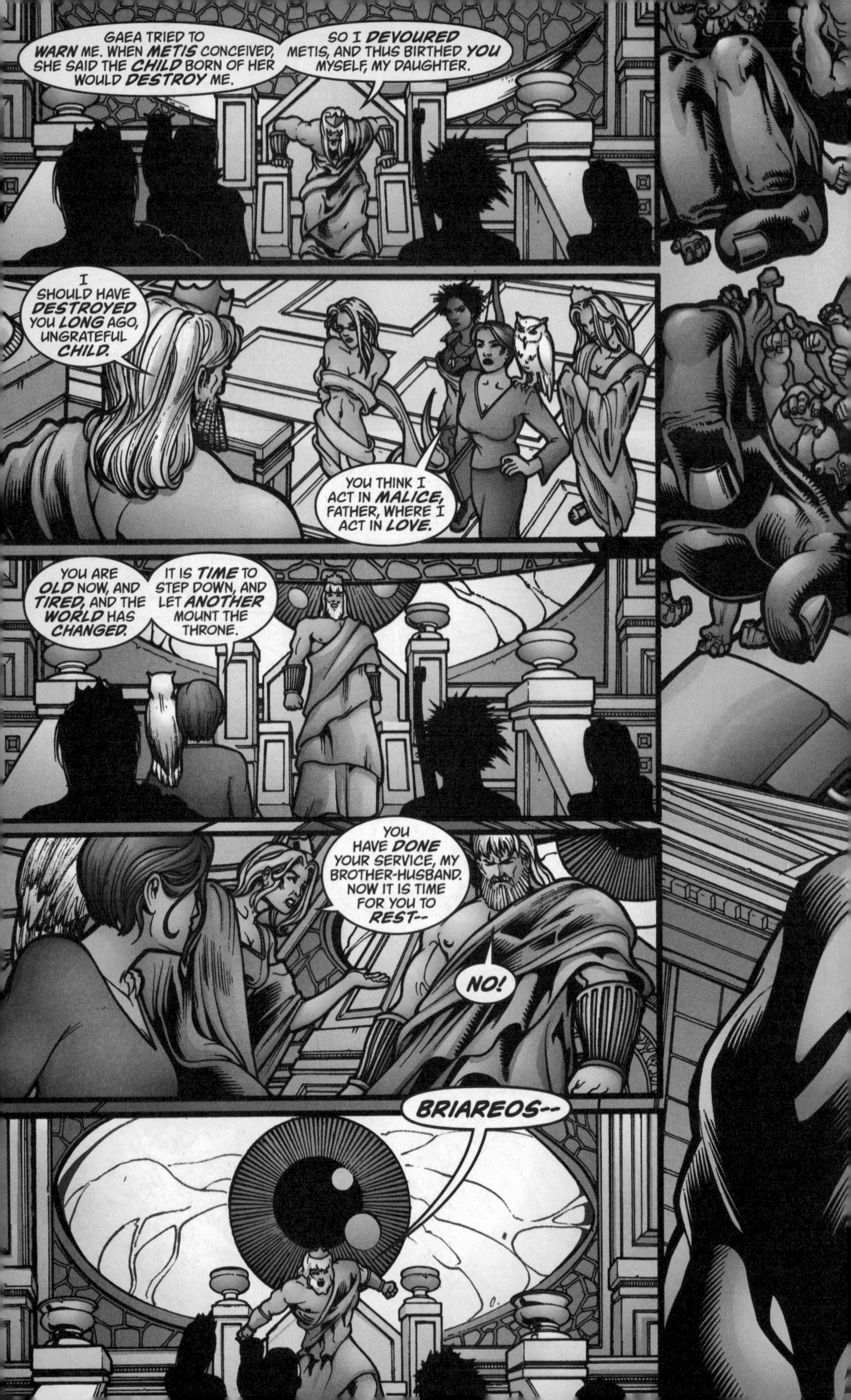
GAEA TRIED TO WARN ME. WHEN METIS CONCEIVED, SHE SAID THE CHILD BORN OF HER WOULD DESTROY ME.
SO I DEVOURED METIS, AND THUS BIRTHED YOU MYSELF, MY DAUGHTER.
I SHOULD HAVE DESTROYED YOU LONG AGO, UNGRATEFUL CHILD.
YOU THINK I ACT IN MALICE, FATHER, WHERE I ACT IN LOVE.
YOU ARE OLD NOW, AND TIRED, AND THE WORLD HAS CHANGED.
IT IS TIME TO STEP DOWN, AND LET ANOTHER MOUNT THE THRONE.
YOU HAVE DONE YOUR SERVICE, MY BROTHER-HUSBAND. NOW IT IS TIME FOR YOU TO REST--
NO!
BRIAREOS--

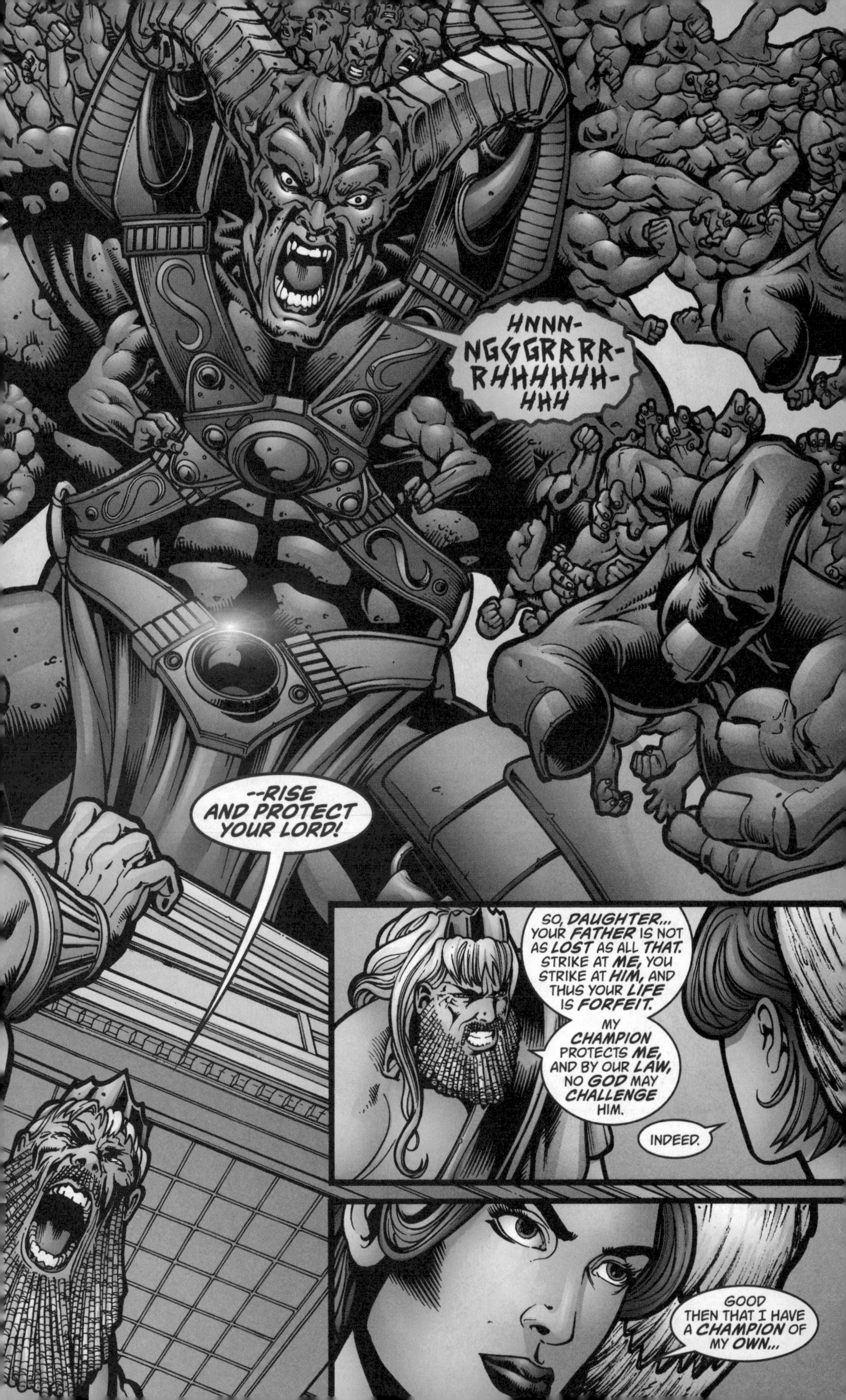
HNNN-NGGGRRRR-RHHHHHH-HHH
--RISE AND PROTECT YOUR LORD!
SO, DAUGHTER... YOUR FATHER IS NOT AS LOST AS ALL THAT. STRIKE AT ME, YOU STRIKE AT HIM, AND THUS YOUR LIFE IS FORFEIT.
MY CHAMPION PROTECTS ME, AND BY OUR LAW, NO GOD MAY CHALLENGE HIM.
INDEED.
GOOD THEN THAT I HAVE A CHAMPION OF MY OWN...

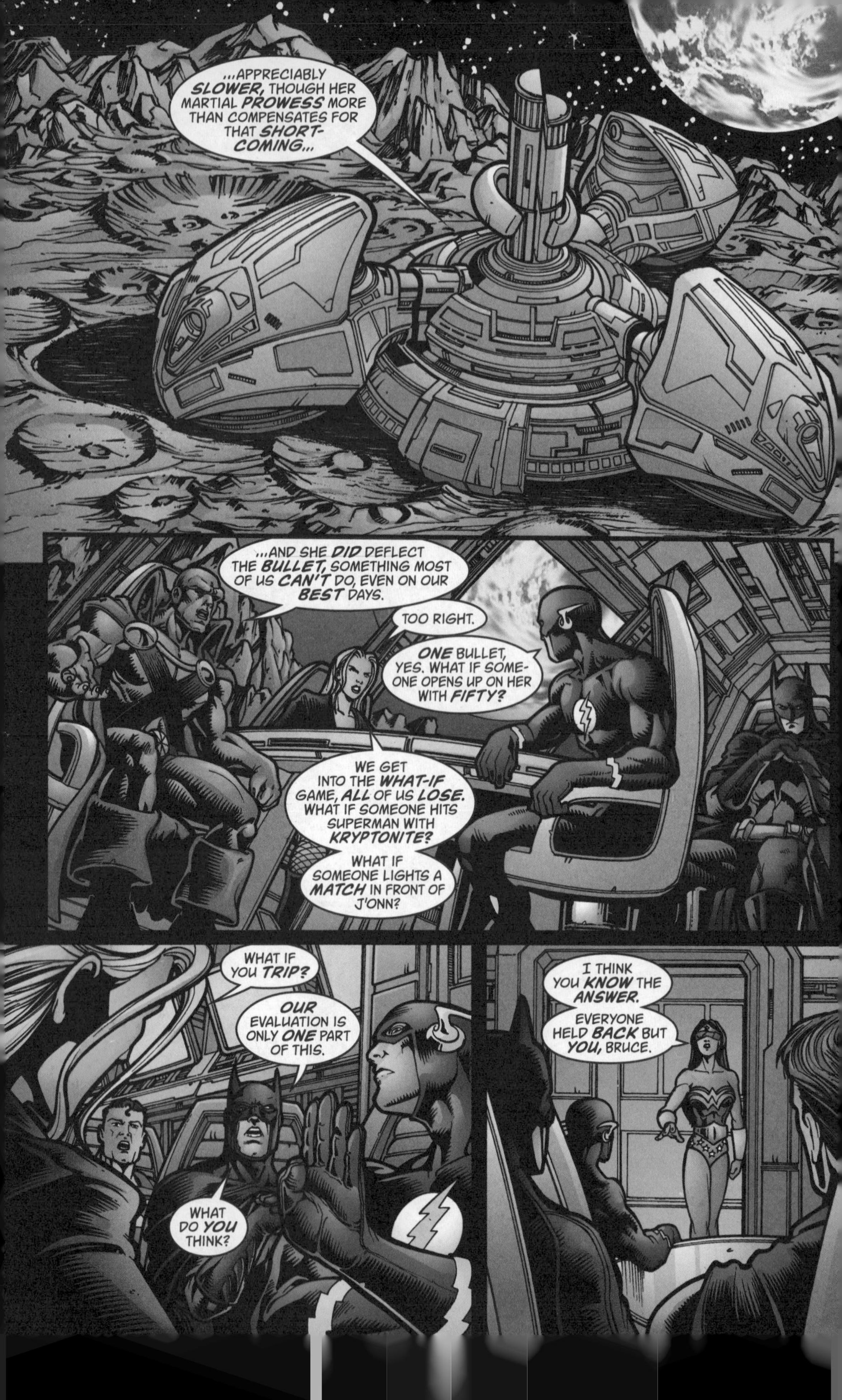
...APPRECIABLY SLOWER, THOUGH HER MARTIAL PROWESS MORE THAN COMPENSATES FOR THAT SHORT-COMING...
...AND SHE DID DEFLECT THE BULLET, SOMETHING MOST OF US CAN'T DO, EVEN ON OUR BEST DAYS.
TOO RIGHT.
ONE BULLET, YES. WHAT IF SOME-ONE OPENS UP ON HER WITH FIFTY?
WE GET INTO THE WHAT-IF GAME, ALL OF US LOSE. WHAT IF SOMEONE HITS SUPERMAN WITH KRYPTONITE?
WHAT IF SOMEONE LIGHTS A MATCH IN FRONT OF J'ONN?
WHAT IF YOU TRIP?
OUR EVALUATION IS ONLY ONE PART OF THIS.
WHAT DO YOU THINK?
I THINK YOU KNOW THE ANSWER.
EVERYONE HELD BACK BUT YOU, BRUCE.

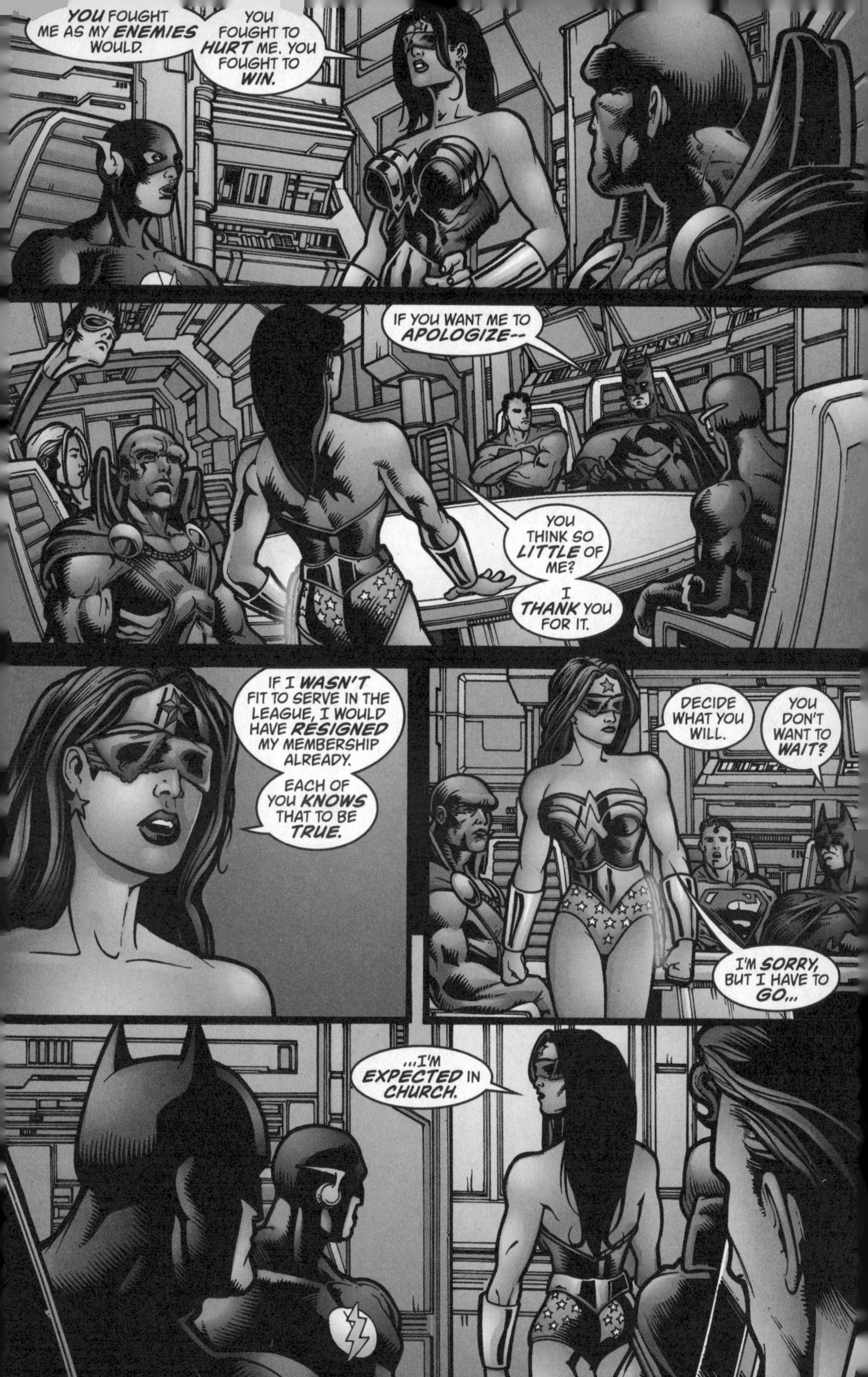
YOU FOUGHT ME AS MY ENEMIES WOULD.
YOU FOUGHT TO HURT ME. YOU FOUGHT TO WIN.
IF YOU WANT ME TO APOLOGIZE--
YOU THINK SO LITTLE OF ME?
I THANK YOU FOR IT.
IF I WASN'T FIT TO SERVE IN THE LEAGUE, I WOULD HAVE RESIGNED MY MEMBERSHIP ALREADY.
EACH OF YOU KNOWS THAT TO BE TRUE.
DECIDE WHAT YOU WILL.
YOU DON'T WANT TO WAIT?
I'M SORRY, BUT I HAVE TO GO...
...I'M EXPECTED IN CHURCH.

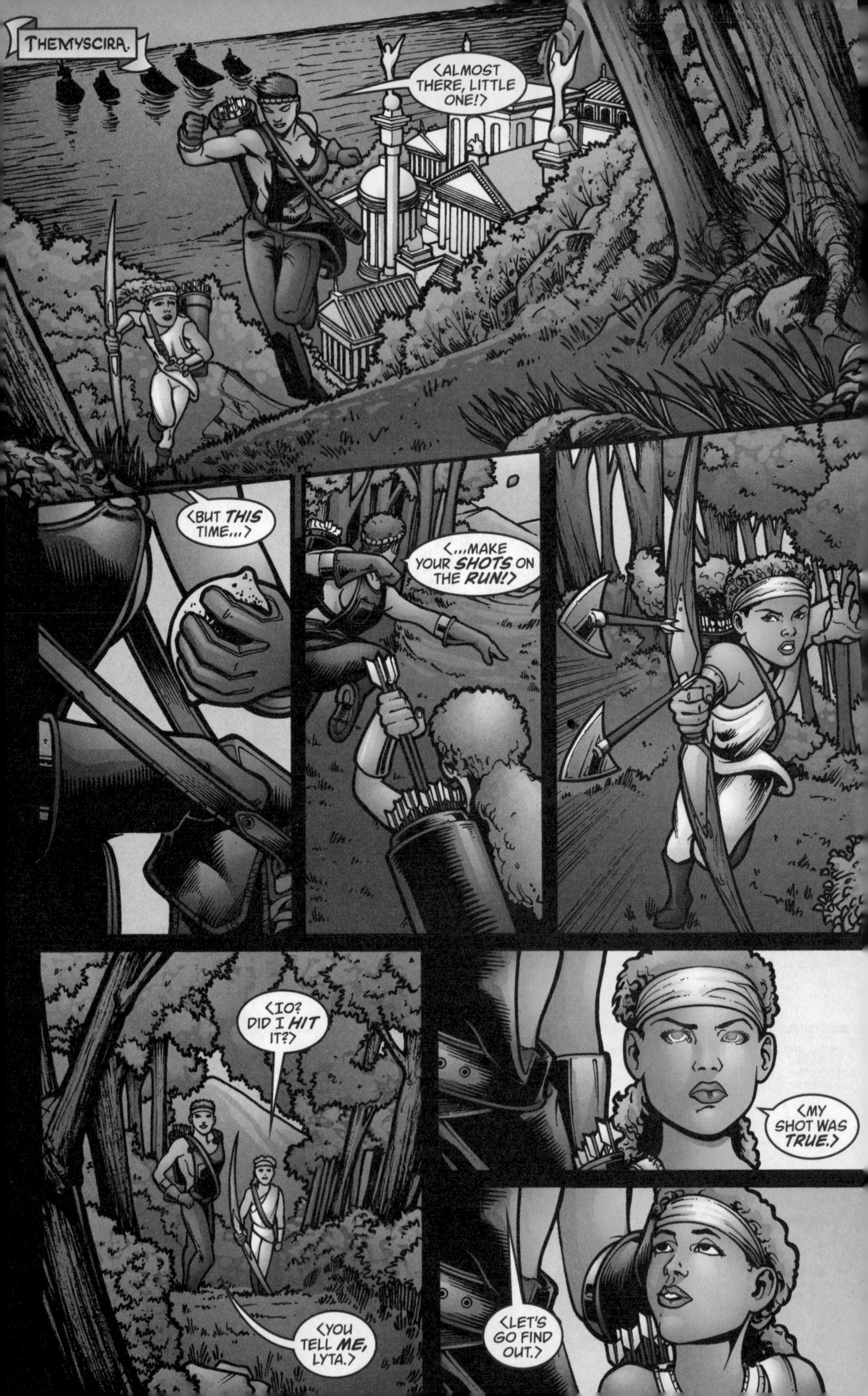
THEMYSCIRA.
<ALMOST THERE, LITTLE ONE!>
<BUT THIS TIME...>
<...MAKE YOUR SHOTS ON THE RUN!>
<IO? DID I HIT IT?>
<YOU TELL ME, LYTA.>
<MY SHOT WAS TRUE.>
<LET'S GO FIND OUT.>

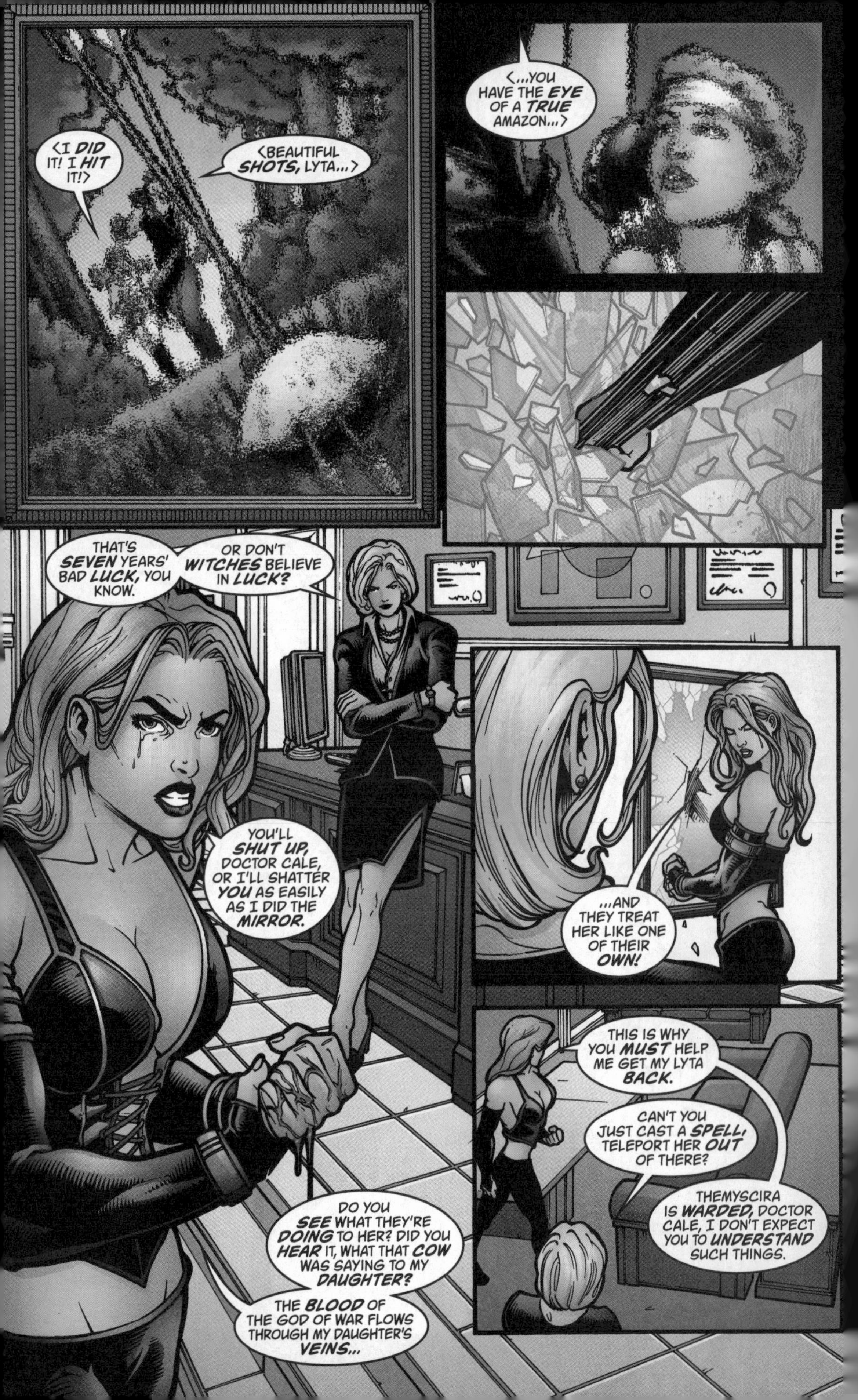

<I DID IT! I HIT IT!>
<BEAUTIFUL SHOTS, LYTA...>
<...YOU HAVE THE EYE OF A TRUE AMAZON...>
THAT'S SEVEN YEARS' BAD LUCK, YOU KNOW.
OR DON'T WITCHES BELIEVE IN LUCK?
YOU'LL SHUT UP, DOCTOR CALE, OR I'LL SHATTER YOU AS EASILY AS I DID THE MIRROR.
DO YOU SEE WHAT THEY'RE DOING TO HER? DID YOU HEAR IT, WHAT THAT COW WAS SAYING TO MY DAUGHTER?
THE BLOOD OF THE GOD OF WAR FLOWS THROUGH MY DAUGHTER'S VEINS...
...AND THEY TREAT HER LIKE ONE OF THEIR OWN!
THIS IS WHY YOU MUST HELP ME GET MY LYTA BACK.
CAN'T YOU JUST CAST A SPELL, TELEPORT HER OUT OF THERE?
THEMYSCIRA IS WARDED, DOCTOR CALE, I DON'T EXPECT YOU TO UNDERSTAND SUCH THINGS.

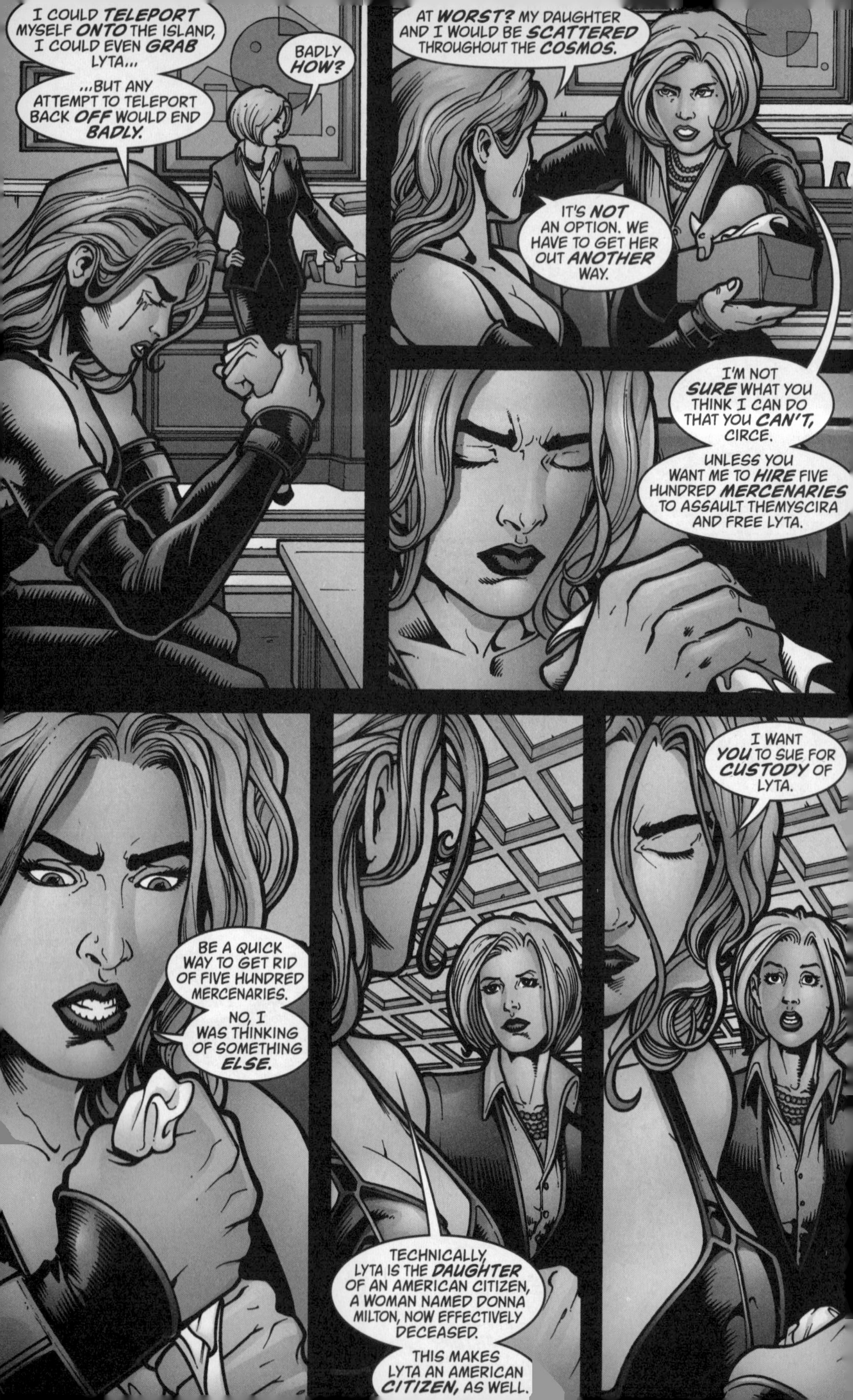
I COULD TELEPORT MYSELF ONTO THE ISLAND, I COULD EVEN GRAB LYTA...
...BUT ANY ATTEMPT TO TELEPORT BACK OFF WOULD END BADLY.
BADLY HOW?
AT WORST? MY DAUGHTER AND I WOULD BE SCATTERED THROUGHOUT THE COSMOS.
IT'S NOT AN OPTION. WE HAVE TO GET HER OUT ANOTHER WAY.
I'M NOT SURE WHAT YOU THINK I CAN DO THAT YOU CAN'T, CIRCE.
UNLESS YOU WANT ME TO HIRE FIVE HUNDRED MERCENARIES TO ASSAULT THEMYSCIRA AND FREE LYTA.
BE A QUICK WAY TO GET RID OF FIVE HUNDRED MERCENARIES.
NO, I WAS THINKING OF SOMETHING ELSE.
I WANT YOU TO SUE FOR CUSTODY OF LYTA.
TECHNICALLY, LYTA IS THE DAUGHTER OF AN AMERICAN CITIZEN, A WOMAN NAMED DONNA MILTON, NOW EFFECTIVELY DECEASED.
THIS MAKES LYTA AN AMERICAN CITIZEN, AS WELL.

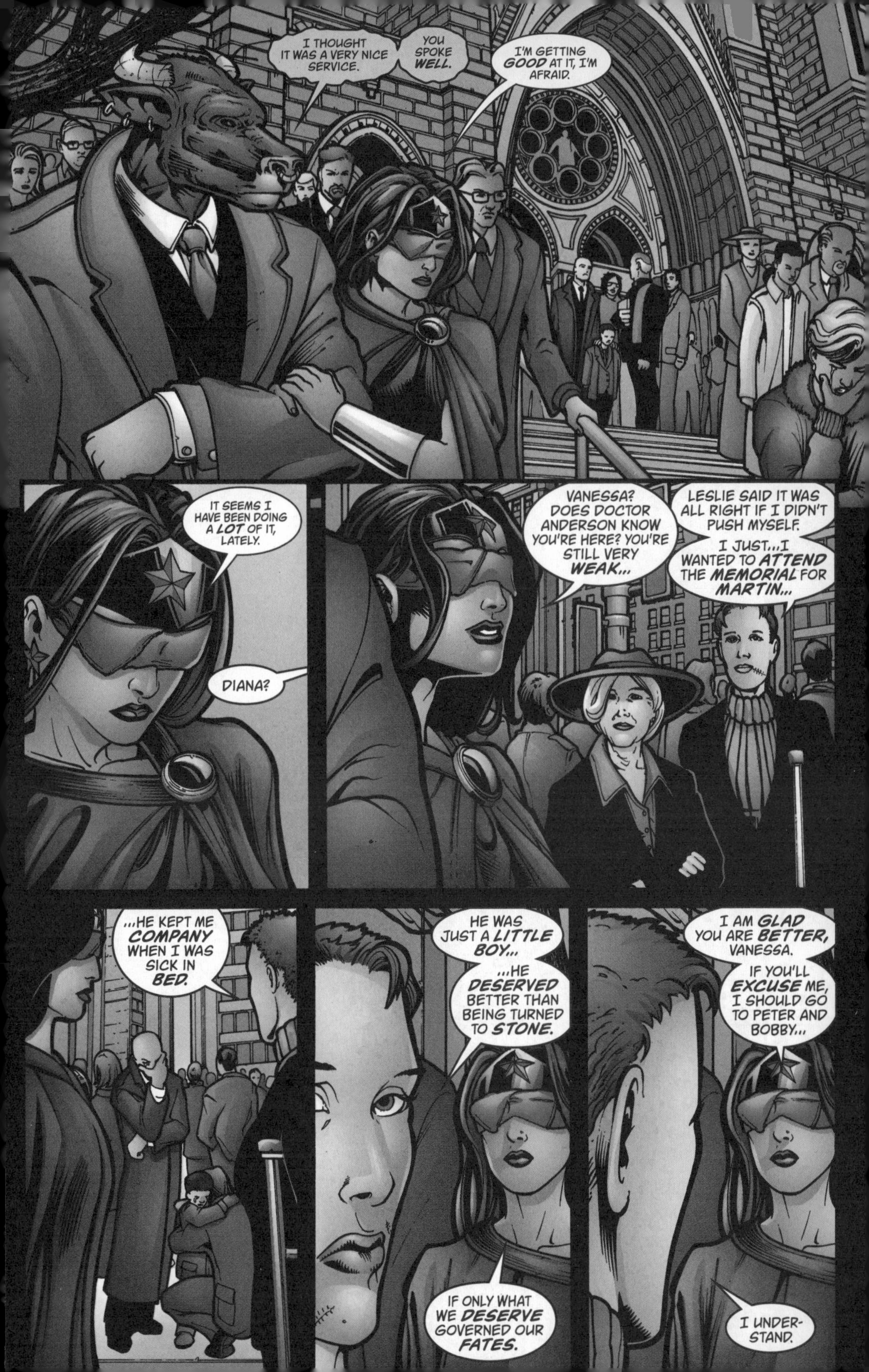
I THOUGHT IT WAS A VERY NICE SERVICE.
YOU SPOKE WELL.
I'M GETTING GOOD AT IT, I'M AFRAID.
IT SEEMS I HAVE BEEN DOING A LOT OF IT, LATELY.
DIANA?
VANESSA? DOES DOCTOR ANDERSON KNOW YOU'RE HERE? YOU'RE STILL VERY WEAK...
LESLIE SAID IT WAS ALL RIGHT IF I DIDN'T PUSH MYSELF.
I JUST...I WANTED TO ATTEND THE MEMORIAL FOR MARTIN...
...HE KEPT ME COMPANY WHEN I WAS SICK IN BED.
HE WAS JUST A LITTLE BOY...
...HE DESERVED BETTER THAN BEING TURNED TO STONE.
IF ONLY WHAT WE DESERVE GOVERNED OUR FATES.
I AM GLAD YOU ARE BETTER, VANESSA.
IF YOU'LL EXCUSE ME, I SHOULD GO TO PETER AND BOBBY...
I UNDER-STAND.

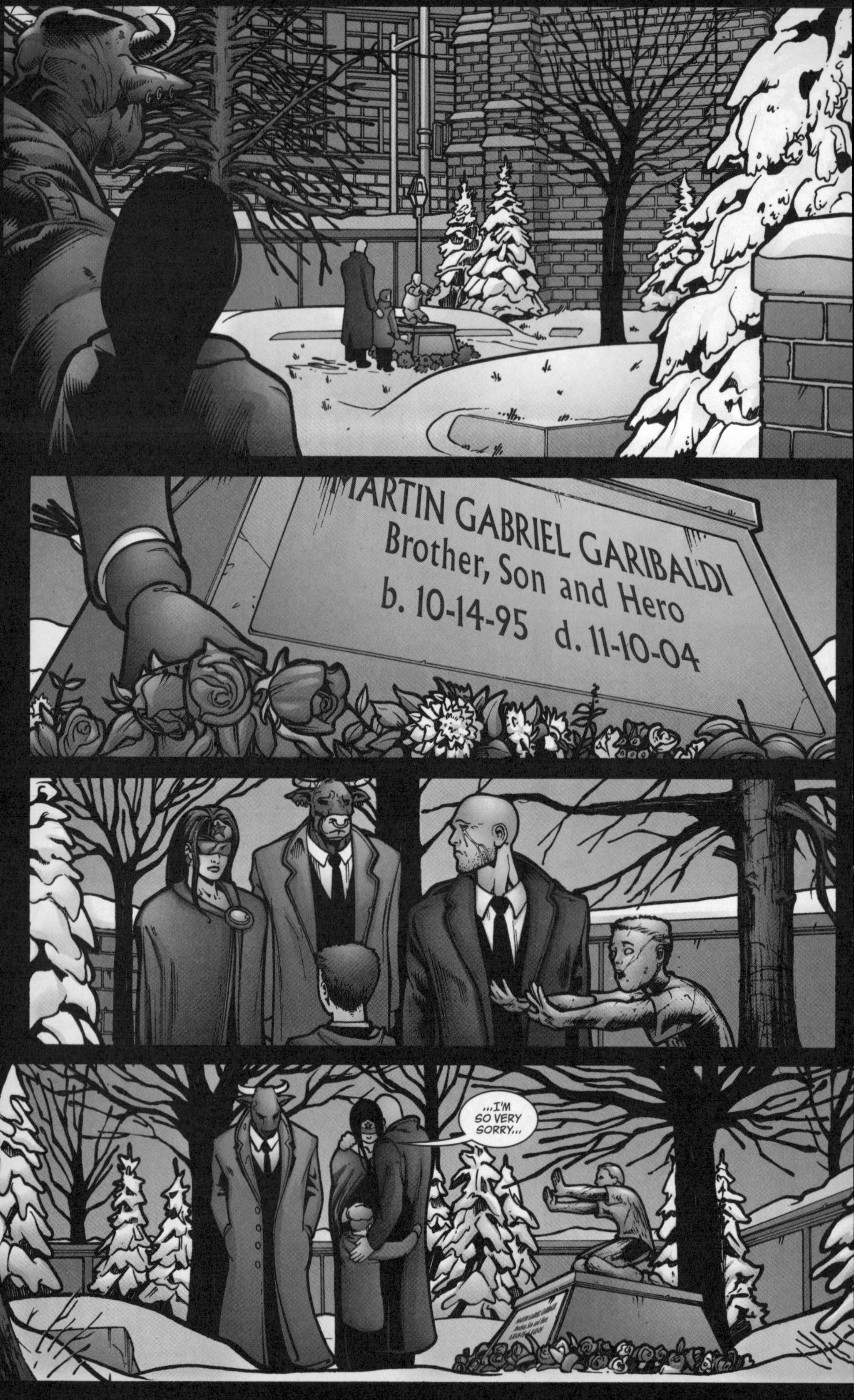
MARTIN GABRIEL GARIBALDI
Brother, Son and Hero
b. 10-14-95 d. 11-10-04
...I'M SO VERY SORRY...

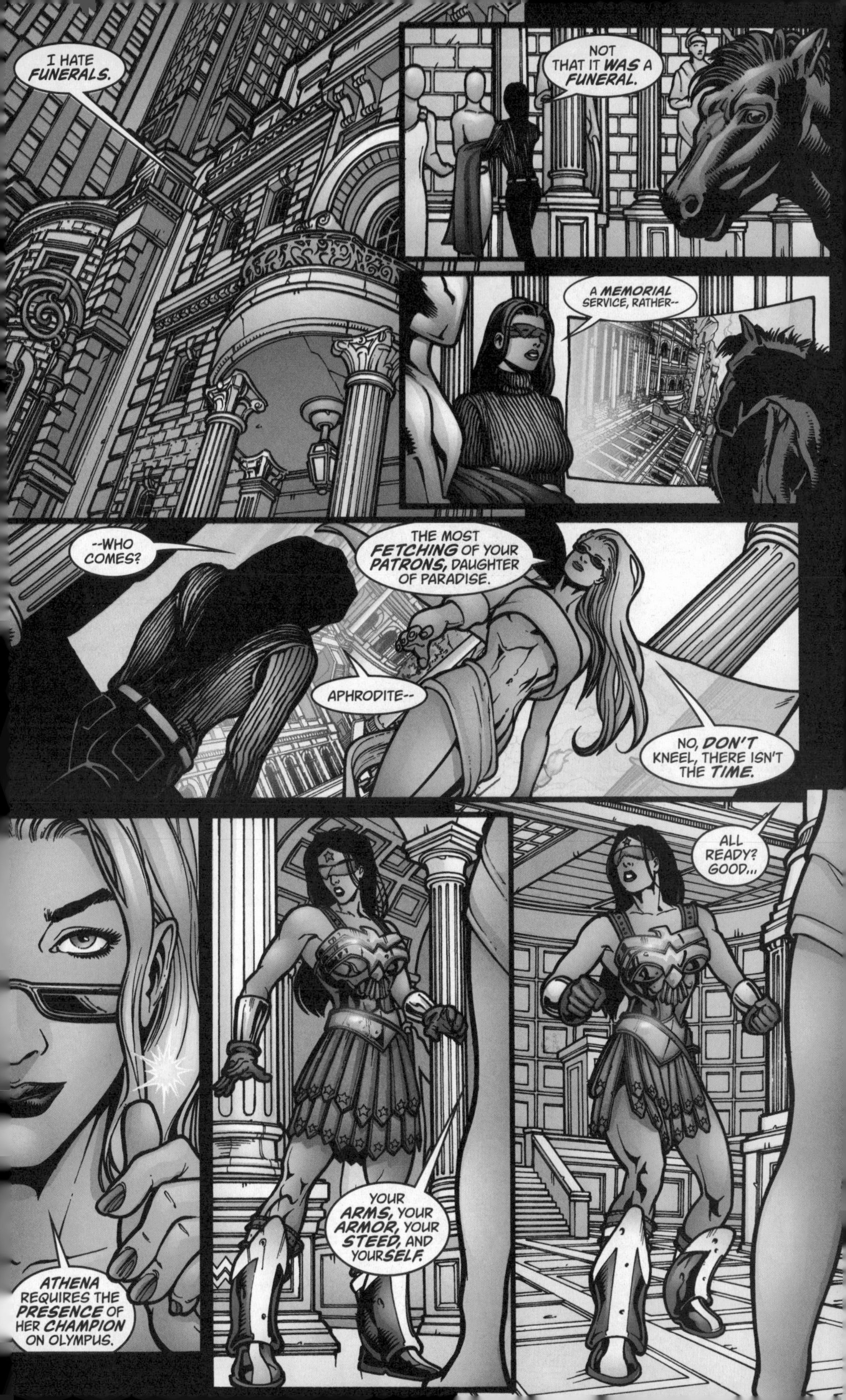
I HATE FUNERALS.
NOT THAT IT WAS A FUNERAL.
A MEMORIAL SERVICE, RATHER--
--WHO COMES?
THE MOST FETCHING OF YOUR PATRONS, DAUGHTER OF PARADISE.
APHRODITE--
NO, DON'T KNEEL, THERE ISN'T THE TIME.
ATHENA REQUIRES THE PRESENCE OF HER CHAMPION ON OLYMPUS.
YOUR ARMS, YOUR ARMOR, YOUR STEED, AND YOURSELF.
ALL READY? GOOD...

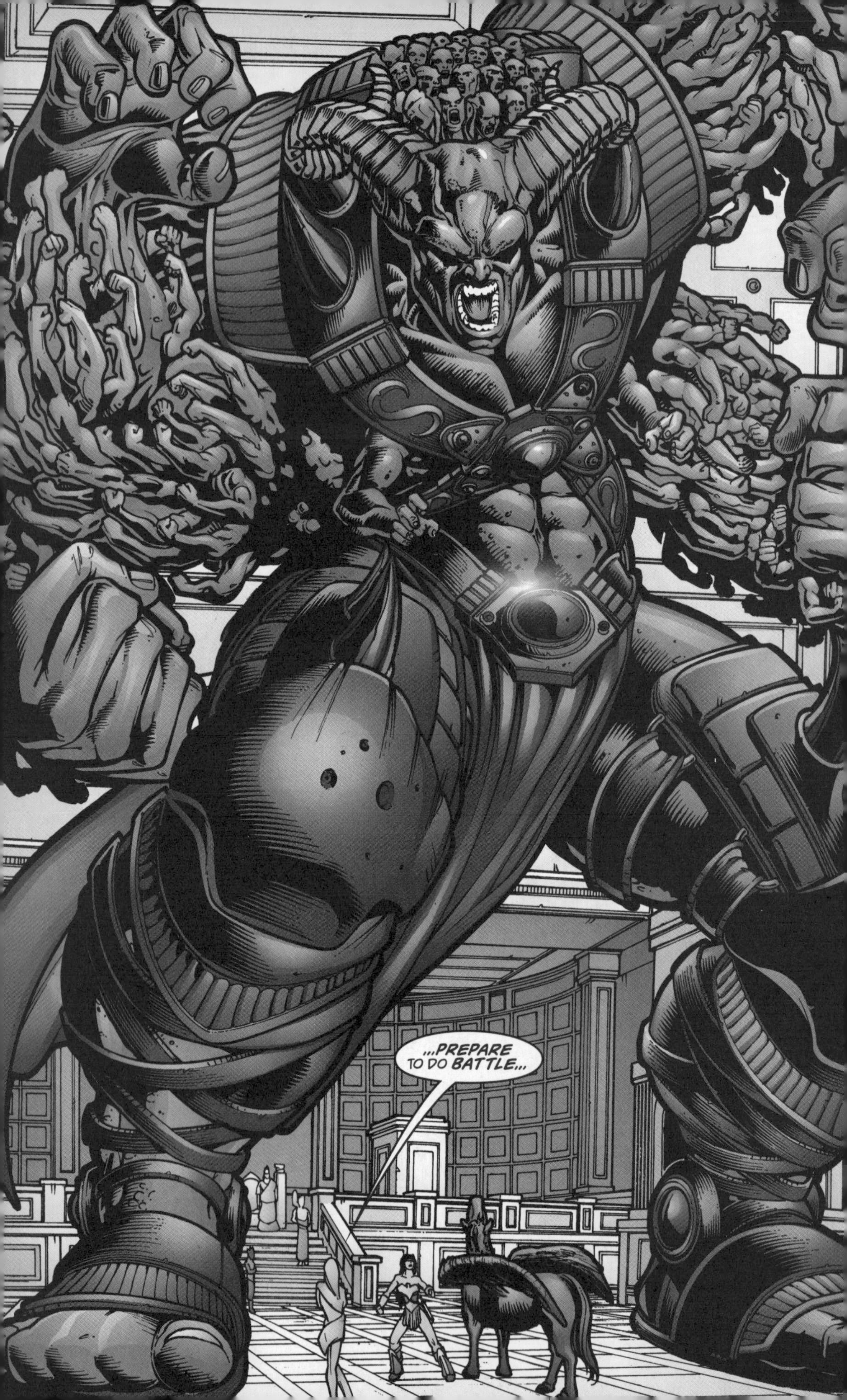
...PREPARE TO DO BATTLE...

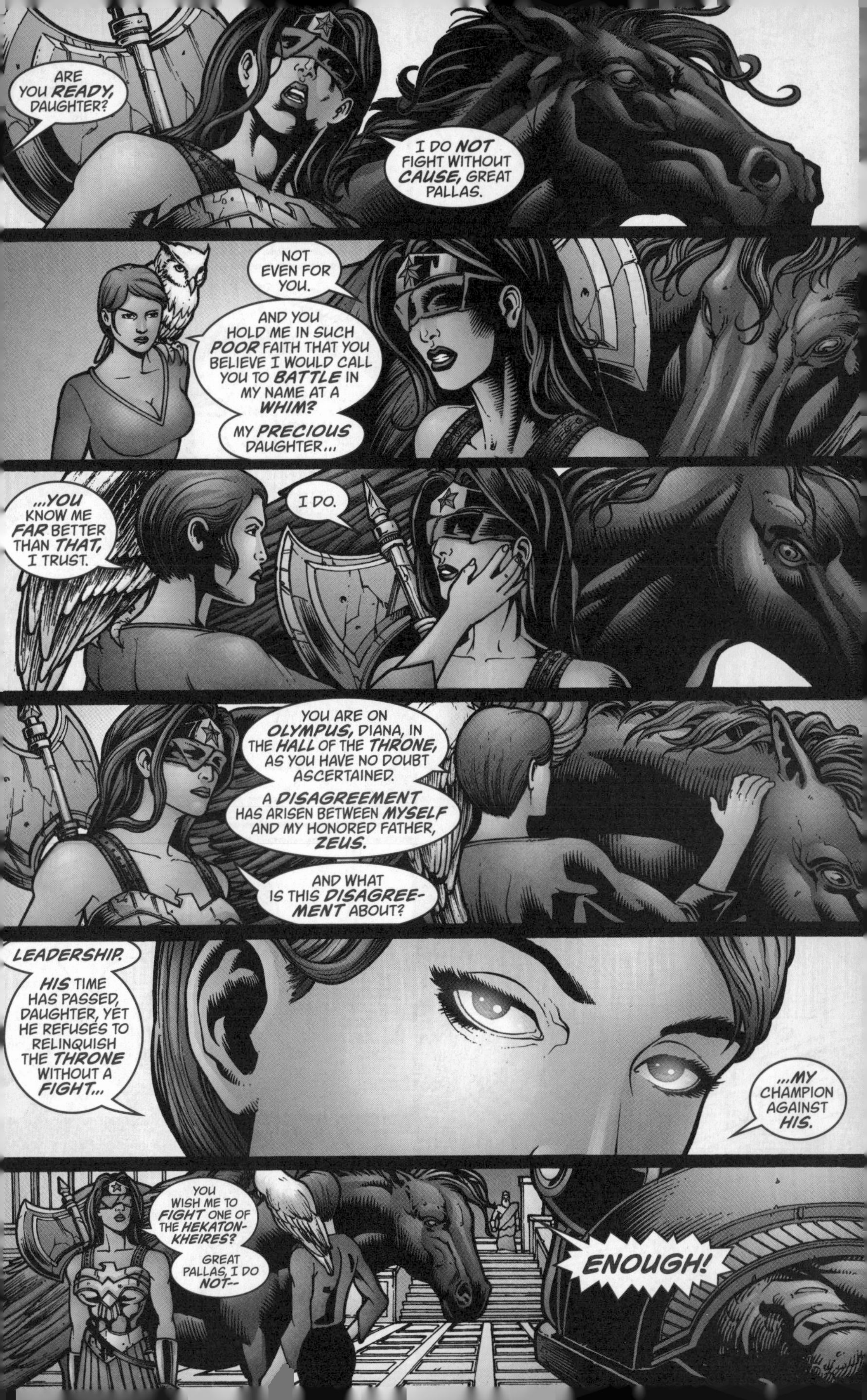
ARE YOU READY, DAUGHTER?
I DO NOT FIGHT WITHOUT CAUSE, GREAT PALLAS.
NOT EVEN FOR YOU.
AND YOU HOLD ME IN SUCH POOR FAITH THAT YOU BELIEVE I WOULD CALL YOU TO BATTLE IN MY NAME AT A WHIM?
MY PRECIOUS DAUGHTER...
...YOU KNOW ME FAR BETTER THAN THAT, I TRUST.
I DO.
YOU ARE ON OLYMPUS, DIANA, IN THE HALL OF THE THRONE, AS YOU HAVE NO DOUBT ASCERTAINED.
A DISAGREEMENT HAS ARISEN BETWEEN MYSELF AND MY HONORED FATHER, ZEUS.
AND WHAT IS THIS DISAGREE-MENT ABOUT?
LEADERSHIP.
HIS TIME HAS PASSED, DAUGHTER, YET HE REFUSES TO RELINQUISH THE THRONE WITHOUT A FIGHT...
...MY CHAMPION AGAINST HIS.
YOU WISH ME TO FIGHT ONE OF THE HEKATON-KHEIRES?
GREAT PALLAS, I DO NOT--
ENOUGH!

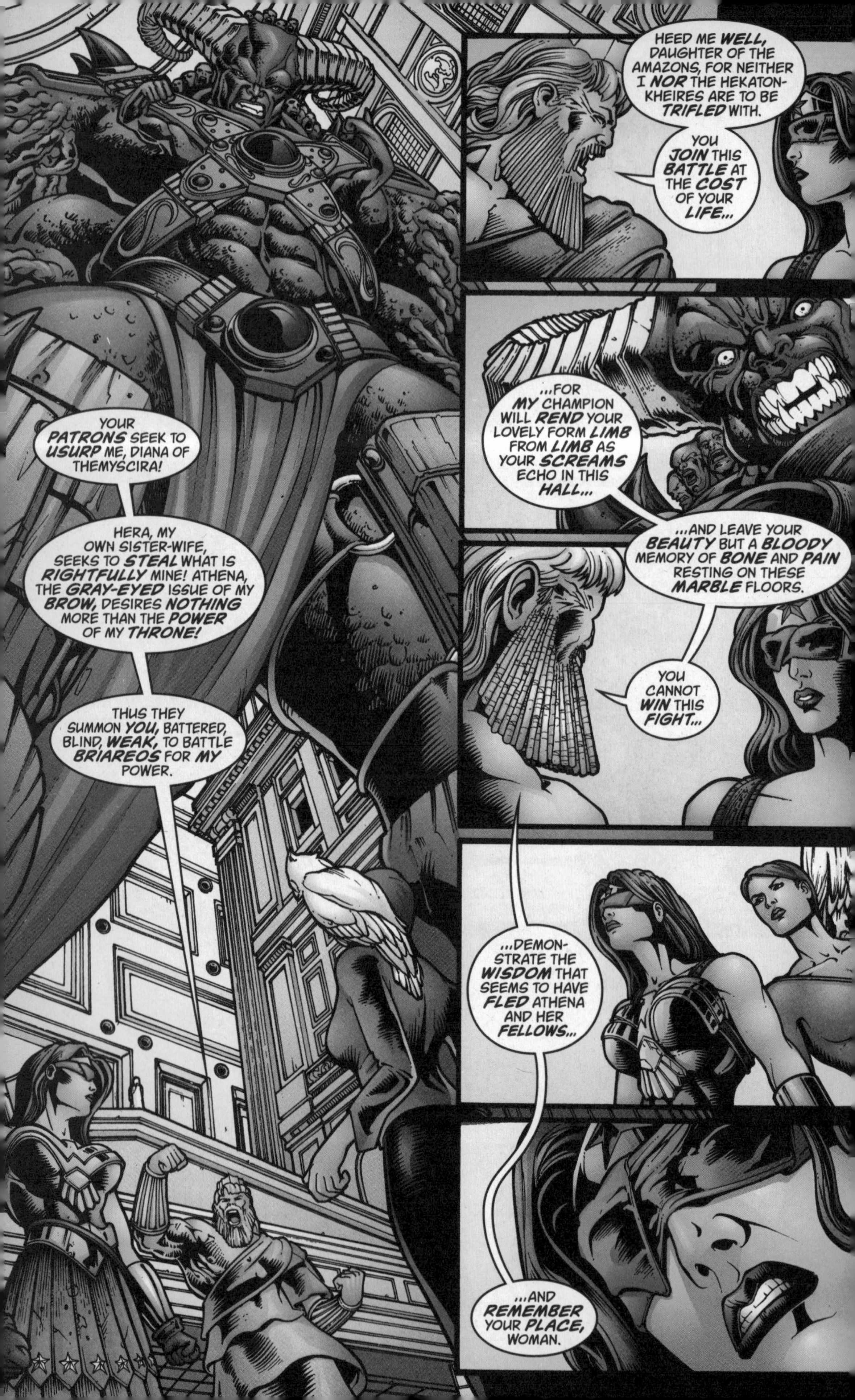
YOUR PATRONS SEEK TO USURP ME, DIANA OF THEMYSCIRA!
HERA, MY OWN SISTER-WIFE, SEEKS TO STEAL WHAT IS RIGHTFULLY MINE! ATHENA, THE GRAY-EYED ISSUE OF MY BROW, DESIRES NOTHING MORE THAN THE POWER OF MY THRONE!
THUS THEY SUMMON YOU, BATTERED, BLIND, WEAK, TO BATTLE BRIAREOS FOR MY POWER.
HEED ME WELL, DAUGHTER OF THE AMAZONS, FOR NEITHER I NOR THE HEKATON-KHEIRES ARE TO BE TRIFLED WITH.
YOU JOIN THIS BATTLE AT THE COST OF YOUR LIFE...
...FOR MY CHAMPION WILL REND YOUR LOVELY FORM LIMB FROM LIMB AS YOUR SCREAMS ECHO IN THIS HALL...
...AND LEAVE YOUR BEAUTY BUT A BLOODY MEMORY OF BONE AND PAIN RESTING ON THESE MARBLE FLOORS.
YOU CANNOT WIN THIS FIGHT...
...DEMON-STRATE THE WISDOM THAT SEEMS TO HAVE FLED ATHENA AND HER FELLOWS...
...AND REMEMBER YOUR PLACE, WOMAN.

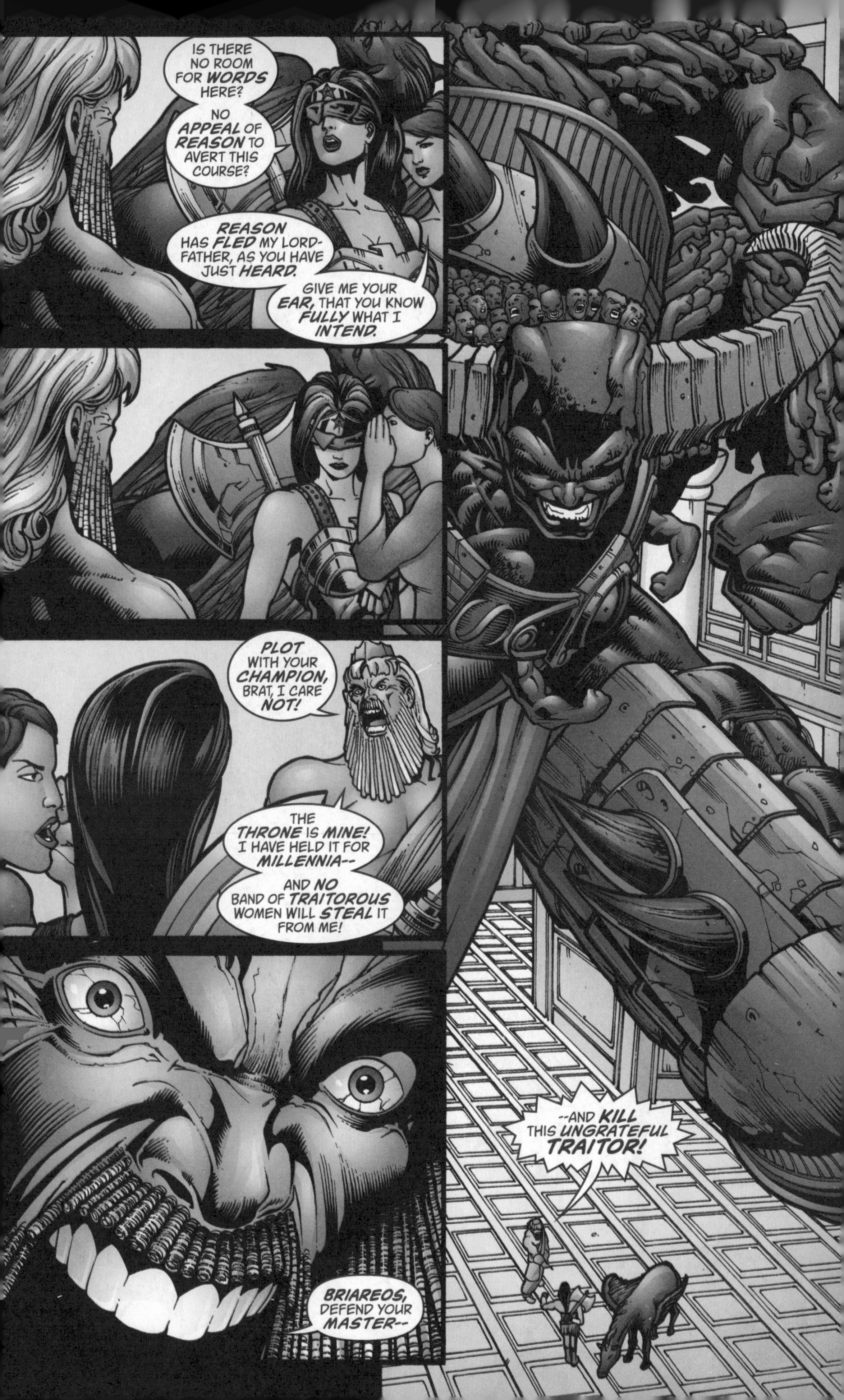
IS THERE NO ROOM FOR WORDS HERE?
NO APPEAL OF REASON TO AVERT THIS COURSE?
REASON HAS FLED MY LORD-FATHER, AS YOU HAVE JUST HEARD.
GIVE ME YOUR EAR, THAT YOU KNOW FULLY WHAT I INTEND.
PLOT WITH YOUR CHAMPION, BRAT, I CARE NOT!
THE THRONE IS MINE! I HAVE HELD IT FOR MILLENNIA--
AND NO BAND OF TRAITOROUS WOMEN WILL STEAL IT FROM ME!
BRIAREOS, DEFEND YOUR MASTER--
--AND KILL THIS UNGRATEFUL TRAITOR!

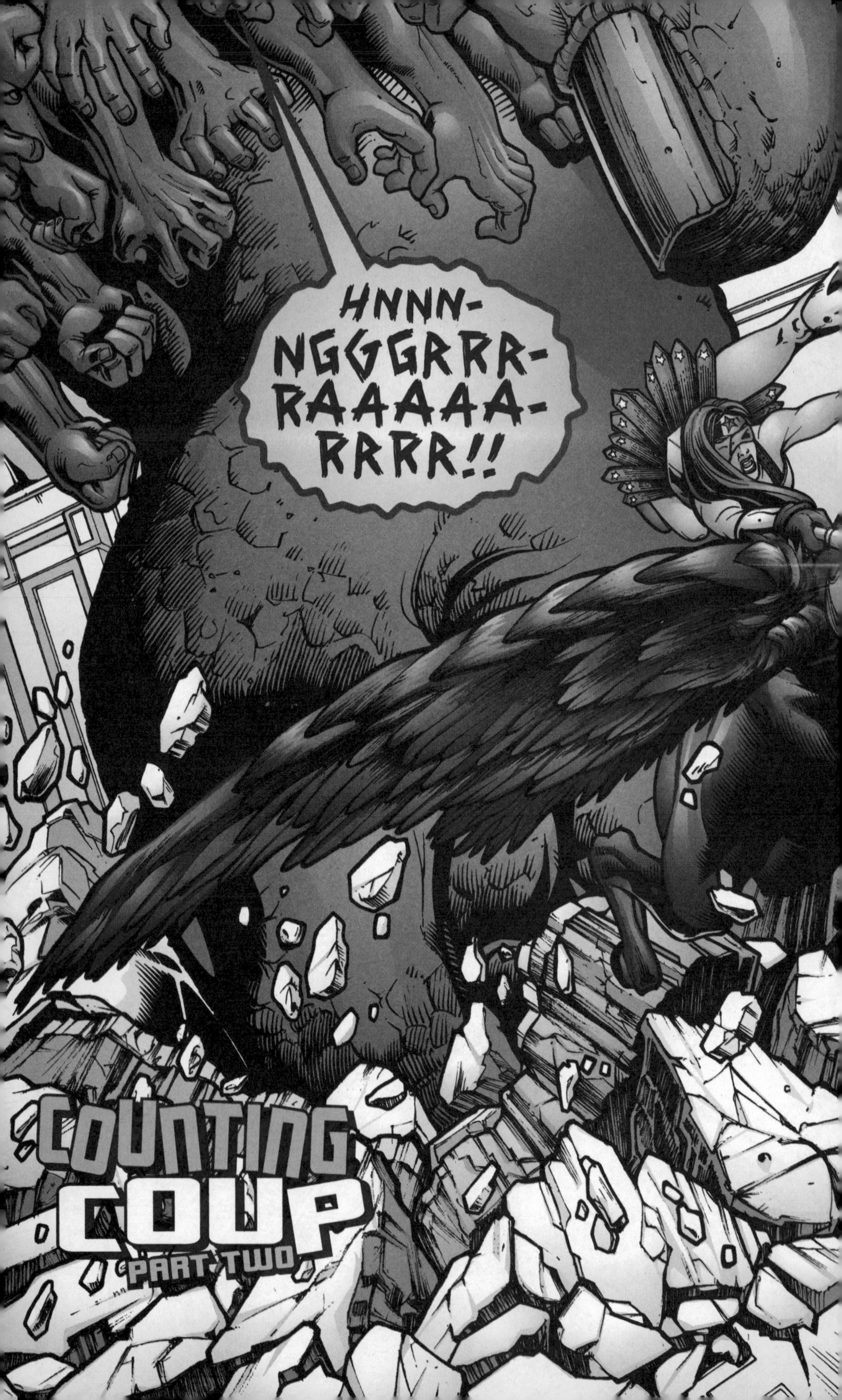
HNNN-NGGGRRR-RAAAAA-RRRR!!
COUNTING COUP
PART TWO

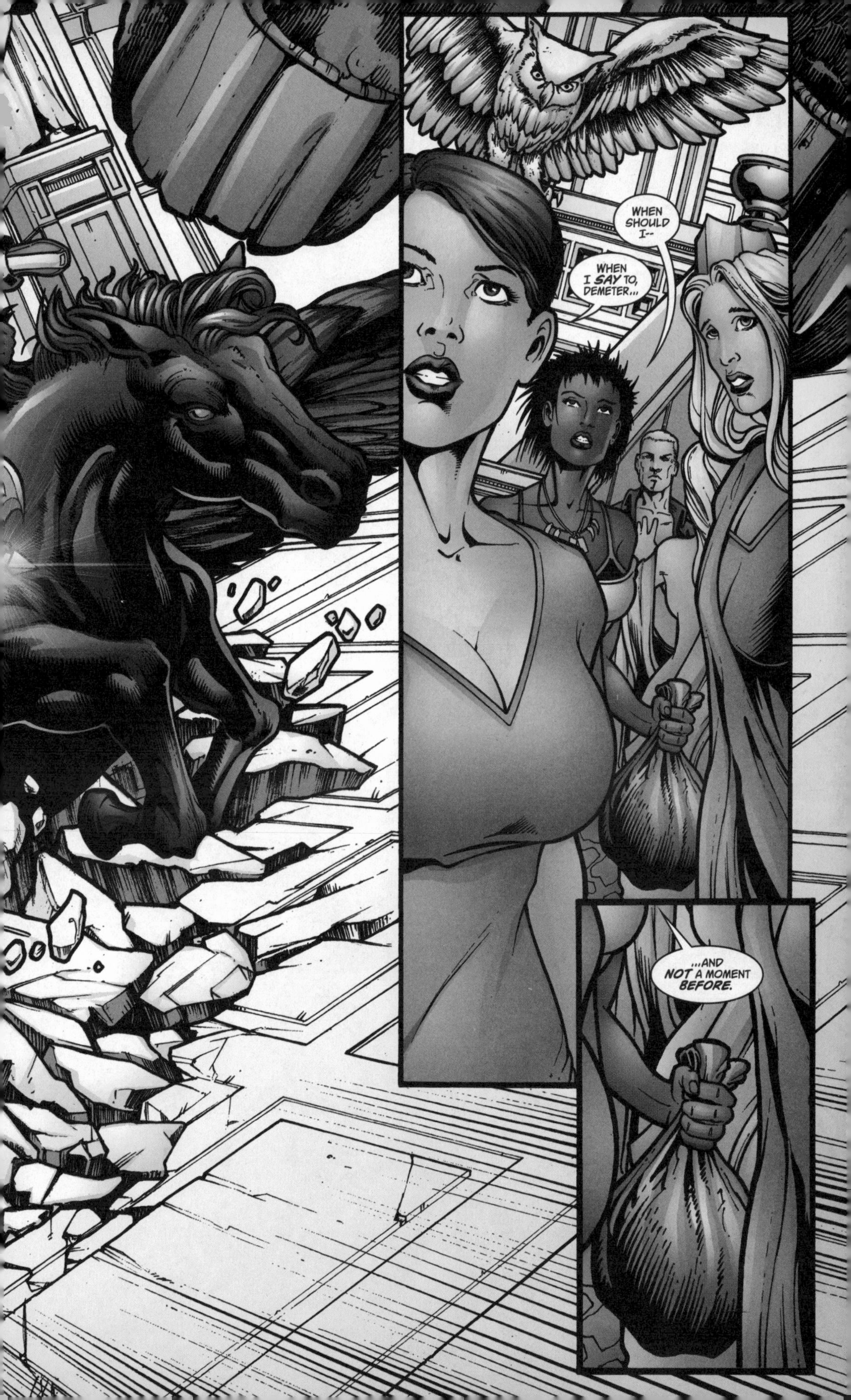
WHEN SHOULD I--
WHEN I SAY TO, DEMETER...
...AND NOT A MOMENT BEFORE.

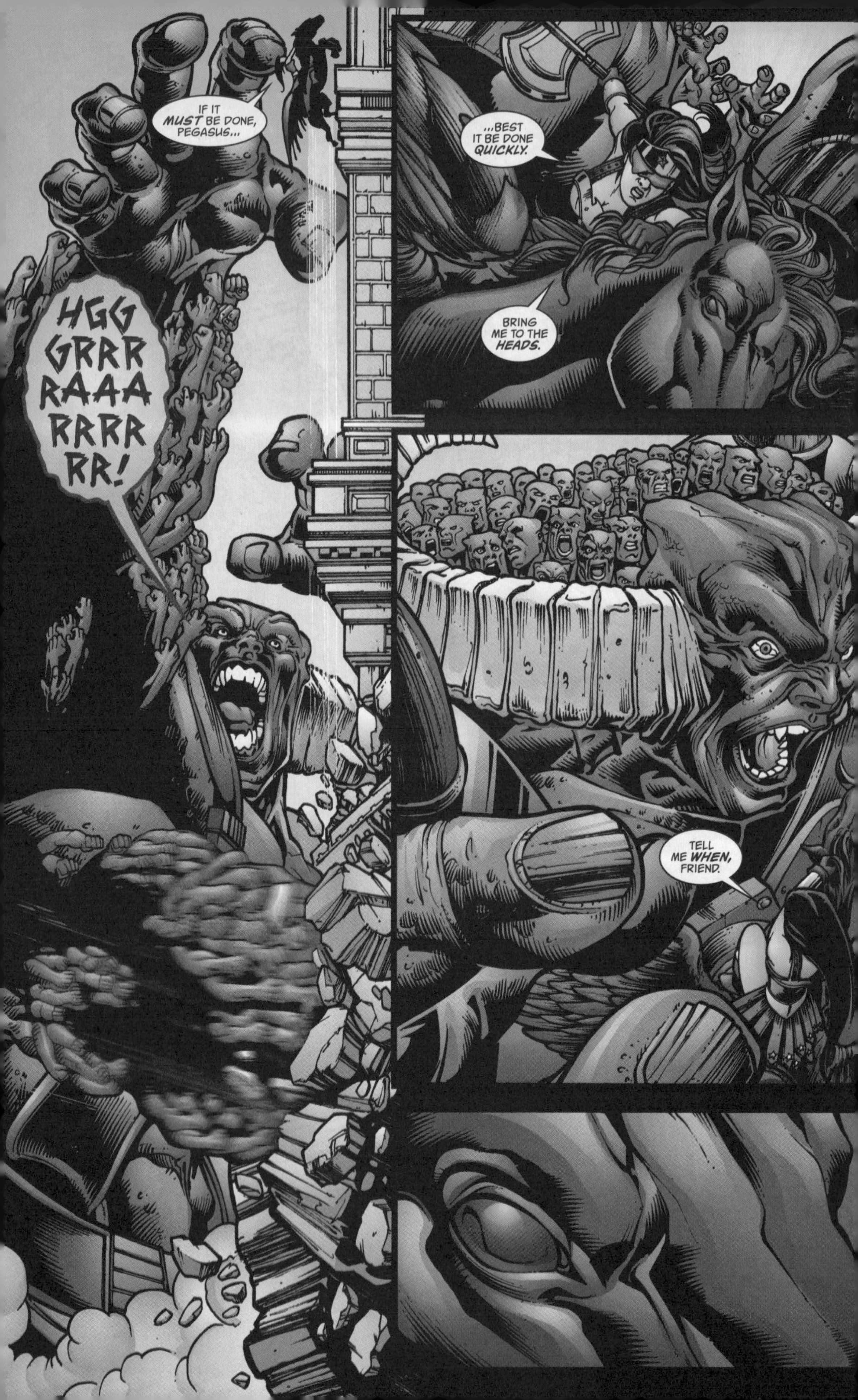
IF IT MUST BE DONE, PEGASUS...
...BEST IT BE DONE QUICKLY.
BRING ME TO THE HEADS.
HGG GRRR RAAA RRRR RR!
TELL ME WHEN, FRIEND.

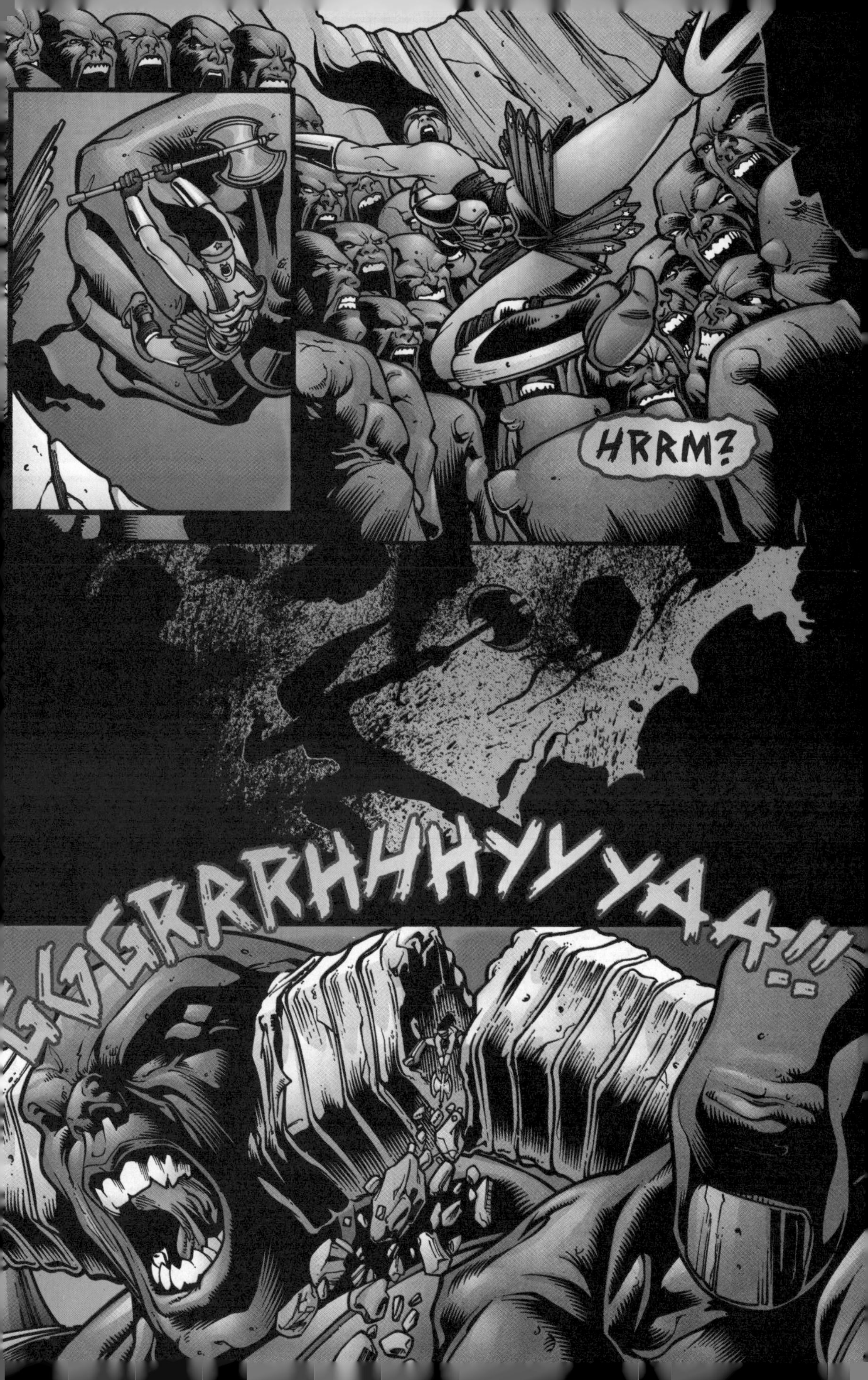
HRRM?
GRRHHHYYYAA!!

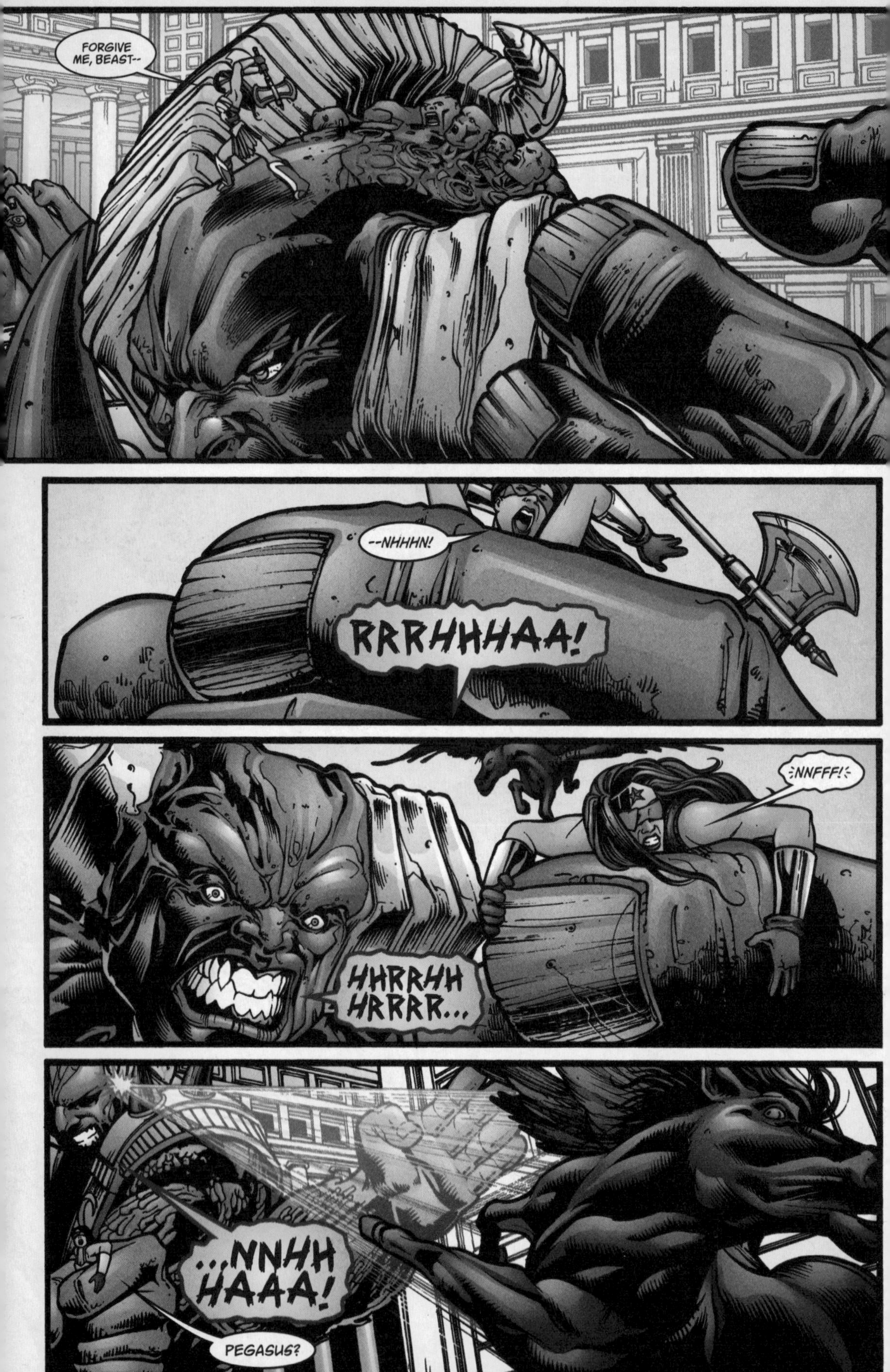
FORGIVE ME, BEAST--
--NHHHN!
RRRHHHAA!
NNFFF!
HHRRHH HRRRR...
...NNHH HAAA!
PEGASUS?

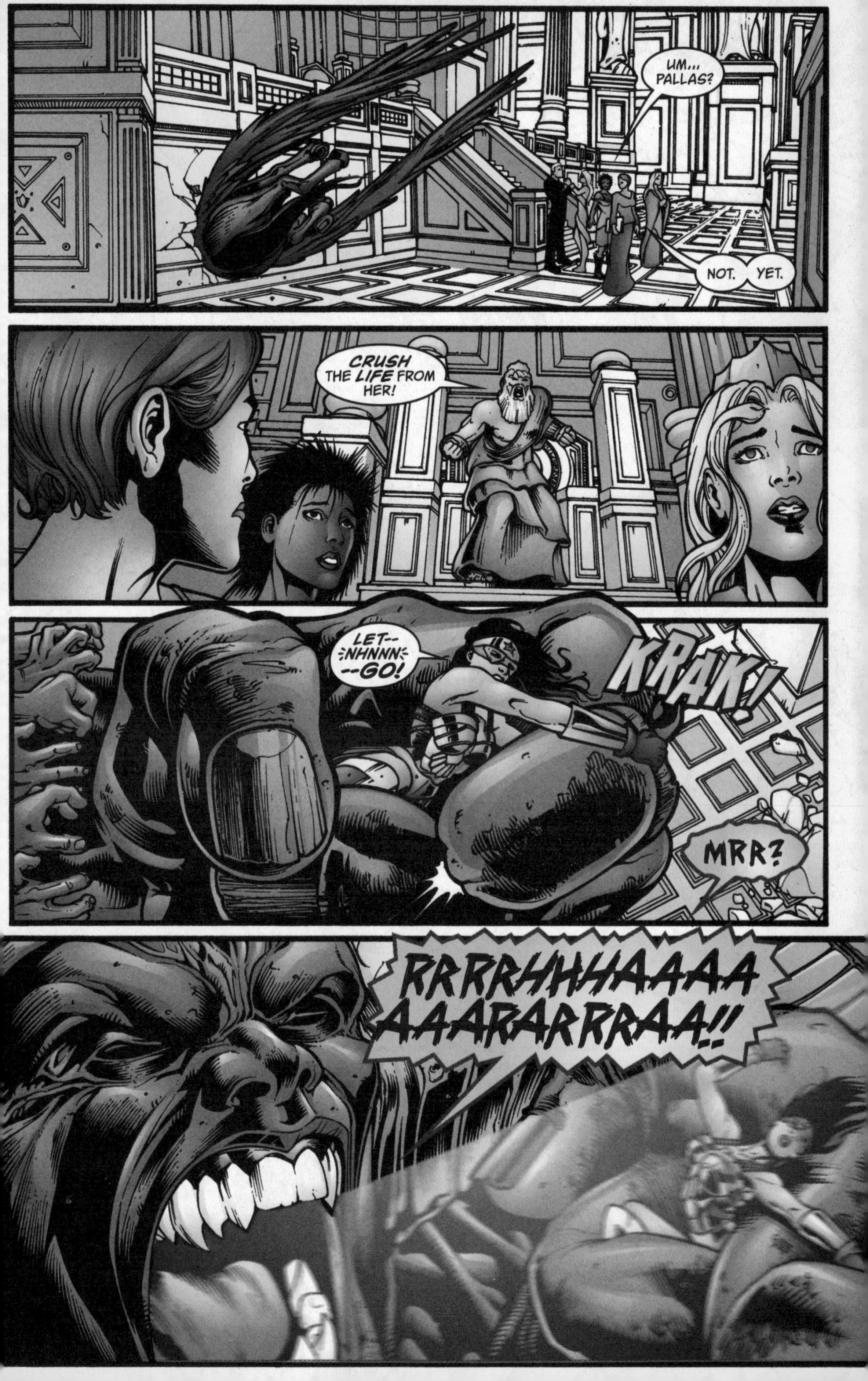
UM... PALLAS?
NOT. YET.
CRUSH THE LIFE FROM HER!
LET-- NHNNN --GO!
KRAK!
MRR?
RRRRHHAAAA AAARARRRAA!!

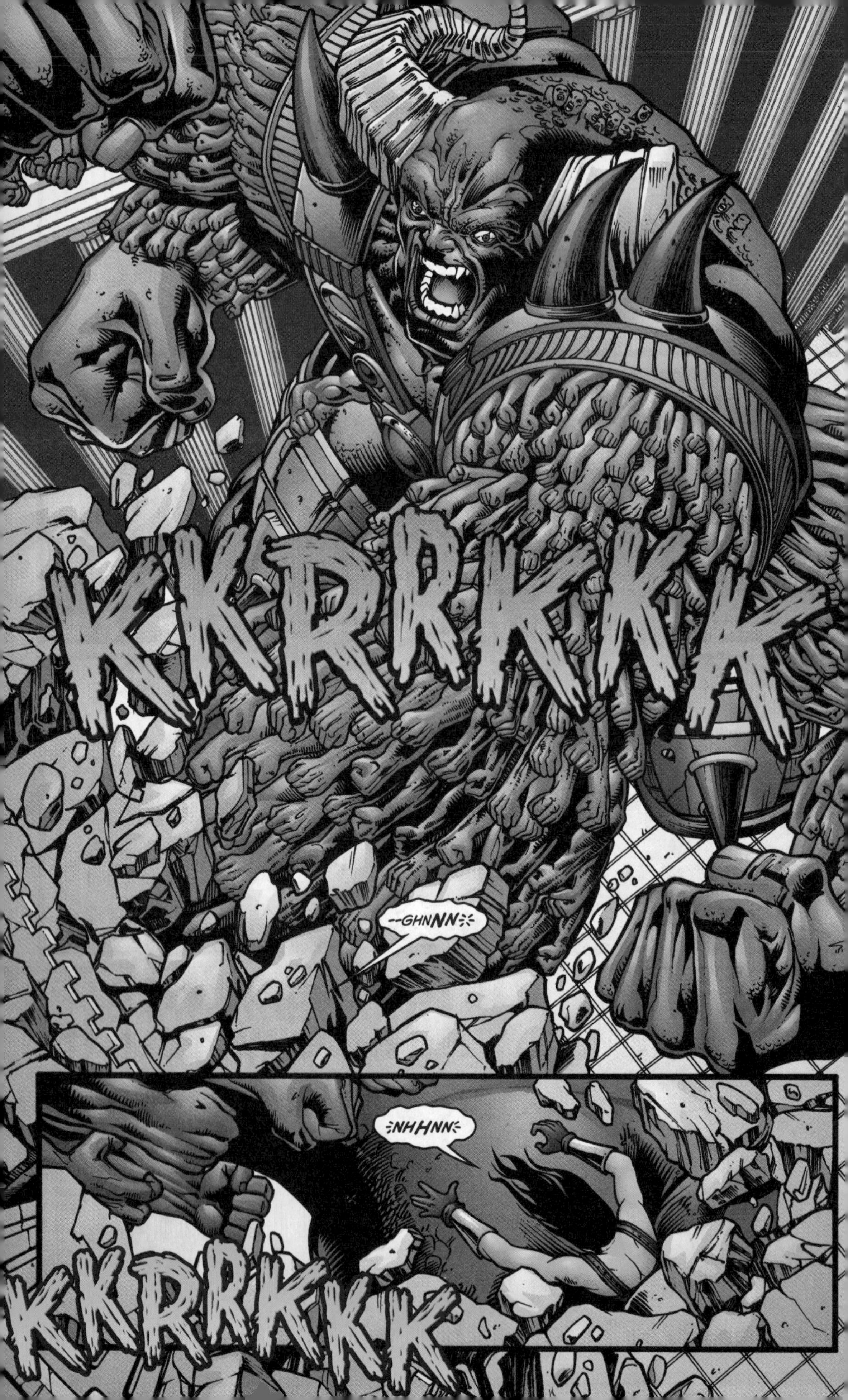
KKRKKK
--GHNNN--
NHHNN
KKRKKK

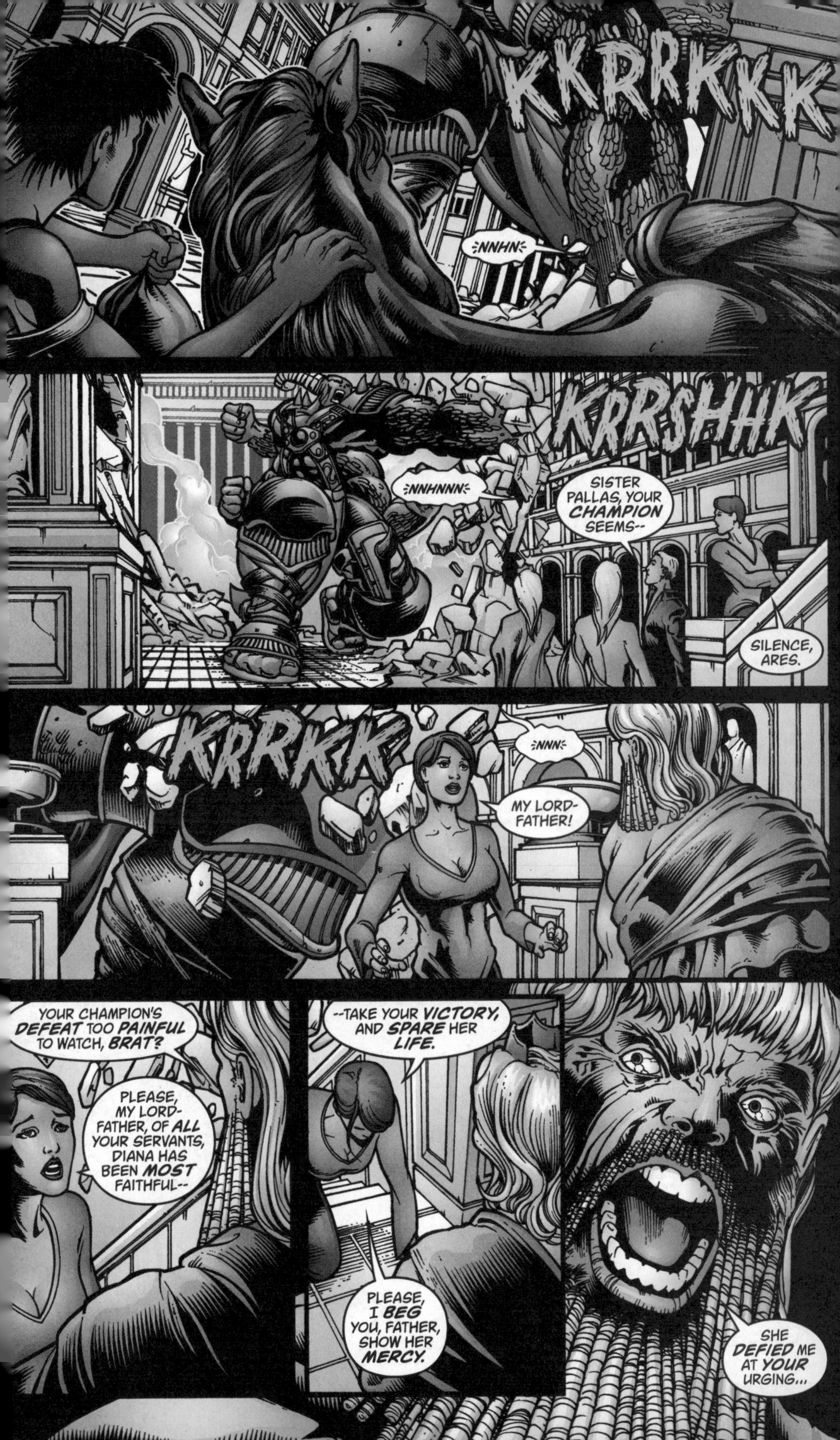
KKRRKKK
NNHN
KRRSHHK
NNHNNN
SISTER PALLAS, YOUR CHAMPION SEEMS--
SILENCE, ARES.
KRRKK
NNN
MY LORD-FATHER!
YOUR CHAMPION'S DEFEAT TOO PAINFUL TO WATCH, BRAT?
PLEASE, MY LORD-FATHER, OF ALL YOUR SERVANTS, DIANA HAS BEEN MOST FAITHFUL--
--TAKE YOUR VICTORY, AND SPARE HER LIFE.
PLEASE, I BEG YOU, FATHER, SHOW HER MERCY.
SHE DEFIED ME AT YOUR URGING...

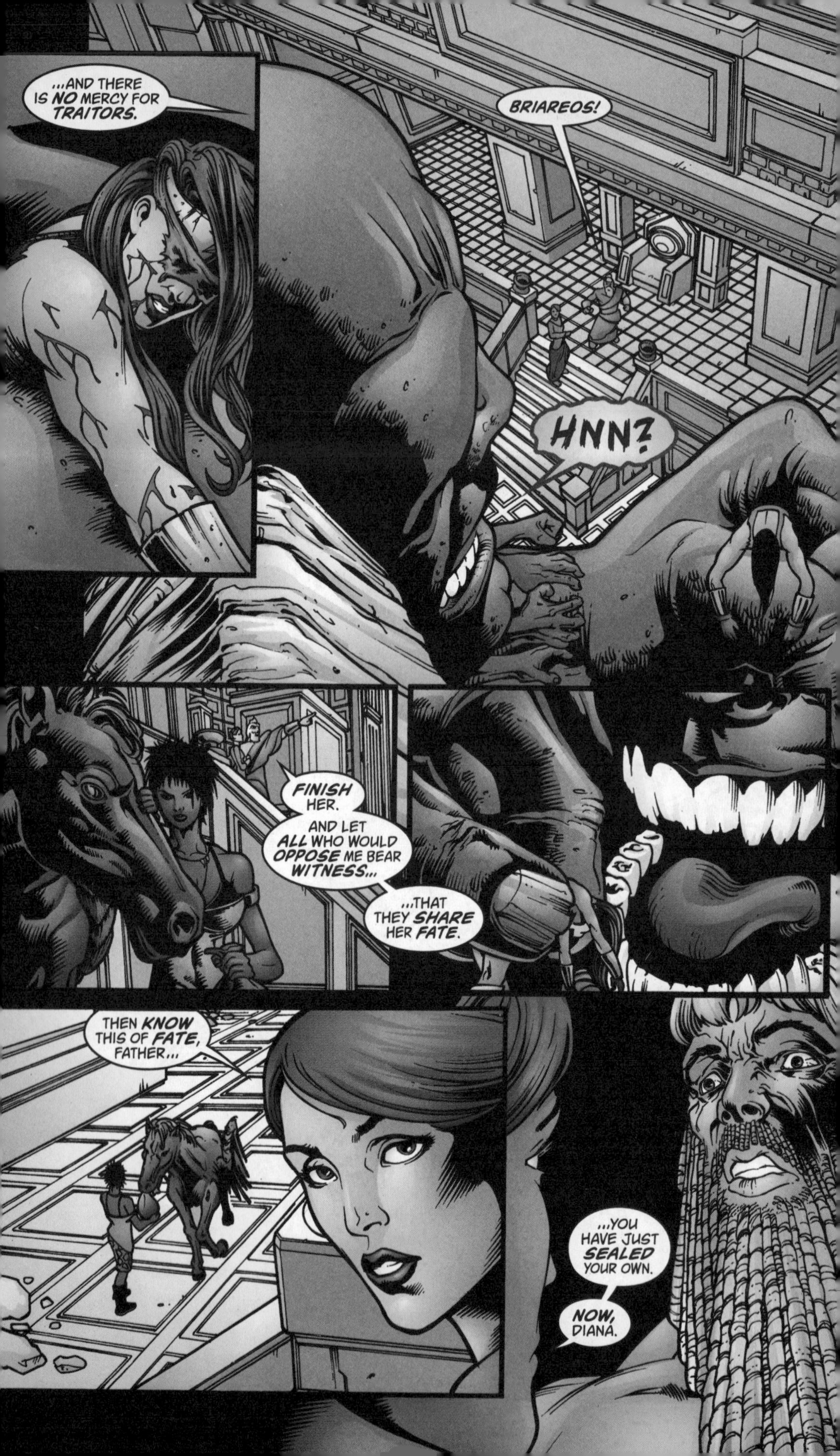
...AND THERE IS NO MERCY FOR TRAITORS.
BRIAREOS!
HNN?
FINISH HER.
AND LET ALL WHO WOULD OPPOSE ME BEAR WITNESS...
...THAT THEY SHARE HER FATE.
THEN KNOW THIS OF FATE, FATHER...
...YOU HAVE JUST SEALED YOUR OWN.
NOW, DIANA.

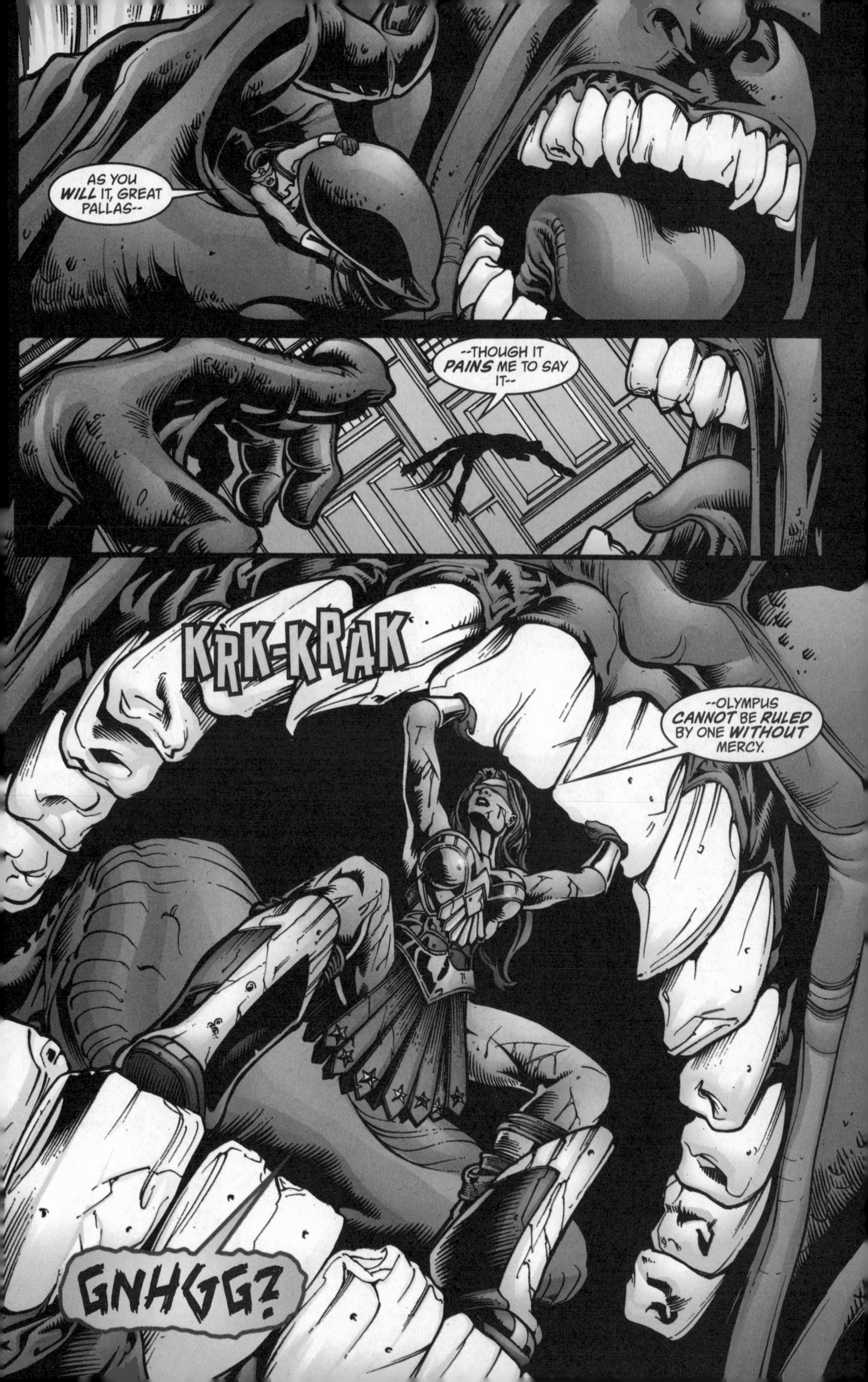
AS YOU WILL IT, GREAT PALLAS--
--THOUGH IT PAINS ME TO SAY IT--
KRK-KRAK
--OLYMPUS CANNOT BE RULED BY ONE WITHOUT MERCY.
GNHGG?

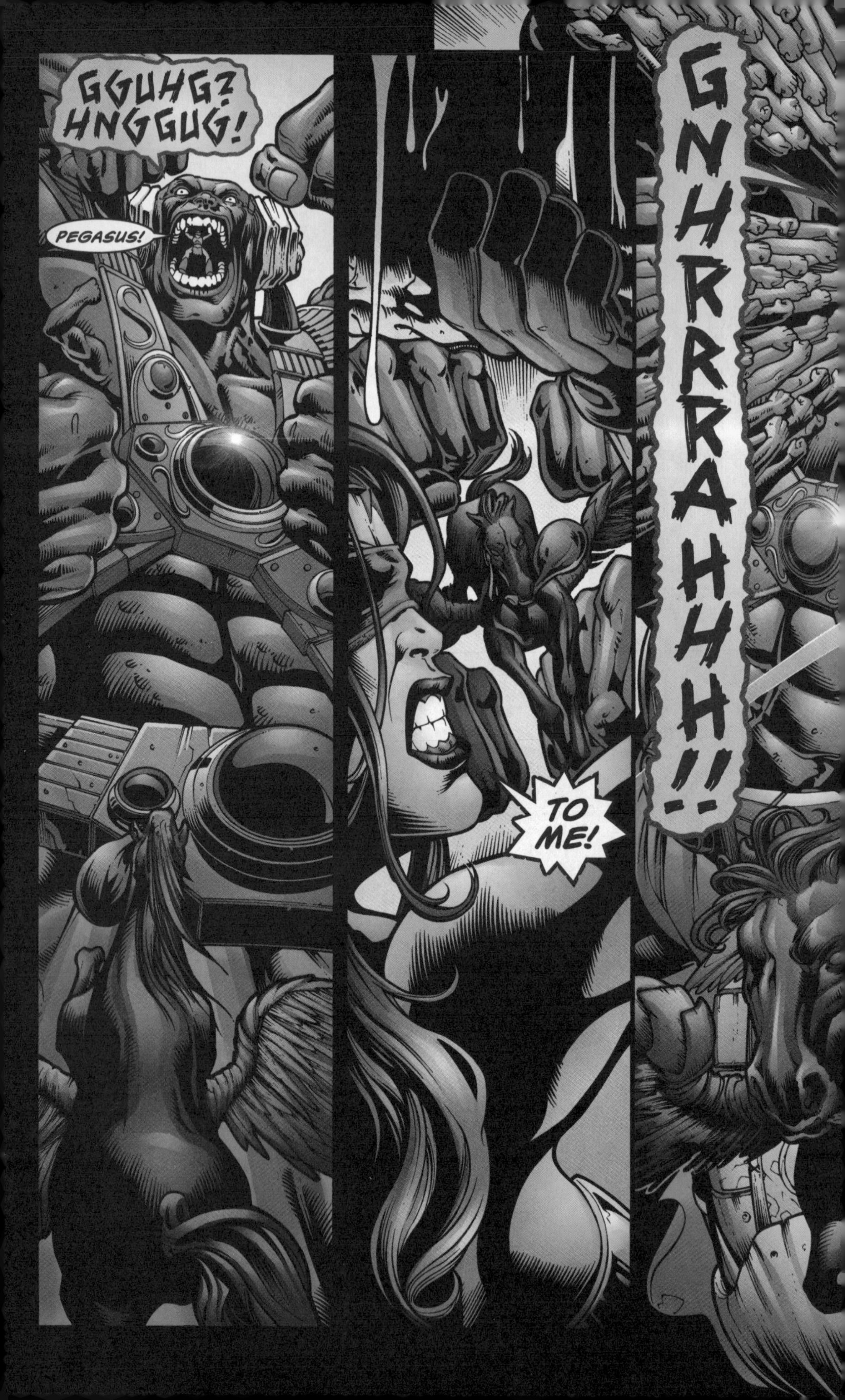
GGUHG? HNGGUG!
PEGASUS!
TO ME!
GNHRRRAHHH!!

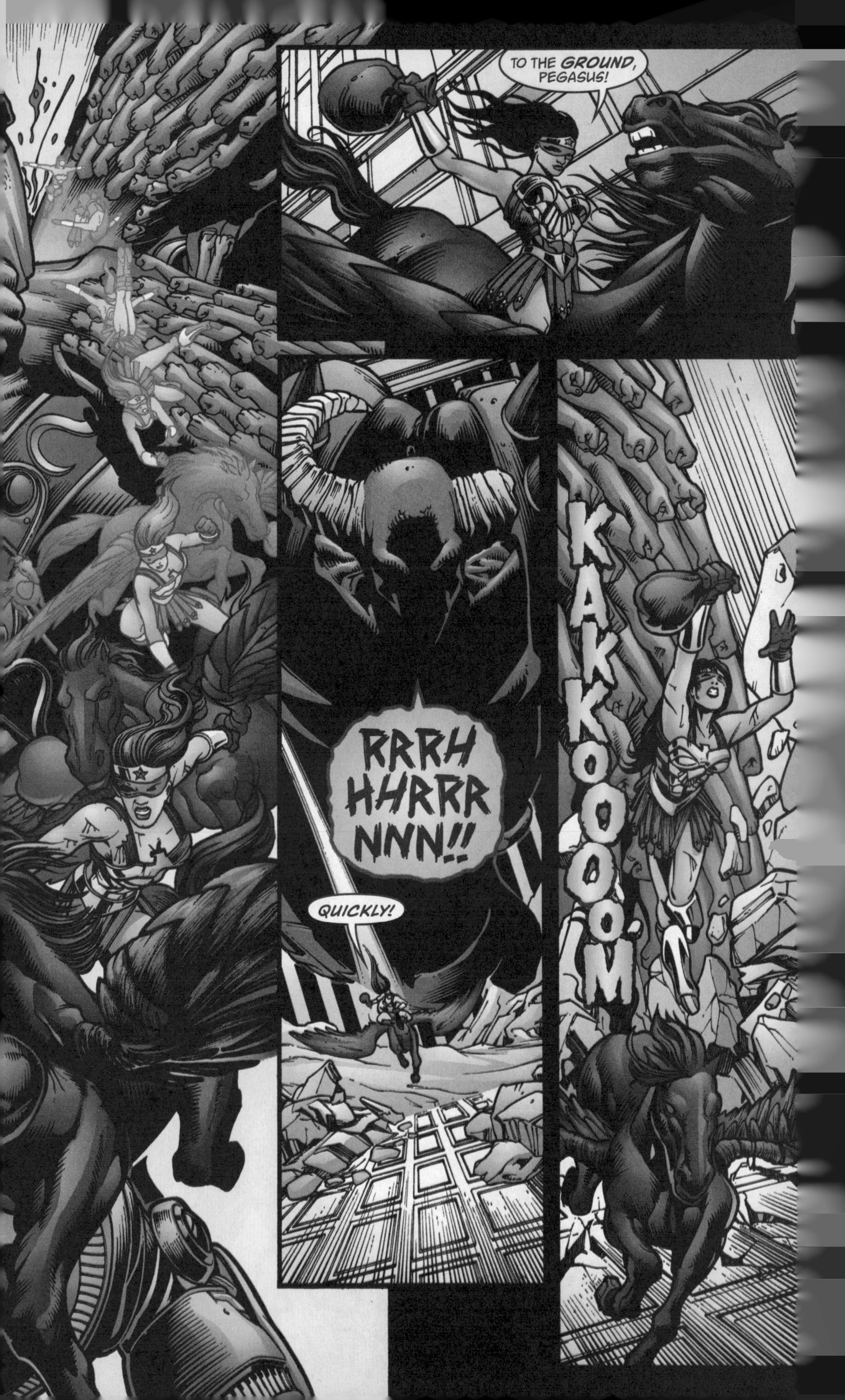

TO THE GROUND, PEGASUS!
RRRH HHRRR NNN!!
QUICKLY!
KAKOOOOM

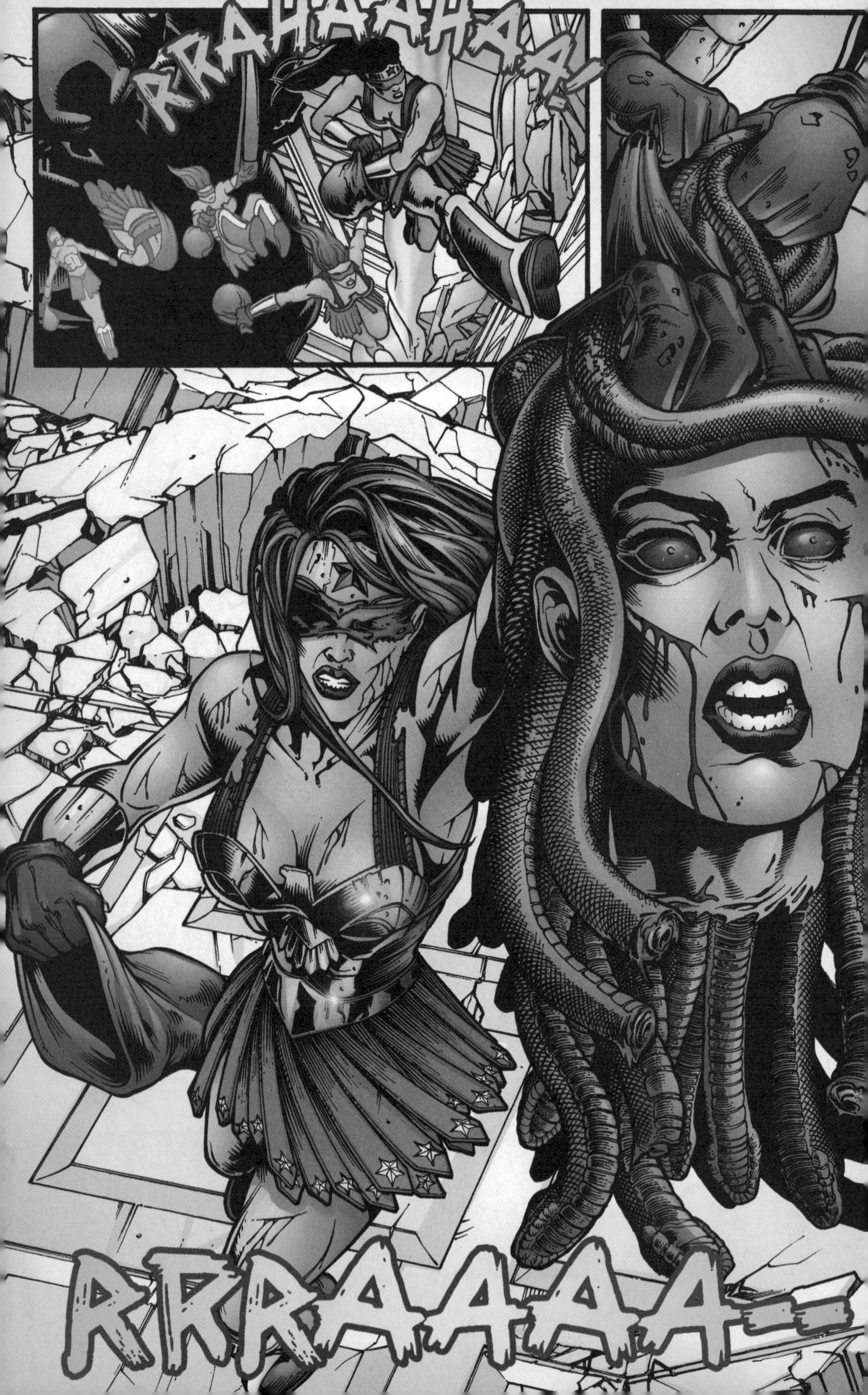
RRAHAAHAA-
RRAAAA-

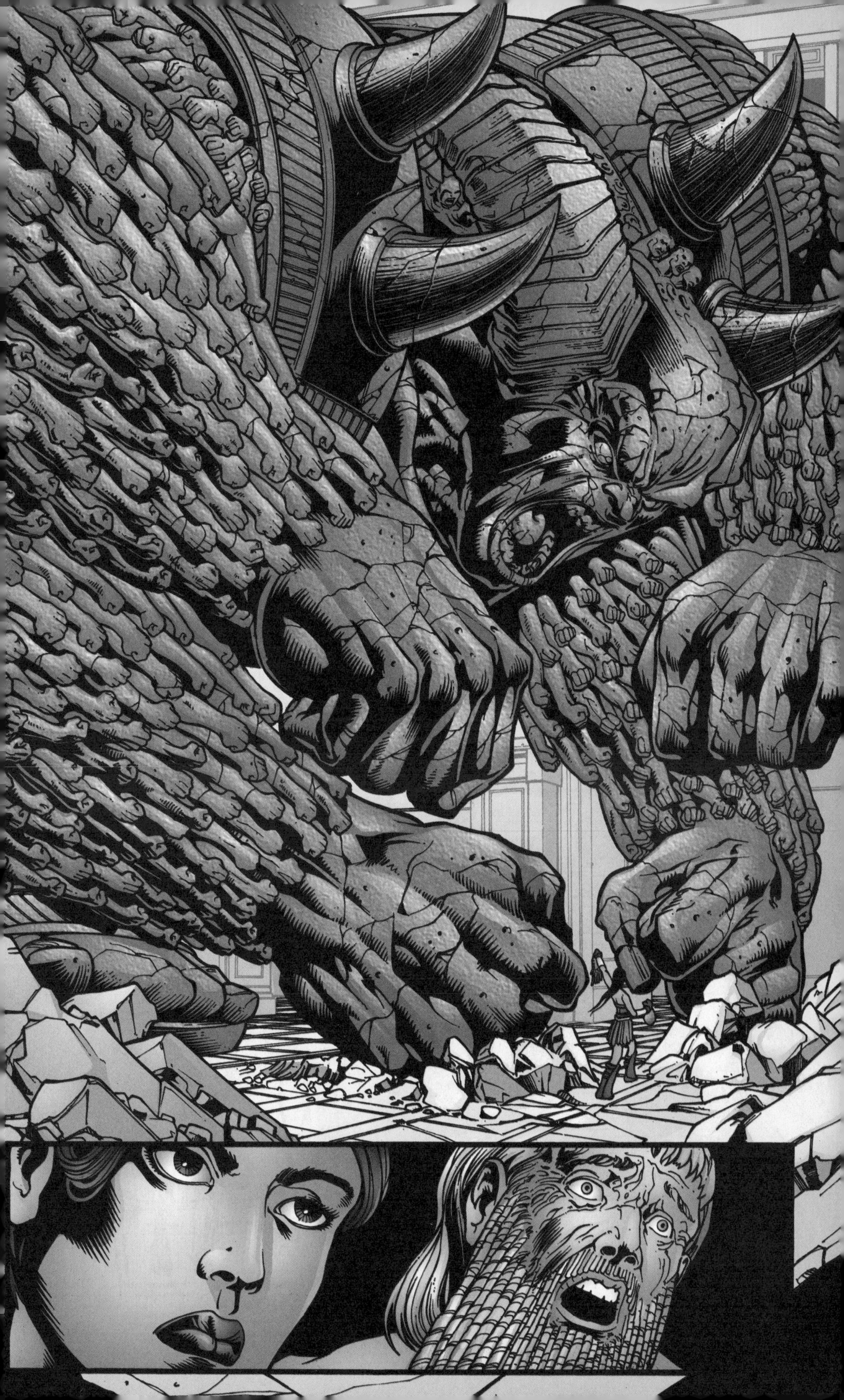

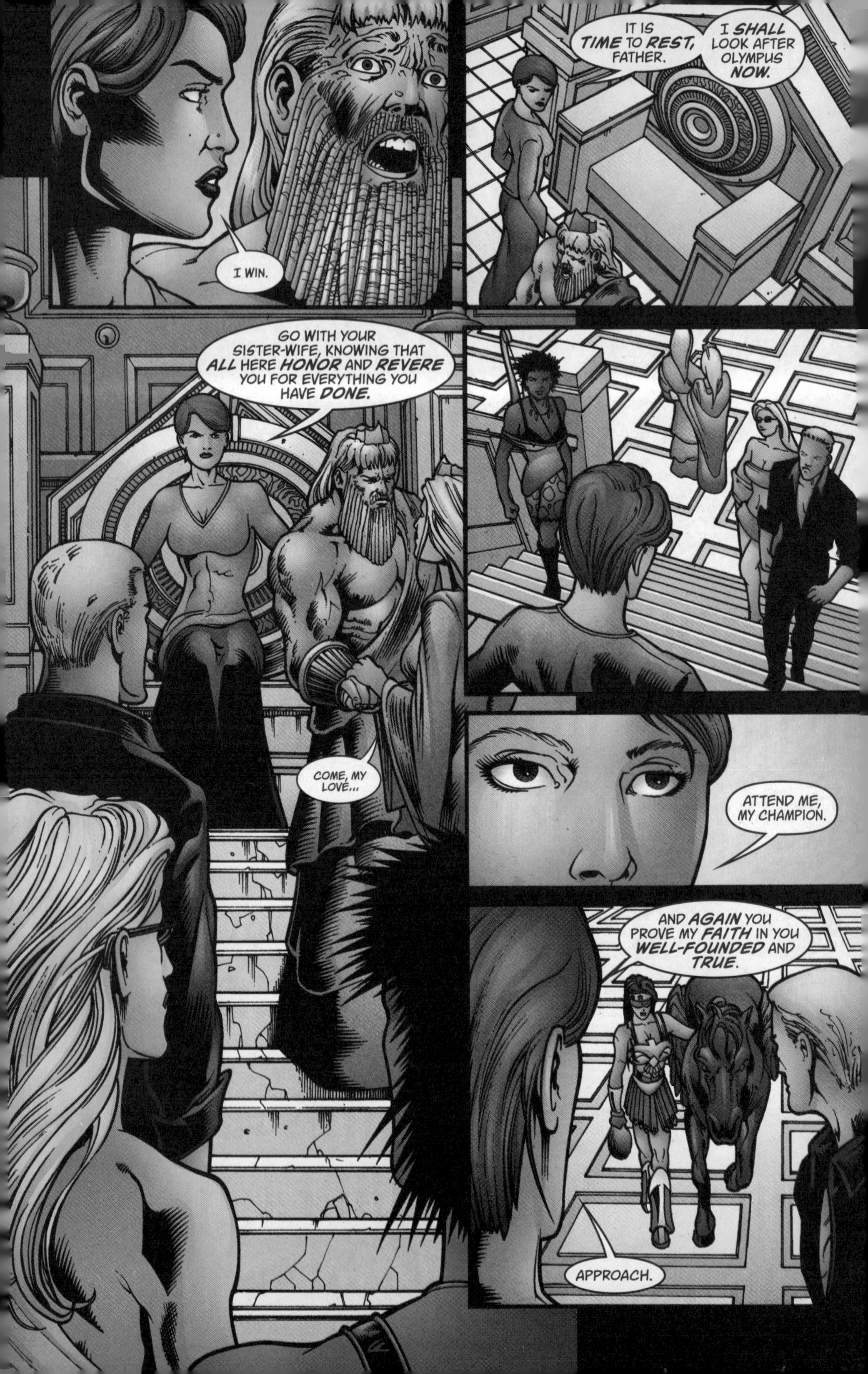
I WIN.
IT IS TIME TO REST, FATHER.
I SHALL LOOK AFTER OLYMPUS NOW.
GO WITH YOUR SISTER-WIFE, KNOWING THAT ALL HERE HONOR AND REVERE YOU FOR EVERYTHING YOU HAVE DONE.
COME, MY LOVE...
ATTEND ME, MY CHAMPION.
AND AGAIN YOU PROVE MY FAITH IN YOU WELL-FOUNDED AND TRUE.
APPROACH.

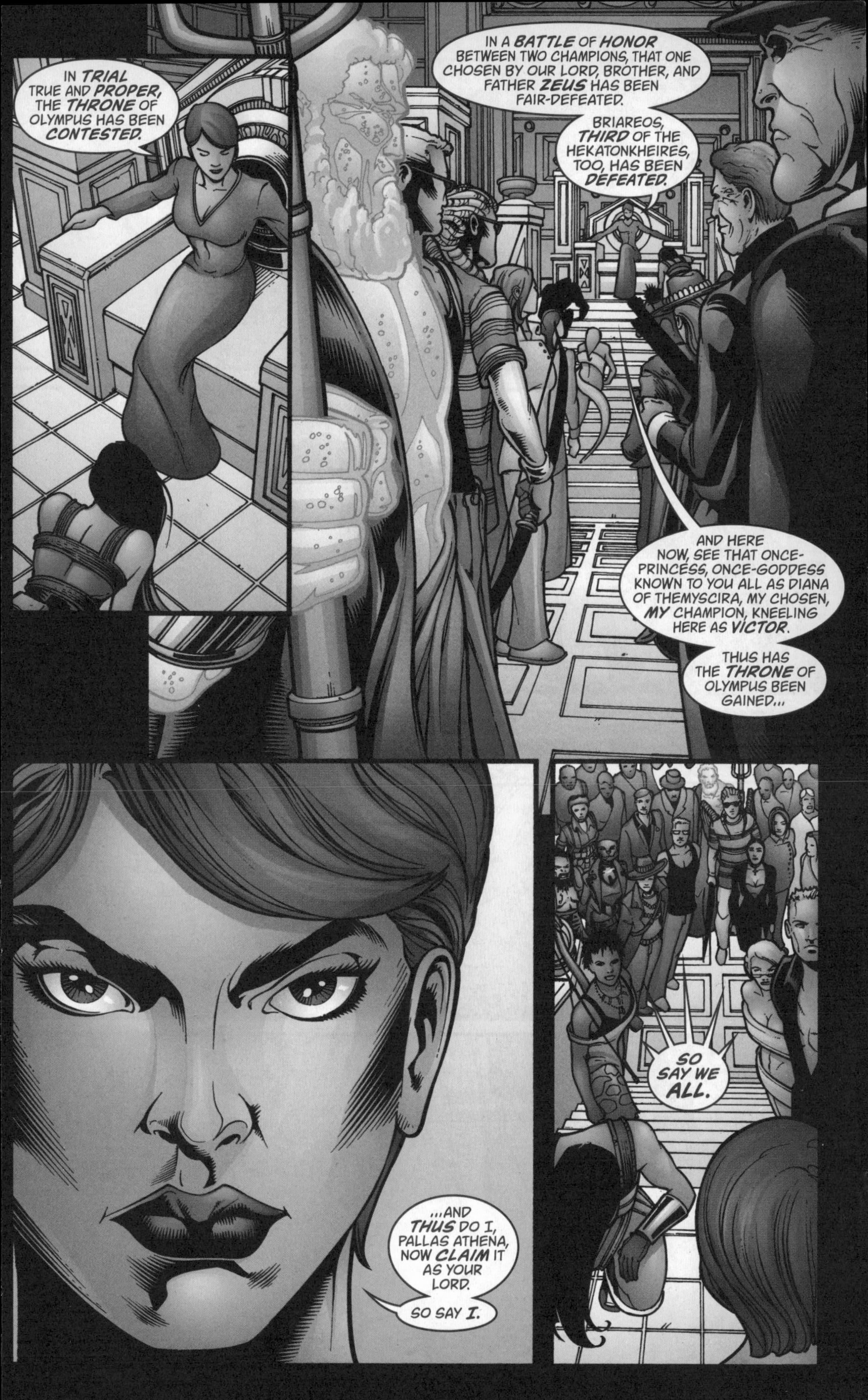
IN TRIAL TRUE AND PROPER, THE THRONE OF OLYMPUS HAS BEEN CONTESTED.
IN A BATTLE OF HONOR BETWEEN TWO CHAMPIONS, THAT ONE CHOSEN BY OUR LORD, BROTHER, AND FATHER ZEUS HAS BEEN FAIR-DEFEATED.
BRIAREOS, THIRD OF THE HEKATONKHEIRES, TOO, HAS BEEN DEFEATED.
AND HERE NOW, SEE THAT ONCE-PRINCESS, ONCE-GODDESS KNOWN TO YOU ALL AS DIANA OF THEMYSCIRA, MY CHOSEN, MY CHAMPION, KNEELING HERE AS VICTOR.
THUS HAS THE THRONE OF OLYMPUS BEEN GAINED...
...AND THUS DO I, PALLAS ATHENA, NOW CLAIM IT AS YOUR LORD.
SO SAY I.
SO SAY WE ALL.

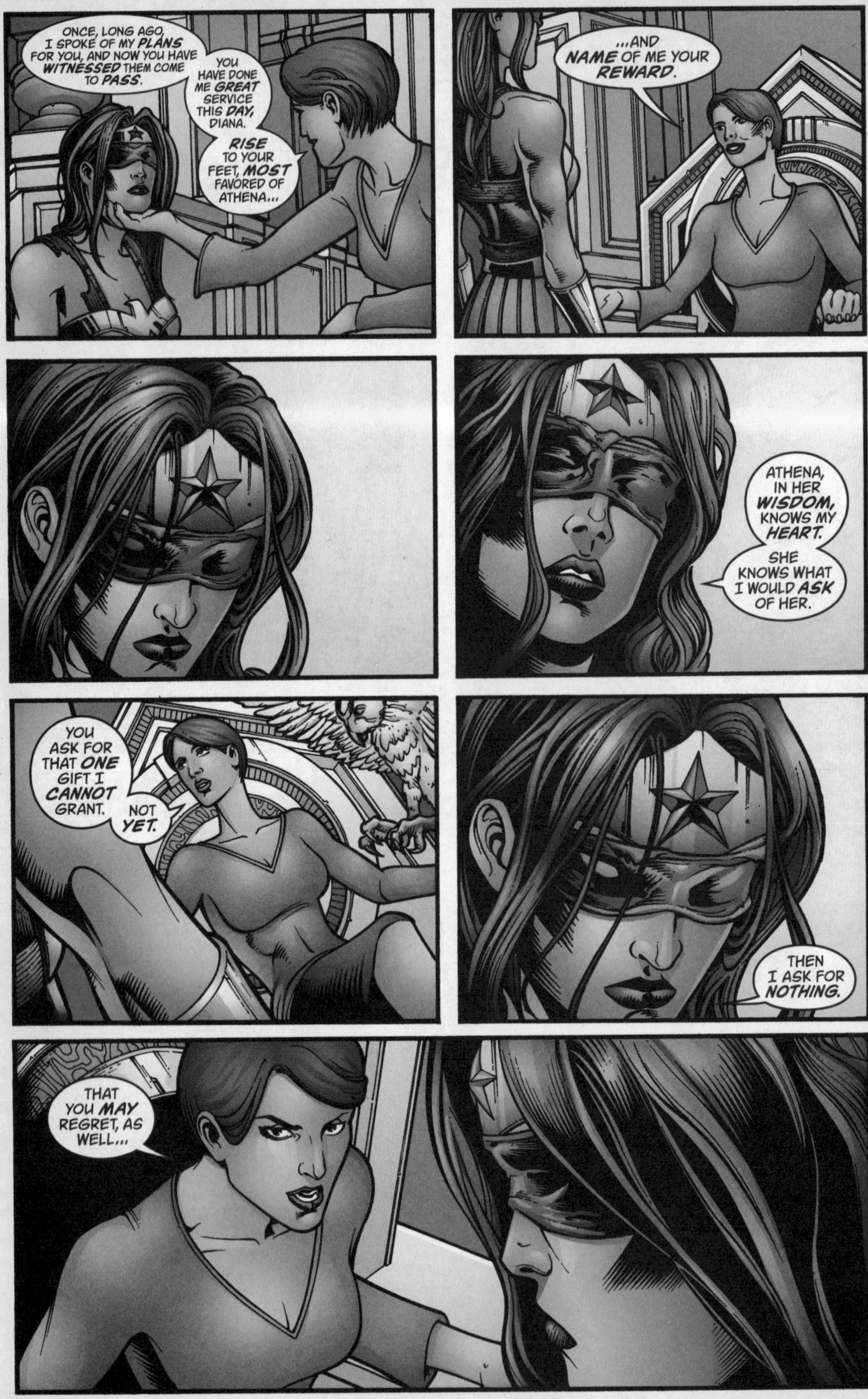
ONCE, LONG AGO, I SPOKE OF MY PLANS FOR YOU, AND NOW YOU HAVE WITNESSED THEM COME TO PASS.
YOU HAVE DONE ME GREAT SERVICE THIS DAY, DIANA.
RISE TO YOUR FEET, MOST FAVORED OF ATHENA...
...AND NAME OF ME YOUR REWARD.
ATHENA, IN HER WISDOM, KNOWS MY HEART.
SHE KNOWS WHAT I WOULD ASK OF HER.
YOU ASK FOR THAT ONE GIFT I CANNOT GRANT.
NOT YET.
THEN I ASK FOR NOTHING.
THAT YOU MAY REGRET, AS WELL...

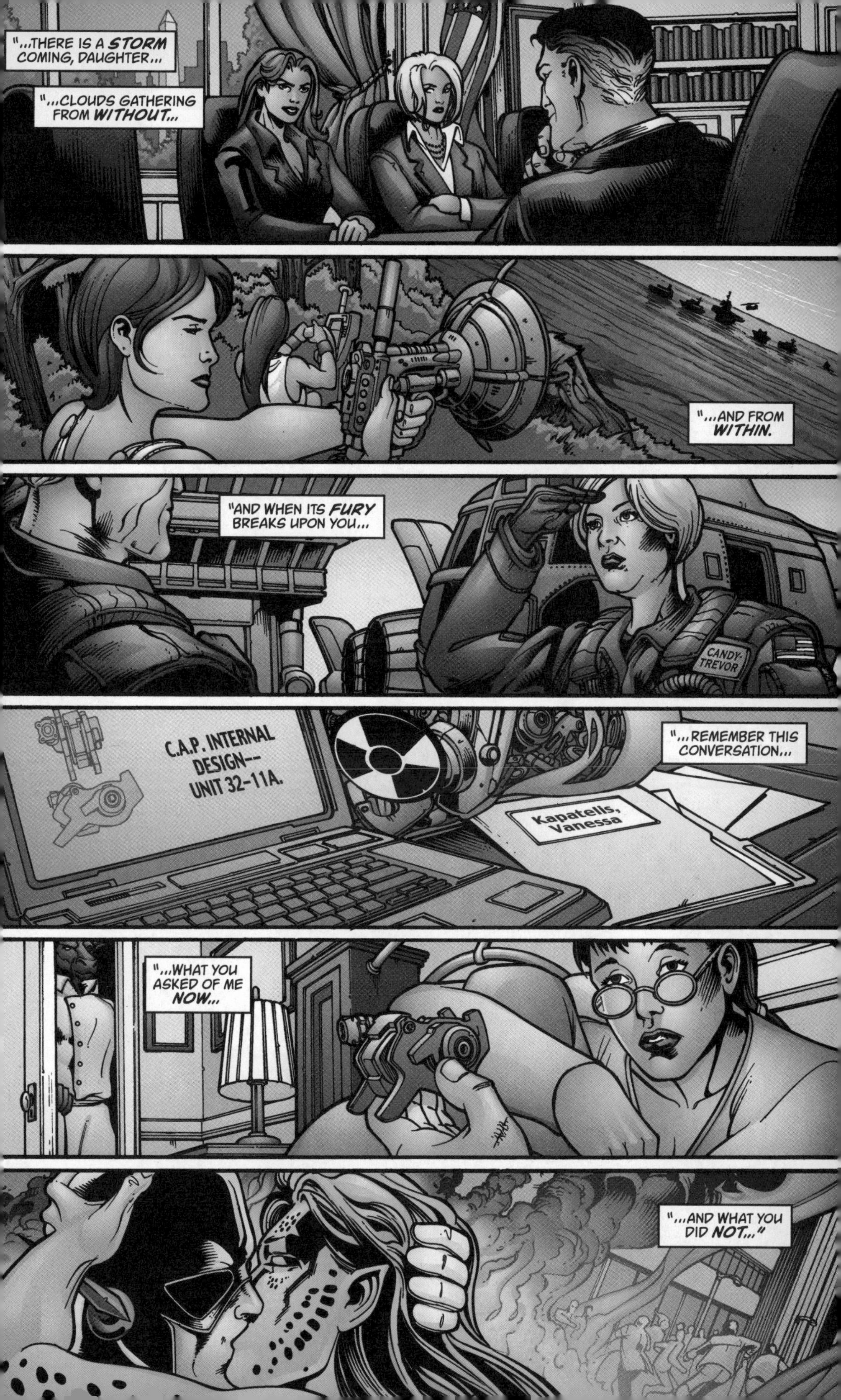
"...THERE IS A STORM COMING, DAUGHTER...
"...CLOUDS GATHERING FROM WITHOUT...
"...AND FROM WITHIN.
"AND WHEN ITS FURY BREAKS UPON YOU...
CANDY-TREVOR
C.A.P. INTERNAL DESIGN-- UNIT 32-11A.
"...REMEMBER THIS CONVERSATION...
Kapatelis, Vanessa
"...WHAT YOU ASKED OF ME NOW...
"...AND WHAT YOU DID NOT..."

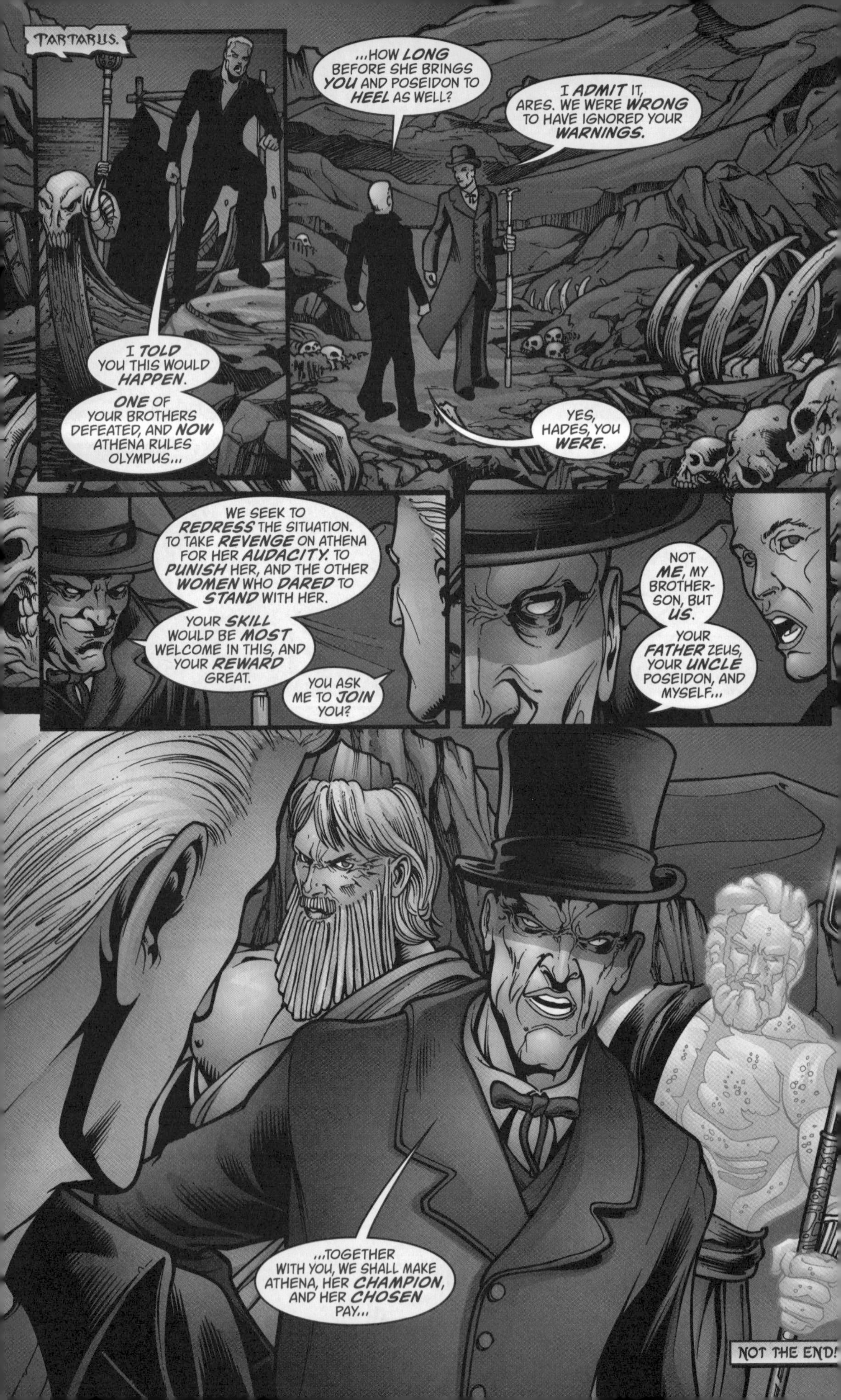
TARTARUS.
...HOW LONG BEFORE SHE BRINGS YOU AND POSEIDON TO HEEL AS WELL?
I TOLD YOU THIS WOULD HAPPEN.
ONE OF YOUR BROTHERS DEFEATED, AND NOW ATHENA RULES OLYMPUS...
I ADMIT IT, ARES. WE WERE WRONG TO HAVE IGNORED YOUR WARNINGS.
YES, HADES, YOU WERE.
WE SEEK TO REDRESS THE SITUATION. TO TAKE REVENGE ON ATHENA FOR HER AUDACITY. TO PUNISH HER, AND THE OTHER WOMEN WHO DARED TO STAND WITH HER.
YOUR SKILL WOULD BE MOST WELCOME IN THIS, AND YOUR REWARD GREAT.
YOU ASK ME TO JOIN YOU?
NOT ME, MY BROTHER-SON, BUT US.
YOUR FATHER ZEUS, YOUR UNCLE POSEIDON, AND MYSELF...
...TOGETHER WITH YOU, WE SHALL MAKE ATHENA, HER CHAMPION, AND HER CHOSEN PAY...
NOT THE END!

WONDER WOMAN

COVERS

WONDER WOMAN #206
ART BY J.G. JONES

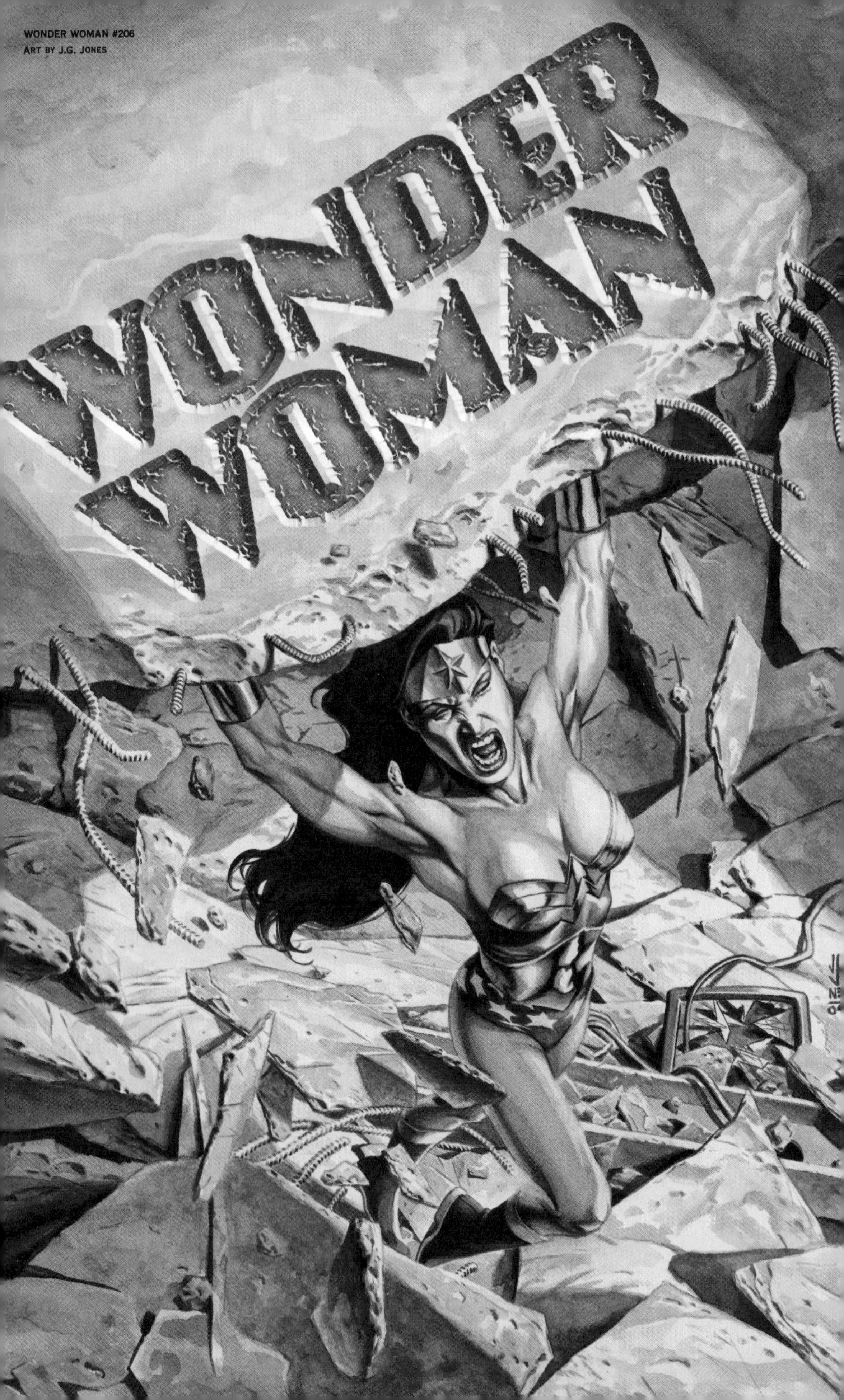
WONDER
WOMAN

WONDER WOMAN #207
ART BY J.G. JONES

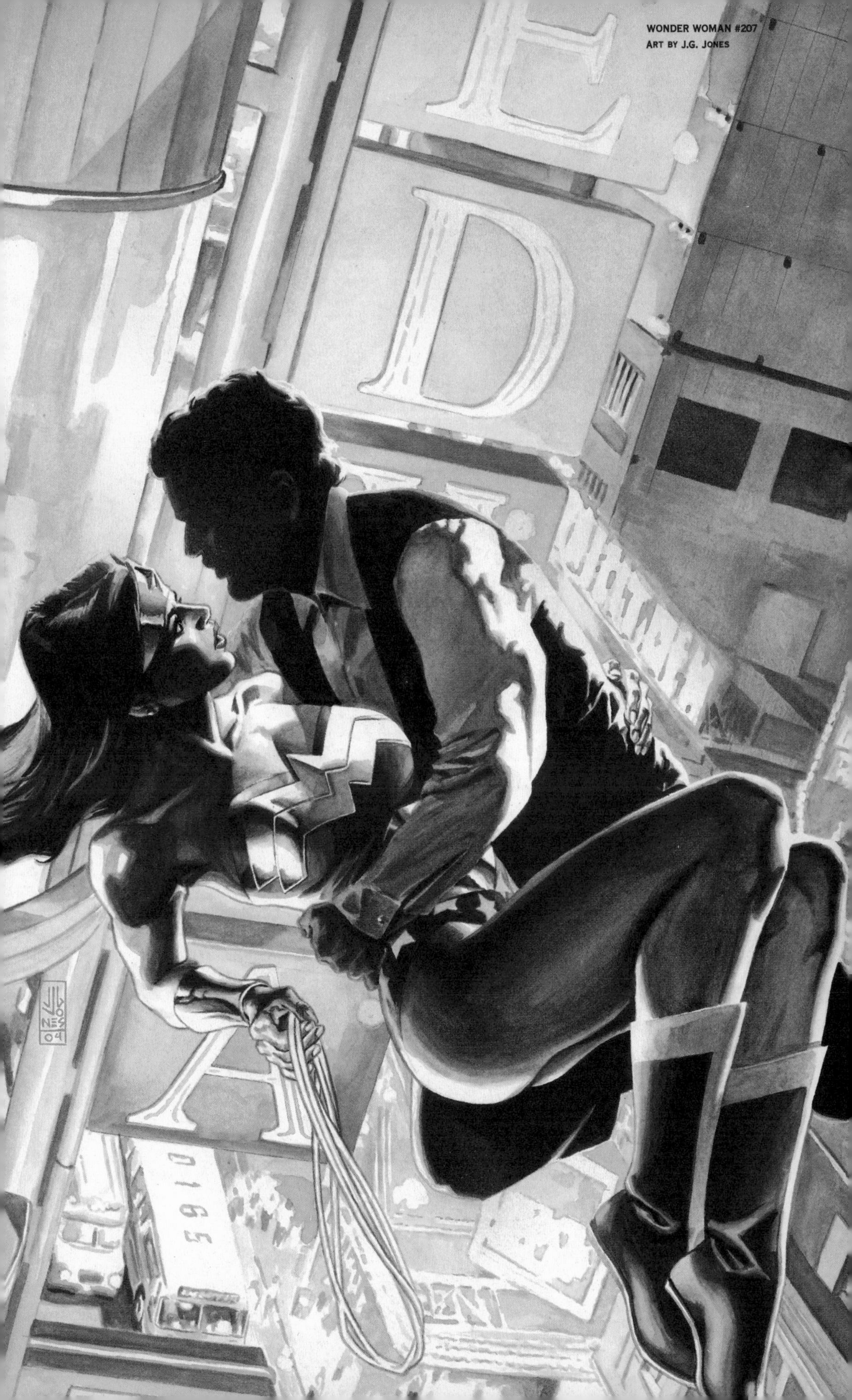

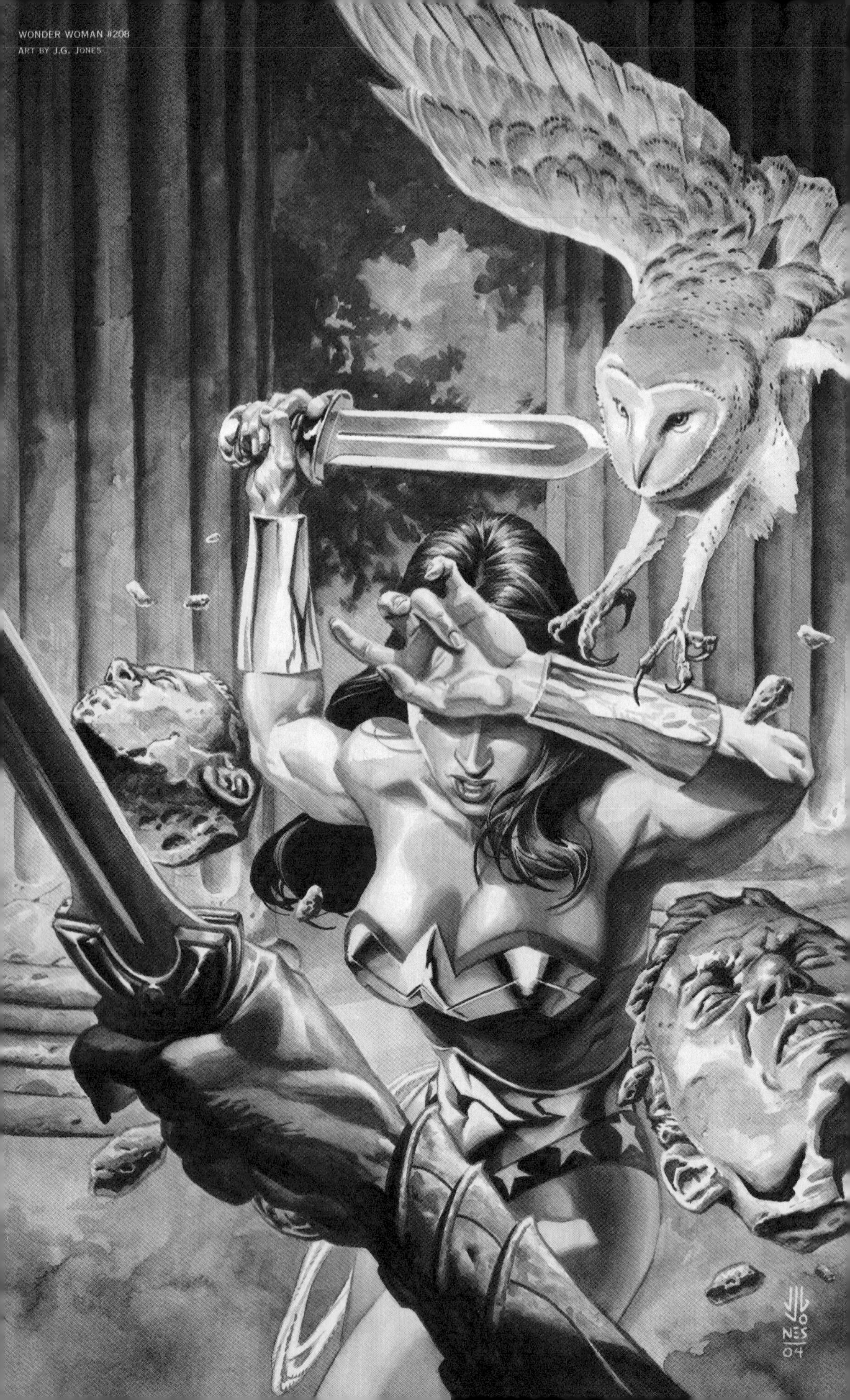

WONDER WOMAN #208
ART BY J.G. JONES

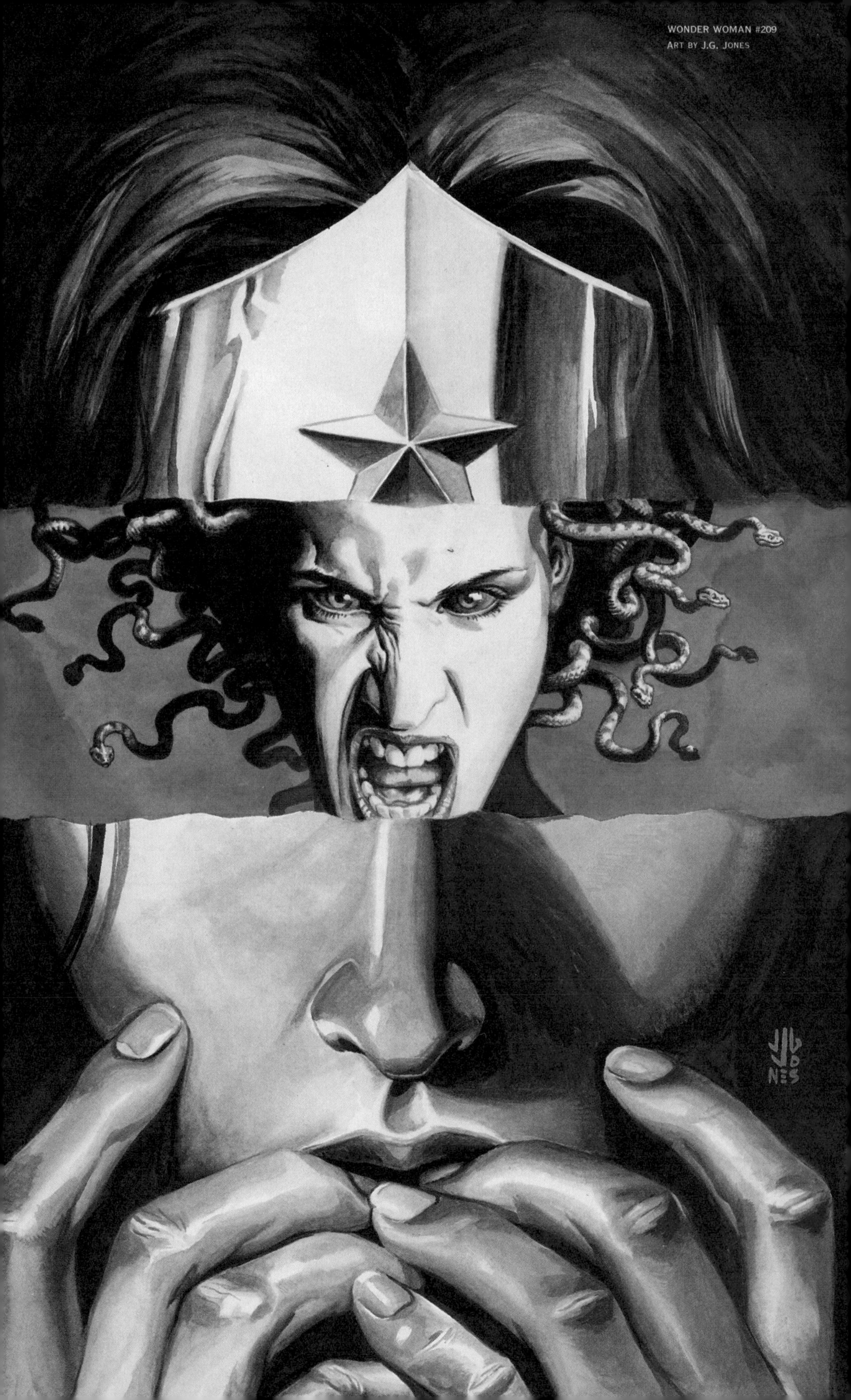

WONDER WOMAN #209
ART BY J.G. JONES

WONDER WOMAN #210

ART BY J.G. JONES

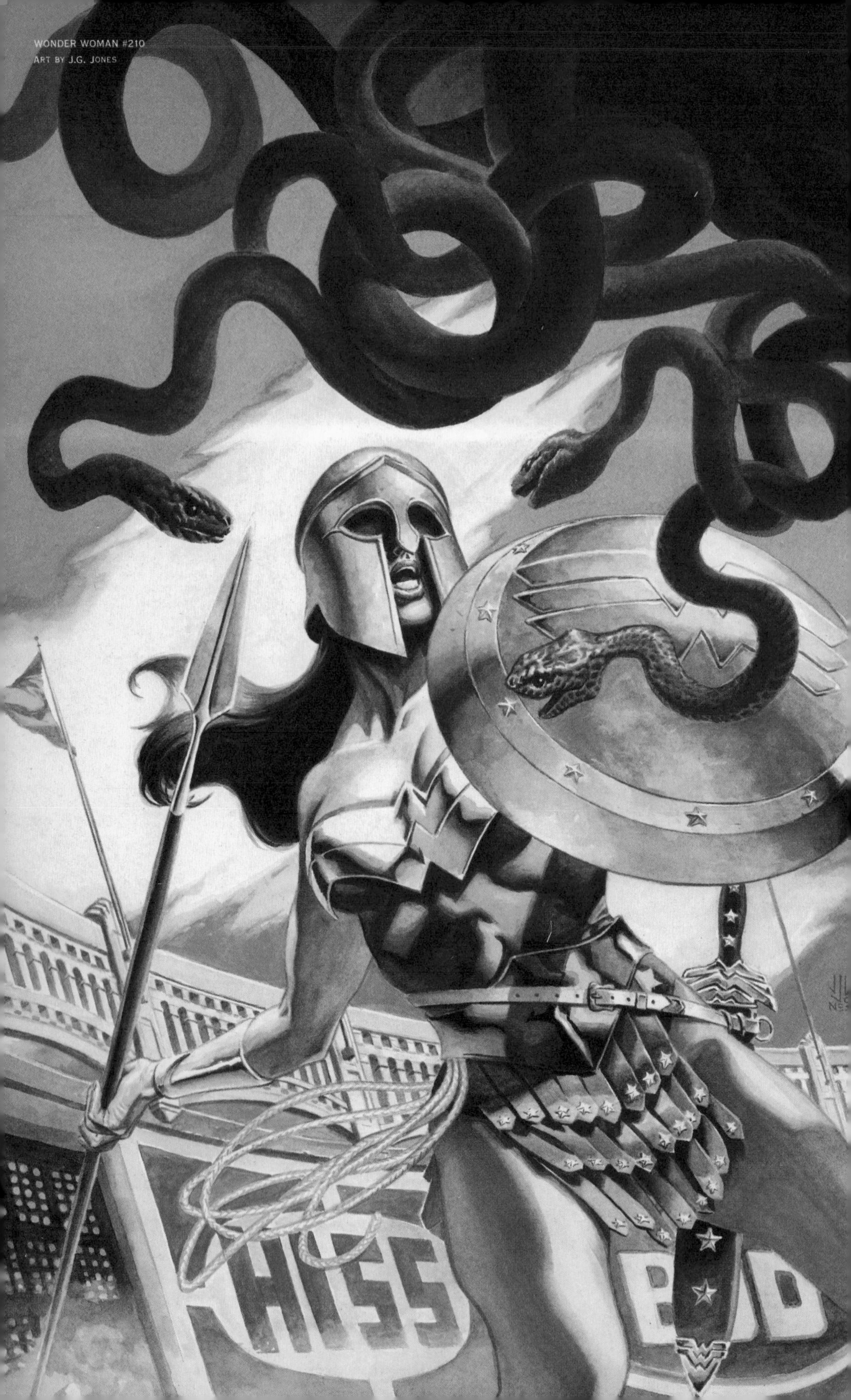
HISS

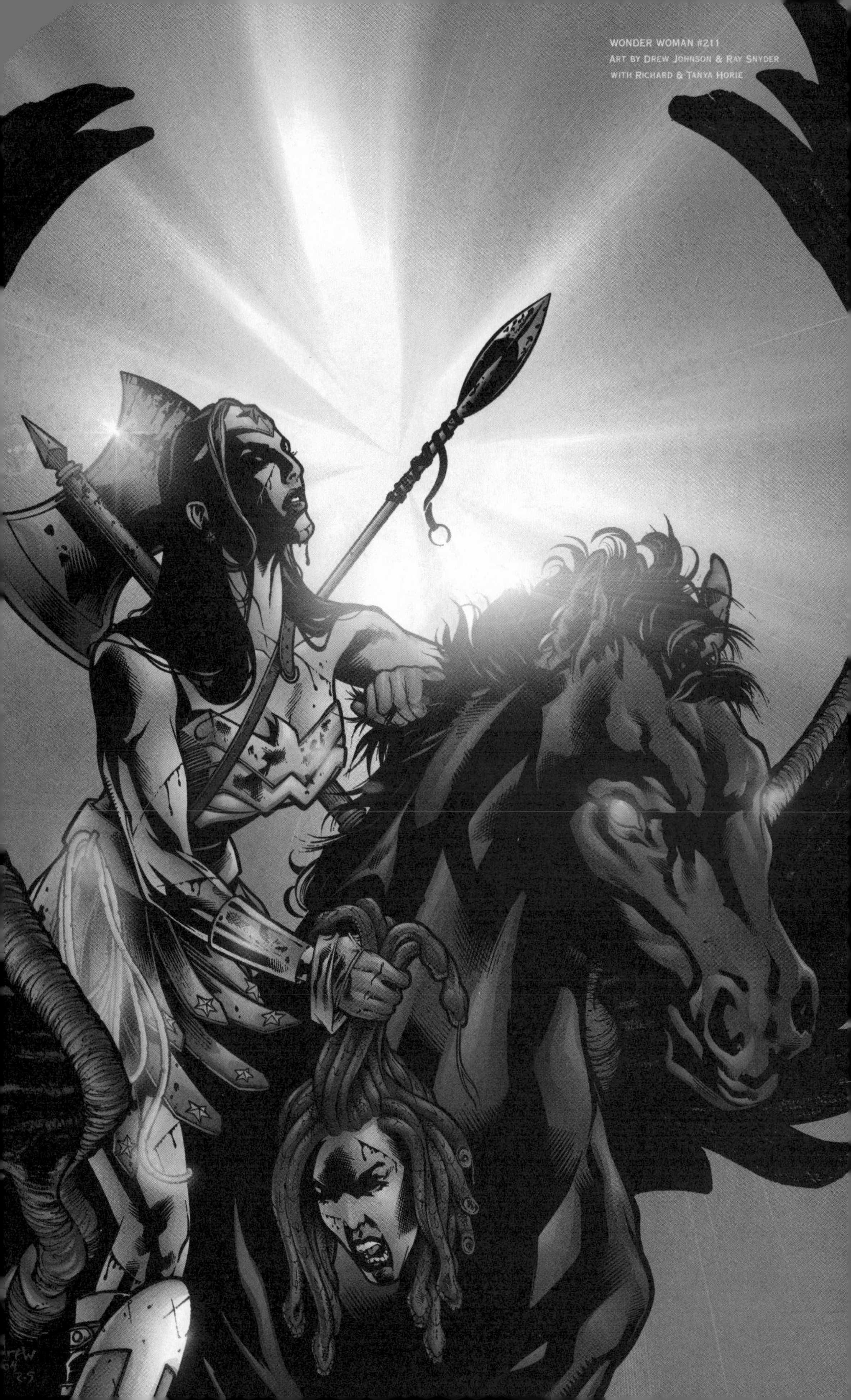

WONDER WOMAN #211
Art by Drew Johnson & Ray Snyder
with Richard & Tanya Horie

WONDER WOMAN #212
Art by J.G. Jones

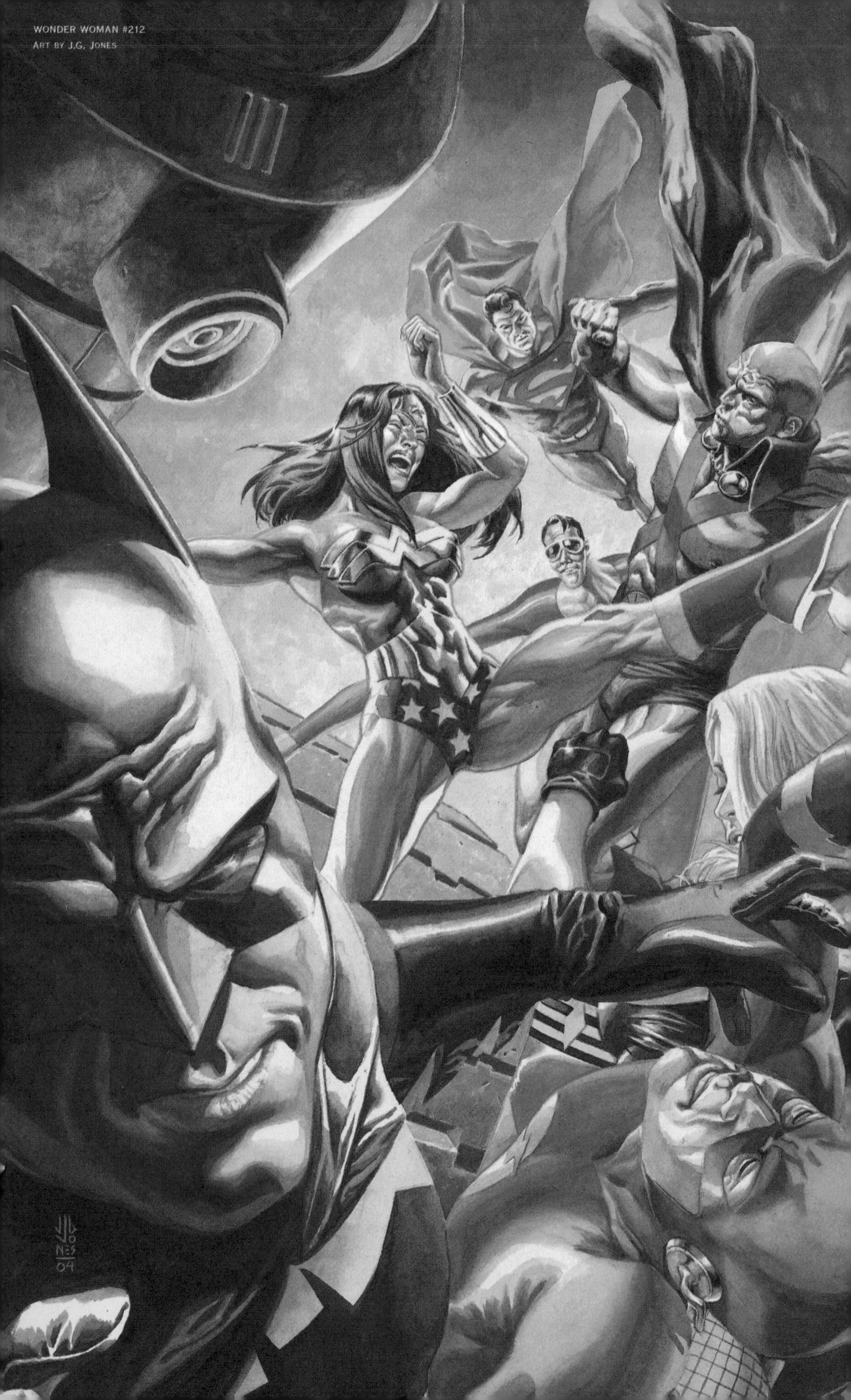

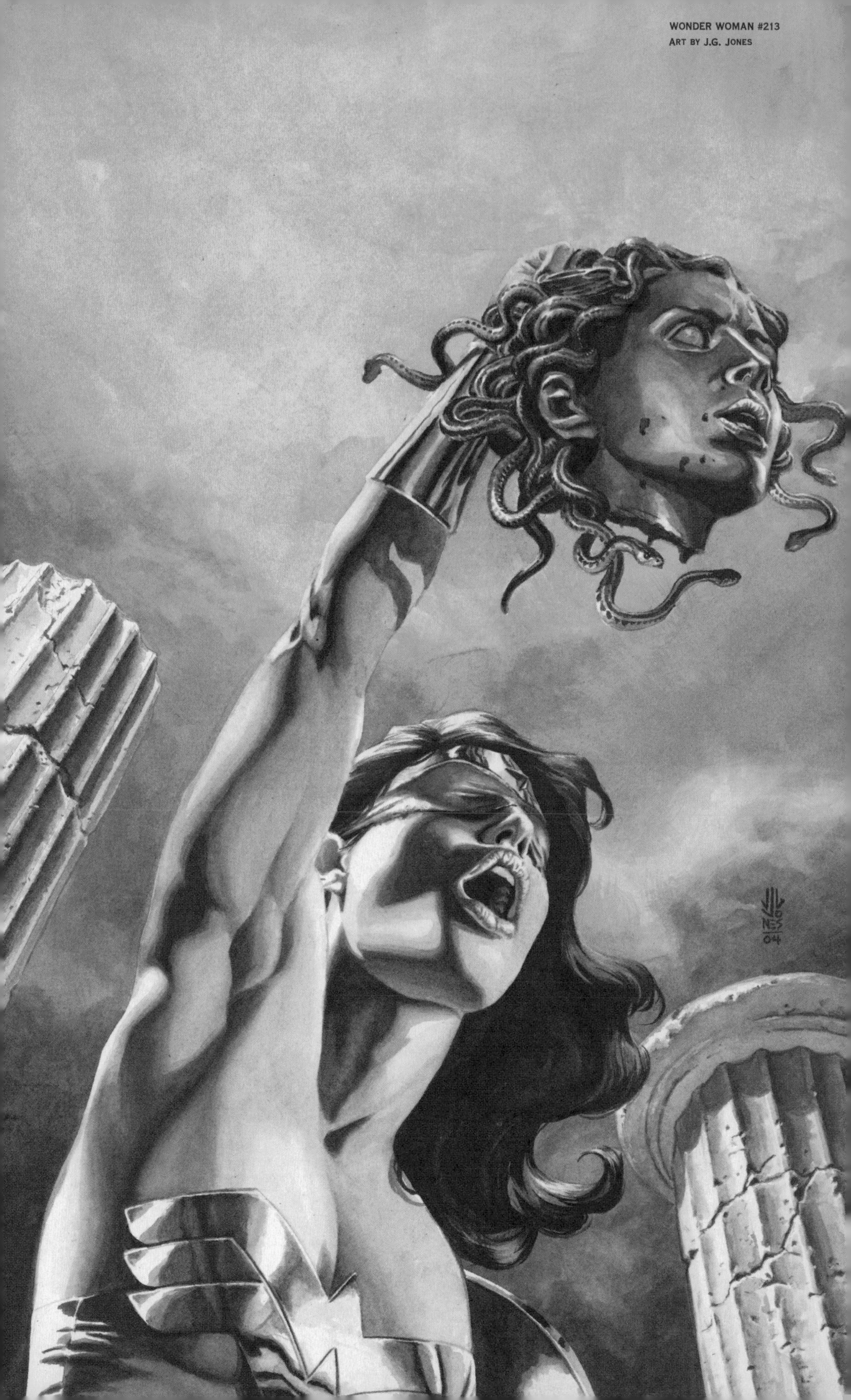

WONDER WOMAN #213
ART BY J.G. JONES